Beyond the American Revolution

Also edited by
Alfred F. Young

The American Revolution

Explorations in the History of American Radicalism

Dissent

Explorations in the History of American Radicalism

Beyond the American Revolution

Explorations

in the

History

of

AMERICAN

RADICALISM

edited by

Alfred F. Young

NORTHERN ILLINOIS UNIVERSITY PRESS

DeKalb   1993

© 1993 by Northern Illinois University Press

Published by the Northern Illinois University Press, DeKalb, Illinois 60115

Manufactured in the United States using acid-free paper ⊗

Design by Julia Fauci

Library of Congress Cataloging-in-Publication Data

Beyond the American Revolution : explorations in the history of American radicalism / edited by Alfred F. Young.
    p.   cm.
    Includes bibliographical references and index.
    ISBN 0-87580-176-5 (clothbound).—ISBN 0-87580-557-4 (pbk.)
    1. Radicalism—United States—History. 2. United States—History—Revolution, 1775–1783—Influence. I. Young, Alfred Fabian, 1925–.
E179.B58   1993
973.3′1—dc20   92-42367
           CIP

Cover painting: "Election Day in Philadelphia" by Lewis Krimmel. Courtesy of Winterthur Museum.

Contents

In Victory and Defeat

Beyond the American Revolution

Introduction

ALFRED F. YOUNG

In 1990, reviewing the last quarter of a century of scholarship on the American Revolution, Linda Kerber concluded that the new research "has tended to restore *rebellions* to histories of the Revolution. Historians have stressed the ways in which marginal peoples—blacks, women and the impoverished—shaped the Revolution and were in turn affected by it." At the same time they have "developed broader conceptualizations of political ideology which permit them to place political theory in an extensive social context." Uniting this recent scholarship on both experience and ideology "is an appreciation of the radicalism—both social and intellectual—of the American Revolution."[1]

This is the third collection of essays in the series *Explorations in the History of American Radicalism* that began in 1968 with the volume *Dissent*, followed in 1976 by *The American Revolution*, and the second to focus exclusively on the American Revolution. Since 1976 a new wave of scholars has appeared to join in the study of radicalism in the era of the Revolution. The three volumes thus serve as benchmarks in the expansion and shifting focus of scholarship on this theme.

"Beyond" in the title *Beyond the American Revolution* can be read in different ways. It implies that there was something more to the Revolution than the War for Independence by which it is still known to most Americans. It suggests a time after the war when radicalism flourished, as the results of the Revolution became apparent. And "beyond" has a political implication: it hints at those large bodies of Americans whose aspirations were not met by the Revolution—not only black people, women, and the impoverished, but middling farmers and artisans—who wanted to push beyond the revolutionary settlement.

What is the meaning of "radicalism" in the subtitle? It requires analysis; it was not a word commonly used at the time. It is neither a word present-day Americans usually associate with the American Revolution, nor is it used with any consensus among historians. In this introduction I will trace the way historians have dealt with this subject over the course of the twentieth century. I will then attempt to define radicalism in the way I think it can best be understood, that is, historically, in the context of available alternatives in a specific period. I will focus on the historic moment of 1775–76, a point at which the multiple radicalisms of the revolutionary era emerged. I will then introduce the essays, which attempt to deal with these many radicalisms. In an afterword I will return to the themes that run through these essays and other recent scholarship that contributes to answering the question, How radical was the American Revolution?

Radical has been commonly used by modern historians of the Revolution to characterize two different trends: the movement for external change that led to separation from Great Britain—independence was a radical break—and the movement for major internal change within the colonies and the newly independent nation. Historians have identified as radical those leaders and movements who from 1765 to 1776 adopted militant tactics in the political resistance to England and were early advocates of independence, men like Samuel Adams and Patrick Henry, and sometimes John Adams and Thomas Jefferson. Secondly, they have used radical as a descriptive term for those Americans who wanted to effect political, economic, and social transformations of all sorts within America. Sometimes the two kinds of radicalism merged; just as often, radicals vis-à-vis Great Britain were not at all radical on internal matters. And "internal" radicals were in some areas indifferent to, or hostile to, the radical patriots seeking independence.

Early in the twentieth century the so-called progressive historians opened up the internal theme, trying to bring these two kinds of radicalism into focus. In 1909 Carl Becker argued that the Revolution "was the result of two general movements; the contest for home rule and independence, and the democratization of American politics" or "if we may so put it, of who should rule at home," a formula that was much repeated. Of the two movements, wrote Becker, "the latter was fundamental." In 1913 Charles Beard, focusing on the Constitution of 1787 as the climax of the Revolution in *An Economic Interpretation of the Constitution,* one of the most influential books in American twentieth-century intellectual life, saw the founders as an economic elite attempting to contain the radicalism of the 1780s rampant in the state legislatures and such temptestuous agrarian upheavals as Shays's Rebellion. In 1926 J. Franklin Jameson, then the dean of the historical profession, broadened the argument, beckoning scholars, as the title of his little book of essays *The American Revolution Considered as a Social Movement* suggested, to explore the "transforming hand of revolution." "The stream of revolution once started," Jameson contended, "could not be confined within thin narrow banks, but spread abroad upon the land. Many economic desires, many social aspirations were set free by the political struggles, many aspects of colonial society profoundly altered by the forces thus set loose."[2]

The progressive historians introduced a much-needed note of realism to the study of the Revolution. In emphasizing the economic origins of the Revolution, they minimized the constitutional dispute with Britain, denigrating ideas as rationalizations of interests. Although they called attention to the participation of ordinary Americans, they often ascribed it to the propaganda and manipulation of elites. In general they looked at "the mob," rural or urban, through the eyes of their manipulators. While they were interested in how much transformation occurred, like most historians until well past the mid-twentieth century, they were inattentive to laboring people, especially African Americans, to women, whatever their status, and to American Indians.[3]

The impression they left of the results of the Revolution, if Charles and Mary Beard's immensely popular *Rise of American Civilization* (1927) is taken as a progressive summa, was that the radicalism of the Revolution was defeated. The Constitution of 1787 was the Thermidor of the American Revolution, taking as a symbolic concept an episode from the French Revolution that stood for a reactionary triumph over radicalism.[4]

A second generation of progressive historians, led by Merrill Jensen, refined and expanded the interpretation. In his first book in 1940 Jensen analyzed the "internal revolution," a phrase he later said he regretted as too sweeping in its implications, but he stuck to the theme, calling one of his last and most insightful works *The American Revolution within America* (1974). For Jensen the "internal revolution" was essentially political, and it was defeated. Neither he nor any of the progressives, old or new, contrary to their critics, ever made a claim for the American Revolution as a social revolution.[5] Jackson Turner Main, Jensen's most prolific student, established the democratizing trends in the new state governments and politics but, taking up the social question raised by Jameson, was skeptical as to the extent of social transformation.[6]

In the 1950s and 1960s the counterprogressives, the so-called consensus historians, believing that their findings had dismantled the progressive edifice block by block, tried to close the door to further consideration of the internal dimensions of the Revolution. Edmund S. Morgan, the senior scholar among them, saw the origins of the Revolution in the principled defense by the colonists of their political and constitutional liberties. Rejecting the progressive social and economic emphasis, he played on Jameson's title to argue for "The American Revolution Considered as an Intellectual Movement." The Revolution ended with the triumph of republican principles, especially equality, in the Declaration of Independence and Constitution, but with only "a host of incalculable, accidental and incidental changes in society." In Morgan's judgment, "to magnify the internal conflict to the same proportion as the revolt against England, is to distort it beyond recognition." It was a conservative revolution in which conflict was contained within a consensus.[7]

In a variant vein Bernard Bailyn contended for *The Ideological Origins of the American Revolution* (1967). "The fear of a comprehensive conspiracy against liberty throughout the English-speaking world," Bailyn was convinced, "lay at the heart of the Revolutionary movement." Assuming a single mind-set in support of this Whig ideology, Bailyn rejected vehemently all efforts to pursue the social or economic origins of the Revolution. Yet he made a case for "The Transforming Radicalism of the Revolution" in the results. For Bailyn the "contagion of liberty" leaped from the dominant Whig political ideology (how is not quite clear) to inspire a presumably pervasive sentiment for the abolition of slavery, religious freedom, political democracy, and the rejection of deference.[8]

Where Bailyn saw a consensus up to 1776, his student Gordon Wood, analyzing the same ideology from 1776 to 1787, revealed "a struggle among Americans for the fruits of independence." Moreover, to Wood the Constitution was "in some sense an aristocratic document designed to curb the democratic excesses of the Revolution." Unwilling to pursue the "reality" underlying the "rhetoric," as he had once proposed, Wood nonetheless ended by inviting scholars to "assess the immense consequences of the social forces released by the Revolution." Thus, while ostensibly repudiating the progressives, he left open the door to variations on Becker, Beard, and Jameson, a door he himself would walk through twenty-five years later.[9]

Meanwhile, by the late 1960s and 1970s the so-called New Left historians opened old doors the counterprogressives tried to close, while historians pioneering the "new social history" opened doors to fields very few historians of any school had ever entered. In 1968 the opening essays in *Dissent,* the first volume in this series, were by two pathbreakers among the New Left historians, Jesse Lemisch and Staughton Lynd. Elsewhere Lemisch pleaded with scholars to examine the Revolution "from the bottom up," rejecting both the unproven assumption of the consensus scholars that the common people shared the ideas of the elites and the widely held conception of the people as a mindless mob manipulated from above. In his 1968 essay Lemisch analyzed the radicalism of the merchant seamen, the "Jack Tars," who played a major role in the crowd actions of the cities acting out of their own long-standing grievances with the British in defense of their own liberty against impressment. He offered a striking demonstration that it was possible to recover the history of the so-called inarticulate, a term he soon put into quotation marks.[10] Lynd, in pursuit of the ideological origins of American radicalism, located a strand of democratic, equalitarian thought among the English Dissenters of the seventeenth and eighteenth centuries to the left of the more moderate thinkers posited by Bailyn and Wood as the primary source of American ideology. Other explorations of tenants and mechanics in New York and of the national conflict over slavery in 1787 took Lynd into a world of complex political struggles, as he put it, "beyond Beard."[11]

By the mid-1970s scholarship about radicalism in the era of the Revolution had so prospered that it was possible to commission, as the second volume in this series, a set of essays devoted exclusively to radical themes of the Revolution. *The American Revolution,* in Edmund Morgan's opinion, "gave a new lease on historiographical life to the contest over who shall rule at home" and was "the most important book on the Revolution yet produced by historians of the New Left." Richard Morris in his presidential address to the American Historical Association relied on the essays to interpret the Revolution as "a People's Revolution." Other scholars saw it as contributing to the breakup of the republican or ideological synthesis. The volume remains popular.[12]

The scholars in *The American Revolution* (1976) focus for the most part on the period before 1776. Essays explore the rural rebellions of the 1760s and 1770s, the urban radicalism that predated political resistance to Britain in 1765, the crowd actions that were the hallmark of resistance from 1765 to 1775, the political economy of the making of the Revolution, the challenge of evangelical religion to the established order, the refusal of the "disaffected" during the war to take part in an aristocratic-led patriot movement, and the democratic artisan-based radicalism articulated by Thomas Paine. The three essayists who address the results of the Revolution deal with the "outsiders" to American political society: African Americans, for whom the "first emancipation, limited as it was," produced "a revolution in black life"; native Americans, who generally fought on the side of their protectors, the British, and for whom the expansion of an American empire proved a disaster; and women, who were active in the patriot movement and the war but for whom, it is argued, the Revolution produced only "the illusion of change."

Many of the authors of essays in *The American Revolution* produced volumes which have since become "standards": on the urban social context of the Revolution; on the political economy of the Revolution; on the complex transformations in Virginia, Maryland, and New York; on the functioning of the crowd in Massachusetts; on the emergence of a free black society; on the evolution of relations between Anglo-Americans and American Indians; and on Thomas Paine, the quintessential radical of the era.[13] From the late 1970s through the 1980s it was possible to probe a wide range of radical themes more deeply, as one field of social history after another bloomed: the history of the laboring classes (artisans, indentured servants, seamen), crowd history, the history of evangelical religion, rural history and the history of small communities, American Indian history, and especially the history of African Americans, antislavery and the history of women.[14] Major works of synthesis by David Brion Davis on antislavery and by Linda Kerber and Mary Beth Norton on women's history opened up for many scholars a new way of thinking about the Revolution as a whole.[15] Conferences explored the Anglo-American origins of radicalism, the limits of radical change, agrarian rebellions and the comparative dimension of the Revolution.[16] New volumes synthesized the new scholarship.[17] College textbooks coauthored by scholars active in the new history incorporated the new findings on the Revolution.[18] Symbolic of the reopening of debate on the once-exiled internal history of the Revolution were the annual conferences sponsored by the United States Capitol Historical Society under the leadership of Ronald Hoffman, a student of Merrill Jensen, each exploring a different theme. The result of Hoffman's organizing efforts was a series of volumes ranging over the changes within the states, the civil war in the Southern backcountry, the economy, the military conflict, and volumes on slavery, women, and religion capped by a volume reviewing the Jameson thesis on the "transforming hand of Revolution."[19]

To recognize that all this scholarship has restored, in Kerber's phrase, "an appreciation of the radicalism of the Revolution" is not to claim it has led to the conclusion that the results of the Revolution as a whole were radical. The question was left open in *The American*

Revolution. Since 1976 some scholars have emphasized the "limits" of the Revolution, minimizing the possibilities for change.[20] Others have been grappling with what they call the "contradictions" or "paradoxes" of the Revolution.[21] Indeed, the sheer volume of scholarship that resulted from the heightened historical consciousness of gender, race, and class, and from doing "history from the bottom up," has required a recasting of the older political and social categories of the debate. To ask how radical the Revolution was means to ask not only how democratic it was politically but how equalitarian.

At this juncture the appearance of Gordon Wood's *The Radicalism of the American Revolution,* an ambitious work of synthesis, is bound to invigorate this debate.[22] Wood has stormed through the door he left ajar in 1967, arguing that "measured by the amount of social change that actually took place, the American Revolution was not conservative at all; on the contrary it was as radical and as revolutionary as any in history." On the one hand, the book confirms much of the scholarship on radical themes of the last twenty-five years. On the other hand, Wood compromised his sweeping claim for the radicalism of the Revolution by excluding any analysis of its consequences for African Americans, women, and native Americans, all subjects central to the new scholarship, by downplaying agrarian rebellion, and by extending the Revolution in time to the era of Andrew Jackson and Alexis de Tocqueville, all the while celebrating capitalism as part of the radical achievement. Historians, to say the least, are in an arena of controversy that may perhaps open more doors, or result at the least in a clearer definition of both radicalism and the Revolution.

Even before the appearance of Wood's book, the axis of debate had shifted. The question is no longer *whether* there was a radical dimension to the American Revolution but *how* radical it was. Thus, the issue of radicalism in the Revolution occupies a central place in historical scholarship and is likely to remain there. The essays in this volume are intended as a contribution to this ongoing debate.

*H*ow should radicalism in the era of the American Revolution be conceptualized? The words *radicalism* and *radical* present a problem. Living in the late twentieth century, most Americans are uncomfortable with the terms, especially after almost a half century of the Cold War, in which radicalism was conflated with communism. Obviously, the words are politically charged. To complicate matters, historically, American radicals, with notable exceptions, have not referred to themselves as radicals. Raymond Williams, everyone's authority on the historic usage of keywords, believes that in England *radical* entered the political vocabulary in the last decade of the eighteenth century and came into common usage early in the nineteenth as a term "to indicate relatively vigorous and far reaching reforms." In the United States the history of the term has not been mapped but in the last half of the twentieth century "the choice of radical . . . can probably be related to the difficulties in the definition of *socialist* and *communist*. Radical seemed to offer a way of avoiding dogmatic and factional associations while asserting the need for vigorous and fundamental change."[23] In the 1960s a wing of the civil rights movement, part of the anti–Vietnam War movement and the youth counterculture, became self-consciously radical. Historians are often inspired by present-day movements to investigate their roots; thus it seemed appropriate in the 1960s and 1970s to conduct explorations into the history of American radicalism, and there seemed to be little need to define the term.[24]

At the time of the American Revolution the word *radical* was used in the general sense of "fundamental" or "thoroughgoing." Thus, John Adams referred to the "radical change in the principles, opinions, sentiments and affections of the people" in the years 1760–75 as "the real American Revolution." In the struggle over the innovative federal Constitution in 1788, Patrick Henry fumed, "Here is a revolution as radical as that which separated us from Great Britain. It is radical, if in this transition our rights and privileges are endangered, and the sovereignty of the States be relinquished."[25]

But *radical* was not a term contemporaries used to identify a person's politics.[26] No political party, faction, or group called itself radical. The word *popular* comes close to it; leaders who were closely identified with the people were sometimes referred to derisively as "popular leaders"; a form of government was "too popular" if it was too democratic. Conservatives had a great many pejorative labels with which they tried to tar their enemies. Politically, they might use "democratic" or "democratical." They might call advocates of economic and social measures which threatened property "levellers" or proponents of "agrarian laws," which meant laws that might equalize property. In the religious world the orthodox often branded proponents of evangelical religion as "enthusiasts" or "fanatics," terms that crossed over into the political world. But none of these pejorative terms stuck as did, for example, "Jacobin" in the French Revolution, a term of opprobrium those who were so labeled wore as a badge of distinction. In the 1790s United States, something like this happened to "democrat," a Federalist term of derision that Republicans softened by calling themselves Democratic Republicans.

Radicalism can be defined with some generalizations that might be applicable to all historical periods, such as advocating fundamental change or analysis that gets to the root of the matter. The word *radical* comes from the Latin word for *root*. But in the last analysis *radical* is a relative term that can only be defined satisfactorily in a specific historic context on the spectrum of available choices. The heart of the problem is that the radicalism of the revolutionary era was so multifaceted. It is hard enough to bring into focus the double political dimension that Carl Becker introduced: "home rule" and "who shall rule at home." The recovery of the history of so many groups of the era has added so many dimensions to the study of the internal history of the Revolution as to confound historians with the best of intentions. Historians must now integrate the unfree (slaves who numbered 500,000 of 2,500,000 Americans), indentured servants (the largest group of immigrants), and apprentices (the most numerous workers in the cities), the free workers (artisans, journeymen, seamen), farmers of all conditions, and women in all classes, let alone the numerous ethnic groups from the British Isles and Europe, as well as native Americans (150,000 of whom were east of the Mississippi).[27]

This very diversity helps to explain why there was not one radicalism but many radicalisms, each more or less rooted in a different group, with an agenda that often developed over time. To define them historically, it may help to focus on one particular historical moment. I suggest 1775–76, not the high point of radicalism, but a point of emergent radicalism at which a number of essays in this volume that deal with elites, the yeomanry, apprentices, and slaves converge. To further focus the discussion, one can try looking at the events of these years through the eyes of a central player, John Adams of Massachusetts, a highly articulate elite leader at the center of the Revolution in Philadelphia, who registered the tremors shaking American society the way a seismograph registers an earthquake.

Present-day Americans are familiar with the events beginning in April 1775 with Paul Revere's ride into the Massachussetts countryside—the battles at Lexington, Concord, and Bunker Hill, the debates of the Continental Congress, the circulation of Thomas Paine's *Common Sense*—and ending with the adoption of the Declaration of Independence in July 1776. These events are fixed in the American imagination thanks to Amos Doolittle's primitive engravings of the skirmishes at Lexington and Concord, Longfellow's poem about the midnight ride of Paul Revere, and John Trumbull's painting of the presentation of the Declaration to Congress.[28]

But the familiar often provides a false sense of security, obscuring the turbulence of the revolutionary upheaval. In 1774–75 Massachusetts had established an extralegal Provincial Congress in defiance of royal authority, and the New England countryside was eager to take up arms. John Adams could look back on ten turbulent years in which he and Samuel Adams had struggled to maintain leadership of city mobs with a will of their own. As lawyer for the British soldiers, John had condemned the rioters at the Boston Massacre, calling them "a motley rabble of saucy boys, negroes and molottoes, Irish teagues and outlandish jack tarrs." Backcountry farmers in Massachusetts who were closing down courts were beyond control. In Philadelphia an illegal congress of delegates from the illegal provincial assemblies turned itself into a government, appointed George Washington as commander-in-chief to organize an army, and authorized committees in every community to police a boycott against British imports. The two Adamses won a reputation as delegates pushing for independence. With war in progress, Congress and the people began to debate whether to abandon reconciliation with Britain.[29]

In January 1776 Thomas Paine's pamphlet *Common Sense* burst on the scene. By the spring it had sold upwards of 100,000 copies, perhaps twenty times more than any previous pamphlet. It precipitated a two-pronged debate: with loyalists over independence and among patriots over what kind of government the new states and nation-to-be should adopt. To argue for independence Paine attacked not only King George III but the principle of monarchy and balanced government, pleading for a republic based on a broadly representative democratic legislature to be drawn up by a constitutional convention. Unlike the pamphlets up to then, Paine's language was plebeian, his tone warmly equalitarian and irreverent, conveying a confidence in the capacity of the common people. And it was suffused with a millennialist idealism: "We have it in our power to begin the world over again. A situation similar to the present has not happened since the day of Noah until now. The Birthday of a new world is at hand."[30]

Paine encapsulated the dual struggle, external and internal, confirming John Adams's worst fears. From his native Massachusetts his correspondents reported "a levelling spirit" and "a spirit of innovation" in the air, "as if everything was to be altered. Scarce a newspaper but teems with new projects."[31] In Philadelphia he witnessed artisans, journeymen, and apprentices forming militia companies, which elected delegates to a Committee of Privates led by Paineite radicals who overturned a recalcitrant assembly and moved the colony to adopt independence and the most radical, that is, the most democratic, constitution of any state.[32]

Adams was soon in print with a pamphlet, *Thoughts on Government*, instructing would-be ruling classes how to draft state constitutions based on the consent of the governed that would "preserve respect for persons in authority." "In New England," he wrote, his proposals would "be displeased because they are not popular enough; in the southern colonies they will be despised and insulted because too popular."[33]

The social dimensions of internal radicalism bloomed in the same heat. In the spring of 1776 with independence looming, Abigail Adams, who corresponded regularly with her husband, out of the blue expressed the hope that in "the new Code of Laws" he and his colleagues would "remember the ladies. . . . Do not put such unlimited power into the hands of the Husbands. Remember all men would be tyrants if they could." Half joking, as if to cushion the radical thrust of her demands, she added, "If perticular care and attention is not paid to the ladies we are determined to foment a Rebellion. . . ." John's reply is as important for registering the shock waves going through society as for his playful put-down of his wife. "As to your extraordinary Code of Laws, I cannot but laugh," he wrote. "We have been told that our Struggle has loosened the bands of Government everywhere. That Children and Apprentices were disobedient—that schools and Colledges were grown turbulent—that Indians slighted their guardians and Negroes grew insolent to their Masters. But your Letter was the first intimation that another tribe more numerous and powerful than all the rest were grown discontented." Abigail, who tried at first to enlist her friend Mercy Otis Warren, the foremost female patriot writer of the day, relented for the moment, but returned in later letters to badger her husband on the need to expand education for women.[34]

Apprentices, John Adams knew, were more than "disobedient" and blacks were more than "insolent." Earlier, Abigail had reported to him "a conspiracy of the Negroes" of Massachusetts to ask the royal governor for freedom.[35] The upsurge for freedom among slaves was at its height in 1775–76. In Virginia the royal governor had offered freedom to slaves and indentured servants who would take up arms for the British. But the slaveholding gentry who ruled Virginia's legislature were pulled hither and yon. To protect their slaves they had exempted their own overseers from military service, arousing a storm from nonslaveholding yeomen that obliged the gentry to repeal their law.

In drawing up the Declaration of Independence, Thomas Jefferson (with support from John Adams, his fellow committee member) withdrew from his draft an indictment of the King for supporting the slave trade and condemned him instead because "he has excited domestic insurrections among us." "The King's real crime," Garry Wills has observed, was "his attempt to *free* Virginia's slaves."[36] Abigail Adams was sympathetic to freedom for slaves; John later helped kill a bill for emancipation in the Massachusetts legislature, fearful of its impact on southern slaveholding patriots.

In the same breath the Declaration condemned the King for his efforts "to bring on the inhabitants of our frontiers, the merciless Indian Savages." The Indian nations, who had long looked to the British as their shield against American expansionism, now took up arms to protect their land and political independence.

In this multidimensional set of struggles, who were the radicals? Clearly, there was not one sphere of struggle but a series of separate spheres that often overlapped, or an array of three-way struggles. On the spectrum of the external conflict with Great Britain, John Adams and Thomas Jefferson were radical, willing "to alter or abolish" and "to throw off" the government that had destroyed their "unalianble rights" as they phrased the right of revolution in the Declaration. The groups who provided the groundswell for independence—the Philadelphia artisans, the yeomanry of the Massachusetts countryside, the readers of Thomas Paine—were radical vis-à-vis Britain, as well as on the spectrum of alternatives, to reshape political institutions. On that spectrum John Adams was someplace in the middle. In the many separate struggles for equality many can be reckoned as radical: Abigail Adams, who wanted at the least equal rights for women in marriage; the Philadelphia militia, who adopted the hunting shirt as their uniform "to level all distinctions"; the Massachusetts farmers with a "levelling spirit"; the Virginia yeomen who rankled at class legislation on behalf of large slaveholders; and the Virginia slaves who fled their masters to join Lord Dunmore's Ethiopian Regiment. The Indian nations taking up arms against the Americans were no different from the signers of the Declaration of Independence in their zeal to preserve their right to self-determination.

The essays in this volume touch on most of the dimensions of the radicalisms that emerged in 1775–76 and others equally important that appeared during and after the Revolution; they carry them into the quarter of a century that followed and often beyond.

*T*he essays in this volume suggest a shift of attention among historians writing in the late 1980s from the origins to the results of the Revolution. Perhaps this is because previous scholarship on the origins of the Revolution has strengthened scholars' grasp of causation and the underlying transforming forces. Many American scholars would agree with Eric Hobsbawm, a British Marxist historian with an enviable command of the vast literature of the comparative history of revolutions, in identifying the "neglected problem [of] how and why revolutions finish."[37]

All the essays that appear here were written specifically for this volume; several have appeared elsewhere in variant form. In inviting scholars to contribute to this volume, I had several criteria. I sought scholars who had not written for the 1976 volume. As before, I invited scholars who were in the midst of a major inquiry to make a progress report and others who had completed a project to distill their findings or broaden its application. And I especially wanted to find a place for historians who were finding new ways to use old original sources or were reexamining little-exploited sources.

In the 1976 volume, two-thirds of the essays deal with the period of the origins of the Revolution or of the war and their focus is for the most part on localized societies. One deals with a truly national figure, Thomas Paine, following him through the war and postwar eras. But only three essayists address the results of the Revolution, and they deal with groups I called, with misleading implications, the "outsiders" to American political society: native Americans, African Americans, and women. The essays in this volume reverse the trend. Most deal either with the Revolution's results or with the long-range trends that helped to frame it. Many scholars are now advancing interpretations that cut across conventional boundaries of time and place. These efforts to link up the Revolution with the rest of American history are overdue. The study of the Revolution has suffered because of self-imposed barriers between specialists of the colonial period and the revolutionary period, and between historians of the Revolution and of early nineteenth century United States. Too many long-range trends occurred that cannot be understood within these artificial boundaries.

I have grouped the essays around three broad themes and in a roughly chronological way. Part 1 addresses the theme, "Who Shall Rule at Home?"; part 2, "Liberty for Whom?"; and part 3, "In Victory and Defeat."

The two essays in part 1 attempt to set the Revolution in the framework of two hundred years of American history, from the early seventeenth to the early nineteenth century. They look at the same Revolution from two different vantage points: the elites, at the top of American society, and the yeomen farmers, who comprised the vast majority of the population.

As might be expected, the authors define class in different ways. "In a country with a ruling class," Gary Kornblith and John Murrin put it colloquially, "the people who own the place also govern it." After analyzing the mechanisms by which the ruling class maintained itself in power in England—"deference, influence and force"—they survey with breathtaking sweep the emergence of elites in the four major colonies, Virginia, Pennsylvania, New York, and Massachusetts. In the revolutionary era these elites attempted to make themselves into a "national ruling class," especially in response to the "popular upheavals" they confronted. In the Kornblith-Murrin scenario the elites were on the verge of success in forging the Constitution of 1787 and in the Federalist ascendancy of the 1790s but then saw their "unmaking" in the Jeffersonian victory in 1801. Subsequent political developments in the states, as these authors see it, ushered in rule by the "middling" classes not at all intended by the would-be ruling classes. If there is any doubt about why an essay on elites should open a volume on radicalism, this should dispel it. The response of the would-be ruling class remains one of the best measures of the impact of the radicalism of popular movements.

Covering the same two centuries, Allan Kulikoff counterpoints the development of an elite to the formation of a yeoman class, a yeoman ideology, and the role of the yeomanry in shaping both the Revolution and its outcome. He attempts to locate the farmers in the larger pattern of the "transition to capitalism," a subject that has drawn increasing attention from American historians. Picking up on the recent debate about the *mentalité* of early American farmers, Kulikoff draws a distinction between yeomen farmers who practiced a "safety first" agriculture and commercial farmers "embedded in a market economy." The yeomanry, he argues, constantly "reinvented themselves as a class" on successive frontiers, developing a consciousness of themselves as a class in conflict with the gentry. The events that Kornblith and Murrin see as landmarks in the formation of a ruling class, Kulikoff sees as embodying both victories and defeats for the yeomanry that set the stage for future conflicts.

The essays in part 2, "Liberty for Whom?" deal with the way liberty was appropriated: how it was redefined by elites and how it was seized by slaves and apprentices, for whom it was not intended.

Edward Countryman focuses "the lens of language" on liberty as a keyword. In the colonial era it was seen by ordinary folk as "the right of small communities to continue their customary ways" and by elites with power in provincial governments as the right to govern themselves free from innovations imposed by Parliament. He traces the way this keyword was transformed from the traditional conservative rights of Englishmen, to "natural rights" in the Declaration of Independence, and then to national law imposed by the federal government over state law and local community custom. The Constitution of 1787, which promised in its preamble "to secure the blessings of liberty," created a host of preconditions for a national market economy that would meet the "needs of the larger scale capitalist American social order that was appearing."

Peter Wood and W. J. Rorabaugh each analyze the way liberty was seized by the "insolent Negroes" and the "disobedient" apprentices who alarmed John Adams. Wood, by looking at the entire range of colonies, establishes a pattern historians have often missed: an upsurge of enslaved African Americans as part of "a cycle of resistance" that peaked in 1775–76. Wood sees blacks in a "pivotal place" in a three-way tug-of-war. By reaching back earlier in the century, Wood also establishes a prior pattern of resistance among slaves shaped by African traditions and the new Protestant evangelical religions.

Rorabaugh sees the profound effect of revolutionary ideology on apprentices who saw masters and journeymen in the forefront of patriot activity and who often took part. Apprentices, actually the most numerous workers within the artisanal system, have been overlooked by historians. Relying on little-used first-person testimony, Rorabaugh shows how during the war apprentices liberated themselves by running off to enlist in the military or on privateering vessels. During and after the war their heightened expectations in a republican society forced a renegotiation of the master-apprentice relationship, eventually contributing to the breakdown of the system.

The long-range transformations taken up in part 1 and the appropriations of liberty during and after the war in part 2 provide a setting for the essays in part 3, "In Victory and Defeat." Devoted to dissenters from the revolutionary settlement, these essays demonstrate the kinds of radicalism that welled up late in the revolutionary era out of a sense of frustration, of promises unfulfilled, or in the case of women, of promises never made.

Alan Taylor, analyzing the settlers who migrated into new backcountries in the North in the decades after the Revolution, finds an "extensive pattern" of resistance to "great proprietors" over acquiring and retaining land. Other scholars have already made clear that the angry rural radicalism that erupted during the 1780s in Shays's rebellion in western Massachusetts and during the 1790s in the Whiskey Rebellion in western Pennsylvania was anything but localized. Taylor finds that in many other areas agrarian resistance to great landowners was protracted and did not end until it was "channelled and mollified" by Democratic Republican politicians.

If the efforts of elites to make themselves into a national ruling class spawned a theorist like James Madison, who sought ways to protect them from "the vices of the political system" (Madison's phrase), it is not surprising that the triumph of elites produced systematic radical thinkers. Michael Merrill and Sean Wilentz examine the thinking of one such person, William Manning, a yeoman and tavern keeper of Billerica, in eastern Massachusetts, an autodidact, a town leader who fought briefly in the patriot militia, was politicized by the Revolution and then radicalized in the 1790s by Hamiltonian finance and Federalist policies. He laid out his thoughts in a long manuscript, which Boston's Jeffersonian editors found too hot to publish during the Federalist "reign of terror" of 1798–99 and for which most scholars of agrarianism or republicanism have not found a place. Unlike other radical farmers, Manning set his face against insurrection. Thus, while convinced that "monied men" had taken over the federal government at the expense of "laboring men," he searched for legal means by which "the Many" could overcome "the Few." He saw it in a national "Labouring Society," which he projected in detail, the first of its kind.

Women did not "foment a Rebelion," as Abigail Adams had threatened—not in 1776 or at any other time in the era. But many participated in the war and underwent a change of consciousness that historians continue to explore. Cathy Davidson tries to get at the thinking of women in the 1790s and early 1800s—the daughters of the patriot generation—by examining the novels they read and rejecting an older notion that these should be dismissed as prescriptive literature. In the eyes of male authority (whether Jeffersonian Republican or Federalist), the novel was "the literary equivalent of a Daniel Shays or a Thomas Paine leading its followers to ruin." Davidson enters the imaginations of women to explore their reception of the first hundred or so American novels from 1790 to about 1820, almost all of which were written "about women, for women, and often by women as well." Because the early American novel "took women seriously," she argues, it was in reality "a subtly subversive form that accorded women a dignity, and perhaps more important, a visibility" not afforded them in public discourse.

The essays in this volume cover a wide range of radical outlooks as well as the response to them. They illustrate the multiple radical agendas that emerged in 1775–76 and continued to develop in the 1780s and 1790s. They do not cover all the popular movements of the era. But taken together with other recent scholarship, they permit us to reflect on two major questions: What were the sources of the radicalism of the era? and What were the results? I offer some reflections on both these themes in an afterword at the end of the book.

NOTES

ACKNOWLEDGMENTS: I wish to express my appreciation to the following who have been helpful in identifying potential contributors to this volume: Michael McGiffert, editor of the *William and Mary Quarterly;* Ronald Hoffman, Director of the United States Capitol Historical Society series "Perspectives on the American Revolution" and of the Institute of Early American History and Culture; Frederick Hoxie, Director of the D'Arcy McNickle Center for the Study of the American Indian, the Newberry Library, and the authors of the 1976 volume. I am also indebted to the scholars who offered criticism to the authors of essays in this volume and especially to Gary Nash, who gave the entire manuscript the benefit of his critical acumen and erudition.

1. Linda Kerber, "The Revolutionary Generation: Ideology, Politics, and Culture in the Early Republic," in Eric Foner, ed., *The New American History* (Philadelphia, 1990), 26, 44.

2. Carl Becker, *The History of Political Parties in the Province of New York, 1760–1776* (Madison, Wis., 1909), 5, 22; Charles Beard, *An Economic Interpretation of the Constitution of the United States* (New York, 1913); J. Franklin Jameson, *The American Revolution Considered as a Social Movement* (Princeton, 1926).

3. Richard Hofstadter, *The Progressive Historians: Turner, Beard, Parrington* (New York, 1968); Peter Novick, *That Noble Dream: The "Objectivity Question" and the American Historical Profession* (New York, 1988); for an extended discussion of the historiography see Alfred F. Young, "American Historians Confront the 'Transforming Hand of Revolution,' " in Ronald Hoffman and Peter J. Albert, eds., *"The Transforming Hand of Revolution": Reconsidering the American Revolution as a Social Movement* (Charlottesville, Va., forthcoming).

4. Charles Beard and Mary Beard, *The Rise of American Civilization,* 2 vols. in one (New York, 1927), vol. 1, chap. 7, "Populism and Reaction."

5. Merrill Jensen, *The Articles of Confederation: An Interpretation of the Social-Constitutional History of the American Revolution, 1774–1789* (Madison, Wis., 1940; paperback ed., 1959, with a new introduction); Jensen, *The New Nation: A History of the United States During the Confederation, 1781–1789* (New York, 1950); Jensen, *The*

American Revolution within America (New York, 1974); for appreciations of Jensen see James Kirby Martin in *The Human Dimensions of Nation Making: Essays on Colonial and Revolutionary America* (Madison, Wis., 1976), 9–22; and Thomas J. Slaughter, "Merrill Jensen and the Revolution of 1787," *Reviews in American History* 15 (1987): 691–701.

6. Jackson T. Main, *The Social Structure of Revolutionary America* (Princeton, 1965); Main, *The Sovereign States, 1775–1783* (New York, 1973); and Main, "The American Revolution and the Democratization of the Legislatures," *William and Mary Quarterly,* 3d series (hereafter cited as *WMQ*) 23 (1966): 391–407.

7. Edmund S. Morgan, *The Birth of the Republic, 1763–89* (Chicago, 1956; 2d ed., 1977), 98; and Morgan, "Conflict and Consensus in the American Revolution," in Stephen G. Kurtz and James H. Hutson, eds., *Essays on the American Revolution* (Chapel Hill, N.C., 1973), 289–309, *The Challenge of the American Revolution* (New York, 1974) collects Morgan's essays.

8. Bernard Bailyn, *The Ideological Origins of the American Revolution* (Cambridge, Mass., 1967; 1992 enlarged ed., with a new preface and concluding chapter); and Bailyn, "The Central Themes of the American Revolution," in Kurtz and Hutson, eds., *Essays on Revolution,* 3–31. *Faces of Revolution* (New York, 1990) collects Bailyn's essays. For an appreciation see Gordon S. Wood, "The Creative Imagination of Bernard Bailyn," in James Henretta, Michael Kammen, and Stanley Katz, eds., *The Transformation of Early American History: Society, Authority, and Ideology* (New York, 1991), 16–50.

9. Gordon S. Wood, *The Creation of the Republic, 1776–1787* (Chapel Hill, N.C., 1969); Wood, "Rhetoric and Reality in the American Revolution," *WMQ* 23 (1966): 3–31; for discussion of Wood's book, see *The Creation of the American Republic, 1776–1787: A Symposium of Views and Reviews," WMQ* 46 (1987): 550–640.

10. Jesse Lemisch, "The American Revolution Seen from the Bottom Up," in Barton Bernstein, ed., *Towards a New Past: Dissenting Essays in American History* (New York, 1967); and Lemisch, "The Radicalism of the Inarticulate: Merchant Seamen in the Politics of Revolutionary America," in Alfred F. Young, ed., *Dissent: Explorations in the History of American Radicalism* (DeKalb, Ill., 1968), 37–82, also published as "Jack Tar in the Streets: Merchant Seamen in the Politics of Revolutionary America," *WMQ* 25 (July, 1968): 371, 407.

11. Staughton Lynd, "Freedom Now: The Intellectual Origins of American Radicalism," in Young, ed., *Dissent,* and in variant form in Lynd, *Intellectual Origins of American Radicalism* (New York, 1968; Princeton, N.J., 1982); Lynd, *Anti-Federalism in Dutchess County,*

New York: A Study of Democracy and Class Conflict in the Revolutionary Era (Chicago, 1962). *Class Conflict, Slavery, and the United States Constitution* (Indianapolis, 1968), collects Lynd's essays.

12. See Edmund S. Morgan, "The American Revolution: Who Were 'the People?' " *New York Review of Books*, 5 Aug. 1976; Richard B. Morris, " 'We the People of the United States:' The Bicentennial of a People's Revolution," *American Historical Review* 82 (1977): 1–19; and Robert E. Shalhope, "Republicanism and Early American Historiography," *WMQ* 39 (April 1982): 333–56. Alfred F. Young, ed., *The American Revolution: Explorations in the History of American Radicalism* (DeKalb, Ill., 1976), now in its seventh printing.

13. See Gary B. Nash, *The Urban Crucible: Social Change, Political Consciousness, and the Origins of the American Revolution* (Cambridge, Mass., 1979); Joseph A. Ernst, *Money and Politics in America, 1755–1775: A Study in the Currency Act of 1764 and the Political Economy of Revolution* (Chapel Hill, N.C., 1973); Rhys Isaac, *The Transformation of Virginia, 1740–1790* (Chapel Hill, N.C., 1982); Ronald Hoffman, *A Spirit of Dissension: Economics, Politics, and the Revolution in Maryland* (Baltimore, 1973); Edward Countryman, *A People in Revolution: The American Revolution and Political Society in New York, 1760–1790* (Baltimore, 1981); Dirk Hoerder, *Crowd Action in Revolutionary Massachusetts, 1765–1790* (New York, 1977); Ira Berlin, *Slaves without Masters: The Free Negro in the Antebellum South* (New York, 1974); Eric Foner, *Tom Paine and Revolutionary America* (New York, 1976); Francis Jennings, *The Invasion of America* (Chapel Hill, N.C., 1975); Jennings, *The Ambiguous Iroquois Empire* (New York, 1984); and Jennings, *Empire of Fortune* (New York, 1988), 3 vols. in the series *The Covenant Chain.*

14. For bibliographic essays see Edward Countryman, *The American Revolution* (New York, 1985), 246–74; Jack P. Greene and J. R. Pole, eds., *Colonial British America: Essays in the New History of the Early Modern Era* (Baltimore, 1984); John J. McKusker and Russell R. Menard, *The Economy of British America, 1607–1789* (Chapel Hill, N.C., 1985); Frederick Hoxie and Harvey Markowitz, *Native Americans: An Annotated Bibliography* (Pasadena, Calif., 1991); Peter H. Wood, " 'I Did the Best I Could for My Day': The Study of Early Black History during the Second Reconstruction," *WMQ* 35 (1978): 185–225. For a selective listing of books, see David L. Ammerman and Philip D. Morgan, comps., *Books about Early America: 2001 Titles* (Williamsburg, 1989); for a very full compilation of books and articles, Ronald L. Gephart, comp., *Revolutionary America 1763–1789: A Bibliography*, 2 vols. (Washington, D.C., 1984).

15. David Brion Davis, *The Problem of Slavery in the Age of Revolution, 1770–1823* (Ithaca, N.Y., 1975); Linda K. Kerber, *Women of the Republic: Intellect and Ideology in Revolutionary America* (Chapel Hill, N.C., 1980); and Mary Beth Norton, *Liberty's Daughters: The Revolutionary Experience of American Women* (Boston, 1980).

16. Margaret C. Jacob and James R. Jacob, eds., *The Origins of Anglo-American Radicalism* (London, 1984; paperback ed. with a new introduction, Atlantic Highlands, N.J., 1991); Robert Gross, ed., *In Debt to Shays: The Legacy of Agrarian Rebellion* (Charlottesville, Va., 1993); for the symposia of the Milan Group in Early United States History on comparative themes, Loretta Valtz Mannuci, ed., *The Language of Revolution* (Milan, *Quaderno* 2, 1989) and Mannucci, ed., *People and Power: Rights, Citizenship and Violence* (Milan, *Quaderno* 3, 1992) [available through Prof. Manucci at the University of Milan].

17. See Countryman, *American Revolution;* and James A. Henretta and Gregory H. Nobles, *Evolution and Revolution: American Society, 1600–1820* (Lexington, Mass., 1987), which incorporates scholarship since Henretta, *The Evolution of American Society, 1700–1815: An Interdisciplinary Analysis* (Lexington, Mass., 1973).

18. See Gary B. Nash et al., *The American People: Creating a Nation and a Society* (New York, 1986); Mary Beth Norton et al., *A People and a Nation* (New York, 1983); James Henretta et al., *America's History* (Chicago, 1987); and Edward Countryman, Marcus Rediker, et al., *Who Built America?* [American Social History Project] (New York, 1990).

19. The following vols. are in the series, "Perspectives on the American Revolution" (Charlottesville, Va.), edited by Ronald Hoffman and Peter J. Albert unless otherwise indicated: *Sovereign States in an Age of Uncertainty* (1981); Hoffman and Ira Berlin, eds., *Slavery and Freedom in the Age of the American Revolution* (1983); *Arms and Independence: The Military Character of the American Revolution* (1984); Hoffman, Albert, and Thad Tate, eds., *The Southern Backcountry during the American Revolution* (1985); *The Economy of Early America: The Revolutionary Period, 1763–1790* (1988); *Women in the Age of the American Revolution* (1989); *Religion in a Revolutionary Age* (forthcoming); *"The Transforming Hand of Revolution"* (forthcoming).

20. See Jack P. Greene, ed., *The American Revolution: Its Character and Limits* (New York, 1987).

21. Henretta and Nobles, *Evolution and Revolution,* 178.

22. Gordon S. Wood, *The Radicalism of the American Revolution* (New York, 1992).

23. Raymond Williams, *Keywords: A Vocabulary of Culture and Society,* rev. ed. (New York, 1983), 251–52.

24. See Novick, *Noble Dream,* chaps. 13–16; and Jon Wiener, "Radical Historians and the Crisis in American History, 1959–1980," *Journal of American History* 76 (1989): 399–434.

25. John Adams to Hezikiah Niles, 13 Feb. 1818, in Adrienne Koch, ed., *The American Enlightenment* (New York, 1965), 228; and Patrick Henry, 5 June 1788, in J. R. Pole, ed. *The American Constitution: For and Against* (New York, 1987), 117.

26. Compare "radical" in *Oxford English Dictionary* (1971 ed.).

27. For recent works dealing with ethnic and cultural diversity see Bernard Bailyn, *The Peopling of British North America: An Introduction* (New York, 1986); Bailyn and Philip D. Morgan, eds., *Strangers within the Realm: Cultural Margins of the First British Empire* (Chapel Hill, N.C., 1991); David H. Fischer, *Albion's Seed: Four British Folkways in America* (New York, 1989); Jack P. Greene, *Pursuits of Happiness: The Social Development of Early Modern British Colonies and the Formation of American Culture* (Chapel Hill, N.C., 1988); and Greene, "Interpretive Frameworks: The Quest for Intellectual Order in Early American History," *WMQ* 48 (1991): 515–30.

28. For the iconography of the Revolution, see Michael Kammen, *A Season of Youth: The American Revolution and the Historical Imagination* (New York, 1978; Ithaca, N. Y., 1988); Alfred F. Young and Terry Fife with Mary Janzen, *We the People: Voices and Images of the New Nation* (Philadelphia, 1993), Introduction.

29. Page Smith, *John Adams,* 2 vols. (Garden City, N.Y., 1962), vol. 1; and John R. Howe, Jr., *The Changing Political Thought of John Adams* (Princeton, 1966). Merrill Jensen, *The Founding of a Nation: A History of the American Revolution, 1763–1776* (New York, 1968), remains the fullest political narrative.

30. Thomas Paine, *Common Sense,* in Merrill Jensen, ed., *Tracts of the American Revolution* (Indianapolis, 1967); Isaac Kramnick, ed., *Common Sense* (London, 1986); Kramnick and Michael Foot, eds., *Thomas Paine Reader* (London, 1987), and many other eds.; Foner, *Tom Paine,* chaps. 3, 4.

31. Smith, *John Adams* 1:245.

32. Stephen Rosswurm, *Arms, Country, and Class: The Philadelphia Militia and the "Lower Sort" during the American Revolution, 1775–1783* (New Brunswick, N.J., 1987); and Richard A.

Ryerson, *The Revolution Is Now Begun: The Radical Committees of Philadelphia, 1765–1776* (Philadelphia, 1978).

33. Smith, *John Adams* 1:247–48; John Adams, *Thoughts on Government, in a Letter to a Friend* (Philadelphia, 1776) in George A. Peek, ed., *The Political Writings of John Adams* (New York, 1985), 83–92.

34. Abigail Adams to John Adams, 31 March 1776; John Adams to Abigail Adams, 17 April 1776; Abigail Adams to Mercy Otis Warren, 27 April 1776; Abigail Adams to John Adams, 9 May, 14 Aug. 1776, in L. H. Butterfield, ed., *Adams Family Correspondence* (Cambridge, Mass., 1963) 1:369–71, 381–83, 396–98, 401–3; 2:94.

35. Abigail Adams to John Adams, 22 Sept. 1774, *Adams Family Correspondence* 1:161–62.

36. Garry Wills, *Inventing America: Jefferson's Declaration of Independence* (Garden City, N.Y., 1978), 74.

37. E. J. Hobsbawm, "Revolution," in Roy Porter and Mikulas Teich, eds., *Revolution in History* (Cambridge, Eng., 1986), 5–46; quotation at 7.

Who Shall Rule at Home?

The Making and Unmaking of an American Ruling Class

GARY J. KORNBLITH

AND

JOHN M. MURRIN

This engraving, "Convention at Philadelphia," appeared in one of the first history books written for American children. Attributed to Elkanah Tisdale, it depicts the harmonious Framers of the Constitution under the leadership of George Washington, to the right. From Rev. Charles A. Goodrich. *A History of the United States of America* (Hartford, Conn., 1823).

Unlike Europe, the United States in the mid-nineteenth century had no visible ruling class. The most prominent old families and the wealthiest men in the country seldom held high office or controlled major policy decisions, nor were their children any more likely than they to exercise public power. Although white laboring men who worked for wages had no chance to hold office and blacks, women, and paupers could not even vote, formal political power had shifted dramatically from the top toward the middle of society.

Most Americans take this situation for granted. They should not. The American colonies seldom lacked ambitious men eager to establish their own claim to rule. The seventeenth century treated them rudely, but for much of the eighteenth the thrust of political and social change favored their goals. The Revolution both challenged and invigorated their aspirations, but they finally failed. They prospered—but they did not govern.

This essay, after describing the devices that England's ruling class used to establish and maintain its dominance, traces similar efforts in the colonies, especially Virginia, Massachusetts, New York, and Pennsylvania. Their founders took it for granted that a sharp boundary ought to separate rulers from the ruled, but none of them could replicate the English system in the seventeenth century. Between 1690 and 1760 this gap between their aspirations and political realities narrowed greatly. The richest and most prestigious families increasingly monopolized high office. At no time in American history have wealth, power, and status coincided more closely. The thrust of social and economic change seemed strongly in their favor until they confronted an unexpected challenge from the British imperial state and its highly developed ruling class. Upper-class colonists in public life had to choose between loyalty to Britain at the cost of popular disfavor, and active resistance to Britain, which meant appealing to and building upon the discontent of ordinary people. Once elite patriots accepted independence, they had to discover whether they still possessed the political resources to control public life in their states. As it became clear that they did not, many of them turned to the continental level to build the leverage they would need to become a *national* ruling class. This struggle turned into one of the most momentous and contested issues of the 1790s. The triumph of the Jeffersonian Republicans over the Federalists after 1800 decisively undermined the effort to establish a national ruling class. Public office went increasingly to middling men, not the very rich.

We are not discussing what to Karl Marx was the greatest transformation in class relations in modern times, the separation of ownership from the means of production and the social and political changes that followed from that shift. We are analyzing the dynamics of class relations before that transition occurred, a problem that has fascinated Marxists, neo-Marxists, and non-Marxists. We are also trying hard not to reify a subject that was always in motion. E. P. Thompson said it well in 1963: "The [class] relationship must always be embodied in real people and in a real context. . . . And class happens when some men, as a result of common experiences (inherited or shared), feel and articulate the identity of their interests as between themselves, and as against other men whose interests are different from (and usually opposed to) theirs." Nor should we expect identical systems to occur in different societies. "Consciousness of class arises in the same way in different times and places," he added, "but never in *just* the same way."[1]

Before proceeding, we need to provide a few basic definitions. *Ruling class* refers to a class that dominates both the socio-economic sphere (or civil society in Marxian terminology) and the political sphere (i.e., the State). A ruling class in the fullest sense of the term exercises direct control over the most powerful agencies of government. Thus it not only rules by means of hegemony but also exercises and controls sovereignty. Put more simply, in a country with a ruling class, the people who own the place also govern it. "It is not a new idea," wrote John Jay in 1810, "that those who own the country are the most fit persons to participate in the government of it."[2]

In preindustrial England, families with the greatest wealth and dignity dominated public life. Components of this ruling class included *aristocrats* with hereditary estates and titles (duke, marquess, earl, viscount, and baron) and the *gentry,* families below the aristocracy with enough landed wealth to live off their rental income. Together, aristocrats and gentry controlled Parliament—indisputably the most powerful institution in the English government by the eighteenth century. In exercising power, they obtained advice and major services from other prominent persons, such as merchants, bankers, and lawyers. These people in turn usually called themselves *gentlemen,* an imprecise but much used word that suggested someone of cultivation and wealth who did not have to work with his hands. (The gentry, unless they had a higher title such as baronet or knight, also called themselves gentlemen, but most gentlemen ranked below the gentry.) Merchants and professionals served the ruling class in important ways, but few really belonged to it.[3]

In the colonies we speak not of a ruling class (or separate ruling classes) but instead of *upper classes* and *elites.* These terms are less precise yet still useful. By *upper class* we mean roughly the wealthiest five percent of provincial society, men who in various ways had distinguished themselves from most of their neighbors. Components of the upper classes differed somewhat from one colony to another but included planters with more than twenty servants or slaves, other landlords with large holdings, the richest merchants, and, eventually, many lawyers. By *elite* we mean the men who held the most important political offices in a colony, including seats in the provincial assembly. In the eighteenth century, as we shall explain, the colonial elites were increasingly comprised of upper-class individuals. Yet because they remained subject to the supreme political authority of Crown and Parliament, we do not consider the various colonial elites to have been genuine ruling classes. From this perspective, it might indeed have taken a revolution to transform separate colonial elites into a consolidated ruling class.

THE REMAKING OF THE ENGLISH RULING CLASS

Throughout the period between the founding of the American colonies and their successful revolution against Great Britain, every European society had a visible ruling class. Usually the wealth of these families came from landed estates. They had formal aristocratic titles, they acquired the cultural and political skills necessary to manage existing governments, and they expected to pass on their status to their descendants. Every viable ruling class also had to have ways of recruiting small numbers of outsiders into its circle, if only because in every generation a fair percentage of dominant families failed to maintain the male line. But the boundary between rulers and ruled was sharp.

"Nothing appears more surprising to those who consider human affairs with a philosophical eye, than the easiness with which the many are governed by the few; and the implicit submission, with which men resign their own sentiments and passions to those of their rulers," wrote David Hume in the mid-eighteenth century. "When we inquire by what means this wonder is effected, we shall find, that, as Force is always on the side of the governed, the governors have nothing to support them but opinion."[4] Hume described what a later generation would call deference, a system of social relationships in which men of inferior resources (family, wealth, education, or all three) willingly defer to the judgment of their superiors in matters of public concern. When deference functioned well, yeomen routinely voted for the largest landholder in their part of the county, as did tradesmen for wealthy merchants in the cities. Nonvoters willingly obeyed the laws passed by their superiors.[5]

But deference was not the only means available to command assent. The state also used influence and, when all else failed, naked force, either legal or military. Those in power could win support from below by distributing favors—patronage, honors, pensions, contracts—among people who might otherwise resist their policies. Recipients of major posts—for example, an army colonel or a commissioner of the board of customs—had lesser favors to bestow on people below them, the whole system constituting a network of *clientage,* which also had its counterpart in the more private world of ascending household economies. Every British ministry in the eighteenth century routinely used large doses of these forms of influence to maintain its majority in the House of Commons.[6]

Like other European states of the same period, the British government tried to maintain a monopoly of violence, first by disarming 90 percent of the population, and—especially after 1660—by building a standing army. Every government relied, in short, on a mix of deference, influence, and force. In England the British government depended primarily on deference and influence, but it was willing to employ force when the stakes were high. It passed the Riot Act in 1715 to make force readily available to local magistrates. The Black Act of 1723 turned the judicial system into a ruthless engine for crushing poachers. Some of the government's efforts to stamp out smugglers resembled small wars against coastal communities. Finally, under threat of the French Revolution, the British state used the law quite mercilessly to smash the radical egalitarians of the 1790s. In Scotland after the union with England in 1707, the emphasis was on influence and force rather than deference, for which few active opportunities were available. Voters there were rarer than college graduates, and the state did not even encourage the creation of a militia of Protestant gentlemen eager to demonstrate their loyalty to the regime. Instead, the Jacobite risings of 1715 and 1745 met savage repression by the British Army. Ireland's aristocracy and gentry relied even more blatantly on the routine use of soldiers to secure obedience. England, Scotland, and Ireland each had a ruling class, in other words, but they dominated their societies in different ways.[7]

Even in England the full system took time to develop. Much of it did not yet exist when the first colonies were founded between 1607 and 1640. The crown had no standing army and very limited patronage to bestow. It governed mostly through the willing services of landed aristocrats and greater gentry, men who could be alienated. It had few resources beyond the network of deference and clientage built into an aristocratic social order. A major rift within this ruling class, especially over a subject as sensitive as religion, could unravel the system that gave those who governed power over others.

Rulers, in short, could be challenged. Between 1640 and 1660 Parliament went to war with King Charles I, executed him in 1649, abolished the House of Lords, and established a commonwealth for eleven years. Real power soon passed to Oliver Cromwell, a puritan general who never lost a battle and who spent the last decade of his life trying to reconcile traditional notions of a proper ruling class with puritan demands that only the godly hold office. Less exalted Englishmen, such as the Levellers and Diggers, demanded a much more radical restructuring of English society. Cromwell's efforts failed even before his death in 1658, and less than two years later the Restoration of Charles II brought back government by king, lords, and commons. The rest of the seventeenth century would show that to achieve stability the aristocrats who governed had to broaden their social base to include most of the gentry.[8]

By 1688 England's ruling class was secure enough to drive out King James II, a Catholic, and invite in the Protestant William of Orange from the Netherlands and make him King William III, all without serious political or social disruption. This Glorious Revolution guaranteed that the House of Commons, a bastion of gentry power, would finally become essential to the entire governing process. It has met every year since 1689, and from 1721 to 1742 Sir Robert Walpole demonstrated that a commoner as prime minister could be far more effective than a lord. Throughout the period the British state became much bigger, greatly expanding the patronage and military force available to the governing few. So long as he had well over a hundred offices to distribute among eager MPs, a prime minister who sat in the Commons was seldom outvoted by any bloc of opposition forces. The British state that the colonists encountered by 1760 was thus quite a different phenomenon from the one the founding generations had known in the first half of the seventeenth century.[9]

WHERE THERE'S A WILL,
THERE'S NOT ALWAYS A COLONIAL WAY

The people who settled colonial America were used to a visible cleavage between the governed and those who rule. They were not accustomed to the routine use of military force in civil government, nor after the very early years did they bring many soldiers with them. Most settlers probably thought that their provincial societies ought to embody the distinction between rulers and the ruled in much the same way that England did before 1640, which meant an emphasis on deference and influence rather than force. They expected a high correlation between status, wealth, and power among the men in office.

Largely through circumstance but partly through choice, no such system took firm hold in the seventeenth century. Only in the eighteenth century would most colonies begin to achieve something resembling a European division of responsibility between rulers and ruled. Nowhere was this process complete, even in the eighteenth century, but it went further in Virginia than anywhere else. Massachusetts, which challenged the English formula in fascinating ways during its period of puritan rule, moved toward a more conventional English system in the eighteenth century, but it did not develop an elite as confident as the planter gentry of Virginia or as capable of passing on its status to its descendants. The gentry, merchants, and lawyers of colonial New York were much more successful at monopolizing high offices, but along the way they encountered frequent resistance to their claims, both from within and from below. Pennsylvania did not lack for gentlemen after about 1720, but their ability to rule was always precarious. A comparison of these four colonies, with occasional glances at others, should illuminate both the potential for creating upper-class political elites in America and the limitations inherent in the process.

Titled aristocrats and landed gentry did not come to America. The few who crossed the ocean seldom stayed. The Crown, the various lord proprietors (such as the successive Lords Baltimore in Maryland or William Penn and his descendants in Pennsylvania), and the corporations that founded colonies (such as the Virginia Company of London and the Massachusetts Bay Company) had to give power to individuals further down the English social scale. They turned to men who had in some way distinguished themselves from ordinary settlers, to those who were in the process of becoming provincial upper classes, or elites. Virginia's largest planters certainly qualified. So did the patroons and manor lords of the Hudson Valley and the wealthiest merchants of Boston, New York City, and Philadelphia. Men with a full or partial college education were also exceptional. The younger sons of minor English gentry, just outside the ruling class in England, had an excellent chance to become justices of the peace, assemblymen, or even members of the governor's council in America. But except in New England, seventeenth-century America offered few chances for education or other refinements. A founder's success in acquiring wealth and office did not guarantee that his sons would possess the same advantages. Early death, of father or sons, often magnified these difficulties.[10]

This necessity to recruit officeholders in America from below the top echelons of the English social hierarchy had important consequences, some of them permanent. Many of the men who acquired office in early America were the younger sons of English gentry or merchants. They showed little inclination to impose primogeniture and entail (the legal devices that sustained the privileges of eldest sons) upon their new societies. Compared with Europe, the English colonies were from the start a paradise for younger sons. That change took root so deeply that it has never been seriously challenged.[11] In like manner the absence of a standing army in most colonies for most of the colonial era compelled the government to insist (except in Quaker societies) that the settlers arm themselves. In no American province did the government establish the monopoly of violence that Europe took for granted by the eighteenth century, and firearms were always and still are more widely available in America than in other Western countries.[12]

The legitimacy of the newcomers' claim to power rested on two sources. One was approval by government and therefore by the English state. The other was willing acceptance by the community they served. Often it was difficult to get both. Legitimacy then remained perilous and could be challenged. This kind of tension made it nearly impossible before the Glorious Revolution of 1688–89 to find men whose right to govern was accepted on both sides of the ocean and who could be confident that their sons would enjoy the same status.[13]

VIRGINIA
The Convergence of Upper Class and Elite

Virginia illustrates all of these problems and the process by which most of them were overcome. A political elite acceptable to both the Crown and to ordinary settlers did not take hold for several generations. Only during the forty years after 1690 or 1700 did the major officeholders of the colony begin to look much more like a traditional ruling class. These men were the economic, political, and social leaders of their society, and everyone knew it.

Virginia in the very early years had many true gentlemen, but when they met disease and death instead of quick wealth, the survivors retreated to England. Power fell to an ambitious group of men who prospered during the tobacco boom of the 1620s, but few of them lived long enough to pass on their advantages to their sons or produced sons who survived long enough to inherit their fathers' status. Instead, at a time when perhaps 85 percent of the Europeans who went to Virginia arrived as indentured servants, the major offices in the colony went to a new wave of free immigrants that contained the first Blands, Byrds, Carters, Harrisons, Jeffersons, Lees, Randolphs, and Washingtons. Often younger sons of minor gentry or London merchant families, they understood political power, and from the 1640s to the 1670s they began to monopolize appointments to the county courts and elections to the House of Burgesses. They had the resources to begin purchasing servants or slaves, and access to power also helped them to acquire large tracts of land. They probably thought of themselves as the first generation of a secure ruling elite for Virginia, at least until Bacon's Rebellion taught them a disturbing lesson in 1676.[14]

Nathaniel Bacon's success revealed the weakness of deference and the brittleness of public authority in Virginia. Several months into a costly war with the Susquehannock Indians, Bacon denounced the governor's reliance on expensive forts (good only for defense) and offered to lead unpaid volunteers in offensive campaigns against neighboring tribes, hostile or neutral. When small planters (those with few or no servants) sided overwhelmingly with Bacon against not only the governor but also a reforming House of Burgesses, the government collapsed during the summer and had to be restored in the autumn months through the armed might of the London tobacco fleet. The upheaval terrified the men around the governor, Sir William Berkeley, and made them far more conscious of their upperclass identity. They castigated the rebels as "an insulting rabble . . . who account the Law their manacles, and like swine turn all into disorder & become insolent [and] abuse all in authority." Bacon, in a famous appeal, mocked the social pretensions of his opponents. They were, he charged, "unworthy favourites and juggling parasites," mere "sponges" who had "sucked up the public treasure." Himself a gentleman by birth, Bacon assured his followers that the governor's men had no better social qualifications than many of the rebels. But this appeal to class resentments never became an explicit class struggle, a demand to destroy a ruling class. Instead, Bacon denied that Virginia had one.[15]

Over the next half century the men who governed Virginia's counties and dominated both houses of its legislature became something much closer to a typical ruling class. By 1700 they already showed considerable success in passing on their wealth and their offices to their sons. By then planters with twenty or more slaves dominated the council. By the 1720s and 1730s big planters also controlled the House of Burgesses, the county courts, and the vestries in those parts of the colony that had passed beyond the frontier stage. The line between small and large planter was not easily bridged. Few could cross it through savings, hard work, or the annual profits from tobacco, but British newcomers who brought capital or education with them could still enter the governing elite.[16]

By the eighteenth century the bastion of power for great planters was the county court, buttressed by the Anglican vestry. Both were co-optive bodies. When vacancies arose, in other words, the existing members decided who would fill them, and the governor merely ratified the result with a formal appointment. With very few exceptions, a planter had to be named by his peers to the county court before he could stand for the House of Burgesses, and the men elevated to the council usually had prior experience in the lower house. Each county also had numerous lesser offices ranging from lowly fence viewers to more exalted grand jurors and, the only position that paid well, tobacco inspectors. The justices distributed these posts among the small planters, apparently with an even hand. Planters who voted were likely to receive some post or other. Modern scholarship has still not determined whether these appointments reflected a general pattern of deference or whether they concealed a system of clientage and influence that linked particular small planters to individual justices. Very likely some combination of both prevailed in different proportions from one county to another, but deference probably outweighed influence in most.[17]

As the great planters built their impressive houses after about 1720, indulged in genteel culture and recreations, and passed on their advantages to their children with ever-less effort, few could doubt that those who governed in Virginia had become an easily recognizable group of interrelated planter dynasties. Except for the coercive relationship that bound slaves to their masters, the system seldom relied upon force. Small planters accepted rule by great planters with little thought of ever creating an alternative system. Virginia had become a participatory oligarchy in which both small and great planters understood their social and political roles.[18]

Virginia's governing elite increasingly resembled England's ruling class but never fully replicated it. Some differences remained critical—the labor systems of the two societies, the commercial origins of most of the colony's first families, the continuing ability of the elite to provide for younger sons, and the relative absence of ties of patronage between great planters and the governor. Successful governors earned support among the burgesses through persuasion, not patronage. For half a century the system worked quite well, long enough to convince the great planters that they deserved to rule.[19]

NEW ENGLAND
From Godly Rule to Upper-class Empowerment

Just as colonial Virginia provided opportunities to rule for people who would have had no such claim in England, early New England also explored social and political possibilities not open in the mother country. The puritans expected to be governed by godly laymen. The gentry among them, such as John Winthrop, intended to limit the active exercise of political power to godly gentlemen. Less exalted puritans fought to gain a share of that power. As religious motivation lost intensity after 1689, a much more secular elite began to emerge. In the eighteenth century these men made formidable gains. The underlying trend was toward the consolidation of power in fewer hands, although the men in office still had to satisfy both the Crown above them and the people below. In 1760 they were not yet a fully secure governing elite, but they had travelled a long way in that direction since the seventeenth century, and the momentum of historical change seemed strongly in their favor.

The most bracing political innovation in seventeenth-century New England was a largely successful effort to create a stable political system built as much upon individual piety as upon social class. The puritan colonies institutionalized what Cromwell had tried only briefly and then abandoned, government by the godly. The leaders of this effort hoped to minimize the difference between what they were actually doing and what they had known in England. John Winthrop, Thomas Dudley, Sir Richard Saltonstall, Theophilus Eaton, and a few other founders were conspicuous "saints" (that is, their neighbors agreed that they had had a valid conversion experience) and also came from at least the outer edges of England's ruling class. Winthrop, Dudley, and Saltonstall all founded political dynasties that exercised power in Massachusetts and Connecticut into the eighteenth century. They expected to make most of the important political decisions for their colonies themselves. They never established that degree of control.[20]

In the 1630s several English puritan aristocrats sought assurances that, if they migrated to New England, they and their heirs would be guaranteed the right to hold high office. John Cotton, speaking for the men already in power, tried to reassure Lord Viscount Saye and Sele that he and his friends were indeed welcome and that Massachusetts would be an aristocracy, not a democracy. But Cotton appealed to scripture in refusing a guarantee of hereditary rule. He could not yield on the main concern of his inquirer, and the puritan lords never did migrate to New England.[21]

Winthrop preferred to have laws made by a small group of "magistrates" elected by the people each year but, in all likelihood, retained in office for life. Puritan voters continually demanded a bigger role for themselves and major restrictions upon the magistrates. Drawing upon the Massachusetts Bay Company charter, they insisted upon electing a House of Deputies to meet four times a year with the magistrates, who in turn emerged as the upper house of the legislature by the 1640s. Winthrop thought of the magistrates as the governing few and the deputies as among the governed, but the deputies would not accept this distinction. They won for themselves an essential share of the power to make laws, and they used it to pass a Body of Liberties in 1641 and a fuller law code in 1648 to restrict the discretionary powers of the magistrates. Neither text had the approval of any authority in England.[22]

After the Restoration, the king became far more threatening to New England's autonomy. Even a charter might not help, as Massachusetts discovered when the Crown revoked the patent of the Massachusetts Bay Company in 1684. From 1686 to 1689 James II ruled Massachusetts through an appointive governor, council, and court system. The House of Deputies was abolished. By 1688 the Crown had merged all of the New England colonies, New York, and East and West New Jersey into a much larger province called the Dominion of New England. Governor Sir Edmund Andros had no intention of confining power to God's elect. He brought into office a number of merchants and other gentlemen who had been excluded on religious grounds before 1686, but by 1689 even many of the newcomers, initially intrigued by the prospect of becoming North America's first intercolonial ruling elite, had grown weary of the autocratic Dominion government. In the wake of England's Glorious Revolution, Boston had one of its own in April 1689 and overthrew the Andros regime. To ensure broad popular support, Massachusetts created several hundred new freemen or voters, in effect abrogating the old government's requirement that they be church members. The era of strict puritan rule was over. In 1691 a new royal charter imposed an appointive governor and justices upon Massachusetts, restored the assembly, and accepted property qualifications, not orthodoxy, as the proper way to limit suffrage.[23]

One result was a drastic change in the people holding office. Few deputies under the old charter became representatives under the new. Partly a generational shift and partly a repudiation of the men who had failed to resist the Dominion of New England adequately, this transformation led to frequent turnover of representatives and considerable uncertainty in government. For two generations godly rule had provided a workable substitute for a conventional ruling class. The province now had to discover whether it could devise a way to do without either or whether it could generate its own ruling families acceptable both to the voters and to British authorities.[24]

In the 1690s about half the representatives in any given assembly were newcomers to the house. By the 1760s that proportion had plummeted to one out of seven. In the 1690s the governor's appointees as justices of the peace (a royal patronage position in Massachusetts in a way that it was not in Virginia) were usually seen as intruders by their towns and seldom elected to the house. By the early 1760s about two-thirds of the representatives were justices, most of whom supported administration policy most of the time. Because the number of offices grew much more slowly than the population, the men who held office stood out more conspicuously over time. And this phenomenon had a pronounced dynastic effect. In two-thirds of the towns that participated actively in provincial politics, four families controlled the office of representative at least two-thirds of the time. In a third of the politically active towns, two families held that post at least half the time. At the highest levels of provincial politics by mid-century, a few families—notably the interrelated Hutchinsons and Olivers—began to act as though Massachusetts owed them its most prestigious appointments, to the great annoyance of such ambitious but less distinguished rivals as the Otises and the Hancocks.[25]

Deference certainly explains much of the success of this emerging elite, but by no means all of it. Far more than in Virginia, royal government in Massachusetts also relied upon influence. Even though their income from fees was never great, those who received appointments from the Crown (the most common were justices and militia officers) and secured election to the legislature were expected to support the governor's policies. But when they voted for highly unpopular measures, the voters could punish them. In times of crisis (the land bank dispute of 1740–41, the controversy over specie resumption after 1748, the excise crisis of 1754), some justices defected to the opposition, and the overall percentage of justices in the house fell sharply, only to climb to greater heights a few years later. The new secular elite had grown accustomed to exercising considerable power, but by 1760 it was still not strong enough to take its position for granted. Even the best families, although they normally got their way, could be challenged. In the hothouse politics of the town of Boston, they usually were.[26]

THE MID-ATLANTIC
The Challenge of Cultural Diversity

The Mid-Atlantic colonies represented still other variations on the same theme. Upper classes emerged in New York and Pennsylvania who laid claim to office on the basis of wealth and family prestige. But ethnic and religious tensions made it difficult to create traditional deference systems that would work effectively across these cultural barriers. These antagonisms almost guaranteed that there would be political conflict within elites, and they greatly complicated the relationship between the elites and ordinary settlers. New York and Pennsylvania devised quite different solutions to these problems.

New York stood out from the rest of North America in one particular. Both under Dutch and English rule it had a small military garrison. Its governors could contemplate the use of overt force in a way that neighboring executives could not. Until about 1700 this threat had a real if unmeasurable impact on public life. Even more characteristic of early New York politics was ethnic conflict, often cast in religious terms. Dutch settlers resented their English conquerors and looked to Calvinism and the Dutch Reformed Church to preserve their way of life. Every English governor, by contrast, hoped to win the cooperation of the most prominent Dutch merchants and landowners. Many of these men accepted public office, and some began to intermarry with the conquerors, a process that threatened to alienate other Dutchmen.[27]

These antagonisms exploded during Jacob Leisler's revolt of 1689, the New York counterpart to the Glorious Revolution in England and Boston. Fearful that Dominion officials in New York would find some way to turn the colony over to Roman Catholic supporters of James II, the Leislerians took control of the fort guarding New York Harbor and, in the months that followed, the whole province. As a group they were heavily Dutch and less prominent and less wealthy than their opponents, but Leislerians typically expressed their anger in religious rather than class terms. For their part, Anti-Leislerians were much more likely to invoke primitive class rhetoric to strip the rebels of any pretension to legitimacy. Leisler, complained Nicholas Bayard, raised "the rabble" against the colony's duly constituted government. To their enemies, Leislerians were "all men of meane birth and sordid Educacon and desperate Fortunes"; all "ye men of best repute for Religion Estates & Integrity" opposed Leisler's regime. As in Virginia, a popular upheaval made upper-class men far more conscious of their social status and far more aware of their vulnerability as a political elite. They responded with indignation. Largely because the Dutch Leislerians could find no effective way to present their case in London to a Dutch king of England, the old elite controlled the appointment of a new governor, returned to New York, and hanged Leisler for treason in 1691.[28]

The resulting hatreds did not subside until the early eighteenth century. As ethnic antagonisms cooled, New York emerged with a pluralistic but intermarried elite that closely controlled access to major offices despite frequent quarrels within the group. After about 1730 the gigantic manorial estates of the Hudson Valley finally began to return good profits, and their owners established regular and close relations with wealthy merchants and prominent lawyers in New York City. Landlord domination of political office went quite far. Of the 137 men who sat in the assembly or the council, acquired a seat on the highest court or practiced law before it, or served as attorney general or register or principal surrogate of the Supreme Court between 1750 and independence, 110 (80.3%) either owned more than a thousand acres or were closely related to someone who did.[29]

Landlord domination of the countryside could generate radicalism in the city by the 1760s. New York's assembly remained quite small—twenty-seven members for most of the eighteenth century. When two landlord factions vied for control, the four seats in New York City often held the balance, and the capital was too large for any one group to dominate for long. The DeLanceys, whose urban links were mostly to commerce, urged voters not to be gulled by the rival Livingstons, whose city spokesmen were mostly lawyers. The Livingstons in turn warned artisans that merchants sought only their own profit and would gladly undersell local crafts with imported English products.[30]

The elite, in short, stimulated class awareness in the city and did a great deal to undermine traditional deference. They sought power to gain access to the influence it brought them. That effort weakened them in some respects, while strengthening them in others. Urban voters began to regard their social superiors with a considerable amount of cynicism. They usually voted against incumbents, only to see the new winners come to terms with the governor in support of unpopular policies.

Pennsylvania's diverse upper class developed still a different pattern. Even more clearly than New York, the colony sustained rival and mutually exclusive elites, one Quaker, the other non-Quaker. In the course of the eighteenth century, the Quakers came to dominate legislative office, while non-Quakers increasingly monopolized executive and judicial posts. Neither alone could become a true ruling class, and politics prevented their convergence. They did not intermarry.

The system took two generations to emerge. Quaker domination of public life through the 1720s permitted frequent factional struggles among members of the Society of Friends. But as Quakers became an ever-smaller minority within the region, they could no longer afford open division. Between 1730 and 1770, wealthy and intermarried Quakers grew less exclusive and less powerful. A highly coherent Quaker Party took shape which controlled the assembly throughout this period, but it evolved from a tight coalition of wealthy Quaker families—the Logans, Pembertons and Norrises stood out—into a more secularized organization led by such non-Quakers as Benjamin

Franklin and Joseph Galloway, men who were willing to respect Quaker scruples but could also negotiate with the Crown in an era of nearly continuous warfare.[31]

The rising non-Quaker gentry—including the Allen, Chew, Hamilton, Shippen, and Willing dynasties—developed in a different direction. Descended from men of established wealth, they emerged as a coherent bloc in the 1730s and 1740s. Capitalizing on the Penn family's defection from the Society of Friends, they captured just about every important office controlled by the proprietors after mid-century—the governor's council, the Supreme Court, the land office, the Philadelphia city corporation, and the College of Philadelphia. Helping themselves to generous shares of proprietary lands, many of them gradually withdrew from trade in a bid to become true gentry. They increasingly intermarried, and found relaxation and amusement only with one another. During the frontier crises of 1755 and 1764, they appealed openly to Scots-Irish Presbyterian and German Lutheran and Reformed voters in an effort to win control of the assembly. They failed, partly because eastern Quaker counties were overrepresented at the frontier's expense, partly also because the proprietary elite had no firm social ties to the people they courted.[32]

In short, the proprietary gentry, for all of their wealth, prestige, exclusiveness, and sense of cohesion, never gained control of the legislative process. Although the aspirations were there, these upper class families were a ruling elite only in a limited sense. Their inability to win elections suggests, at best, weak links of deference between them and the artisans and farmers of Pennsylvania. Their monopoly of high office gave them great potential influence, but they had little impact on a Quaker assembly, few of whose members were interested in military rank, war contracts, or even judicial appointments that would require them to administer oaths.

The governing elites of New York and Pennsylvania differed from both Virginia's and New England's in another important particular. Their prestige and influence crossed colonial boundaries, a phenomenon that became characteristic of the Mid-Atlantic region.[33] Lewis Morris and James Alexander held high office in both New York and New Jersey. Robert Hunter Morris became chief justice of New Jersey and governor of Pennsylvania. John Kinsey served as speaker of the house in both New Jersey and Pennsylvania. This pattern continued into the Revolution. William Livingston achieved political prominence in New York, then moved to New Jersey shortly before independence, and was there elected governor every year from 1776 until his death in 1790. John Dickinson acted as chief executive for Pennsylvania and Delaware at different times. Thomas McKean, who began his public life in Delaware, eventually became governor of Pennsylvania. Gouverneur Morris, who started in New York, represented Pennsylvania in the Constitutional Convention. Although no systematic study of this phenomenon has ever been made, numerous other examples could be cited involving such families as the Smiths of Burlington and Philadelphia, the Antills, Edsalls, Chews, Tilghmans, and Coxes.

Only in this region did prominent families think of themselves as an intercolonial governing class even before independence. They did so, in all probability, because the ethnic and religious groups that made up the region paid little heed to formal colonial boundaries. Jersey Quakers gathered with Pennsylvania Quakers at the yearly meeting of the Society of Friends, while the Dutch long outweighed all rivals in the Hudson Valley and in Bergen County, New Jersey.[34] Scots settled in the Mohawk Valley of New York, at Perth Amboy and its hinterland in New Jersey, and in Pennsylvania, and the Scots-Irish were also widely dispersed through the Mid-Atlantic colonies and the southern backcountry.[35] The Presbyterian Church was always an intercolonial institution, even when it split into Old Side and New Side synods between 1741 and 1758, the first remaining in Philadelphia, the second locating in New York.[36] So from its founding was the College of New Jersey, organized by Presbyterians in the 1740s primarily to meet the church's needs throughout the region, in parts of New England, and increasingly in the upper South as well.[37] Status acquired in one place could carry over to another.

TOWARD A RULING CLASS BY 1763?
Achievements and Limits

On the eve of the revolutionary struggle, how did the colonial elites compare with the English ruling class? The answer to that question depends in good part on understanding how the larger system of class relationships in the colonies compared with Britain's. North America was much more rural and had no set of men as wealthy as the families that governed England. England had no class of laborers as exploited as the slaves in America. The most affluent 1 percent in England probably controlled over 40 percent of the wealth, and the richest 5 percent owned over 70 percent of the kingdom's land and personal property. In the colonies the yeomanry—roughly 60 percent of white householders—controlled 70 percent of the land. The wealthiest 5 percent in colonial society claimed only 30 percent. The most distinctive feature of the colonies was the relative economic autonomy of the middling orders. Thus colonial society had a lower basement and a lower ceiling than England, and it also had far more people crowded into the middle. Yet as the decades passed, the upper classes were becoming more exclusive, more distinctive, and more successful at capturing and holding office.[38]

Relations with social inferiors affected the ability of elites to govern. Virginia's great planters had successfully neutralized overt class conflict by enslaving the people who did most of the physical work in their society and by granting real social privileges to all whites. The officeholders of Massachusetts always faced greater potential opposition from politically alert and increasingly literate middling settlers. The competing upper-class factions of New York often frustrated one another's ambitions, although the DeLancey family did very well for itself in the third quarter of the century. Pennsylvania's rival elites never coalesced, and never dared make many political demands on ordinary settlers. In no province were clientage networks as dense as in Britain, for the goal of family autonomy remained a highly plausible target throughout the large stratum of middling persons. Thus no colony had an upper class as secure as Britain's, but in every colony the men in power by 1760 had more convincing credentials for becoming a traditional ruling class than had been true in 1690. Wealth, power, and status were converging in ways that might eventually have created one or more ruling classes in North America.[39]

Wealth and status earned in the private sphere needed some kind of public sanction to become a right to rule in North America, and the king's representatives in the provinces usually decided who received these favors. The system of titles used throughout the continent by the mid-eighteenth century reflected this hierarchy. Only the governor was addressed as "Your Excellency." In royal colonies he was appointed directly by the Crown, and in Maryland and Pennsylvania by the lord proprietor. Only Rhode Island and Connecticut retained direct election of their chief executives. Members of the council, also royal appointees in most colonies, were called "Honorable" as were justices of a colony's supreme court and the county courts of common pleas. Justices of the peace bore the title "Esquire." Military officers went by their militia rank and, of course, tended to move upwards in the normal course of the life cycle, but not every lieutenant could expect to rise to colonel. Most men seem to have used for the rest of their life the highest title they had ever claimed, even after resigning a civil or military commission. As in England, the title "gentleman" had almost no legal meaning and was used by many individuals, some of whom doubtless had few claims to any such distinction. Between the death of the founding generation and the 1750s, few men appropriated the title in Connecticut, which had no royal governor or court, but it was widespread in Massachusetts and other royal provinces.[40]

Even in Virginia the need to seek Crown approval limited the ability of the planters to become a ruling class. They did not control the ultimate sources of political power in their society. On the other hand, the very existence of the governor's royal court in a province stimulated emulation of Britain's ruling class and roused the continuing ambition among the colonial elite to become more than they were at any particular moment.

For all of their differences, the separate provincial elites shared two common traits. The most conspicuous was similar tastes in consumption—Georgian architecture and furnishings, the latest clothing fashions from London, an interest in similar reading materials— all of which tended to set them apart from less-refined settlers. The other characteristic was an ambiguous relationship to British authority, which they used to ratify their social and political pretensions but which nearly all of them had some experience in resisting on one occasion or another. After 1760 Crown and Parliament would increasingly force the colonial elites to choose whether to rally social inferiors to resist British demands, or retain Britain's good favor at the risk of losing popular acceptance in their colonies.[41]

REVOLUTION
Between Parliament and People

Between the close of the Seven Years' War and the outbreak of the American Revolution, some segments of the colonial elites began to transform themselves into a ruling class capable of governing North America without the support of Whitehall. At first, most of them probably thought of themselves more as part of a local than a continental ruling class, but the imperatives of resistance before independence, and political survival after, broadened their awareness and their ambitions. They were repelling assaults on their prerogatives by the British ruling class, and at the moment of independence in 1776, they probably enjoyed the confidence of most white male Americans. At that point they were not at all certain whether to concentrate their energy at the state or the continental level. In turning to the people at large for support in the struggle against British authority in their own states, the elites promoted a process of political mobilization that acquired its own momentum and proved hard to control. Hence even as they fought off the imperial threat from above, they faced a new democratic challenge from below.

It is highly conceivable that Anglo-American history could have followed a different course. In 1764 Sir Francis Bernard, the royal governor of Massachusetts, proposed the creation of an American "*Nobility* appointed by the *King* for life" as a way to recognize and reinforce the status and authority of the colonial elites. But after the Seven Years' War, London officials adopted a contrary approach. Confronted with the costs of managing an empire of global proportions, they sought to augment the power of the metropolitan ruling class at the colonial elites' expense. The combination of Sugar, Stamp, and Currency Acts passed by Parliament in 1764–65 represented a direct attack on both the elites' economic interests and their political authority.[42]

To rebuff this attack, the elites joined together as never before in protesting Parliament's actions as a violation of the rules of empire. To be sure, there were important differences over questions of strategy and substance. The Virginia House of Burgesses divided almost evenly over Patrick Henry's resolutions boldly challenging parliamentary taxation on grounds of principle. The Hutchinson faction in Massachusetts advocated petitions framed in terms of customary "privileges" rather than constitutional "rights." Yet the intercolonial Stamp Act Congress which met in New York in October 1765 took only two weeks to agree on a basic line of defense, one that reserved to colonial legislatures the exclusive authority to tax the settlers.[43]

The achievement of unity among colonial elites did not, by itself, cause the metropolitan ruling class to relent. Without the action of urban mobs who blocked implementation of the Stamp Act in the fall of 1765, Parliament would probably not even have given serious consideration to the demand for repeal.[44]

Scholars disagree over the extent to which urban crowds acted under upper-class direction during the Stamp Act crisis. Although street organizers such as Ebenezer MacIntosh in Boston and Alexander McDougall in New York City evidently enjoyed the patronage of wealthy sponsors, urban mobs on several occasions clearly exceeded the wishes of their social betters in the resistance movement. After the gutting of Thomas Hutchinson's Boston mansion, for example, Josiah Quincy, Jr., decried "the fury and instability of the populace" and reaffirmed his faith in "that glorious medium, the British Constitution" as a source of protection against anarchy as well as tyranny.[45]

In retrospect, however, what appears most notable about the Stamp Act riots is how the fears and resentments of the participants were focused rather narrowly on stamp distributors and their sympathizers, not on the rich or powerful in general. In mobilizing against the Stamp Act, urban crowds defended not only the principle of home rule, but also the prerogatives of many of those who ruled at home. Some men, such as Thomas Hutchinson in Massachusetts, suffered a loss of prestige that they would never be able to recover. But in New York both the Livingstons and the DeLanceys took sufficiently dramatic stands against the Stamp Act to retain credibility. In Virginia the widespread elite reluctance to encourage resistance quite evaporated between May and September 1765. Philadelphia's Quaker elite, eager to replace proprietary with royal government, permitted protest but discouraged resistance, which proprietary leaders helped to provoke.[46]

Repeal of the Stamp Act in the spring of 1766 represented a major victory for the colonial elites, who had upheld their authority by emphasizing the shared rights and interests of all colonists—or at least of all free adult white males. Yet concurrent disturbances in the countryside suggest the enormous risks run by the elites when they turned to the populace at large for support. Developments in New York provide a case in point. While residents of New York City celebrated the news of repeal, thousands of tenants and squatters in the Hudson Valley rioted in protest against the manorial claims of several of the colony's largest landlords. Not surprisingly, although the Livingstons and other lordly sorts had eagerly joined the fight against the Stamp Act, they raised no cry of tyranny when the royal governor ordered British soldiers to suppress the land riots. In this instance, the use of military force worked. But it also highlighted the weakness of deference and influence as mechanisms of social control in rural New York.[47]

During the decade between the Stamp Act crisis and the Declaration of Independence, the colonial elites divided internally over how best to protect their interests in the face of renewed efforts by the British ruling class to reduce their power and status. On one side were loyalists (or Tories) who accepted colonial subordination as a prerequisite for social and political stability; on the other side were patriots (or Whigs) who dared to risk disorder for the sake of preserving, and enhancing, American autonomy. Although a full explanation of why the elites of some colonies were overwhelmingly patriots, while those of other colonies contained a sizable number of loyalists, remains elusive, there seems to have been a general pattern to elite allegiances. In many colonies, at least, the ultimate division over independence followed longstanding partisan lines and was anticipated by conflicting responses to the Townshend Acts.[48]

Whereas the Stamp Act had served to bring together various elite factions in mutual opposition to British policy, the more limited challenges embodied in the Townshend Acts tended to drive these groups apart. The external character of the Townshend duties (as distinct from the direct or internal tax imposed by the Stamp Act) as well as the intention of using their revenues to pay the salaries of high government officials meant that members of "court" factions already aligned politically with the governors had less to lose and something to gain from the legislation. Thus the Hutchinsons and Olivers in Massachusetts and, after their electoral triumph in 1769, the DeLanceys in New York openly defended the legitimacy of the Townshend Acts. The Quaker Party in Pennsylvania again hesitated to encourage overt resistance. There was no "Townshend Acts Congress," and nonimportation agreements were only belatedly achieved and partially enforced. Yet colonial rhetoric escalated as members of "country" parties already aligned politically against the governors increasingly dominated the leadership of the resistance movement. Well schooled in the logic of English opposition thought, these radical Whigs attacked imperial policy not only as a violation of the rules of empire but also as a ministerial conspiracy to reduce the colonists to abject slavery.[49]

Partial repeal of the Townshend duties eased tensions temporarily, but fear took control on both sides of the Atlantic after passage of the Tea Act in 1773. It prompted the Boston Tea Party, which led in turn to the Boston Port Act, the Massachusetts Government Act, and other efforts to single out Massachusetts for punishment. Instead, these Coercive (or Intolerable) Acts made the plight of Massachusetts the common cause of colonists across the continent. The consensus that developed in 1774–75 was broader than that of 1765–66. While court factions within the elites tended to fall away, for the first time a large proportion of the yeomanry joined actively in resistance to British authority.[50]

Colonial outrage over the Coercive Acts led to the creation of an institutional framework for leadership by an intercolonial patriot elite—the Continental Congress—and the restructuring of authority at all levels of society. By initially entrusting the enforcement of its directives to local committees and provincial congresses and conventions, Congress acknowledged that it lacked the police powers of a full-fledged ruling body. Yet its prestige exceeded its might, and it rapidly expanded its executive functions. Between 1774 and 1776, in a process that might be termed "reciprocal legitimation," the various levels of the patriot counterregime conferred authority on each other, while organizing the populace at large first to support a trade embargo, then to fight a war, and eventually to endorse independence. At the apex rested Congress, which ought to be conceptualized, not as an American legislature or counterpart to Parliament, but as a plural executive for the continent, a substitute for the imperial Crown.[51]

From a continental perspective, the process appears remarkably smooth. No comprehensive analysis of congressional membership is available, but a survey of the delegates who served between 1774 and 1776 reveals that three-fifths boasted prior experience in provincial assemblies—a rough indication of the elite status most had in common.[52] As the imperial crisis intensified, militant and moderate delegates alike recognized the need for compromise and cooperation to survive against the British threat. The year-long delay between the creation of the Continental Army and the Declaration of Independence reflected this central concern for unity. Despite the continuing reservations of some delegates, the final break with Great Britain proved relatively simple to make: the overthrow of imperial authority did not require the physical elimination of the king or the metropolitan ruling class.[53] In 1765 the colonial elites had looked to those below them on the social scale for validation of their authority in the face of the challenge launched from abroad and above. In 1776 the wisdom of their strategy seemed confirmed when ordinary settlers overwhelmingly accepted the judgment of Congress about which regime in which colony was legitimate. Congress had indeed replaced George III, a truly revolutionary event.

Yet the continental perspective can be misleading. As resistance developed into war, and war into massive revolution and independence, many members of Congress left to take up other duties. Some, like George Washington and Benjamin Franklin, accepted military commands or diplomatic posts in continental service. Many others, such as Patrick Henry and Samuel Adams, returned to their states and resumed their roles as local rather than "national" leaders. By the late 1770s even congressmen often complained that their body could not hold a sufficient corps of talented men. To the extent that an interstate ruling elite was beginning to appear in these years, its center was more in the officer corps of the Continental Army than in Congress.[54]

Within the states, the transition from resistance to Revolution often created great turmoil. Especially in provinces where a high proportion of the colonial elite remained loyal to the Crown, well-to-do patriots out of necessity welcomed "new men" from lower social ranks into positions of power. These newcomers possessed their own interests and pursued their own agendas, generating controversy and conflict within the patriot movement.[55]

Nowhere were the results more dramatic than in Pennsylvania, where the resistance movement discredited virtually the entire Quaker Party (except Franklin) and many proprietary leaders as well. Men of humbler origins quickly rose to prominence. Beginning as lesser partners in Philadelphia's patriot coalition, artisans after 1774 jumped to positions of command within successive committees of resistance. By early 1776 mechanics comprised fully 40 percent of Philadelphia's committeemen—more than the proportion of merchants and lawyers combined. When John Dickinson and other prominent Pennsylvania patriots hesitated to cut all ties with Britain, artisan leaders went their own way and pressed energetically for independence.[56]

In seizing the revolutionary initiative, artisans repudiated deference both in practice and in principle. A letter circulated by the Philadelphia militia during the summer of 1776 articulated the mechanics' position. When choosing delegates to draft a state constitution, the militiamen warned, "great and over-grown rich Men will be improper to be trusted, they will be too apt to be framing Distinctions in Society because they will reap the Benefits of such Distinctions." This was not a call for the redistribution of private wealth, but a demand for the restructuring of the social order by choosing political decision-makers from outside the upper class.[57]

In selecting delegates to Pennsylvania's constitutional convention, voters followed the militiamen's advice and elected men without impressive wealth or elite connections. The delegates in turn drafted a constitution conferring the right to vote and hold office on all adult male taxpayers and providing for a unicameral assembly, annually elected and open to public view. Yet the convention declined to endorse the principle of an "agrarian law" to prevent the concentration of property. In a market economy devoid of business corporations, the fear of tyranny focused on the abuse of political prerogatives rather than on exploitation by capital in the private sphere. Democratic control of government seemed an adequate solution to the problem.[58]

Simultaneously the surviving leaders of the proprietary party began to regroup within an Anticonstitutionalist or "Republican" opposition (opposed, that is, to the radical constitution of 1776). They proved quite adroit at mobilizing various discontented groups, including even Quakers and other pacifists, against the radicals. For the first time the two old elites, proprietary and Quaker, showed signs of merging. They would soon begin thinking in national terms as well.[59]

REVOLUTION
The Expanding Challenge of Popular Upheaval

The upheaval in Pennsylvania in 1776 foreshadowed conflicts that would vex Americans for the next dozen years and both hinder and promote, in different ways, the formation of a national ruling class. The challenge from below came with greater force and coherence than ever before, but it also gave a new urgency to elite efforts to unite and regain control of public affairs. As a diverse population struggled with Thomas Paine's challenge "to begin the world over again," lines of cleavage appeared at all levels of the polity. Upper-class patriots struggled among themselves for dominance in the Continental Congress, while they were repeatedly challenged from below in state legislatures. However, with the drafting and ratification of the Constitution in 1787–88, prospects for the creation of a national ruling class acquired unprecedented plausibility as Federalists sought to establish a central government with the power and prestige to bring order out of tumult.

In combining to oppose the British ruling class, patriot leaders had overcome longstanding intercolonial prejudices, but they could not erase differences of economic interest, social organization, and cultural tradition. Hence it took the state legislatures four years to ratify the Articles of Confederation, a document that resembled a treaty for mutual defense more than a framework for national government. Nor did the shared experience of the War for Independence solidify ties among the state elites. As a result, the Continental Congress emerged from the war more divided and less respected than when it entered the struggle. So weak was the chain of authority in 1783 that Congress fled Philadelphia to escape harassment by soldiers demanding back pay. When they regrouped in Princeton, New Jersey, many delegates doubted that the American Union could long survive the end of the war which had called it into existence.[60]

Within Congress, disputes over financial, frontier, and foreign policy reflected and reinforced a spirit of sectional antagonism. Analyses of Congressional voting behavior during and after the Revolution reveal an evolving pattern of geographically based parties. During the late 1770s North (or East) opposed South, usually successfully. Then in the early 1780s a newly formed Mid-Atlantic bloc of reluctant revolutionaries turned ardent nationalists took charge. Since they were the heirs of the only colonial elites with extensive intercolonial experience, their nationalism was not surprising. But they lost both their control of Congress and their internal cohesion with the advent of peace. By the mid-1780s Southerners battled Northerners over questions of commercial reform and westward expansion. The split over John Jay's treaty negotiations with Spain in 1786 generated open talk of dividing the United States into two or more separate confederacies.[61]

Meanwhile, challenges to elite control within the states came from two distinct quarters: artisans and laborers in urban centers on the one hand, and farmers, especially in the backcountry, on the other. In general, both groups rallied to the support of elite patriots at the beginning of the Revolution, but each group grew disaffected as the War for Independence dragged on and dragged it down. While the economic impact of the war is difficult to quantify, one recent effort suggests that, on average, Americans' personal income fell dramatically over the course of the conflict. After the war British policy prevented the revival of conventional trading patterns. Consequently, the return of peace produced neither prosperity nor consensus.[62]

Major seaports were among the first areas to suffer the war's negative economic consequences, including enemy occupation, inflation, unemployment, and food shortages. Crowds gathered not only to toss Tories out of town but to seize the property of genteel Whigs suspected of engrossing necessities in a time of collective emergency. From Boston to Charleston the patriot coalition threatened to dissolve along class lines. After the war urban artisans organized to demand government intervention on their behalf. In New York City, for instance, they founded the General Society of Mechanics and Tradesmen and nominated their own candidates for state offices. In Boston they formed the Association of Tradesmen and Manufacturers and lobbied successfully for a state protective tariff. By such means the "mechanic interest" asserted its autonomy and, usually without resort to riots, put political pressure on the patriot elite.[63]

A greater but separate challenge to elite control came from the countryside. Early in the war many of the economic dislocations that fueled tensions in the cities worked to the benefit of farmers in the hinterlands. Domestic food shortages brought higher prices for surplus crops. Inflated paper currency made it easier to pay taxes, which were also more fairly apportioned than before in most states when reforms in the mode of property assessment transferred a greater part of the total burden onto the rich. As a result, farmers found the early rewards of independence enticing—perhaps too enticing for their long-term good.[64]

For upper-class patriots, tax reform was part of "the price of Revolution" they had to pay to retain the allegiance of the rural majority. Many Whig grandees also bought government securities to help finance the war effort, sometimes risking their personal fortunes for the common welfare. Once victory seemed assured, however, wealthy creditors throughout America called for full funding of state and national debts, hard money, and heavy taxes to make good on public obligations as soon as possible. When depression set in shortly after the war's conclusion, they also demanded speedy repayment of private debts in specie, partly because many of them owed large sums to British merchants.[65]

Backcountry farmers reacted to these demands with alarm. Having become increasingly alert to market opportunities during the war, rural producers in the flush of peace and victory took advantage of easy credit to purchase substantial quantities of foreign imports. Given the general shortage of specie in postwar America, large payments due in coin threatened widespread financial ruin in the countryside. Disillusioned by the record of elite leadership, rural voters overcame deferential habits and began to exercise their democratic rights. Exploiting electoral changes wrought by the new state constitutions, farmers from interior regions increasingly chose persons like themselves to represent them in the state legislatures. The result was a series of political confrontations within state governments across the continent over questions of monetary policy, taxes, and debt relief—and eventually the outbreak of Shays's Rebellion in Massachusetts.[66]

Not coincidentally, Pennsylvania, with its highly democratic political framework, was the first state to introduce paper money as legal tender during the postwar crisis. By contrast, in Virginia, where the gentry retained political control, the assembly never gave paper money serious consideration, although it did delay collection of, and then lower, taxes. New York followed a middle course. By the mid-eighties a yeoman-based legislative bloc tied to Governor George Clinton had put the likes of Robert R. Livingston, Gouvernour Morris, and John Jay on the defensive in state politics. Yet descendants of New York's colonial elite remained influential in the upper house. Three times the New York Assembly passed a paper money bill only to have the Senate reject it. Finally, on the fourth attempt, the Senate gave way, and New York issued paper currency usable for tax purposes and certain private debts.[67]

The rebellion in Massachusetts reveals both the utility and futility of influence as a means of upper-class rule in postwar America. Although farmers comprised nearly half of the lower house and almost one third of the upper house in the 1780s, the Massachusetts General Court refused time and again either to issue paper money or to provide alternative means of tax or debt relief. The key to this puzzle lies in the dynamics of governmental patronage. Most officeholders who served in the legislature shared the upper class's interest in upholding public credit and private contracts. Together they stood firm against agrarian calls for help.[68]

Government intransigence prompted rural insurgence, especially in western communities in which prewar deference networks had disintegrated. What began as a series of courthouse riots developed, during the fall of 1786, into a concerted armed revolt. Having exhausted other means of political control, Governor James Bowdoin and his council opted for the application of brute force. After efforts to raise troops under congressional auspices came to naught, Boston merchants in January 1787 agreed to finance a special state army to crush the rebellion. The soldiers did their job, and before winter was out, law and order—but not harmony—were restored across the state.[69]

Had Boston's artisans rallied to the cause of rural debtors, the outcome might have been different. But Boston's mechanics remained loyal to the government during the crisis. Although they, too, suffered severely from the dislocations of the postwar economy, the memory of wartime inflation and food shortages prompted a distrust of paper money and, more generally, of the motives of the "landed interest." In Massachusetts, as elsewhere, artisans and farmers challenged the patriot elite separately, but not as a united front.[70]

THE FEDERAL CONSTITUTION AND THE MAKING OF AN AMERICAN RULING CLASS

Faced with this dual threat from below and concerned to resolve conflicts among themselves at the top, upper-class patriots more than ever before turned to national consolidation as a solution to political and social disorder. Most of the fifty-five delegates who gathered at Philadelphia during the summer of 1787 to draft the federal Constitution fit this description. Two-thirds were rich, and three-fifths were well-born or well-married. A large majority had participated in earlier continental conclaves: three had attended the Stamp Act Congress, eight had signed the Declaration of Independence, and forty-two had served in the Continental Congress. Twenty-two saw military service during the Revolution, including George Washington, two other generals, and three members of his staff.[71] Yet who the delegates were was less important than what they tried to do. With a keen sense of urgency, they sought to create a political structure capable of appeasing the concerns of urban artisans, reducing the power of backcountry farmers, and promoting the development of a national ruling class that would "think continentally," rather than in sectional, state, or regional terms.[72]

Few delegates were prepared to endorse Alexander Hamilton's call for a national political hierarchy capped by a chief executive and senate serving for life—a plan self-consciously modeled on the British Constitution and also reminiscent of the proposal made a quarter century before by Sir Francis Bernard for the creation of an American nobility with lifetime titles.[73] Nobody called for the introduction of hereditary privilege. But most delegates agreed on the need to curb "the excess of democracy," as Elbridge Gerry put it, that seemed to plague the state legislatures. He favored a requirement of popular elections in the federal government only "if it were so qualified that men of honor & character might not be unwilling to be joined in the appointments." "The people," agreed Roger Sherman, "[immediately] should have as little to do as may be about the Government. They want information and are constantly likely to be misled." In tracing the source of "the evils under which the U. S. laboured," Edmund Randolph affirmed that "every man had found it in the turbulence and follies of democracy." Comfortable with the secrecy in which they debated, delegates could speak their minds about the people.[74]

Working from James Madison's blueprint, the delegates designed a central government whose republican architecture would be supported by the pillars of deference, influence, and force. They intended to strengthen all three. Although the drafting process itself was marked by sharp contention, the final document reflected a broad consensus over who should rule at home. Thus the question of how to select and apportion the Senate generated great debate, yet delegates on opposing sides shared John Dickinson's conviction that it should "consist of the most distinguished characters, distinguished for their rank in life and weight in property, and bearing as strong a likeness to the British House of Lords as possible." When Charles Pinckney questioned whether conditions in the United States were conducive "to the rapid distinction of ranks," Madison responded in the affirmative. "In all civilized Countries," he explained, "the people fall into different classes hav[in]g a real or supposed difference of interests." While he acknowledged that America was more egalitarian than European nations, he insisted that "we cannot however be regarded even at this time as one homogeneous mass," and he predicted that in the future both social inequality and class resentment would increase. "No agrarian attempts [i.e., efforts to pass legislation limiting property holdings] have yet been made in the Country," he warned, "but symptoms of a leveling spirit . . . have sufficiently appeared in . . . certain quarters to give notice of the future danger." By this logic, a high-toned Senate was not only feasible, it was necessary to preserve liberty and justice in a stratified republic.[75]

Just as significant as the framers' preference for a high-toned Senate was their plan for a compact lower house. Notwithstanding their last-minute decision to raise the maximum number of representatives from one per forty thousand inhabitants to one per thirty thousand, the body was designed to be small—65 members at the start, virtually the same size as the assemblies of New York and

Pennsylvania, and considerably smaller than the Virginia House, much less the Massachusetts assembly, which numbered over 200 members in 1787. By Madison's own reckoning, the ratio of one representative to thirty thousand inhabitants approximated that achieved in the British House of Commons—with the large proportion of MPs from pocket boroughs excepted. Embedded in this calculation was a strategy for reestablishing a safe political distance between the people and those who governed in their name.[76]

Madison explained this strategy elegantly in *The Federalist* no. 10. On the one hand, the large size of electoral districts would favor the selection of "men who possess the most attractive merit, and the most diffusive and established characters." Only men of reputation—the upper class—would be known to all voters throughout a large district of 30,000 people, which was about twice the size of Boston or Baltimore. On the other hand, the large size of the republic would inhibit the formation of an "unjust and interested majority" bent on subverting the rights of others, especially their right to property. Madison assumed that deference would prevail so long as voters chose representatives on the basis of their general reputation, not the particular interests they advocated. He did not justify upper-class rule for its own sake, but he insisted that the enlightened few could better judge the public good and protect private liberty than the impassioned many. Since the foremost danger came from below during the 1780s (in the form of "a rage for paper money, for an abolition of debts"), the solution lay in shifting power to those above.[77]

At the same time that they sought to revive deferential politics, the framers of the Constitution intended to give the federal government enough power to rule the United States as a single nation-state, rather than as a league of sovereign units. Although they made no attempt to eliminate the separate state governments, they did wish to establish a central regime capable of subordinating sectional and localistic interests to the national good. The Constitution gave the federal government independent means both to raise revenue and enforce its will. By conferring upon Congress (in conjunction with the president) the authority not only to levy imposts and direct taxes, but also to create an executive bureaucracy, a standing army, and even a nationally coordinated militia, the framers provided the basis for a stronger concentration of influence and force than Parliament had had at its disposal within America when attempting to reform the colonies after 1763.[78]

Yet the framers also realized that the means for transferring power to a high-toned central government had to rest upon the people's broad commitment to popular sovereignty. The convention had to draw upon the revolutionary experience of ordinary citizens at the state level. It had to build upon active consent. "Notwithstanding the oppression & injustice experienced among us from democracy," George Mason reminded his fellow delegates early in the proceedings, "the genius of the people is in favor of it, and the genius of the people must be consulted." The delegates could create a government capable of using effective force, but they could not use force to impose such a government. Legitimacy required popular ratification.[79]

The ratification struggle revealed that while not everyone accepted Madison's diagnosis, proponents and opponents of the document alike understood the elitist implications of his remedy. Most ominous from the Antifederalist point of view was the prospect that rule by the enlightened few would devolve into an aristocratic oligarchy along European lines. As young John Quincy Adams noted in his diary, "If the Constitution be adopted it will be a grand point in favor of the aristocratic party: there are to be no titles of nobility; there will be great distinctions; and those distinctions will soon be hereditary, and we shall consequently have nobles, but no titles."[80] What to the Federalists was a framework for responsible self-government seemed to their antagonists a program for class oppression.

Central to the dispute was the question of what sort of men should rule a republic. Whereas Madison argued for entrusting power primarily to those at the apex of the social order, Antifederalist Melancton Smith of New York contended that "those in middling circumstances have less temptation; they are inclined by habit, and the company with whom they associate, to set bounds to their passions and appetites." "When the interest of this part of the community is pursued, the public good is pursued," Smith explained, "because the body of every nation consists of this class, and because the interests of both the rich and the poor are involved in that of the middling class." Hence members of the "middling class" ought to predominate in a republican legislature—as indeed they increasingly did within the states.[81]

Notwithstanding the popular appeal of such Antifederalist logic, the Federalists won the contest over ratification. They did so in part because the dual threat from below never coalesced into a single force. Backcountry farmers proved highly suspicious of the Constitution, but urban artisans responded warmly to the prospect of a national government strong enough to promote economic growth. More generally, the Federalists out-organized their foes and made further concessions—such as the promise of a Bill of Rights—when these proved necessary.[82]

The framers, in short, believed that they had found a way to secure popular consent for the establishment of a genuine ruling class in

which they, of course, would play a prominent role. Few of them realized that they had also created a system that could give ordinary
citizens a far more active voice in continental affairs than any of
them had ever had before. Over the short term, Madison's understanding prevailed. Over the long run, however, Melancton Smith's
vision would be largely realized—ironically, with Madison's help.

THE UNMAKING OF AN AMERICAN RULING CLASS

Initially it appeared that the Constitution would produce the sort of
political leadership the framers desired. The First Congress had a
distinctly more elite cast to it than contemporary state legislatures.
Nearly half of its members hailed from prominent colonial families,
most were rich, and only a small minority were practicing farmers.[83]
This pattern persisted through the federal government's first decade
of operation, especially after the capital moved back to Philadelphia,
where ambitious public figures from every state had numerous opportunities to socialize and even intermarry with the nationalizing
elite of the nation's largest city. Their efforts suggest that real potential existed for the consolidation of a national ruling class based
primarily on wealth and breeding.[84]

But contrary to colonial tendencies and Antifederalist fears, the
federal Congress did not evolve into a hereditary oligarchy akin to
the British Parliament. Partisan conflicts during the 1790s prevented the integration of the patriot elites and stimulated new efforts to mobilize the citizenry at large against established authority.
The defeat of the Federalists in 1800 marked an end of the trend toward centralized government by a national ruling class. It also sig-
nalled the effective convergence, as in 1774–76, of artisans and
farmers under the same party banner.

The very effort to solidify a continental ruling class began its unmaking. As the first secretary of the treasury, Alexander Hamilton
sought to accomplish indirectly through federal fiscal policy what he
could not do directly through the institutional framework of the Constitution. Again he turned to Great Britain for his example and proposed a program true to English precedent. If he could not have a
chief executive and Senate serving for life, at least he would have a
substantial national treasury to pay for energetic government and to
promote unity within the top echelons of society. Full funding of the
federal debt, assumption of the state debts, and the creation of a national bank promised to tie wealthy creditors throughout the country
to the federal government, while affording them added economic leverage within their respective states. The purport of Hamilton's pro-

gram, in brief, was to use the influence of the federal government to speed the transition of state elites into a national ruling class.[85]

Hamilton did not anticipate that his program would generate fierce contention rather than mutual cooperation among state elites. Like the Continental Congress before it, the federal Congress during the early 1790s divided sharply along sectional lines. The cleavage was rooted in differing upper-class interests. Harder hit by the war and more inclined to speculate in western lands and slaves than in government securities, southern planters had less to gain from Hamilton's funding program than northern merchants, especially the 150 or so who were the windfall winners in the assumption sweepstakes.[86] Similarly, southern congressmen perceived in the national bank and Hamilton's friendly policy toward Great Britain a design to sacrifice the welfare of the landed interest to that of the commercial, and to pass control of the government from proper representatives to northern stock jobbers.[87] By 1794 the efforts of the Constitution's framers to balance "the two great divisions of Northern & Southern interests" had seemingly come to naught. Instead, the process was already under way whereby, for the first time in the history of the republic, the elite of one section was learning how to undermine the bonds of deference and influence that supported the elite in another section. Reasonably secure as rulers within their own states, southern planters, often working through radical English and Irish émigré journalists, discovered how to appeal directly to farmers and artisans in the Mid-Atlantic states against their Federalist officeholders. For the time being, Federalist New England remained largely immune to these efforts.[88]

Thanks in good measure to Madison, the battle over Hamilton's fiscal program developed into a broad-based partisan rivalry. Having attempted through the Constitution to filter out the passions of the multitudes and reestablish elite predominance in government, Madison in the early 1790s dramatically switched course and moved to mobilize the multitudes against the Federalist administration he had helped to put in place. Not that he was as inconsistent in his positions as Hamilton alleged. To Madison's mind, the primary threat to the public good in the 1790s was quite different from what it had been in the 1780s. Then the peril had come from unjust majorities dominating various state governments; now the danger consisted of an unjust sectional minority manipulating the national government. "If a faction consists of less than a majority," Madison had noted in *Federalist* no. 10, "relief is supplied by the republican principle, which enables the majority to defeat its sinister views by a regular vote."[89] With Thomas Jefferson as his great collaborator, Madison set about organizing the Republican party in order to rally a virtuous (as opposed to factious) majority of voters nationwide to rescue the country from subversion by Hamilton and his corrupt cabal.[90]

In the South, Republicans found plenty of allies among the state elites. Consequently, although a number of prominent southerners remained loyal to the Federalist cause, the growth of Republican opposition there in the 1790s tended to reinvigorate rather than subvert deferential attitudes.[91]

In the North, however, the rise of the Republican party had democratic implications. In New England and the Mid-Atlantic states, Republican leadership quite often went to men who lacked elite credentials. It also included many upwardly mobile merchants and manufacturers, some of whom became quite wealthy, whose personal prospects were threatened by Hamilton's program. Northern Jeffersonians challenged the better-established Federalists by appealing to the economic interests and social resentments of artisans and farmers. Writing in the Philadelphia press in the fall of 1792, Madison outlined the strategy. He portrayed the Federalists as men "more partial to the opulent than to the other classes of society" who hoped that "the government itself may by degrees be narrowed into fewer hands, and approximated to an hereditary form." "[H]aving debauched themselves into a persuasion that mankind are incapable of governing themselves," he charged, "it follows with them, of course, that government can be carried on only by the pageantry of rank, the influence of money and emoluments, and the terror of military force."[92]

Federalists denounced Republicans in equally virulent terms. Against the backdrop of the French Revolution and the outbreak of war in Europe, Hamilton and his supporters interpreted the Republican challenge as a fundamental assault on the political stability of the new nation. They railed against the dangers of Jacobinism and mobocracy, and savaged the Democratic-Republican societies for assuming the right to agitate against the policies of the nation's duly elected rulers.[93] Turning provisions of the Constitution to their advantage, the Federalists employed influence to promote their cause. As Hamilton had explained some years before, "the reason of allowing Congress to appoint its own officers of the Customs, collectors of the taxes and military officers of every rank is to create in the interior of each State, a mass of influence in favor of the Federal Government." Once in power he put this strategy into practice. A study of the civil service during the 1790s demonstrates that partisan considerations played a critical part in the choice of customs officers, postmasters, and other lower-echelon federal officials. These men in turn helped build the Federalist party at the local level.[94]

When deference and influence proved inadequate to uphold federal authority, the Federalists resorted to coercion. By calling out a massive army to crush the Whiskey Rebellion in 1794, the Washington administration aimed not only to enforce the excise tax on liquor in western Pennsylvania, but also to demonstrate the capacity of the national government to command obedience over the full domain of the United States. By passing the Alien and Sedition Acts in 1798, congressional Federalists sought not only to protect the nation from foreign provocateurs during a war scare but also to silence the Republican press. In both cases, the Federalists followed the example of the British ruling class in aggressively suppressing domestic dissent.[95]

If the Federalists had won an enduring victory, they most probably would have built something like another England in America. But they failed. Why? The question defies a simple answer and has received little scholarly attention in recent years. Any explanation must be tentative.

The Mid-Atlantic nationalists do seem to have made their biggest mistakes in their home territory. Their triumph in Pennsylvania politics from the mid-1780s into the mid-1790s depended upon the ability of former proprietary men to merge with and represent Quakers and German sectarians who, as the wartime victims of Constitutionalist disfranchisement policies, helped give the Federalists (Anticonstitutionalists in state politics) a solid popular majority. The use of force against whiskey rebels and later against John Fries's tax rioters broke the still-fragile deferential links between Federalist leaders and their voting base. In England force was usually an emergency expedient called upon to restore the more peaceful devices of deference and influence. In Pennsylvania it killed both, at least for the Federalists. By the late 1790s the struggle for that state was all but over, with the Jeffersonian Republicans as huge winners, despite the continuing threat of a French war.[96]

Of course Pennsylvania was not the nation, or even the whole Mid-Atlantic region, but in a country tightly balanced between Federalist New England and the Jeffersonian South, it counted heavily. Elsewhere, the Republican party's expansive democratic appeal contributed greatly to Federalism's defeat at the polls in 1800, and yet the first party system was more than a contest between democracy and aristocracy, even in the North. Federalists enjoyed popular support where their fiscal and commercial policies produced concrete economic benefits, particularly in New England. While they alienated large numbers of urban artisans in Mid-Atlantic cities during the 1790s, they made significant inroads among frontiersmen and some farmers who had opposed ratification of the Constitution. New York,

New Jersey, and Delaware all became closely contested battle-grounds, with New York proving decisive.[97]

To a large extent, the fate of the Federalists after the Whiskey Rebellion rested on European developments over which they had little control, but to which they might have responded more adroitly. Although widespread outrage at Jay's Treaty put their pro-British foreign policy to the test in 1795, three years later the groundswell of patriot fervor after the XYZ Affair presented the Federalists with an enormous opportunity. Had President John Adams asked for an official declaration of war against France in 1798 (as Hamilton and other Federalist leaders desired), the Federalists might have been able to discredit their opponents for good in most northern states and even in parts of the South, much as the Republicans later used the War of 1812 to destroy Federalist credibility. But after arousing passionate Republican opposition through his support of the Alien and Sedition Acts, Adams pursued a more pacific course, one that left the Federalists deeply divided and opened the way for Republican victory in 1800.[98]

REFLECTIONS
Private Wealth and Public Power in Republican America

Republican ascendancy after 1800 had profound implications. Thomas Jefferson in his first inaugural address proclaimed that henceforth, in principle, the majority would rule. More important, in practice he and his party set about shrinking the scope and functions of the federal government. As a result, during his first term in office the momentum toward political centralization was reversed, and power began to shift from the national level back to the states, where the ratio of legislative representatives to the general population was much higher than in Congress. Although this trend was interrupted by the Embargo of 1807–9 and the War of 1812, it was resumed with the "Era of Good Feelings." By the 1820s state governments were taking the lead in shaping economic and social policy.[99] "The federal government is hardly concerned with anything but foreign affairs," Alexis de Tocqueville concluded after his tour of the United States in 1831–32; "it is the state governments which really control American society." He was right.[100]

With the resurgence of state authority in the early nineteenth century, political power moved down the social scale, much as it had during the revolutionary era. When Tocqueville decried "the tyranny of the majority," he was referring to the operation of state governments, not the national regime. Modern studies on the composition of state legislatures indicate that men of moderate circumstance predominated in these assemblies.[101] Contrary to the hopes of the Constitution's framers, Melancton Smith's vision of middle-class democracy was largely realized by the Age of Jackson, although a few southern states held out longer than others. Nowhere else in the Western world was political power more sharply separated from wealth and breeding. Tocqueville saw that pattern quite clearly. "In the United States," he wrote, "it is men of moderate pretensions who engage in the twists and turns of politics. Men of parts and vaulting ambition generally avoid power to pursue wealth."[102]

The main theme of this essay has been that this result represented a fundamental break with the pre-revolutionary pattern of political development. In the seventeenth century, hardly anyone doubted that those who governed should be set apart from the people they ruled, although demographic and economic circumstances inhibited the emergence of stable colonial elites. During the first half of the eighteenth century, as colonies became more socially complex, upper-class families established their right to rule at the provincial level, deliberately emulating as much as possible aristocratic English norms. Within the imperial context, however, the colonial elites remained clearly inferior to the increasingly cohesive ruling class of the mother country. When the metropolitan ruling class sought to curb longstanding colonial rights and privileges after the Seven Years' War, the colonial elites had no alternatives but to yield or turn to those below them on the social scale for help in resisting this challenge to their authority. They proved successful in rallying mass support, but once mobilized, urban artisans and backcountry farmers began to press new demands of their own. By the end of the conflict, congressional authority was on the wane at the continental level, and in the mid-1780s patriot elites also found themselves losing control of public policy to men of middling status within the states.

Through the creation of a stronger central government, the framers of the Constitution sought to reverse the decline in the political prospects of America's upper classes. Federalists envisioned a national regime dominated by "the wise, the rich, and the good," as Hamilton put it, and thus endowed with sufficient prestige and power to command popular loyalty and obedience. But conflicts between elites of different states and regions prevented the consolidation of a national ruling class in the 1790s. Neither deference, influence, nor force could stop the Jeffersonian victory in the "Revolution of 1800."

Because of the Jeffersonians the divergence from English precedent became decisive. After 1800 power shifted away from the national government and toward the state legislatures comprised of middling men. Tocqueville, whatever his faults, grasped this basic democratic fact of American life. Men of great wealth and breeding did not disappear from American society. Indeed, they grew far richer than their predecessors had ever been, but they acquired no hegemony over politics. Few of them even held office. This pattern took firm hold before the United States transformed itself from a society of autonomous producers into one of employers and employees, and the consequences, though less conspicuous now than in 1850, are still highly visible.

The Jeffersonian revolution even transformed the meaning of corruption in American politics. Both before and right after the Revolution, the fear of corruption concentrated on the possibility that the executive would undermine the legislature and seduce assemblymen or private citizens through the favors it could offer. The public sphere always seemed capable of destroying the integrity of the private. In the nineteenth century corruption increasingly came to mean that private wealth might undermine the integrity of the public sphere. Influence peddling no longer implied an initiative from government. It meant that wealthy citizens would be able to buy favors from less affluent officials. That anxiety remains a central concern of American politics, the price that the republic has learned to pay for the way that it has divorced its political and economic hierarchies.[103]

As the nineteenth century unfolded, and as the Marxian transition to a nation of owners and wage laborers took firm hold, the Jeffersonian revolution began to acquire new ironies. Rich Americans acquired fortunes that matched Europe's grandest. Yet they still did not govern, a situation that shocked one onlooker, British Prime Minister William E. Gladstone. He learned in 1877 that railroad baron Cornelius Vanderbilt had left to his son the world's first $100-million industrial fortune (equal to more than a third of the entire federal budget). Wealth on so gigantic a scale ought not to exist accompanied by no "obligation to society," Gladstone declared. "The government ought to take it away from him, as it is too dangerous a power for one man to have." Yet William Vanderbilt doubled that fortune before his own death eight years later, and John D. Rockefeller had amassed $900 million—more than double the federal budget—when he retired in 1897. By then the families of Rockefeller and Andrew Carnegie alone had amassed fortunes that approached 10 percent of the gross national product of the entire country, which was $14.6 billion. None of these men held office in the United States or answered to any kind of political constituency. Yet their routine business decisions altered the lives of thousands of their countrymen and seriously affected millions more. By then it was a distinctive American pattern—enormous economic power without political accountability.[104]

As every subsequent reform movement has asked, citizens had to wonder what to make of America's political economy. Had the Revolution destroyed the ruling class? Or had it created a system in which the wealthiest families had finally learned how to rule without the need to govern? Had the influence of private citizens upon government overwhelmed the authority of government over powerful citizens? And had a new kind of corruption become a routine and essential part of that process? In a capitalist society that generates huge extremes of wealth and want, democracy is ever at risk.

NOTES

1. E. P. Thompson, *The Making of the English Working Class* (London, 1963), 9, 10.

2. Tom Bottomore, ed., *A Dictionary of Marxist Thought* (Cambridge, Mass., 1983), s.v. "ruling class"; John Jay to William Wilberforce, 25 October 1810, quoted in Dixon Ryan Fox, *The Decline of Aristocracy in the Politics of New York, 1801–1840* (New York, 1919), 9.

3. See Lawrence Stone and Jeanne C. Fawtier Stone, *An Open Elite? England, 1540–1880* (Oxford, 1984), especially chaps. 6–7. See also E. P. Thompson, "Eighteenth-Century English Society: Class Struggle without Class?" *Social History* 3(1976): 133–65.

4. David Hume, *Essays and Treatises on Several Subjects* [1742], new ed. (Edinburgh, 1825), 1: 27. By "Force" in this context, Hume meant that the governed always outnumber their governors. If really determined to resist, they would succeed.

5. See J. G. A. Pocock, "The Classical Theory of Deference," *American Historical Review* 81(1976): 516–23.

6. Modern analysis of this system began with Sir Lewis B. Namier, *The Structure of Politics at the Accession of George III*, 2d ed. (London, 1957). See also his *Crossroads of Power: Essays on Eighteenth-Century England* (London, 1962).

7. Of the vast literature on England, perhaps the best place to begin is with Lawrence Stone, *The Crisis of the Aristocracy, 1558–1641* (Oxford, 1965), especially chap. 5; and J. H. Plumb, *The Growth of Political Stability: England, 1675–1725* (Boston, 1967). See also J. R. Western, *The English Militia in the Eighteenth Century: The Story of a Political Issue, 1660–1802* (London, 1965); E. P. Thompson, *Whigs and Hunters: The Origin of the Black Act* (New York, 1975); Douglas Hay et al., *Albion's Fatal Tree: Crime and Society in Eighteenth-Century England* (New York, 1975); and Albert Goodwin, *The Friends of Liberty: The English Democratic Movement in the Age*

of the French Revolution (Cambridge, Mass., 1979), especially chaps. 8–10. For Scotland, compare Bruce Lenman, *The Jacobite Risings in Britain, 1689–1746* (London, 1980) with John Robertson, *The Scottish Enlightenment and the Militia Issue* (Edinburgh, 1985). For the Irish contrast, see John Phillip Reid, *In a Defiant Stance: The Conditions of Law in Massachusetts Bay, the Irish Comparison, and the Coming of the American Revolution* (University Park, Pa., 1977), especially chaps. 13–14; and Francis Godwin James, *Ireland in the Empire, 1688–1770: A History of Ireland from the Williamite Wars to the Eve of the American Revolution* (Cambridge, Mass., 1973).

8. For a survey that is both recent and balanced see Derek Hirst, *Authority and Conflict: England, 1603–1658* (Cambridge, Mass., 1986).

9. See J. R. Western, *Monarchy and Revolution: The English State in the 1680s* (London, 1972); J. R. Jones, *The Revolution of 1688 in England* (New York, 1972); John Brewer, *The Sinews of Power: War, Money, and the English State, 1688–1783* (New York, 1989); and, for the dynamics of opposition, Linda Colley, *In Defiance of Oligarchy: The Tory Party, 1714–60* (Cambridge, Eng., 1982).

10. Serious analysis of these problems began with Bernard Bailyn, "Politics and Social Structure in Virginia," in James Morton Smith, ed., *Seventeenth-Century America: Essays in Colonial History* (Chapel Hill, N.C., 1959), 90–115.

11. Easily the most thoughtful study of this process is Martin H. Quitt, "Immigrant Origins of the Virginia Gentry: A Study of Cultural Transmission and Innovation" *William and Mary Quarterly,* 3d series (hereafter cited as *WMQ*), 45(1988): 629–55.

12. No study has yet been made analyzing the significance of an armed population in colonial America at a time when ordinary people in Europe were being systematically disarmed, but this contrast is basic to several major interpretations of military events in early America. See especially Richard Slotkin, *Regeneration through Violence: The Mythology of the American Frontier, 1600–1860* (Middletown, Conn., 1973); John E. Ferling, *A Wilderness of Miseries: War and Warriors in Early America* (Westport, Conn., 1980); William L. Shea, *The Virginia Militia in the Seventeenth Century* (Baton Rouge, La., 1983); and Fred Anderson, *A People's Army: Massachusetts Soldiers and Society in the Seven Years' War* (Chapel Hill, N.C., 1984).

13. See Kenneth A. Lockridge, *Settlement and Unsettlement in Early America* (New York, 1981).

14. In a rich literature the most powerful single book is Edmund S. Morgan, *American Slavery, American Freedom: The Ordeal of Colonial Virginia* (New York, 1975). See also Thad W. Tate and David L.

Ammerman, eds., *The Chesapeake in the Seventeenth Century: Essays on Anglo-American Society* (Chapel Hill, N.C., 1979).

15. "Virginia's Deploured Condition," Massachusetts Historical Society, *Collections,* 4th series, 9(1871): 176; Bacon's manifesto of 1676, in Merrill Jensen, ed., *American Colonial Documents to 1776,* vol. 9 of *English Historical Documents,* ed. David C. Douglas (New York, 1962), 581–82.

16. See Martin H. Quitt, *Virginia House of Burgesses, 1660–1706: The Social, Educational, and Economic Bases of Political Power* (New York, 1989); David Alan Williams, *Political Alignments in Colonial Virginia Politics, 1698–1750* (New York, 1989); Aubrey C. Land, "Economic Behavior in a Planting Society: The Eighteenth-Century Chesapeake," *Journal of Southern History* 33(1967): 471–85, especially 482; and Jack P. Greene, "Foundations of Political Power in the Virginia House of Burgesses, 1720–1776," *WMQ* 16(1959): 485–506.

17. See David Alan Williams, "The Small Farmer in Eighteenth-Century Virginia Politics," *Agricultural History* 43(1969): 91–101; Robert J. Dinkin, *Voting in Provincial America: A Study of Elections in the Thirteen Colonies, 1689–1776* (Westport, Conn., 1977), especially 194, 198; and Robert E. Brown and B. Katherine Brown, *Virginia, 1705–1786: Aristocracy or Democracy?* (East Lansing, Mich., 1964), chap. 9.

18. See Allan Kulikoff, *Tobacco and Slaves: The Development of Southern Cultures in the Chesapeake, 1680–1800* (Chapel Hill, N.C., 1986).

19. See Thad W. Tate, "The Coming of the Revolution in Virginia: Britain's Challenge to Virginia's Ruling Class," *WMQ* 19(1962): 323–43.

20. For the centrality of the conversion experience to life in early New England, see Edmund S. Morgan, *Visible Saints: The History of a Puritan Idea* (New York, 1963). See also Richard S. Dunn, *From Puritans to Yankees: The Winthrop Dynasty in Colonial New England, 1630–1717* (Princeton, 1962); William A. Polf, "Puritan Gentlemen: The Dudleys of Massachusetts, 1576–1686" (Ph.D. diss., Syracuse University, 1973); and on Governor Eaton of New Haven, Gail Sussman Marcus, " 'Due Execution of the Generall Rules of Righteousnesse': Criminal Procedure in New Haven Town and Colony, 1638–1658," in David D. Hall, John M. Murrin, and Thad W. Tate, eds., *Saints and Revolutionaries: Essays on Early American History* (New York, 1984), 99–137.

21. For this exchange see Edmund S. Morgan, ed., *Puritan Political Ideas, 1558–1794* (Indianapolis, 1965), 160–73.

22. See Edmund S. Morgan, *The Puritan Dilemma: The Story of John Winthrop* (Boston, 1958); and Robert E. Wall, Jr., *Massachusetts Bay: The Crucial Decade, 1640–1650* (New Haven, 1972).

23. See especially Richard R. Johnson, *Adjustment to Empire: The New England Colonies, 1675–1715* (New Brunswick, N.J., 1981).

24. The most important recent studies of Massachusetts politics in this period are Robert M. Zemsky, *Merchants, Farmers, and River Gods: An Essay on Eighteenth-Century American Politics* (Boston, 1971); William Pencak, *War, Politics & Revolution in Provincial Massachusetts* (Boston, 1981); and Richard L. Bushman, *King and People in Provincial Massachusetts* (Chapel Hill, N.C., 1985).

25. See Edward M. Cook, Jr., *The Fathers of the Towns: Leadership and Community Structure in Eighteenth-Century New England* (Baltimore, 1976); and John M. Murrin, "Review Essay," *History and Theory* 11(1972): especially 245–72.

26. For the period before 1715 the percentage of justices in the assembly (anyone listed as "Esquire") has been tabulated from *Acts and Resolves, Public and Private, of the Province of Massachusetts Bay* . . . (Boston, 1869–1922), vols. 7–9; for 1715 through 1774 we have used the first 50 volumes of *Journals of the House of Representatives of Massachusetts Bay,* reprint edition by the Massachusetts Historical Society (Boston, 1919–81). John J. Waters, Jr., and John A. Schutz, "Patterns of Massachusetts Colonial Politics: The Writs of Assistance and the Rivalry between the Otis and Hutchinson Families," *WMQ* 24(1967): 543–67 is a fine case study. See also Gary B. Nash, "The Transformation of Urban Politics, 1700–1760," in his *Race, Class, and Politics: Essays on American Colonial and Revolutionary Society* (Urbana, Ill., 1986), 140–70.

27. The best general histories of New York in this period are Robert C. Ritchie, *The Duke's Province: A Study of New York Politics and Society, 1664–1691* (Chapel Hill, N.C., 1977); and Joyce D. Goodfriend, *Before the Melting Pot: Society and Culture in Colonial New York City, 1664–1730* (Princeton, 1992). On more specific points see Stanley M. Pargellis, "The Four Independent Companies of New York," in *Essays in Colonial History Presented to Charles McLean Andrews by His Students* (New Haven, 1931), 96–123; Randall H. Balmer, *A Perfect Babel of Confusion: Dutch Religion and English Culture in the Middle Colonies* (New York, 1989); John M. Murrin, "English Rights as Ethnic Aggression: The English Conquest, the Charter of Liberties of 1683, and Leisler's Rebellion in New York," in William Pencak and Conrad Edick Wright, eds., *Authority and Resistance in Early New York* (New York, 1988), 56–94; and Murrin, "The Menacing Shadow of Louis XIV and the Rage of Jacob Leisler: The

Constitutional Ordeal of Seventeenth-Century New York," in Stephen L. Schechter and Richard B. Bernstein, eds., *New York and the Union: Contributions to the American Constitutional Experience* (Albany, N.Y., 1990), 29–71.

28. See Minutes of the Council, 4 June 1689, New-York Historical Society, *Collections* 1(1868): 269–70; and Nicholas Bayard and William Nicolls, "Answer to Blagge's Memorial," in E. B. O'Callaghan, ed., *The Documentary History of the State of New York*, octavo ed. (Albany, N.Y., 1849–51), 2:388, 390.

29. See generally Sung Bok Kim, *Landlord and Tenant in Colonial New York: Manorial Society, 1664–1775* (Chapel Hill, N.C., 1978). For the statistics on officeholding see Irving Mark, *Agrarian Conflicts in Colonial New York, 1711–1775*, 2d ed. (New York, 1965), 85–94.

30. See especially Roger Champagne, "Family Politics versus Constitutional Principles: The New York Assembly Elections of 1768 and 1769," *WMQ* 20(1963): 57–73.

31. See Gary B. Nash, *Quakers and Politics: Pennsylvania, 1681–1726* (Princeton, 1968); Thomas Wendel, "The Keith-Lloyd Alliance: Factional and Coalition Politics in Colonial Pennsylvania," *Pennsylvania Magazine of History and Biography* 92(1968): 289–305; Alan Tully, *William Penn's Legacy: Politics and Social Structure in Provincial Pennsylvania, 1726–1755* (Baltimore, 1977); and Richard Alan Ryerson, "Portrait of a Colonial Oligarchy: The Quaker Elite in the Pennsylvania Assembly, 1729–1776," in Bruce C. Daniels, ed., *Power and Status: Officeholding in Colonial America* (Middletown, Conn., 1986), 106–35.

32. See especially G. B. Warden, "The Proprietary Group in Pennsylvania, 1754–1764," *WMQ* 21(1964): 367–89; Stephen J. Brobeck, "Changes in the Composition of Philadelphia Elite Groups, 1756–1790" (Ph.D. diss., University of Pennsylvania, 1976); and Brobeck, "Revolutionary Change in Colonial Philadelphia: The Brief Life of the Proprietary Gentry," *WMQ* 33(1976): 410–34.

33. On Middle Colony regionalism and politics see Wayne Bodle, "The 'Myth of the Middle Colonies' Reconsidered: The Process of Regionalization in Early America," *Pennsylvania Magazine of History and Biography* 113(1989): 527–48.

34. For prominent studies of Quaker reform with an intercolonial emphasis, see Sydney V. James, *A People among Peoples: Quaker Benevolence in Eighteenth-Century America* (Cambridge, Mass., 1963); and Jean R. Soderlund, *Quakers & Slavery: A Divided Spirit* (Princeton, 1985). Jack D. Marietta, *The Reformation of American Quakerism, 1748–1783* (Philadelphia, 1984) is, by contrast, confined

to events in Pennsylvania. Balmer, *Perfect Babel,* contrasts Dutch religious behavior in New York and New Jersey.0

35. See Ned C. Landsman, *Scotland and Its First American Colony, 1683–1765* (Princeton, 1985); and Elizabeth I. Nybakken, "New Light on the Old Side: Irish Influences on Colonial Presbyterianism," *Journal of American History* 68(1981–82): 813–32.

36. See Leonard J. Trinterud, *The Forming of an American Tradition: A Reexamination of Colonial Presbyterianism* (Philadelphia, 1949).

37. See Thomas J. Wertenbaker, *Princeton, 1746–1896* (Princeton, 1946), chaps. 1–3.

38. On wealth distribution compare John A. James, "Personal Wealth Distribution in Late Eighteenth-Century Britain," *Economic History Review,* 2d series, 41 (1988): 543–65, especially 559–60; Alice Hanson Jones, *Wealth of a Nation to Be: The American Colonies on the Eve of the Revolution* (New York, 1980), chaps 6–7; Hermann Wellenreuther, "A View of the Socio-Economic Structures of England and the British Colonies on the Eve of the American Revolution," in Erich Angermann, Marie-Luise Frings, and Hermann Wellenreuther, eds., *New Wine in Old Skins: A Comparative View of Socio-Political Structures and Values Affecting the American Revolution* (Stuttgart, 1976), 16–19; Gary B. Nash, *The Urban Crucible: Social Change, Political Consciousness, and the Origins of the American Revolution* (Cambridge, Mass., 1979), 4; Jackson Turner Main, *The Social Structure of Revolutionary America* (Princeton, 1965); and James A. Henretta, "Wealth and Social Structure," in Jack P. Greene and J. R. Pole, eds., *Colonial British America: Essays in the New History of the Early Modern Era* (Baltimore, 1984), 175–88, 281–83.

On elite success in holding power see generally Jack P. Greene, "Legislative Turnover in British America, 1696 to 1775: A Quantitative Analysis," *WMQ* 38(1981): 442–63; Greene, "The Growth of Political Stability: An Interpretation of Political Development in the Anglo-American Colonies, 1660–1760," in John Parker and Carol Urness, eds., *The American Revolution: A Heritage of Change* (Minneapolis, 1975), 26–52; and Colin Bonwick, "The American Revolution as a Social Movement Revisited," *Journal of American Studies* 20(1986): 355–73.

39. For a recent synthesis of an enormous literature emphasizing both the emergence of colonial elites and the significance of family autonomy, see Jack P. Greene, *Pursuits of Happiness: The Social Development of Early Modern British Colonies and the Formation of American Culture* (Chapel Hill, N.C., 1988).

40. This discussion of titles derives mostly from our reading of public records. For Connecticut's exceptional pattern see Jackson Turner Main, "New Views on the Colonial Past: From the Regional Perspective," paper presented at the annual meeting of the Organization of American Historians (Minneapolis, April 1985), 1.

41. Richard L. Bushman, "American High Styles and Vernacular Cultures," in Greene and Pole, eds., *Colonial British America,* 345–83; and John M. Murrin, "Political Development," in ibid., 408–56 summarize the relevant literature.

42. See Francis Bernard, "Principles of Law and Polity, Applied to the Government of the British Colonies in America" (1764), nos. 86–89, in Jack P. Greene, ed., *Colonies to Nation, 1763–1789: A Documentary History of the American Revolution* (New York, 1975), 11; Edmund S. Morgan and Helen M. Morgan, *The Stamp Act Crisis: Prologue to Revolution* (Chapel Hill, N.C., 1953), chaps. 2–5; and John L. Bullion, *A Great and Necessary Measure: George Grenville and the Genesis of the Stamp Act, 1763–1765* (Columbia, Mo., 1982).

43. Morgan and Morgan, *Stamp Act Crisis,* chap. 7.

44. See ibid., chap. 16; P. D. G. Thomas, *British Politics and the Stamp Act Crisis: The First Phase of the American Revolution* (Oxford, 1975); and Paul Langford, *The First Rockingham Administration, 1765–1766* (New York, 1973).

45. Greene, ed., *Colonies to Nation,* 63. For differing interpretations of Stamp Act crowds, see Morgan and Morgan, *Stamp Act Crisis,* chaps. 8–9, 11; and Pauline Maier, *From Resistance to Revolution: Colonial Radicals and the Development of American Opposition to Britain, 1765–1776* (New York, 1972), chaps. 3–4; and Nash, *Urban Crucible,* chap. 11.

46. See Morgan and Morgan, *Stamp Act Crisis,* chaps. 9–10, 12–14. See also Patricia U. Bonomi, *A Factious People: Politics and Society in Colonial New York* (New York, 1971), chap. 7; James H. Hutson, *Pennsylvania Politics, 1746–1770: The Movement for Royal Government and Its Consequences* (Princeton, 1972); and Benjamin H. Newcomb, *Franklin and Galloway: A Political Partnership* (New Haven, 1972), especially chaps. 4–5.

47. Kim, *Landlord and Tenant,* chap. 8; and Edward Countryman, *A People in Revolution: The American Revolution and Political Society in New York, 1760–1790* (Baltimore, 1981), chap. 2, discuss this episode from the point of view of landlords and rioters, respectively.

48. Recent studies that identify the formative character of the Townshend Crisis include John W. Tyler, *Smugglers and Patriots:*

Boston Merchants and the Advent of the American Revolution (Boston, 1986), chaps. 3–4; and Thomas M. Doerflinger, *A Vigorous Spirit of Enterprise: Merchants and Economic Development in Revolutionary Philadelphia* (Chapel Hill, N.C., 1986), 189–99; Doerflinger, "Philadelphia Merchants and the Logic of Moderation, 1760–1775," *WMQ* 40(1983): 197–226. For a provocative analysis that locates the roots of revolutionary allegiance in earlier partisan alignments, see Marc Egnal, *A Mighty Empire: The Origins of the American Revolution* (Ithaca, N.Y., 1988). James Kirby Martin, *Men in Rebellion: Higher Governmental Leaders and the Coming of the American Revolution* (New York, 1973) explores social and political factors that influenced the pattern of loyalties within the provincial elites.

49. Merrill Jensen, *The Founding of a Nation: A History of the American Revolution, 1763–1776* (New York, 1968), chaps. 8–14, is an outstanding narrative history of the Townshend Crisis. For the evolving ideology of resistance see Maier, *From Resistance to Revolution*, especially chaps. 5–7.

50. See Benjamin W. Labaree, *The Boston Tea Party* (New York, 1964); Ira D. Gruber, "The American Revolution as a Conspiracy: The British View," *WMQ* 26(1969): 360–72; Bernard Bailyn, *The Ideological Origins of the American Revolution* (Cambridge, Mass., 1967), especially 144–59; and David Ammerman, *In the Common Cause: American Response to the Coercive Acts of 1774* (Charlottesville, Va., 1974).

51. See Jerrilyn Greene Marston, *King and Congress: The Transfer of Political Legitimacy, 1774–1776* (Princeton, 1987).

52. Compilation based mainly on data in *Biographical Directory of the American Congress, 1774–1989*. For a useful analysis of the signers of the Declaration of Independence, see Richard D. Brown, "The Founding Fathers of 1776 and 1787: A Collective View," *WMQ* 33(1976): 465–80.

53. See Jack N. Rakove, *The Beginnings of National Politics: An Interpretive History of the Continental Congress* (New York, 1974), chaps. 3–5.

54. See Arnold M. Pavlovsky, " 'Between Hawk and Buzzard': Congress as Perceived by Its Members, 1775–1783," *Pennsylvania Magazine of History and Biography* 101(1977): 349–64; and Edwin G. Burrows, "Military Experience and the Origins of Federalism and Antifederalism," in Jacob Judd and Irwin H. Polishook, eds., *Aspects of Early New York Society and Politics* (Tarrytown, N.Y., 1974), 83–92.

55. Richard A. Ryerson, *The Revolution Is Now Begun: The Radical Committees of Philadelphia, 1765–1776* (Philadelphia, 1978), 248.

56. See ibid., especially chaps. 2–3, 8–9; and Charles S. Olton, *Artisans for Independence: Philadelphia Mechanics and the American Revolution* (Syracuse, N.Y., 1975), chaps. 4–6.

57. See Steven R. Rosswurm, *Arms, Country, and Class: The Philadelphia Militia and the "Lower Sort" during the American Revolution* (New Brunswick, N.J., 1987), especially 101.

58. See Eric Foner, *Tom Paine and Revolutionary America* (New York, 1976), chap. 4.

59. See Douglas M. Arnold, *A Republican Revolution: Ideology and Politics in Pennsylvania, 1776–1790* (New York, 1989); and Owen S. Ireland, "The Crux of Politics: Religion and Party in Pennsylvania," *WMQ* 42(1985): 453–75.

60. See Rakove, *Beginnings of National Politics*. For the fear of disunion, see Eugene R. Sheridan and John M. Murrin, eds., *Congress at Princeton, Being the Letters of Charles Thomson to Hannah Thomson, June–October 1783* (Princeton, 1985), especially 19, 29–31.

61. See H. James Henderson, *Party Politics in the Continental Congress* (New York, 1974); Joseph L. Davis, *Sectionalism in American Politics, 1774–1787* (Madison, 1977); and Drew R. McCoy, "James Madison and Visions of American Nationality in the Confederation Period: A Regional Perspective," in Richard Beeman, Stephen Botein, and Edward C. Carter II, eds., *Beyond Confederation: Origins of the Constitution and American National Identity* (Chapel Hill, N.C., 1987), 226–58.

62. See John J. McCusker and Russell R. Menard, *The Economy of British America, 1607–1789* (Chapel Hill, N.C., 1985), chap. 17.

63. On economic conditions and class tensions in the cities, see Dirk Hoerder, *Crowd Action in Revolutionary Massachusetts, 1765–1780* (New York, 1977), chaps. 13–14; Nancy Fisher Chudacoff, "The Revolution and the Town: Providence, 1775–1783," *Rhode Island History* 35(Aug. 1977): 71–90; Foner, *Tom Paine*, chap. 5; James K. Alexander, "The Fort Wilson Incident of 1779: A Case Study of the Revolutionary Crowd," *WMQ* 31(1974): 589–612; and Richard Walsh, *Charleston's Sons of Liberty: A Study of the Artisans, 1763–1789* (Columbia, S.C., 1959), 77–87. On artisanal organization after the war, see Staughton Lynd, "The Mechanics in New York Politics, 1774–1788," *Labor History* 5(1964): 235–41; and Gary J. Kornblith, "From Artisans to Businessmen: Master Mechanics in New England, 1789–1850" (Ph.D. diss., Princeton University, 1983) 1:56–67.

64. See Robert A. Becker, *Revolution, Reform, and the Politics of American Taxation* (Baton Rouge, La., 1980), pt. 2; Ronald Hoffman, *A Spirit of Dissension: Economy, Politics, and the Revolution in Maryland* (Baltimore, 1973), chap. 9; Stephen E. Patterson, *Political*

Parties in Revolutionary Massachusetts (Madison, Wis., 1973), chaps. 6–7; and Robert A. Gross, *The Minutemen and Their World* (New York, 1976), 141–42.

65. See Hoffman, *Spirit of Dissension,* chap. 10 and p. 210 (quotation); Jackson Turner Main, *Political Parties before the Constitution* (Chapel Hill, N.C., 1973), 49–62, and chaps. 4–11; Norman K. Risjord, *Chesapeake Politics, 1781–1800* (New York, 1978), chap. 4; and David P. Szatmary, *Shays' Rebellion: The Making of an Agrarian Insurrection* (Amherst, Mass., 1980), chap. 2.

66. Thus the proportion of farmers (excluding large landowners) in the New York Assembly rose from 25 percent in 1769 to 42 percent in 1785, and the proportion of farmers in Virginia's lower house increased from 13 percent in 1773 to 26 percent in 1785. In Pennsylvania farmers comprised 37 percent of the men elected to the assembly between 1780 and 1788, and in Massachusetts they constituted 47 percent of those elected to the lower house between 1784 and 1788. See Jackson Turner Main, "Government by the People: The American Revolution and the Democratization of the Legislatures," *WMQ* 23(1966): 391–407; Main, *Political Parties,* 93 (table 4.2), 175 (table 7.1). For changes in the composition of the upper houses, see Main, *The Upper House in Revolutionary America, 1763–1788* (Madison, Wis., 1967).

67. See Merrill Jensen, *The New Nation: A History of the United States during the Articles of Confederation* (New York, 1950), chap. 16.

68. See Van Beck Hall, *Politics without Parties: Massachusetts, 1780–1791* (Pittsburgh, 1972), chaps. 2–4.

69. See ibid., chaps. 6–7; Szatmary, *Shays' Rebellion,* chaps. 4–6; and Robert J. Taylor, *Western Massachusetts in the Revolution* (Providence, R.I., 1954), chaps. 6–7. For an important study of how Shays's Rebellion related to deference patterns, see John L. Brooke, "To the Quiet of the People: Revolutionary Settlements and Civil Unrest in Western Massachusetts, 1774–1789," *WMQ* 46(1989): 425–62. Brooke points out that the most indebted communities were not the ones to take up arms.

70. Szatmary, *Shays' Rebellion,* 86.

71. On the background of the delegates see Forrest McDonald, *We the People: The Economic Origins of the Constitution* (Chicago, 1958), chap. 3; and Richard B. Morris, *The Forging of the Union, 1781–1789* (New York, 1987), 268–75.

72. Of the vast literature on the framing of the Federal Constitution, the most useful studies for the purposes of the present essay have been Gordon S. Wood, *The Creation of the American Republic, 1776–1787* (Chapel Hill, N.C., 1969), pt. 5; Wood, "Interests and Dis-

interestedness in the Making of the Constitution," in Beeman et al.,
eds., *Beyond Confederation,* 69–109; Alfred F. Young, "Conservatism,
the Constitution, and the 'Spirit of Accomodation,'" in Robert A.
Goldwin and William A. Schambra, eds., *How Democratic Is the Constitution?* (Washington, D.C., 1980), 117–47; Forrest McDonald, *Novus Ordo Seclorum: The Intellectual Origins of the Constitution*
(Lawrence, Kans., 1985); and Isaac Kramnick, "The 'Great National
Discussion': The Discourse of Politics in 1787," *WMQ* 45(1988): 3–32.

73. For the Hamilton Plan see Max Farrand, ed., *The Records of
the Federal Convention of 1787,* rev. ed. (New Haven, 1937) 1:
282–311.

74. Ibid., 1: 48, 50, 51. The bracketed word in the Sherman quotation is an insertion Madison made in his Convention notes years
later. Its effect is to align Sherman against direct elections of representatives, but not the indirect elections used under the Articles of
Confederation.

75. Ibid.,1:150(Dickinson),400(Pinckney),and422–23(Madison).

76. See Jacob E. Cooke, ed., *The Federalist* (Middletown, Conn.,
1961), no. 56, especially 382–83.

77. See ibid., 56–65. For a recent analysis of Madison's views
see Edmund S. Morgan, *Inventing the People: The Rise of Popular
Sovereignty in England and America* (New York, 1988), chap. 11.

78. On the framers' vision of a national military establishment,
see Lawrence Delbert Cress, *Citizens in Arms: The Army and Militia
in American Society to the War of 1812* (Chapel Hill, N.C., 1982),
chap. 6. For what Richard H. Kohn calls the founder's "murder of the
militia system" in the early 1790s, see his *Eagle and Sword: The Beginnings of the Military Establishment in America* (New York, 1975),
chap. 7.

79. See Young, " 'Spirit of Accommodation,' "; and John M. Murrin, "1787: The Invention of American Federalism," in David E. Nar-
rett and Joyce S. Goldberg, eds., *Essays on Liberty and Federalism:
The Shaping of the U. S. Constitution* (College Station, Tex., 1988),
20–47. For Mason's speech, see Farrand, ed., *Records of Federal Convention* 1: 101.

80. David Grayson Allen et al., eds., *Diary of John Quincy Ad-
ams* (Cambridge, Mass., 1981), 2: 302–3. The fullest compilation of
Antifederalist writings is Herbert J. Storing, ed., *The Complete Anti-
Federalist,* 7 vols. (Chicago, 1981).

81. Jonathan Elliot, ed., *The Debates in the Several State Conventions on the Adoption of the Federal Constitution, as Recommended by the General Convention at Philadelphia in 1787,* 2d ed.
(Washington, D.C., 1854) 2: 247–48. See also Alfred F. Young, *The*

Democratic Republicans of New York: The Origins, 1763–1797 (Chapel Hill, N.C., 1967), 103–5.

82. The intensity and complexity of the ratification struggle is best conveyed by Merrill Jensen et al., eds., *The Documentary History of the Ratification of the Constitution* (Madison, Wis., 1976–). For a fine narrative see Robert Allen Rutland, *The Ordeal of the Constitution: The Antifederalists and the Ratification Struggle of 1787–1788* (Norman, Okla., 1966). For an analysis of how little Madison thought he was conceding with the Bill of Rights that he and the First Congress drafted, see Kenneth R. Bowling, " 'A Tub to the Whale': The Founding Fathers and Adoption of the Federal Bill of Rights," *Journal of the Early Republic* 8(1988): 223–51.

83. See Jack N. Rakove, "The Structure of Politics at the Accession of George Washington," in Beeman et al., eds., *Beyond Confederation*, 276–79; and *Biographical Directory of the Amerian Congress, 1774–1989*.

84. See Ethel E. Rasmussen, "Democratic Environment—Aristocratic Aspiration," *Pennsylvania Magazine of History and Biography* 90(1966): 155–82.

85. See Gerald Stourzh, *Alexander Hamilton and the Idea of Republican Government* (Stanford, Calif., 1970), 87–91; Lance Banning, *The Jeffersonian Persuasion: Evolution of a Party Ideology* (Ithaca, N.Y., 1978), 128–41; E. James Ferguson, "Political Economy, Public Liberty, and the Formation of the Constitution," *WMQ* 40(1983): 404–8; and John R. Nelson, Jr., *Liberty and Property: Political Economy and Policymaking in the New Nation, 1789–1812* (Baltimore, 1987), chap. 2.

86. See E. James Ferguson, *The Power of the Purse: A History of American Public Finance, 1776–1790* (Chapel Hill, N.C., 1961), 251–86, 335–36; and Whitney K. Bates, "Northern Speculators and Southern Debts: 1790," *WMQ* 19(1962): 30–48, especially table 12.

87. See Banning, *Jeffersonian Persuasion*, chap. 5; Drew R. McCoy, *The Elusive Republic: Political Economy in Jeffersonian America* (Chapel Hill, N.C., 1980), chap. 6; Richard Buel, Jr., *Securing the Revolution: Ideology in American Politics, 1789–1815* (Ithaca, N.Y., 1972); chap. 1; and Robert E. Shalhope, *John Taylor of Caroline, Pastoral Republican* (Columbia, S.C., 1980), chap. 2.

88. See Mary P. Ryan, "Party Formation in the United States Congress, 1789 to 1796: A Quantitative Approach," *WMQ* 28(1971): 523–42; H. James Henderson, "Quantitative Aproaches to Party Formation in the United States Congress: A Comment," *WMQ* 30(1973): 307–24; Henderson, *Party Politics*, chap. 15; and Michael Durey, "Thomas Paine's Apostles: Radical Émigrés and the Triumph of Jef-

fersonian Republicanism," *WMQ* 44(1987): 661–88. The quotation is from Farrand, ed., *Records of Federal Convention* 2:450.

89. Cooke, ed., *Federalist,* 60; see also Lance Banning, "The Hamiltonian Madison: A Reconsideration," *Virginia Magazine of History and Biography* 92(1984): 3–28.

90. See Noble E. Cunningham, *The Jeffersonian Republicans: The Formation of Party Organization, 1789–1801* (Chapel Hill, N.C., 1957), chaps. 1–4; and McCoy, *Elusive Republic,* chaps. 6–7.

91. See Nelson, *Liberty and Property,* 76; Norman K. Risjord and Gordon Denboer, "The Evolution of Political Parties in Virginia," *Journal of American History* 60(1973–74): 961–84; Lisle A. Rose, *Prologue to Democracy: The Federalists in the South, 1789–1800* (Lexington, Ky., 1968); and Richard R. Beeman, *The Old Dominion and the New Nation, 1788–1801* (Lexington, Ky., 1972).

92. See Paul Goodman, "Social Status of Party Leadership: The House of Representatives, 1797–1804," *WMQ,* 25(1968): 465–74; Goodman, *The Democratic-Republicans of Massachusetts: Politics in a Young Republic* (Cambridge, Mass., 1964); and Joyce Appleby, *Capitalism and a New Social Order: The Republican Vision of the 1790s* (New York, 1984), chap 4. The quotations are from Madison, "A Candid State of Parties" *National Gazette,* 22 September 1792, in William T. Hutchinson et al., eds., *The Papers of James Madison* (Chicago, 1962–) 13:371.

93. See Marshall Smelser, "The Jacobin Frenzy: Federalism and the Menace of Liberty, Equality, and Fraternity," *Review of Politics* 13(1951): 457–82; John R. Howe, Jr., "Republican Thought and the Political Violence of the 1790s," *American Quarterly* 19(1967): 147–65; and Buel, *Securing Revolution,* 97–105.

94. See Carl E. Prince, *The Federalists and the Origins of the U. S. Civil Service* (New York, 1977). The quotation is from "The Continentalist," no. 6, *New-York Packet,* 4 July 1782, in Harold C. Syrett et al., eds., *The Papers of Alexander Hamilton* (New York, 1961–81) 3: 105.

95. See Thomas P. Slaughter, *The Whiskey Rebellion: Frontier Epilogue to the American Revolution* (New York, 1986), chap. 12; and Manning J. Dauer, *The Adams Federalists* (Baltimore, 1953), chap. 10.

96. See Owen S. Ireland, "The Ethnic-Religious Counter-Revolution in Pennsylvania, 1784–1786" (paper presented at the Philadelphia Center for Early American Studies, 22 January 1988); Ireland, "The People's Triumph: The Federalist Majority in Pennsylvania, 1787–1788," *Pennsylvania History* 56(1989): 93–113; Roland M. Baumann, "Philadelphia's Manufacturers and the Excise Taxes of

1794: The Forging of the Jeffersonian Coalition," *Pennsylvania Magazine of History and Biography* 106(1982): 3–39; and Kenneth W. Keller, "Rural Politics and the Collapse of Pennsylvania Federalism," *American Philosophical Society Transactions* 72, pt. 6 (1982).

97. See David Hackett Fischer, *The Revolution of American Conservatism: The Federalist Party in the Era of Jeffersonian Democracy* (New York, 1965), 201–26; Hall, *Politics without Parties,* chap. 11; Young, *Democratic Republicans,* especially chap. 12; Nelson, *Liberty and Property,* chaps. 6–7; Carl E. Prince, *New Jersey's Jeffersonian Republicans: The Genesis of an Early Party Machine, 1789–1817* (Chapel Hill, N.C., 1964); and John A. Munroe, *Federalist Delaware, 1775–1815* (New Brunswick, N.J., 1954).

98. See Jerald A. Combs, *The Jay Treaty: Political Battleground of the Founding Fathers* (Berkeley, Calif., 1970); Dauer, *Adams Federalists,* chaps. 9–16; Stephen G. Kurtz, *The Presidency of John Adams: The Collapse of Federalism, 1795–1800* (Philadelphia, 1957); and Jacob E. Cooke, "Country above Party: John Adams and the 1799 Mission to France," in Edmund P. Willis, ed., *Fame and the Founding Fathers: Papers and Comments presented at the Nineteenth Conference on Early American History, March 25–26, 1966* (Bethlehem, Pa., 1967), 53–77.

99. See John M. Murrin, "The Great Inversion, or Court versus Country: A Comparison of the Revolution Settlements in England (1688–1721) and America (1776–1816)," in J. G. A. Pocock, ed., *Three British Revolutions: 1641, 1688, 1776* (Princeton, 1980), 423–25; Carter Goodrich, *Government Promotion of American Canals and Railroads, 1800–1890* (New York, 1960), chaps. 1–3; Stuart Bruchey, *The Roots of American Economic Growth, 1607–1861: An Essay in Social Causation* (New York, 1968), chap. 6; and Robert H. Wiebe, *The Opening of American Society: From the Adoption of the Constitution to the Eve of Disunion* (New York, 1984), especially chap. 10.

100. Alexis de Tocqueville, *Democracy in America,* ed. J. P. Mayer, trans. George Lawrence (Garden City, N.Y., 1966, 1969) 1:246n.

101. Ibid., 1:260n. For data on the social and economic backgrounds of state legislators during the early and middle decades of the nineteenth century, see Harold Joseph Counihan, "North Carolina, 1815–1836: State and Local Perspectives on the Age of Jackson" (Ph.D. diss., University of North Carolina at Chapel Hill, 1971), 19–24; Horace B. Davis, "The Occupations of Massachusetts Legislators, 1790–1950," *New England Quarterly* 24(1951): 89–100; Philip Shriver Klein, *Pennsylvania Politics, 1817–1832: A Game without Rules* (Philadelphia, 1974), 26–29; Peter D. Levine, *The Behavior of*

State Legislative Parties in the Jacksonian Era: New Jersey, 1829–1844 (Rutherford, N.J., 1977), chap. 3; J. Mills Thornton III, *Politics and Power in a Slave Society: Alabama, 1800–1860* (Baton Rouge, La., 1978), chap. 2; Ralph A. Wooster, *The People in Power: Courthouse to Statehouse in the Lower South, 1850–1860* (Knoxville, Tenn., 1969), chap. 1; and Wooster, *Politicians, Planters, and Plain Folk: Courthouse and Statehouse in the Upper South, 1850–1860* (Knoxville, Tenn., 1975), chap. 1. In a challenge to Tocqueville's portrait of the United States as an egalitarian society, Edward Pessen has documented a large upper-class presence in the municipal governments of Boston, Brooklyn, New York, and Philadelphia. He ignores the composition of state governments, however. *Riches, Class, and Power before the Civil War* (Lexington, Mass., 1973), especially chap. 13. Philip H. Burch, Jr., also neglects the state level of government in his lengthy *Elites in American History,* 3 vols. (New York, 1981).

102. Tocqueville, *Democracy in America* 1:205. Compare 1:198.

103. For the very real reluctance to come to terms with this transition in the early republic, see John M. Murrin, "Escaping Perfidious Albion: Federalism, Fear of Aristocracy, and the Democratization of Corruption in Post-Revolutionary America," in Richard K. Matthews, ed., *Virtue, Corruption, and Self-Interest* (Bethlehem, Penn., forthcoming).

104. Matthew Josephson, *The Robber Barons* (New York, 1934), 183, 184 (italics removed); and Robert A. Divine et al., *America Past and Present,* brief ed. (Glenview, Ill., 1986), 298. For the federal budget see U.S. Bureau of the Census, *Historical Statistics of the United States, Colonial Times to 1970* (Washington, D.C., 1975) 2: 1104.

The American Revolution, Capitalism, and the Formation of the Yeoman Classes

ALLAN KULIKOFF

VENERATE THE PLOUGH

The motto and image are from a medal offered by the Philadelphia Society for Promoting Agriculture, a group of "gentlemen farmers," as a prize for the best plan for agricultural improvement. It appeared, together with the winning plan for the design of a farmyard, in [Philadelphia] *Columbian Magazine,* vol. 1 (1786).

In July 1775, fearing slave rebellions in time of civil unrest, Virginia's revolutionary assembly, composed of wealthy slaveholders, exempted overseers of four or more adult slaves from militia musters and army drafts. They particularly sought to protect slave property from the interference of Governor John Dunmore, the last royal governor of Virginia, who had offered to free any slave who would fight the rebels. The exempt raised a firestorm of dissent from yeoman tobacco planters—nonslaveholders or men who owned but a few chattels. Hundreds of angry men petitioned the assembly. For instance, two hundred and twenty-five petitioners from Lunenburg County, a frontier county south of the James River, complained that the law exempting overseers "from bearing arms in the Militia & also Excus'd from being Drafted as Soldiers" led "many persons" to "become Overseers that Otherways wou'd not . . . to Secure themselves from Fighting in defense of their Country as well as their Own Property." The law was clearly unjust to poor *freeholders,* as men who owned land absolutely were called. When they were drafted, as they must because so many overseers were exempted, they would leave their families without support, forcing them to go "up & down the County abeging or [stay] at home aSlaving, and at the same time quite unable to help them to the Necessaries of life, while the Overseers are aliving in ease & Affluence at the Expense of their Employers."[1]

These Virginia *yeomen,* who constituted three-fifths of the white heads of families in the colony, owned land and knew that freeholding land tenure was their only claim to political participation, their only security against impoverishment. They sold tobacco to Scottish merchants in their midst, but grew sufficient food to feed their families and traded with neighbors for what they could not make themselves. Although willing to accept advances from these merchants until their crops were sold, they avoided incurring large debts that might lead to loss of their land. Landownership guaranteed them some economic autonomy and allowed them to direct the labor of their wives and children. As long as *gentlemen* ensured their status as freeholders, most Virginia yeomen had acquiesced in the rule of gentlemen. These men, the gentry, about a tenth of the white population, members of a few hundred interrelated families who owned as many as one-third of Virginia's 200,000 slaves and thousands of acres of land, and who dominated both local and provincial government, comprised the colony's ruling class.[2]

The Virginia petitioners saw the exemption of overseers as an attempt to deprive them of their property. Coming from southside Virginia, where yeomen had adopted an evangelical religion that put

them in opposition to the gentry-dominated Anglican culture and religion, they challenged any political attack from gentlemen. They
linked household and state: like all married men, they were obligated to support their families and they wanted state policy to advance that goal. Exemption from militia musters and military
service for overseers not only threatened yeomen with loss of land
and even poverty, it was also inequitable, creating a leisured class,
safe from the dangers of war. Clearly, if yeomen were to support the
Revolution and its gentry leaders, the exemption had to be ended.
Listening to petitions like this one, the gentry in the legislature
abandoned the law in May 1776, just seven months after Dunmore's
offer of freedom to slaves.

Such petitions and their success raise important questions about
the loyalty of yeomen to the revolutionary cause. Historians who
have studied this issue sometimes assume that gentlemen persuaded
farmers to join the Revolution and made them politically aware, and
that once farmers were incorporated into the body politic, they supported the goals of gentlemen.[3] The success of the Lunenburg, Virginia, petitioners suggests otherwise. They were patriots but
rejected gentry control. Through actions like theirs, patriotic men in
every region sought democratic participation as freeholders, without
any tinge of what they considered to be aristocratic control over
policy-making.[4] They insisted that they be respected as citizens of
the Republic. Not only did they give new meaning to the political declarations of gentlemen and merchants, they composed their own documents, often appropriating the rhetoric of Whig patriots to their
own ends. Forced by wartime military needs, gentlemen acquiesced
frequently to yeoman demands. In the 1780s, when gentlemen sought
to reassert hegemony, yeomen tried to salvage the democratic republic they believed their blood had created by electing legislators who
would do their bidding, supporting Shays's Rebellion, or fighting ratification of the Constitution. Although gentlemen, merchants, and
lawyers suppressed rural uprisings and used the Constitution to reestablish a representative republican government they might control, they still had to search for votes. Yeomen had long believed that
their frugality and independence made them virtuous and productive
citizens, an ideal ratified by their blood during the Revolution. To
gain votes in the 1790s and beyond, gentlemen, especially Jeffersonian Republicans, placed this yeoman self-image at the center of their
message, thereby legitimating and co-opting the political rhetoric of
the sturdy yeoman.

We have no vision to help us understand these dramatic political
themes over the last three decades of the eighteenth century. This

essay explores the Revolution ordinary rural folk made. Focusing on those farmers who supported the revolutionary cause, it will try to disentangle the social and political bases of patriotism.[5] To explain revolutionary events we must place them in the context of the history of class relations in rural America. The American Revolution was the most important event in the history of the small property-holding yeoman class. It can be seen as a key event in the development of capitalism and the outlook of *possessive individualism*.

Our analysis examines three subjects. First, we will show how yeoman classes formed in the eighteenth century and how these yeomen shaped an ideology. Second, we will turn to the problem of explaining rural loyalty to the patriot cause from the 1760s to the 1780s. And third, we will examine the ways yeomen helped shape revolutionary institutions. We close with an exploration of the economic consequences of the Revolution in the countryside, struggles between yeomen and capitalists in both the city and countryside, a legacy that would dominate the history of rural America in the nineteenth century.

THE FORMATION OF THE AMERICAN YEOMAN CLASSES[6]

This yeomanry did not emerge fully developed until sometime in the eighteenth century, after the ownership of land, the means of agricultural production, had become widespread. Hector St. John Crèvecoeur, a French immigrant who became a gentleman farmer in the Hudson Valley of New York, expressed the link between land and yeoman class identity. Writing in the guise of a simple American farmer of the 1770s, he explained the value of land. "What should we American farmers be without the distinct possession of the soil? It feeds, it clothes us; from it we draw . . . our best meat, our richest drink. . . ." But land meant more than physical well-being; it created the "only philosophy of the American farmer." A man's labor improved the soil, sustained his ownership of land, and gave him a political identity. "This formerly rude soil has been converted by my father into a pleasant farm," Crèvecoeur adds, "and in return, it has established all our rights; on it is founded our rank, our freedom, our power as citizens. . . ."[7]

This yeomanry was formed out of seventeenth- and eighteenth-century struggles: English class conflicts, which continued in the colonies, warfare with Indians, and contests among colonists over who should rule at home. Despite these obstacles, settlers made thousands of new homes on American frontiers. Both these struggles and the reality of landownership slowly led yeomen to become conscious of their role as citizens and to create a class ideology in the decades before the Revolution.

The Revolution in rural America, this essay argues, can be seen as a key event in the division of farmers into classes of yeomen and capitalists. We need to define such terms as *yeoman* and *capitalist* carefully. *Yeomen* were small, producing farmers who owned land and participated in markets to sustain familial autonomy and local exchange. Practicing "safety first" agriculture, they grew much of the food they consumed and tried to procure the rest through trade with neighbors. Avoiding entangling debts, they retained the independence needed to make virtuous political decisions. Yeoman farmers can be contrasted with *capitalist farmers,* who sought greater market embeddedness, concentrated on staple crops, and on occasion bought financial instruments. Unlike yeomen, they often hired wage laborers to increase their output and profits. They became part of a capitalist economy, one where profits were divided between the original producers (farmers, artisans, small urban capitalists, wage laborers) and a class of capitalists who owned and controlled the means of production and who expropriated part of the value of goods every producer made.[8]

Revolutionary ideology legitimated the power of the yeomanry. The success of farmers in justifying yeoman democracy was predicated upon *possessive individualism,* the idea that they, like all men, possessed political rights as individuals (rather than as members of groups) and that these rights protected their property.[9] Possessive individualism, however, was a cornerstone of a capitalist outlook, one that reduced each male person to a discrete individual attached to community only by freely made contracts. The emerging capitalist class sought integrated markets and intense economic development of the countryside. Even before the Revolution, urban merchants found many allies among middling and wealthy commercial farmers who had become comfortable with full market embeddedness, transferable credit instruments, and the use of wage labor. As a capitalist economy began to develop during and after the war, capitalist farmers grew in number.[10]

Our analysis begins in England. The first migrants to our shores—*husbandmen* (a term for all those who worked the land, whether as tenants or owners), former husbandmen, and urban workers—had lived through the birth of English capitalism. Although feudal lords had coerced peasants into making extraeconomic payments, in return peasants had controlled most of England's lands. During the sixteenth and seventeenth centuries, capitalist landlords had expropriated the lands of these peasants, renting the land to improving tenants. Forced into agricultural labor or into the urban work force, these new proletarians protested regularly, tearing down hedges that enclosed common lands, flooding drained swamplands, rioting for a fair price for bread. In the revolution of the 1640s, they supported the radical democrats. Believing wage labor to be debased, they dreamed of regaining land they or their parents had lost.[11]

When they left England behind, the first white Americans of the seventeenth century carried with them a craving for independence from lordship and an ardor for secure control over land. These goals were difficult to achieve. Fleeing religious persecution or dispossession, English migrants rejected the new capitalist order and its insistence that humankind sell its labor power on free markets, yet a majority of them had to sell themselves into temporary servitude as indentured servants to pay their passage to America. But they also rejected the feudalism that had disappeared long ago, when capitalists in the guise of feudal lords had taken their lands. Repudiating feudalism, they rarely held property in common; disliking capitalism, they nonetheless espoused private property in land, and the land markets, economic interdependence, and capitalist development that they disliked inevitably followed.[12]

The search for land led seventeenth-century colonists to enmesh themselves in innumerable struggles with native Americans. Notwithstanding epidemics caused by white diseases, native villages could be found everywhere in the early seventeenth-century colonies. European settlers found themselves a minority (or a small majority) of the population, their villages interspersed with those of Indians. Temporarily lacking the military power needed to subjugate their neighbors, the colonists (especially those living away from their core settlements) searched for accommodation, a middle ground with the American Indians. As long as they tolerated the Indians, acquiescing in their control over hunting lands, the colonists could not turn the forests and meadows around them into the private property they all sought. But when colonists achieved numerical and military superiority, they demanded more land, killing native Americans in battle and eventually sending them into exile far beyond the limits of white settlement. Whites thereby created an uninhabited wilderness where native communities had lived before.[13]

Everywhere colonists fought incessantly among themselves over who would rule their communities. The search for secure land (and opposition to continued native American occupation of it) sometimes lay behind these conflicts. Bacon's Rebellion in Virginia in 1676 is a good illustration of the complex relation between conflicts over political power and struggles for land. Since the beginning of settlement, indentured servants had defied their masters by demanding rights, running away, and refusing to obey orders. As long as ex-servants eventually got land, they worked more or less willingly as agricultural laborers. But access to land was critical. When Nathaniel Bacon, an English gentleman, fomented rebellion and warfare in 1676 to obtain political power, he gained numerous adherents among the freedmen of frontier counties, whose goal was land and who feared that unless the native Americans were massacred, there would be no land for them to possess.[14]

Settlers came, in part, to find land of their own, but they had no reason to expect that they could gain landownership easily. Gentlemen, who had taken their land in England, sometimes migrated with them. Even more important, contrary to the American myth of opportunity, until the end of the seventeenth century there was land scarcity in America. So much land—but no capital to develop it; so much land—but much of it in settlers' minds a "howling wilderness"; so much land—but American Indians controlled much of it and threatened to force them off the rest. What little land colonists could develop had to be carefully exploited. Living in scarcity in the midst of abundance, seventeenth-century colonists rejected the complex system of land tenure in England but did not immediately create a capitalist land market, where all land had a price and anyone could buy or sell it. The founders of New England communities who held land in common for a generation and then slowly dispersed it to the sons of early settlers acted prudently. In contrast, southern colonies gave land away to anyone who financed his own voyage to the colonies.[15]

Events at the end of the seventeenth century increased the supply of land and created a capitalist land market. Over the seventeenth century large numbers of men in New England and the Chesapeake colonies had become used to owning land. Capitalist land markets developed in these places after lands were distributed to the initial settlers. By the early eighteenth century these colonists had conquered sufficient land from the Indians to meet the needs of several generations. Similar events soon occurred in most of the other colonies. When he founded Pennsylvania in the 1680s, William Penn made peace with the native Americans, thereby opening much new land to white settlement, which he immediately sold to speculators and settlers, creating a capitalist land market. Now there was *uninhabited* wilderness, ready for white habitation.[16]

This new American reality of plentiful land combined with the inherited goals of the descendants of settlers led ordinary white families to forge a new class system based upon widespread landownership. By the last half of the eighteenth century between two-thirds and three-quarters of farm operators in the colonies were freeholders who owned land—a far greater proportion than in England. They lived within societies as disparate as Connecticut, eastern Massachusetts, Long Island, eastern New Jersey, and Tidewater Virginia. As population grew, land became scarce, and sons of yeomen migrated to new frontiers, taking up unimproved land rather than adding to the level of tenancy.[17]

Thus, pioneer farmers, on their way to becoming yeomen, had to reinvent their class on every new frontier, re-creating the material base necessary to sustain familial autonomy, local exchange, and market agriculture. At the outset of settlement in new areas, few pioneers owned land. Instead, they squatted on land owned by others. Once large numbers of families arrived, however, residents either registered ownership of land or left. Since land remained abundant, the proportion of landowners rose to high levels. For example, in frontier Lunenburg County, Virginia, in 1750, a decade after the first settlers arrived, just over half the heads of family owned land, but by the 1760s between three-quarters and four-fifths of them had land. Within a decade of initial settlement, three-quarters to four-fifths of householders owned land in new communities scattered from Massachusetts to Piedmont Virginia.[18]

As land ownership spread in older communities, labor shortages inevitably grew. Men who knew they could farm their own land married in their early to middle twenties, rather than work on their parents' farms. Northern farmers relied upon exchanges of labor with neighbors, an occasional hired hand, and particularly upon their own families and the large numbers of children their wives bore. In contrast, southern farmers, even yeomen, solved the problem of farm labor with slaves. The high demand for tobacco and rice in England gave wealthy southerners access to slave markets, and yeomen often owned a slave or two, crucial additions to scarce family labor.[19]

Yeoman expectations of landownership were not fulfilled everywhere in the eighteenth-century colonies. Great landlords who rented land to tenants dominated counties in the Hudson River valley, southern Maryland, and the northern neck of Virginia. During the early years of seventeenth-century settlement in New York, Dutch landlords enticed few farm families, for they could procure land on nearby frontiers. Only low rents and long terms, often lifetime leases that were almost the equivalent to freehold land tenure, attracted yeomen. As settlement proceeded and land became scarce, landlords adapted income-generating tenancies at will and by the 1750s, granted only annual leases at high rents.[20]

Most farmers who sought economic independence, however, avoided tenancy. Whenever rich men threatened secure land tenure, yeomen

and their sons resisted being reduced to a state of dependency, sometimes with violence. In 1730 in Virginia, for example, when the assembly passed a tobacco inspection act that diminished tobacco
output of yeomen, small planters (yeomen and tenants) in several
counties burned down the inspection warehouses. In the 1750s and
1760s Massachusetts farmers who had moved to Hudson Valley land
owned by New York landlords revolted several times, rejecting tenancy and demanding freehold land tenure and Massachusetts sovereignty in the contested areas they farmed.[21] Such resistance led
yeomen to greater self-definition as a class.

Gentlemen, whose connections to English capital and complex
marriages within their class assured their wealth and continued political prominence, learned that secure land tenure for ordinary men
ensured social peace. They procured millions of acres of undeveloped
land through land speculation, grants from provincial governments,
or inheritance. With land supplies abundant, most wealthy men sold
off undeveloped land to yeomen, often retaining economic power by
granting credit. By the second third of the eighteenth century gentlemen in settled parts of New England, the Chesapeake colonies,
and Pennsylvania had accepted yeoman aspirations.[22] They expected
social and political deference from the yeomanry; in return, they
guaranteed yeomen the security of the land and control over their
own farms and families. In New England gentlemen granted credit to
sons in older towns to buy land, formed land companies, and sold off
land cheaply. In the South they imported enough slaves to supply the
needs of many poorer planters, thereby creating a great class barrier
between all whites (as free men) and all people of color.[23]

Yeomen were active agents in this process of class formation.
Within the constraints of an increasingly capitalist world market,
they invented a traditional household economy. They desired to sustain their competency, making enough to keep the family from de-
meaning wage labor. These small farmers decided what crops to
produce, how to divide farm tasks among family members, if and
when to grow crops for distant commodity markets. Cooperation
among family members was necessary for economic independence,
with men assuming authority over their wives and children. Wives of
yeomen, whose labor in garden and dairy and exchanges with neighbors made farms viable, had neither separate political nor separate
legal identities. Yeoman families produced much of the food they ate
and tried to obtain the rest by trading with neighbors. To sustain familial autonomy and finance the exchange of labor, food, and local
manufactures with neighbors, they sold surpluses at local markets
for cash or goods. Participation in these commodity markets (ab-

stract institutions that set prices based upon supply and demand) mandated certain payment and impersonal credit relations; local exchange was informal, based upon friendship or kinship, and characterized by barter of "gifts" over long periods of time.[24]

All yeomen in the colonies lived in a capitalist world economy as well. The strategies they pursued to achieve economic independence—what crops they grew, how deeply they committed themselves to market production, what tools they purchased, how often they hired workers or bought slaves—were shaped by English, European, and West Indian demand for agricultural commodities. Yeomen in the Chesapeake colonies, where nearly every farmer sold tobacco for foreign markets, felt these constraints especially severely. Although the largest planters created nearly self-sufficient plantations based on the labor of numerous slaves, smaller slaveowners and men without slaves had to participate in staple markets without such advantages. Over the eighteenth century, however, they grew more food crops and devised local exchange networks as intensive as those of their northern neighbors.

Northern farmers who lived near cities or along navigable rivers, an important minority, turned to commercial agriculture, sending large surpluses to market, lending money at interest, and renting land near towns to increase their profits. Grain deficits in Southern Europe particularly propelled many Delaware Valley farmers into international grain commodity markets. For all such farmers, local exchange networks diminished in importance.[25]

A traveler to the colonies in 1750 would have found peaceful class relations and intensive exchange networks in New England, the Chesapeake Colonies, and parts of the Middle Colonies. By contrast, Hudson River Valley landlords and men who financed backcountry settlement from Pennsylvania to Georgia sought greater political control. Numerous conflicts over land ensued, beginning in New Jersey in the 1730s and touching Vermont, the Hudson River Valley, backcountry Pennsylvania, western North Carolina, and western South Carolina by the 1770s. Land speculators, landlords, and merchants confronted yeomen farmers, seeking to protect their property from the burdens of debt, from uncertain land titles, from the lack of government, from bandits, or from unfair taxation.

EMERGENCE OF A YEOMAN IDEOLOGY

The yeoman response to the American Revolution should be seen in the context of this process of class formation, class conflict, and the development of a yeoman class ideology. Eighteenth-century yeomen often had little consciousness of themselves as a class. The origins of a public yeoman class ideology can be traced to justifications of their rights to land when either gentlemen or native Americans threatened the security of their land tenure. When threats were imminent, yeomen petitioned legislatures, rioted, or took up arms. Although, even in the heat of conflict, class language was often subsumed in communal, ethnic, or religious rhetoric, with yeomen aspiring to no greater political end than a redress of grievances, during local conflict they developed a class outlook. Each conflict strengthened their folk memory of gentry oppression and their need for secure land tenure. To legitimate their rights to land, yeomen embraced a labor theory of value, one they had carried over with them from England, but that lay dormant until conflict broke out. Land, they insisted, was made valuable only by labor that improved it, and therefore farmers who worked the land should own it, even if speculators were the legal owners. A freeholder became an independent man, owing his livelihood to no one and thereby able to vote.[26]

Indian sovereignty over lands they hunted and cultivated made development of extensive private property—essential for any yeoman ideology—impracticable. From the outset of the conquest of America English colonists attacked Indian use of land, especially as hunting grounds, as unproductive. Indians, John Winthrop (the first governor of Massachusetts Bay Colony) insisted, "enclose noe Land, neither have any setled habytation, nor any tame Cattle to improve the Land by," and therefore had no right to retain ownership of it. Only human labor improved the land, thereby bestowing ownership rights upon it. Once the native Americans had been vanquished, colonists implicitly set their productive use of land against the wilderness left behind; attack on their property and persons posed a threat, especially for those who lived closest to the edge of white habitation.[27]

Statements spawned by conflicts over land in Massachusetts, New York, and the Carolinas suggest the widespread diffusion of this class ideology by 1770. In Massachusetts agrarian fear of dispossession began early. In 1687, when Governor Edmund Andros suggested that local land titles might be in doubt, Samuel Sewall reported that local farmers were "very averse from complying with anything that may alter the Tenure of their lands." Yeoman fears of threats to secure land tenure persisted, especially in debates of the late 1740s and 1750s over the expansion of paper currency. Farmers who wanted paper money viewed creditors opposed to it as conspirators seeking to reduce them to dependence: "We must sell our lands to pay them; then go and work upon their Farms; or Starve, or go to Sea as their Slaves, or go to—Jail." Although few Massachusetts farmers in the late colonial era lost land because of debt, they understood how vulnerable their land might become if tyranny returned.[28]

In New York yeomen, mostly from New England, vigorously defended their land rights during the Hudson Valley land riots of 1766. When land in New England was fully cultivated, settlers poured into New York, where great landlords owned the best land. In order to gain freeholds or at least to avoid short-term tenancy, the New Englanders resorted to violence. Their grievances were clear from their petitions and in their trial records. As some tenants put it in a 1764 petition, they had worked the land "for near 30 years past and had manured and cultivated" it thinking it was theirs, but now their landlords "would not lease the land" to them under good terms ("3 lives or twenty years") but "would oblige them to buy their farms paying money down for it or else remove immediately." When Dutchess County landlords ejected some settlers and put new tenants in their place, the former tenants, under William Prendergast, formed a militia and took back their old homes or tried to get the new tenants to pay them for their improvements. At his trial for treason Prendergast said he led the rebellion "on accot. of Largeness of rents and Shortness of Leases" and because he "pitied poor people who were turned out of possession." He and his supporters sought a settlement "to compell their Landlords to alter their Rents." They *had made him a desperate Man.* After all, "it was hard that they were not allowed to have any *property.*" Because "there was no Law for poor Men," Prendergast urged his followers to "pay their honest Debts but not their Rents until Settlemt. with their landlords." Prendergast himself had never paid rent, withholding payment "for the good of the Country." Such testimony suggests that the rioters had a fully articulated ideology.[29]

In the backcountry of the Carolinas participants in the Regulator movements vigorously expressed yeoman concerns about land security. During the late 1760s and early 1770s in North Carolina, western men of poor to middling stature opposed to high taxes were in sharp conflict with autocratic gentry rule by eastern creditors and their local allies. Calling themselves "farmers," "planters," and "poor industrious peasants," they contrasted themselves with rich and powerful men, who expropriated the fruits of their labor. Anson County Regulators made three demands in a 1769 legislative petition: more equitable taxation, less venal local government, and fairer land distribution. "The poor Inhabitants," they wrote, "are much oppress'd by reasons of disproportionate Taxes," and their inability, unlike eastern farmers, to pay their taxes with produce. The monopoly on the best unimproved lands enjoyed by friends of the Governor and Council, moreover, increased that burden, for "great numbers of poor people" had to "toil in the cultivation of bad Lands whereon they hardly can subsist" while great men left their land stand idle.[30]

In South Carolina, when provincial authorities refused to organize local government in the backcountry and bring bandits to justice in the late 1760s, Regulators rebelled, justifying their action as a defense of their labor, lands, and rights. "We are *Free-Men*—British Subjects—Not Born Slaves—We contribute our Proportion in all Public Taxations" yet they enjoyed few rights. Secure property was the key to all rights: "Property is of no Value, except to be secure" and theirs was very insecure, with their cattle stolen, horses "carried off," and personal property "plunder'd." Without local courts, with bandits running loose, "No improvements are attempted—No New Plans can take Place. . . . And (shameful to say) our Lands (some of the finest in *America*) lye useless and uncleared being rendered of small Value from the many licentious Persons intermixed among Us, whom We cannot drive off without Force or Violence." Therefore, they were "obliged to defend our Families, by *our own Strength*: As *Legal Methods* are beyond our Reach."[31]

By the mid-eighteenth century yeomen had their own agenda—sustaining familial autonomy (and male authority over the family), landownership, a modest freeholder egalitarianism. Northern merchants and wealthy southern planters may have started the revolt against England, but they needed widespread support to succeed. How rural Americans would respond to their demands—whether they became patriots or joined the disaffected—depended upon prior relations between yeomen and gentlemen and how well revolutionary governments responded to the wishes of yeomen for a more egalitarian social order of men of property.

YEOMEN AND THE MAKING OF THE REVOLUTION

How the yeomen made *their* Revolution, then, is a significant issue for historical inquiry.[32] As the conflict with England deepened in the 1760s and 1770s, Whig gentlemen tried to mobilize poorer freeholders. Many yeomen interpreted these calls to action through the lens of their own democratic agenda, thereby pushing the Revolution toward greater participation of male property holders. The Revolution for yeomen was a cumulative process that started slowly in the Stamp Act crisis in 1765–66, accelerated in the crises of 1774–76, and reached political maturity during the war. By the mid-1770s yeoman political participation rose to levels never before achieved. If some yeoman patriots tried to democratize the Revolution, others joined the English because they feared that Whig gentlemen would dispossess them of their lands as they had attempted to do earlier in the century.

At first, yeomen in almost all colonies listened to the Whig political program with some indifference; after all, the Stamp Act of 1765, with its tax on legal and commercial papers, deeds, wills, newspapers, almanacs, land warrants, and surveys affected urban folk—merchants, lawyers, even artisans—more often than yeomen. In towns the tax would be a daily nuisance; in the countryside, an infrequent and irregular one, when a man appeared at court, procured land, bought an almanac, or died.[33] Moreover, the rhetoric of Whig leaders during this crisis harkened back more to the country ideology of eighteenth-century England than the democracy of radicals in the English Revolution of the 1640s. Corruption had led the English Parliament to reduce colonial rights, and luxuries from England threatened to undermine colonial virtue. The merchants' stress on the virtue of the people (defined narrowly), the public interest, and communal consensus and their attack on conspicuous consumption may have been an attempt to unify their own class (the only people "wallowing in luxury") while passively incorporating poorer folk.

Such appeals worked in the towns where most of the Stamp Act riots occurred, but they gained little active response in the countryside. Here and there yeomen participated in crowd actions. For example, in Virginia's northern neck about fifty yeomen (a tiny part of that class) joined an equal number of gentlemen (nearly the entire class) and marched on Leedstown to prevent a merchant from distributing stamps; in two western Massachusetts towns inhabitants rioted to prevent imprisonment of debtors lacking stamped papers that would permit them to sell land to pay their debts.[34]

Rural folk interpreted the arguments of the Whig "Sons of Liberty" about the Stamp Act in the light of their beliefs about land and labor, as well as the underground tradition of a wide franchise and a smallholder republic, taken from the English Levellers and other radicals of the 1640s.[35] John Adams, who rode the legal circuit in Massachusetts and understood the countryside well, incorporated rural economic concerns in the instructions on the Stamp Act he wrote for his hometown of Braintree to its representative; more than forty other towns adopted his language. The Stamp tax was "a burthensome tax because the duties are so numerous and so high . . . that it would be totally impossible for the people to subsist under it," and considering "the present scarcity of money, we have reason to think the execution of that act for a short . . . time would drain the country of its cash, strip multitudes of their property and reduce them to absolute beggary." The Stamp tax, he concluded, was inherently unfair because "the public money of this country is the toil and labor of the people."[36]

On the other hand, yeomen engaged in struggle with the gentry often applied Whig ideas about the Stamp Act to their own ends. William Prendergast and the tenants he led against Whig landlords in the New York land riots called themselves "Sons of Liberty." Rioters in Scarborough, Maine, calling themselves "Suns of liburty," linked the merchant Richard King, who had "destroyed the poor and taken away Peoples Estates," with English ministers who drafted the Stamp Act.[37]

Whig leaders came to understand that to gain the support of white property holders they had to appeal to the lived experience of yeomen, to their fears of losing their land. In the crisis of 1774 and 1775 throughout the colonies gentlemen and merchants organized mass meetings to gain the support of ordinary folk. In Virginia patriot leaders like Patrick Henry spoke with an evangelical fervor many of their auditors shared. New England Whigs argued that English ministers, in Samuel Adams's words, threatened to "take away your Barn and my house." This aristocracy, John Adams wrote, was bent on "reducing the country to lordships" by taxing land and property, making virtuous yeomen into tenants and servile laborers, much like seventeenth-century English landlords. In June 1774, in a letter to rural towns, the Boston Committee of Correspondence directly appealed to this fear. What "if a favorite of a perverse Governor should pretend title to our lands," they wrote. "Of what value are our lands or estates to us if such an odious government should be established among us? Can we look with pleasure . . . on the field cultivated by our own industry?"[38]

Yeomen in New England took their own, radical initiatives, refusing to listen to the moderate counsel of their betters. Seeing a relation between taxes imposed by Parliament and the security of their own land, they expanded upon the Whig message. Between the passage of the Intolerable Acts in 1774 and the outbreak of war in April 1775, they sometimes took over the revolutionary movement, pushing the colonies closer to independence. The Intolerable Acts, which closed the port of Boston and curtailed the Massachusetts government, and the Quebec Act, which tolerated Catholics, aroused more New England yeomen into political action. "The common people," reported Anne Hulton, sister of a British customs commissioner, feared taxes would dispossess them of their land, with customs commissioners having "an *unlimited* power given them to tax even their lands, & that in order to raise a Revenue for supporting . . . Bishops that are coming over." They attended illegal town meetings, insisted that courts be closed, or democratically appointed their own judges, both to defy the British and to help poor rural debtors. Dramatic evidence of the response of yeomen and their wives took place in late 1774, when a rumor spread that General Gage had captured colonial arms and powder stored in Charlestown. As many as fifty thousand Massachusetts, Connecticut, and New Hampshire militiamen marched toward Boston. Ezra Stiles, an eyewitness, reported that "all along were armed Men rushing forward . . . , at every house Women and Children making Cartridges, Running Bullets, . . . crying and bemoaning and at the same time animating their Husbands and Sons to fight for their Liberties."[39]

In New York freeholders who were fearful that the colonial or English government might evict them from their land vigorously supported independence, in contrast to most tenants who hoped the king might dispossess their Whig landlords. In late 1774 citizens of Newtown, on Long Island, linked their attack on the Intolerable Acts to land. The acts "absolutely tended to deprive" them of their "most inestimable rights and privileges," their property rights, adding that "man ought to have the disposition of his property either by himself or his representatives." The Green Mountain Boys of Vermont, who captured Fort Ticonderoga from the British in May 1775, saw the war as continuing their long battle with New York landlords. They tied support for independence to separation from New York, arguing that the landlords had deprived them "by frawd viollance and oppression" of "thire property and in particularly thire Landed interest."[40]

Yeomen in other colonies took radical action. In 1775 Virginia gentlemen sometimes lost control over revolutionary committees to small planters. In 1776 Pennsylvania, Delaware Valley, and backcountry farmers united with Philadelphia artisans and journeymen to support the state's democratic constitution, a document that enraged conservatives by rejecting the mixed government of England and the other colonies. In June 1776 several militia companies in rural Anne Arundel County, Maryland, drafted a radical constitution; one month later 855 men—about two-fifths of the county's white men—demanded universal white manhood suffrage.[41]

One can find hints that neither gentlemen or yeomen could control the radicalism of the Revolution from spreading to farm women. Many women had actively fomented revolt, supporting nonimportation by spinning American fabrics and boycotting tea, urging husbands and sons to support the war. Listening carefully to male rhetoric in the 1760s and early 1770s, middling farm women took advantage of the revolutionary ferment, slowly becoming more conscious of themselves as potential citizens and implicitly rejecting yeomen efforts to limit democratization to males.[42]

In the war years between 1776 and 1781 the yeomanry made a revolution for themselves, one that disrupted and might have transformed relations of power and production. Because they fed the soldiers of the fledgling nation and they and their sons defended their states against the English foe, they deserved a more democratic polity. The 200,000 men who served in either the militia or the regular army—many of them poor—expected decent pay, respect, the franchise, and sufficient land after the war to remain yeomen or to pull themselves up from the ranks of the dispossessed. "The strength of the country," as Abraham Yates of Albany, New York (an Antifederalist foe of the landlords), put it, "lays in the yeomanry thereof, who . . . had been upon hard militia duty, in which a man worth no more than ten pounds had to do equal duty with a gentleman of 10,000 pounds . . . ; if the rich intended to avail themselves of the yeomanry . . . to fight for their riches, it would require to shew them . . . that they intended no partiality." As Yates's language suggests, yeomen radicalized revolutionary rhetoric about slavery and freedom, taxation and representation, tyranny and popular sovereignty. For them, "the sovereignty of the people" suggested a democracy of property holders in which their views would be paramount, not merely a legal relation between voter and representative. The people would make policy through assemblies, but if these bodies ignored them, yeomen could resort to other means to assert their will.[43]

Politicized by the war, patriot farm women tried to act as good citizens, circulating petitions, testifying against Tories, managing farms, making cloth and clothes, tending to the domestic needs of the Continental Army, and giving goods and money to the revolutionary cause. Women linked their activity both to their status as virtuous housewives and to the war against English bondage. Ideas of independence and individualism espoused by revolutionary leaders seemed to offer them greater autonomy from their husbands, or at least greater respect than they received in patriarchal farm households. Yeomen opposed such aspirations for they attacked the patriarchal base of yeoman citizenship.[44]

The overall pattern of yeoman allegiance seems clear. The success of the appeal of revolutionaries depended upon prior relations between yeomen and gentlemen. Where Whig gentlemen protected yeoman property, yeomen often joined the patriot cause, paying taxes to the new governments and enlisting in militia or army. In these places yeomen expected democratic social change. Such patriotism was most common in New England, most of New Jersey, eastern Pennsylvania, the Chesapeake region, and the eastern parts of the

Carolinas. In New England the long tradition of vigorous town meetings and local autonomy gave ordinary citizens a voice (even if subordinate) in political affairs and linked the destiny of gentleman and yeoman. Local custom, which gave citizens control of resources such as water and pasturelands, constrained the behavior of wealthy men. In the Chesapeake colonies, where yeomen acquiesced in gentry rule in return for protection of their land and slaves, yeomen often borrowed money from gentlemen to purchase slaves.

In contrast, wherever yeomen (or would-be yeomen among tenants) saw Whig gentlemen as enemies, they joined the British or stayed neutral. Partisan warfare between Whigs and Tories broke out in the Hudson River Valley, in Vermont, and in the Carolina backcountry, where landlords or wealthy planters had ignored or suppressed the demands of yeomen. Such violence led many farm families to run for cover, away from both patriots and loyalists. Others, like residents of Livingston Manor in New York, joined the British, hoping that the British would distribute land to them. And where loyalist gentlemen or landlords had maintained good relations with farmers—along Virginia's eastern shore—rural folk stayed loyal.[45]

YEOMEN AND THE SHAPING OF REVOLUTIONARY INSTITUTIONS

In patriot regions yeomen extracted a steep price from gentlemen for their support, insisting upon a direct role in making public policy. Of course, they could not establish direct democracy, deciding political action as a group. Yet they achieved remarkable success. They attended mass meetings, they sent some of their number to the new enlarged state assemblies, they voted for representatives to conventions to draft state constitutions, they signed a multitude of petitions on public issues, and—quite remarkably—they sometimes achieved substantial success in creating or vetoing laws.

In the late 1770s and 1780s, written constitutions were new and untried vehicles to restrain government. As popular pressure on legislatures grew, states replaced constitutions written by legislatures in 1776–77 with those composed by special conventions, where delegates sometimes received instructions from constituents. Reacting to demands for popular democracy, writers of the later constitutions (1777–86) in Massachusetts, New York, Vermont, and New Hampshire included more frequent and direct instances of consent by the people as a whole or through their legislators. The constitution writers in New York and Massachusetts rejected democracy, but they understood that to maintain any political control, they had to accommodate the democratic desires of the yeoman and mechanic majority.[46]

Massachusetts, alone among states, sent its new constitutions to the people for ratification at town meetings. Practicing their right of consent, the citizens of Massachusetts rejected the first proposed constitution in 1778. In town after town they voted against the document, usually reaching a consensus. Underneath the legal language of small-town returns, the concerns of yeomen for local autonomy, security, and freeholder democracy shine brightly. Inhabitants of various towns raised demands for emancipation of slaves, a universal male franchise (or at least one that included all men of property), election of militia officers and justices of the peace, laws favoring debtors, local control over the militia, limited powers for the governor, and a bill of rights.[47]

Listening to ordinary freeholders, the town leaders who wrote attacks on the proposed constitution espoused egalitarian ideals and an implicit labor theory of value. Townsmen in Lenox, located in western Massachusetts, insisted that since "all Men were born equally free and independent," they had rights to "enjoying and defending Life and Liberty and acquiring, possessing and protecting Property." The 1778 constitution, by excluding free Negroes and those too poor to pay taxes from the polls made "Honest Poverty a Crime for which a large Number of the true and faithfull Subjects of the State who perhaps fought and bled in their Countrys Cause are deprived of [these rights,] for how can a Man be said to [be] free and independent, enjoying and defending Life and Liberty and protecting property, when he has not a voice allowed him in" electing legislators who "can make laws to bind him." Not surprisingly, they also decried the way the courts reduced men to subservience, complaining that the law "obligated a poor Debtor to go through a course of Law and pay the extravigant Costs, when he was willing to confess Judgment and submit to justice, which is an oppressive and Tyrannical Law and beneficial to none but Attornies."[48]

In the colonial era freeholders had frequently petitioned assemblies for redress of local grievances—location of the courthouse, contested local elections, creation of new countries. But the Revolution empowered ordinary men to launch petition campaigns on broader political issues. In Virginia a deluge of petitions aiming at a more democratic society, for instance, reached the assembly between 1776 and 1782. Most petitions still concerned local issues. But yeoman planters now demanded policy action on a multitude of issues: disestablishing the Anglican Church, reducing the high prices speculators charged for land, paying debts in kind or paper money rather than specie, repealing unjust poll and commodity taxes, equalizing land taxes, and confirming titles of land farmed by squatters. These campaigns often generated opposition; the assembly also received petitions asking that taxes be raised to restore the credit of the state or to keep the established church. Residents of Orange County, alone, sent remonstrances to the legislature on the inequities of the land tax, the necessity of home manufactures, the operation of the militia, and freedom of religion. On average a tenth of the county's white men signed each petition.[49]

In almost every state yeomen circulated similar petitions, reasserting through their diversity a reinvented moral economy, centered around a demand for political and economic equality. They defined equality in everyday terms of ready access to unimproved land, relief from the burdens of debt, and taxes proportionate to ability to pay. Petitioners, for instance, wished to pay debts and taxes in paper money because they had little specie. Poll taxes forced everyone to pay at the same rate, despite differences in wealth; land taxes usually taxed the improved land of yeomen more heavily than the large unimproved holdings of speculators. The state, petitioners concluded, had an obligation to ensure the land tenure of poorer freeholders by issuing paper money or taxing the wealthy proportionately more. They believed state action necessary because a republic could survive only if a majority of her citizens were independent freeholders capable of making political choices without servile dependence upon patron, creditor, or employer.[50]

Not only did the formation of new governments encourage local attempts at instructing legislators through petitions, but voters elected more farmers of middling wealth to state legislatures, hoping men like themselves would be receptive to their views. From the 1760s to the 1780s, the number of men of moderate wealth elected to lower houses in New Hampshire, New York, and New Jersey increased from a sixth to more than three-fifths, and the proportion of farmers rose from a quarter to over a half. Even in the South, which changed less, the percentage of farmers (excluding gentlemen) more than doubled, from an eighth to over a quarter. The election of their own kind gave yeomen hope that their petitions would be heard and the instructions they contained be made into policy. Given the divisions of opinion on most issues, petitioners gained approval with remarkable frequency.[51]

One might expect to find few successful petitions in Virginia, with its great planter ruling class. Yet, even there, yeomen sometimes persuaded their supposed betters. We have seen how petitioning led to repeal of the law exempting overseers from service in county militias.

Other examples can be found. When citizens of Kentucky County complained in October 1779 that the four hundred acres granted them for defending the county was insufficient, the assembly gave them more land. In 1780 petitioners from Amelia County who desired both dissolution of church vestries and the right of dissenting ministers to perform marriages succeeded in getting several bills introduced and passed. And in 1780 citizens of Amherst County gained an extension of time to pay their taxes. When the legislature failed to grant relief—as was often the case on the issue of the religious establishment—a committee aired the issue, leaving hope for eventual favorable action.[52]

In state after state the success of the yeomanry in influencing public policy during the war and postwar years led yeomen to believe that they, the majority of voters, could rule. In every state legislature yeomen and their allies made up a significant minority that supported minimal government expenditures, low taxes, credit relief, and paper money. But merchants, great planters, and small capitalists who still ruled the states opposed the yeomanry, often frustrating the actions yeomen desired. In the 1780s, when yeomen failed to gain relief, they turned to the traditional rural remedy of crowd action adopted in the 1760s and 1770s. Shays's Rebellion of 1782–86 is the most famous example. Debtor farmers in western Massachusetts tried, but failed, to gain legislative relief. In 1786, after a decade of endemic riots against tax collectors and auctions of property seized for debt, and fearing debtors prison and the loss of their lands, they closed the courts, preventing the operation of credit laws. Similar debtor agitation occurred elsewhere in New England and in Maryland, South Carolina, New Jersey, Virginia, and Pennsylvania. All these agrarian upheavals were suppressed.[53]

The gentry ruling class and its allies observed this growth of democracy with horror and set about reimposing discipline upon an unruly rural population. Classical republican texts suggested the gentry's cause was virtuous and worthy of consensual support. Instead, the mob had insisted upon instructing their betters, the natural aristocracy, in the business of government, had destroyed the economy, had elected venal men as state legislators who then passed class legislation favoring debtors, and in Massachusetts had revolted against constituted republican authority.[54]

The intolerance of men of means toward popular democracy can be seen in their frenzied reaction to rural uprisings in the 1780s. In the 1760s gentlemen had accepted, but attempted to control, riots, sometimes thought of as an extension of government, more often an example of class tensions. But since American states were now republics whose people were sovereign, any crowd action, they argued, constituted rebellion against the people. Governments used military force to end crowd actions like Shays's Rebellion. Once they had ended dissension, political leaders often incorporated local men of wealth and middling farmers who had supported the yeomen into the political system. Men unwilling to work within this new political system found themselves thrust out of politics altogether.[55]

YEOMEN AND THE AMERICAN CONSTITUTION

In 1787–88 yeoman farmers helped incite wealthy Whigs to reform the government of the Confederation. Tiring of what they saw as democratic chaos created by governments of small farmers, wealthy Whigs organized the Constitutional Convention in order to create a republic that constrained popular legislative behavior and the *people-out-of-doors*. James Madison reflected these concerns in a memorandum in early 1787. The Confederation had failed to "guaranty to the states of their Constitutions & Laws against internal violence," increasing the odds that a minority of voters would unite with "those whose poverty excludes them from a right of suffrage, and who . . . will be more likely to join the standard of sedition than that of the established government." State legislatures, influenced by debtors, were equally pernicious, reducing the rights of creditors. "Paper money, instalments of debts, occlusion of Courts, making property a legal tender," Madison wrote, "affect the Creditor State, in the same manner they do its own citizens who are relatively creditors toward other citizens."[56]

Most delegates to the Philadelphia Convention sought a stronger national government, with the power to tax, regulate commerce, suppress internal conflict, and encourage economic development. They uniformly opposed *agrarian* laws, a term used to imply the redistribution of wealth and the leveling of property. Not surprisingly, the document they produced reflected the interests of the commercial classes—merchants, great planters, lawyers, master craftsmen, commercial farmers. Nevertheless, the delegates had to pay attention to the agenda of the people-out-of-doors, if for no other reason than to get it ratified. Although some sympathized with Alexander Hamilton's plan to establish a nation-state with a president for life and an absolute veto over the states, they understood that the people would absolutely reject it. In this spirit, they rejected attempts to establish national property qualifications for voting or officeholding that would have disenfranchised many urban mechanics and poorer rural folk.[57]

Farmers divided over support of the Constitution. To a considerable

extent, the little evidence we have suggests, the political division reflected the split between yeomen and capitalist farmers oriented
toward commodity markets a national government might open. Most
yeoman farmers living in the large states opposed it. Following the
views of rural property holders, ratifying conventions in the popu-
lous states of Massachusetts and New York initially opposed the Constitution, and the final vote in these states and Virginia was very
close. But capitalist farmers, especially those living near cities,
joined urban artisans in supporting a Constitution that created
stable and larger markets for their goods and that eliminated trade
barriers between states. Western farmers were probably more ambiguous: on the one hand, they wanted a strong national government,
capable of dispossessing the Indians of their homelands and securing
land for them; on the other, they wished to be left alone to create a
sufficiency, without paying taxes they considered burdensome. Given
the numerical predominance of yeoman farmers in long-settled areas, the Constitution probably would have been rejected if it had
been put to a national plebiscite of property holders.[58]

Although few essays by yeoman farmers survive from the ratification controversy, some writers reflected their concerns. Yeomen believed that a few wealthy and prominent men would dominate the
new federal government and oppress common freeholders. Their old
concerns about land security resurfaced. In the language of the eighteenth century, yeomen feared "aristocracy." Not only would these
"aristocrats" ignore the legitimate demands of the yeomanry, they
would support creditors and land speculators and raise unfair taxes.
Yeomen unable to pay taxes or debts could lose their land and, with
it, their class identity as yeomen, their ability to support their families, and their status as patriarchal heads of their own households.[59]

The mood of the debate led commentators to adopt the language of
class. An Antifederalist satire, "Address of the Lowborn" by "John
Humble," published in a Philadelphia newspaper, resonated with
yeoman anger. Denying the greater virtue of the six hundred "well-
born" men over "three millions of *lowborn* American slaves," he insisted that "yet our feeling, through the medium of the plow, the hoe,
and the grubbing axe is as acute as any nobleman's in the world."
The Constitution, "Humble" contended, replicated the aristocracy of
England, replacing *"kings, lords,* and *commons"* with *"President,
Senate,* and *Representatives,"* the only government the wellborn believe "can save this our country from inevitable destruction."[60]

Yeomen demanded political respect because of their control of productive land, their large numbers, and their virtue. As Melancton
Smith (a yeoman's son who became a successful merchant and an An-

tifederalist leader) argued at the New York Convention, "those in middling circumstances . . . are inclined by habit and company with whom they associate, to set bounds to their passions and appetites . . . hence the substantial yeomanry of the country are more temperate, of better morals and less ambition than the great." For these reasons, "a representative body, composed principally of the respectable yeomanry is the best possible security to liberty."[61]

A debate between two farmers over the Constitution at the Massachusetts ratifying convention, one insisting that it took property, the other that it cured the anarchy of Shays's Rebellion, illuminates the rural conflict over ratification. Amos Singletary, a farmer from Worcester County, repeated Antifederalist fears of tyranny and aristocracy. Like Great Britain in 1775, the Constitution "claimed a right to tax us and bind us," taxing our land, thereby taking "all we have—all our property. [The aristocrats and the wealthy] get all the power and all the money into their own hand, and then they will swallow up all us little folks, like the great *Leviathan*, . . . ; yes, just as the whale swallowed up *Jonah*." Jonathan Smith's response supporting the Constitution is revealing. "I am a plain man," he began, "and get my living by the plough. I am not used to speak in public, but I beg your leave to say a few words to my brother ploughjoggers." Then he explained the "effects of anarchy, that you may see the reasons I wish for good government," arguing that men took up arms to defend their property. When he "saw this Constitution, I found that it was a cure for these disorders. . . . I got a copy of it, and read it over and over," trying to understand it, looking for "checks and balances of power" and finding "them all here." Just as a small farmer would want his neighbor's support, even if a wealthy "man of learning," when his "title was disputed," farmers should politically support wealthy men for "these lawyers, these moneyed men, these men of learning, are all embarked in the same cause with us . . . ; and shall we throw the Constitution overboard because it does not please us alike?"[62]

Notwithstanding widespread opposition among the yeomanry, the Constitution was ratified by "the people." If the Constitution had a popular mandate, then any challenge to constitutional federal government could be construed as an attack on "the people." Rural democratic movements that depended upon the people-out-of-doors thereby lost legitimacy and, like farmers in the antitax Whiskey Rebellion of 1794, faced the iron hand of federal power. To influence government, yeomen had to work through electoral politics.

Once yeomen were willing to accept the dictates of majority rule, no matter how remote the majority, they could legitimately gain a place in politics. In the 1790s, even though the national government from the outset was dominated by men of wealth, as Antifederalists had feared, yeomen insisted on their right to a hearing. They participated in republican politics, electing and attempting to influence their representatives. Party politics became an arena for complex class negotiations between yeomen and rulers, negotiations often mediated by ethnicity, region, religion, and occupation.[63]

In pushing for greater freeholder democracy in the 1780s and 1790s, yeomen became more conscious of themselves as a political class, distinct from gentlemen and merchants. They placed their desire for secure land on state and national political agendas. But other classes—merchants, gentlemen, artisans, commercial farmers—remained powerful. How the struggles between yeomen and their adversaries would conclude was unclear even in 1800.

LEGACY OF THE REVOLUTION

The Revolution, then, was a crucial event for the American yeomanry. It brought the problems of rural life to the forefront of politics. Because politicians all sought farm votes, they universally connected the plow to liberty. But was agrarian virtue the yeoman vision of familial autonomy and local exchange, or was it the capitalist vision of intensive development and improving agriculture? Historians have just begun to uncover the extent of this conflict, but we can suggest the contours of the struggle. In the Northeast, capitalist agriculture threatened to engulf the yeomanry but in the West, where the Revolution had opened up millions of "virgin" acres, the yeomanry had room to grow and struggle with capitalist adversaries—land speculators, creditors, commercial farmers—over land policy, credit, and commercial agriculture.

Yeomen in the backcountry still had to protect their land, as the chronic tax uprisings described above and the Indian wars show. Confrontations between western yeomen and Indians in the Ohio Valley and the Old Southwest deepened the yeomen's attachment to land they took from Indians, but considered their own, and helped perpetuate a distinctive yeoman ideology. After two decades of conflict and war, which had prevented white migration to the West, thousands of eastern families streamed into the Ohio Valley, where they encountered equal numbers of native Americans, many of whom colonists had forced to vacate lands east of the mountains. Settlers refused to share the land on this middle ground and insisted, as squatter John Emerson put it in 1785, "that all mankind, agreeable to every constitution formed in America, have an undoubted right to pass into every vacant country." Secretary of War Henry Knox saw the consequences of the settlers' behavior upon Indians not yet clearly defeated in war: while American Indians "anxiously defend their lands which the other [whites] avariciously claim," the "slightest offence occasions death—revenge follows which knows no bounds." Settlers massacred them (even when allies), inciting guerilla warfare, and then insisting that the federal government join their crusade to rid the region of native Americans. White settlers in the Ohio Valley welcomed the military campaigns of the 1790s that ultimately ended what they saw as the Indian menace.[64]

Out of conflicts with native Americans, creditors, and landlords, small landowners devised a democratic language to describe themselves that legitimated their place in society. Yeomen insisted that they were the country's most productive class, whose small surpluses when added together accounted for much of the nation's wealth. Because land gained value only through labor, they demanded the ownership of the land they farmed. Northeastern yeomen sought rapid settlement of unimproved lands, but opposed intensive economic development that might force them from farm to workshop. These ideas set yeomen against anyone who threatened to take their land from them and sell it at the highest price the market would bear. Creditors tied them so firmly to the commodity markets in which their grains and foodstuffs were sold that loss of their land was possible; capitalist farmers perfected new, capital-intensive techniques, making older strategies of communal self-sufficiency in food difficult, if not impossible.[65]

These yeoman ideals influenced the political leaders who created a powerful ideology that historians have commonly called "Jeffersonian agrarianism," but which might better be dubbed "agrarian realism."[66] *Agrarian realists* like Thomas Jefferson contended that the best possible society was one dominated by small, independent producers. Only widespread distribution of land could prevent usurpation of power and destruction of the republic by the wealthy. Jefferson even drafted legislation that would have given all freemen in Virginia seventy-five acres of improved land upon marriage. In these ideas Jefferson and his followers faithfully reflected yeoman views. But agrarian realists linked small-scale farming to agricultural improvement in ways that implied greater participation in the market than yeomen who sought only a vent for small surpluses desired. Unlike yeomen, agrarian realists were committed to the search for foreign markets and rapid economic development. Since landowners reaped all the profits of their toil, agrarian realists argued, they should rapidly improve their property and seek ever-more productive ways to increase output and raise exports.

The Revolution was a watershed for northeastern farmers, who

slowly turned to capitalist agriculture. However much they agreed
with yeomen on the virtue of farming, the capitalist farmers devised
a different ideology, one based on their growing reliance on the market and their desire for intensive rural development. When inflation
reduced the value of their "book" debts during the war, they invested
in commercial paper, exchangeable in financial markets; when the
growth of cities created more integrated regional markets at the
same time as European markets opened up, they eagerly expanded
their output.[67]

The Philadelphia Society for Promoting Agriculture illuminates
the improving spirit that animated capitalist farmers. Founded in
1785 by merchants, doctors, and gentlemen (including Benjamin
Rush and Robert Morris), nearly all of whom opposed Pennsylvania's
democratic constitution of 1776 and applauded the federal Constitution of 1787, the society gave its first prize, a gold medal inscribed with
the words "Venerate the Plough," to George Morgan, a gentleman
farmer from Princeton, New Jersey. The medal shows a farmer plow-
ing his fields with the allegorical female figure of liberty at his side.
Yeomen would surely have applauded such imagery. Beneath a picture of a neat barn and farmhouse the *Columbian Magazine* reprinted Morgan's plan for an efficient barnyard, "for affording the
best shelter for cattle and procuring the greatest quantity of ma-
nure" necessary to improve output for the market. The agrarianism of
the Philadelphia Society thus varied sharply from that of yeomen.[68]

Middling farm women, wives of commercial farmers, tried as best
they could to gain the fruits of their patriotic participation in the
war. Capitalist agriculture, with its emphasis upon productivity and
market ethics over family custom, gave farm wives in the urbanizing
Northeast the potential for political participation, however limited.
If individual virtue and productivity were to be the farmer's goal,
then women's contributions arguably should be recognized as equal
to their husbands. Although Whig leaders had encouraged the
Daughters of Liberty in patriotic activities, they suppressed almost
every attempt women made to claim their rights as citizens. For instance, opponents ridiculed the New Jersey law that enfranchised female landowners from 1790 to 1807 as starting "a government in
petticoats." Lacking any possibility of gaining a public political role,
wealthier women either kept their political opinions within their
homes or diverted politics inward upon the household. They assumed
the role of republican mothers, with the political duty of training the
next generation of republican men and women. How far this ideology
of republican motherhood, which required that women be educated
in politics and morality, spread through the countryside is not clear,

but many northeastern rural women seem to have interpreted it to sustain not only child nurture but rational management of farm kitchens and taking part in the market.[69]

If a vanguard of capitalist farmers seemed ready to eliminate yeoman farming in the East, the vast western frontier, won from the British and conquered from the Indians, provided opportunity for yeomen searching for secure land and the maintenance of patriarchal families. During the early decades of the new nation, hundreds of thousands of whites migrated to the new frontiers in northern New England, western New York and Pennsylvania, Ohio, Georgia, and other new states.[70] In order to attain relative autonomy, migrating yeomen needed cheap frontier land and control over their family's labor. Thus, they included those who felt most adamant about their traditional familial role and who left older areas overrun by commercial farms on which women practiced a kind of domestic economy that implied more equal marriages.[71]

The goal of western farmers to own land led to a century of conflict. The issues in the debate over the distribution of frontier land—land prices, the minimum acreage a pioneer could buy, credit to purchasers, the rights of squatters to stay on lands they improved—set land speculator against yeoman. If men should have the fruits of their labor, then free land to farmers was the best policy. Free distribution of land by the state might limit capitalist land markets; it might sustain yeoman familial independence, but it would reduce the profits of speculators. Men of wealth, fearing the "savagery" they thought inevitable if men were permitted to squat on unimproved land without paying for it, sought a capitalist land system. Insisting that location and the fertility of land, not the labor put into it, created value, they wanted the states (which controlled much unimproved land in the new nation) and the federal government to sell land at market prices. If frontier families became self-sufficient rather than market-oriented, those who looked to fostering commerce and manufactures believed that American development would slow (there would be fewer farm exports to finance development) and infant American industries atrophy (self-sufficient farmers could not afford to buy American manufactures).[72]

In retrospect, the American Revolution was the most important event in the history of the small property-owning yeoman class. Long before the Revolution, yeoman farmers—influenced by the republican values of their ancestors and the wide availability of land in the colonies—had devised farm strategies that placed them between full self-sufficiency and the market. Wherever gentlemen had attempted to gain greater control over yeoman property, yeomen devised a class ideology, based upon their version of a labor theory of value, to legitimate their rights to land.

The American Revolution transformed class relations and created something new—a yeoman class imbued with democratic ideas. Not content with passively voting for one's betters, yeomen believed that small landowners, as the most independent and virtuous of classes, had a right to rule. In the ferment of the 1770s and 1780s, they sometimes succeeded; more often, gentlemen, capitalist farmers, merchants, and bankers dominated the legislatures, and rural folk turned to the venerable tactics of closing courts or harassing tax collectors. State and federal governments refused to acquiesce, and widespread violence disrupted rural America from the 1770s to the early 1800s. Only after 1800 did yeomen pull back from crowd actions and willingly become part of the republican body politic.

The defeat of yeoman popular democracy in the revolutionary era was only the first stage in the struggle of yeomen to maintain their communal social order. On every frontier yeomen reinvented their class and remade a world of patriarchal family government, food-producing farms, and communal self-sufficiency. As capitalist farmers expanded on the northern frontiers, conflicts with yeomen ensued. In the South, on the other hand, the struggles between large planters and yeomen were different and tended to ensure the continued viability of yeoman society. Still, the direction of change was clear. Ultimately, the yeoman farmers, precariously poised between local self-sufficiency and the market, succumbed to capitalist agriculture. Only the radical legacy of the Revolution sustained yeoman democracy for so long, nurturing the yeomanry through their protracted struggles of the nineteenth century.

NOTES

ACKNOWLEDGMENTS: Research for this paper was supported by a summer research grant from Northern Illinois University. I am indebted to Stanley Engerman and Gary Nash for criticism of earlier drafts and to Alfred Young, whose primary source suggestions and extraordinarily valuable comments on earlier versions focused my thinking and sharpened the argument of the essay.

PUBLISHING NOTE: A revised version of this essay appears in Allan Kulikoff, *The Agrarian Origins of American Capitalism* (Charlottesville, Va., 1992). Used with permission from the University Press of Virginia.

1. Robert L. Scribner and Brent Tarter, eds., *Revolutionary Vir-*

ginia: The Road to Independence, vol. 6, The Time for Decision, 1776: A Documentary Record (Charlottesville, Va., 1981), 474–77. I have placed this incident in broader perspective in The Agrarian Origins of American Capitalism (Charlottesville, Va., 1992), chap. 6.

2. See Allan Kulikoff, Tobacco and Slaves: The Development of Southern Culture in the Chesapeake, 1680–1800 (Chapel Hill, N.C., 1986), chaps. 3, 4, and 7; and, for other gentry classes, Gary Kornblith and John Murrin, "The Making and Unmaking of the American Ruling Class," this volume. Precise counting of yeomen, gentlemen, and poor whites is speculative. Perhaps a third of white heads of household were tenants, squatters, or sons waiting to inherit land. Kulikoff, Tobacco and Slaves, chap. 4.

3. Richard D. Brown, Revolutionary Politics in Massachusetts: The Boston Committees of Correspondence and the Towns, 1772–1774 (Cambridge, Mass., 1970) is an example of this kind of argument.

4. Ruth Bogin, "Petitioning and the New Moral Economy of Post-Revolutionary America," William and Mary Quarterly, 3d series (hereafter cited as WMQ), 45(1988): 391–425, provides a framework for understanding petitioning.

5. Rural conditions and culture are summarized in Allan Kulikoff, "The Transition to Capitalism in Rural America," WMQ 46 (1989): 120–44; and Daniel Vickers, "Competency and Competition: Economic Culture in Early America," WMQ 47(1990): 3–29. Richard L. Bushman, "Massachusetts Farmers and the Revolution," in Richard M. Jellison, ed., Society, Freedom, and Conscience: The Coming of the Revolution in Virginia, Massachusetts, and New York (New York, 1976), 77–124, is the seminal examination of rural ideology. For rural revolts see Edward Countryman, " 'Out of the Bounds of the Law': Northern Land Rioters in the Eighteenth Century," in Alfred F. Young, ed., The American Revolution: Explorations in the History of American Radicalism (De Kalb, Ill., 1976), 39–69; Richard Maxwell Brown, "Back Country Rebellions and the Homestead Ethic in America, 1740–1799," in Brown and Don E. Fehrenbacher, eds., Tradition, Conflict, and Modernization: Perspectives on the American Revolution (New York, 1977), 73–99; Alan Taylor, "Agrarian Independence: Northern Land Rioters after the Revolution," this volume; David P. Szatmary, Shays' Rebellion: The Making of an Agrarian Insurrection (Amherst, Mass., 1980); and Thomas P. Slaughter, The Whiskey Rebellion: The Frontier Epilogue to the American Revolution (New York, 1986).

6. For details of issues covered in this section see my book The Rise and Destruction of the American Yeoman Classes (Chapel Hill, N.C., 1992).

7. J. Hector St. John de Crèvecœur, *Letters from an American Farmer and Sketches of Eighteenth-Century America,* ed. Albert E. Stone (New York, 1981), 54. Nothwithstanding Crèvecœur's paeans to American classlessness and his blindness to American poverty and diversity, his portrayal of land and yeoman identity rings true. See Durand Echeverria, *Mirage in the West: A History of the French Image of American Society to 1815* (Princeton, 1957), 147–55.

8. For definitions of capitalism and the American transition to capitalism, see Kulikoff, "Transition to Capitalism," 120–44, and *Agrarian Origins,* chap. 1.

9. For yeomen and capitalist farmers see Kulikoff, "Transition to Capitalism," 140–44. The term (and idea) of *possessive individualism* was coined by C. B. McPherson, *The Political Theory of Possessive Individualism* (London, 1962).

10. The rise of capitalist agriculture is summarized in Kulikoff, "Transition to Capitalism," 129–32; and Winifred B. Rothenberg, "The Market and Massachusetts Farmers, 1750–1855," *Journal of Economic History* 41(1981): 283–314. A commercial farmer participates actively in commodity markets, but often retains the "safety first" goals of yeomen; a capitalist farmer is a commercial farmer who embeds himself into the capitalist world economy, hires wage labor, and seeks to maximize utility and profits.

11. The classic account remains Karl Marx, *Capital: A Critique of Political Economy,* trans. Ben Fowkes (1867; New York, 1977), vol. 1, chaps. 26–30. Examples of more recent works include Brian Manning, "The Peasantry and the English Revolution," *Journal of Peasant Studies* 2(1975): 133–58; Peter Linebaugh, "All the Atlantic Mountains Shook," *Labour/Le Travailleur* 10(1982): 87–121; Alice Clark, *Working Life of Women in the Seventeenth Century* (1919; London 1982), introduction, chaps. 3–4, and Christopher Hill, "Pottage for Freeborn Englishmen: Attitudes to Wage-Labour," in his *Change and Continuity in Seventeenth-Century England* (Cambridge, Mass., 1975), 219–38.

12. See David Galenson, *White Servitude in Colonial America* (Cambridge, England, 1981); Edmund S. Morgan, *American Slavery, American Freedom: The Ordeal of Colonial Virginia* (New York, 1975); David Cressy, *Coming Over: Migration and Communication between England and New England in the Seventeenth Century* (Cambridge, England, 1987), especially chaps. 2–3, 7; and Stephen Innes, *Labor in a New Land: Economy and Society in Seventeenth-Century Springfield* (Princeton, 1983).

13. The troubled relations between Indians and whites and the impact of Indians on yeoman society and ideology are beyond the

scope of this essay. For a sampling of the issues ethnohistorians have raised, see William Cronon, *Changes in the Land: Indians, Colonists, and the Ecology of New England* (New York, 1983), especially chaps. 4, 6–7; Richard White, *The Middle Ground: Indians, Empires, and Republics in the Great Lakes Region, 1650–1815* (Cambridge, England, 1991), especially 50–53 and chaps. 9–11; James H. Merrell, *The Indian's New World: Catawas and Their Neighbors from European Contact through the Era of Removal* (Chapel Hill, N.C., 1989), especially chaps. 5–7; Merrell, " 'The Customes of Our Countrey': Indians and Colonists in Early America," in Bernard Bailyn and Philip D. Morgan, eds., *Strangers within the Realm: Cultural Margins of the First British Empire* (Chapel Hill, N.C., 1991), 117–56, especially 117–22; and Francis P. Jennings, *The Invasion of America: Indians, Colonialism, and the Cant of Conquest* (Chapel Hill, N.C., 1975).

14. For conflicting views of Bacon's Rebellion see Wilcomb E. Washburn, *The Governor and the Rebel: A History of Bacon's Rebellion in Virginia* (Chapel Hill, N.C., 1957); Morgan, *Slavery, Freedom,* chaps. 11–14; and Stephen Saunders Webb, *1676: The End of American Independence* (New York, 1984), bk. 1.

15. The classic essay on land abundance in America is Frederick Jackson Turner, "The Significance of the Frontier in American History," in *The Frontier in American History* (New York, 1920), 1–38, but see also Henry Nash Smith, *Virgin Land: The American West as Symbol and Myth* (Cambridge, Mass., 1950). For land law and distribution see David Thomas Konig, "Community Custom and the Common Law: Social Change and the Development of Land Law in Seventeenth-Century Massachusetts," *American Journal of Legal History* 17(1974): 148–64; Morgan, *Slavery, Freedom,* 94, 171–73, 218–23; Carville V. Earle, *The Evolution of a Tidewater Settlement System: All Hallow's Parish, Maryland, 1650–1783* (Chicago, 1975), chaps. 1, 5, 7.

16. See note 13 above for land systems. For the impact of Indian warfare on white settlement, see Morgan, *Slavery, Freedom,* chap. 13; and Lois Kimball Mathews, *The Expansion of New England: The Spread of New England Settlement and Institutions to the Mississippi River, 1620–1865* (Boston, 1909), chap. 3. Pennsylvania's land system is described in Gary B. Nash, *Quakers and Politics: Pennsylvania, 1681–1726* (Princeton, 1968), chaps. 1–2, especially 15–19, 52–53.

17. See Jackson Turner Main, *Society and Economy in Colonial Connecticut* (Princeton, 1985), 123–25, 160–61; Bettye Hobbs Pruitt, "Agriculture and Society in the Towns of Massachusetts, 1771: A Statistical Analysis" (Ph.D. diss., Boston University, 1981), 112,

map 8; Kulikoff, *Tobacco and Slaves,* 86–90; Alfred F. Young, *The Democratic Republicans of New York: The Origins, 1763–1797* (Chapel Hill, N.C., 1967), 585–88; and Dennis P. Ryan, "Landholding, Opportunity, and Mobility in Revolutionary New Jersey," *WMQ* 36(1979): 571–92.

18. See Kulikoff, *Tobacco and Slaves,* 156; Young, *Democratic Republicans,* 585–88; Pruitt, "Agriculture and Society," 112, and maps 9 and 11; James Lemon, *The Best Poor Man's Country: A Geographical Study of Southeastern Pennsylvania* (Baltimore, 1972), 92–96; Michael Nicholls, "Origins of the Virginia Southside, 1703–1753: A Social and Economic Study" (Ph.D. Diss., College of William and Mary, 1972), chaps. 2–3. This pattern may hold for other areas, like Piedmont North Carolina, but no systematic studies of landholding have appeared.

19. See Richard S. Dunn, "Servants and Slaves: The Recruitment and Employment of Labor," in Jack P. Greene and J. R. Pole, eds., *Colonial British America: Essays in the New History of the Early Modern Era* (Baltimore, 1984), 157–94; Marcus Rediker, " 'Good Hands, Stout Heart, and Fast Feet': The History and Culture of Working People in Early America," *Labour/Le Travailleur* 10(1982): 123–44; Vickers, "Competency and Competition," 3–29; Vickers, "Working the Fields in a Developing Economy: Essex County, Massachusetts, 1630–1675," and Paul G. E. Clemens and Lucy Simler, "Rural Labor and Farm Household in Chester County, Pennsylvania, 1750–1820," in Stephen Innes, ed., *Work and Labor in Early America* (Chapel Hill, N.C., 1988), chaps. 1, 3.

20. For tenants see Sung Bok Kim, *Landlord and Tenant in Colonial New York, 1664–1775* (Chapel Hill, N.C., 1978), vii, and chaps. 3–6; Edward Countryman, *A People in Revolution: The American Revolution and Political Society in New York, 1760–1790* (Baltimore, 1981), chap. 1; Gregory A. Stiverson, *Poverty in a Land of Plenty: Tenancy in Eighteenth-Century Maryland* (Baltimore, 1981), chaps. 2–4, and 144–45; Willard F. Bliss, "The Rise of Tenancy in Virginia," *Virginia Magazine of History and Biography* 108(1950): 427–41; and Kulikoff, *Tobacco and Slaves,* 132–35.

21. For Virginia see Kulikoff, *Tobacco and Slaves,* chap. 3; for New York see the contrasting views of Kim, *Landlord and Tenant,* chaps. 7–8; and Countryman, *People in Revolution,* chap. 1.

22. Kulikoff, *Tobacco and Slaves,* chap. 7; Edward M. Cook, Jr., *Fathers of the Towns: Leadership and Community Structure in Eighteenth-Century New England* (Baltimore, 1976); and Michael Zuckerman, *Peaceable Kingdoms: New England Towns in the Eighteenth Century* (New York, 1970), especially chaps. 5–6, provide op-

posing views of this process.

23. See Kornblith and Murrin, "Making and Unmaking." Kulikoff, *Tobacco and Slaves,* chaps. 3, 4, 7, provides a case study; see Charles S. Grant, *Democracy in the Connecticut Frontier Town of Kent* (New York, 1961), chaps. 2–5, for land speculation and sales.

24. The analysis of this paragraph and the next one borrow heavily from Kulikoff, "Transition to Capitalism," 128–44. For alternative visions of the behavior of small farmers and their relation to capitalism, see Michael Merrill, "Cash Is Good to Eat: Self-Sufficiency and Exchange in the Rural Economy of the United States," *Radical History Review* 4(Winter 1977): 42–71; James A. Henretta, "Families and Farms: *Mentalité* in Pre-Industrial America," *WMQ* 35(1978): 3–32; Rothenberg, "Market and Farmers," 283–314; and Vickers, "Competency and Competition," 3–29.

25. Rothenberg, "Market and Farmers," 283–314; and Thomas M. Doerflinger, "Farmers and Dry Goods in the Philadelphia Market Area, 1750–1800," in Ronald Hoffman et al., eds., *The Economy of Early America: The Revolutionary Period* (Charlottesville, Va., 1988), 166–95, provide case studies.

26. See the contrasting analyses in R. M. Brown, "Back Country Rebellions," 73–99; Taylor, "Agrarian Independence"; and Kim, *Landlord and Tenant,* chaps. 4–6.

27. See Cronon, *Changes in Land,* chap. 4 (quotes on 56–57), and sources cited in note 13 above.

28. Bushman, "Farmers and Revolution," 104–7 (Sewall quote on 105), 111–20; Bushman, *King and People in Provincial Massachusetts* (Chapel Hill, N.C., 1985), 200–201 (second quote on 201).

29. For differing versions of the riots see Staughton Lynd, *Anti-Federalism in Dutchess County, New York: A Study of Democracy and Class Conflict in the Revolutionary Era* (Chicago, 1962), chap. 2 (first quote on 48); Kim, *Landlord and Tenant,* chap. 8; and Irving Mark and Oscar Handlin, "Land Cases in Colonial New York, 1765–1767: The King v. William Prendergast," *New York University Law Quarterly Review* 19(1942): 165–94 (quotes on 172, 175, 177, 181, 191).

30. Class language quoted in Marvin L. Michael Kay, "The North Carolina Regulation, 1766–1776," in Young, ed., *American Revolution,* 72–123 (quotes on 74–75); petition reprinted in Jack P. Greene, ed., *Colonies to Nation, 1763–1789: A Documentary History of the American Revolution* (New York, 1975), 105–7. For other views of the North Carolina Regulation, see A. Roger Ekrich, "The North Carolina Regulators on Liberty and Corruption, 1766–1771," *Perspectives in American History* 11(1977–78): 199–256; Kay, "North Carolina Regulation"; and James P. Whittenberg, "Planters, Mer-

chants, and Lawyers: Social Change and the Origins of the North Carolina Regulation," *WMQ* 34 (1977): 215–38.

31. Remonstrance reprinted in Greene, ed., *Colonies to Nation,* 99–105 (quotes on 100, 102). Richard Maxwell Brown, *The South Carolina Regulators* (Cambridge, Mass., 1963) is the key work on South Carolina Regulators.

32. See Ronald Hoffman, "The 'Disaffected' in the Revolutionary South," and especially Alfred F. Young, "Afterword," in Young, ed., *American Revolution,* 273–318, 451–54.

33. See Edmund S. Morgan, ed., *Prologue to Revolution: Sources and Documents on the Stamp Act Crisis, 1764–1766* (Chapel Hill, N.C., 1959), 35–43, for a copy of the act.

34. For the general absence of rioting in rural Massachusetts, see Gregory H. Nobles, *Divisions throughout the Whole: Politics and Society in Hampshire County, Massachusetts, 1740–1775* (Cambridge, Mass., 1983), 157–58; and Bushman, "Farmers and Revolution," 79–81. The examples are found in Kulikoff, *Tobacco and Slaves,* 306; and Dirk Hoerder, *Crowd Action in Revolutionary Massachusetts, 1765–1780* (New York, 1977), 132–38. Kornblith and Murrin, "Making and Unmaking," explains the response of gentlemen to the Stamp Act.

35. Alfred F. Young, "English Plebian Culture and Eighteenth-Century American Radicalism," in Margaret Jacob and James Jacob, eds., *The Origins of Anglo-American Radicalism* (London, 1984), 185–212.

36. John Adams, "Instructions of the Town of Braintree to Their Representative," in George A. Peek, Jr., ed., *The Political Writings of John Adams: Representative Selections* (New York, 1954), 22–25; and R. D. Brown, *Revolutionary Politics,* 24–26.

37. Mark and Handlin, "Land Cases," 183; Hoerder, *Crowd Action,* 134–35.

38. R. D. Brown, *Revolutionary Politics;* and Rhys Isaac, *The Transformation of Virginia, 1740–1800* (Chapel Hill, N.C., 1982), chaps. 11–12, detail popular mobilization. For the changing ideological appeal to yeomen see Bushman, *King and People,* 190–210 (quotes on 202–3, 198); Bushman, "Farmers and Revolution," 77–124; and Gordon Wood, *The Creation of the American Republic, 1776–1787* (Chapel Hill, N.C., 1969), chaps. 2–3, 8–9; the letter from the Boston Committee can be found in Peter Force, comp., *American Archives . . . ,* 4th series, (1837?)1:397–98.

39. Ann Hulton, *Letters of a Loyalist Lady* (Cambridge, Mass., 1927), 30 June 1768, p. 13–14; Bushman, "Farmers and Revolution," 80–81 (quote); see also Hoerder, *Crowd Action,* 276–97, 301–4; and

Stephen E. Patterson, *Political Parties in Revolutionary Massachusetts* (Madison, Wis., 1973), chap. 4.

40. Jessica Kross, *The Evolution of an American Town: Newtown, New York, 1642–1775* (Philadelphia, 1983), 199–201; Countryman, *People in Revolution,* chap. 5 (quote on 156).

41. See Kulikoff, *Tobacco and Slaves,* 306–8; Kulikoff, "Tobacco and Slaves: Population, Economy, and Society in Eighteenth-Century Prince George's County, Maryland" (Ph.D. diss., Brandeis University, 1976), 429; David Curtis Skaggs, *Roots of Maryland Democracy, 1753–1776* (Westport, Conn., 1973), 183–86, 220–26; Robert Gough, "Notes on the Pennsylvania Revolutionaries of 1776," *Pennsylvania Magazine of History and Biography* 96(1972): 89–103; Theodore Thayer, *Pennsylvania Politics and the Growth of Democracy, 1740–1776* (Harrisburg, Pa., 1953), chap. 13, especially 179, 182–89.

42. See Linda K. Kerber, *Women of the Republic: Intellect and Ideology in Revolutionary America* (Chapel Hill, N.C., 1980), chap. 2; and Mary Beth Norton, *Liberty's Daughters: The Revolutionary Experience of American Women, 1750–1800* (Boston, 1980), chap. 6.

43. Young, *Democratic Republicans,* 18 (Yates quote). For revolutionary war service see John W. Shy, "The Legacy of the American Revolutionary War," in Larry R. Gerlach, James A. Dolph, and Michael Nicholls, eds., *Legacies of the American Revolution* (Logan, Utah, 1978), 43–60, but especially 45–46; Charles Royster, *A Revolutionary People at War: The Continental Army and American Character, 1775–1783* (Chapel Hill, N.C., 1979), chap. 1, appendix; and Kulikoff, *Agrarian Origins,* chap. 6.

44. See Kerber, *Women of Republic,* chaps. 3–4; Norton, *Liberty's Daughters,* chaps. 6–7.

45. See Wallace Brown, "The American Farmer during the Revolution: Rebel or Loyalist?" *Agricultural History* 42(1968): 327–38; Edward Countryman, "Consolidating Power in Revolutionary America: The Case of New York, 1775–1783," *Journal of Interdisciplinary History* 6(1976): 645–77; Kulikoff, *Tobacco and Slaves,* 300–13; Hoffman, " 'Disaffected' in South," 273–318; Young, "Afterword," 451–54.

46. See Jackson Turner Main, *The Sovereign States, 1775–1783* (New York, 1973), chap. 5; Wood, *Creation of Republic,* chaps. 4–5, 8–9; Donald S. Lutz, *Popular Consent and Popular Control: Whig Political Theory in the Early State Constitutions* (Baton Rouge, La., 1980), 38–52, and chap. 6. Lutz and Main agree, except on South Carolina in 1778 (Main calls it Whig; Lutz finds ten instances where consent was required) and on North Carolina in 1776 and Georgia in 1777 (Main calls them radical; Lutz finds consent required in only

three or four instances).

47. See Oscar Handlin and Mary Handlin, eds., *The Popular Sources of Political Authority: Documents on the Massachusetts Constitution of 1780* (Cambridge, Mass., 1966), 21–23, 190–323.

48. Ibid., 253–58. The Lenox response is more radical than those from most towns, especially those from commercial towns. In 1780 Massachusetts towns did ratify a constitution.

49. For a general analysis see Bogin, "New Moral Economy," 391–425. For Virginia see James E. Bailey, *Popular Influence upon Public Policy: Petitioning in Eighteenth-Century Virginia* (Westport, Conn., 1979); Randolph W. Church, comp., *Virginia Legislative Petitions: Bibliography, Calendar, and Abstracts from Original Sources 6 May 1776–21 June 1782* (Richmond, Va., 1984); and Kulikoff, *Tobacco and Slaves*, 309–10 (Orange County) and 423–24.

50. This paragraph relies heavily upon Ruth Bogin's important work "New Moral Economy," 402–25, and summarizes some of her arguments.

51. For instructions see Wood, *Creation of Republic*, 188–96; for lower houses see Jackson Turner Main, "Government by the People: The American Revolution and the Democratization of the Legislatures," *WMQ* 23(1966): 391–407.

52. Church, comp., *Virginia Legislative Petitions*, 303, 356, 363; and for the campaign over the church establishment, see Thomas E. Buckley, *Church and State in Revolutionary Virginia* (Charlottesville, Va., 1977).

53. Jackson Turner Main, *Political Parties before the Constitution* (Chapel Hill, N.C., 1973), especially chaps. 12 and 13, discusses yeoman politics. See Szatmary, *Shays' Rebellion* for rural uprisings in the 1780s (chap. 7 for the spread of crowd actions); Van Beck Hall, *Politics without Parties: Massachusetts, 1780–1791* (Pittsburgh, 1972), chaps. 6 and 7 (184–89 for early 1780s violence); and Taylor, "Agrarian Independence."

54. See Main, *Political Parties*, especially chaps. 12–13; and Wood, *Creation of Republic*, chap. 10.

55. For changes in gentry reactions to the people-out-of-doors after the Revolution, see Wood, *Creation of Republic*, 319–28, 411–13; and Taylor, "Agrarian Independence."

56. James Madison, "Vices of the Political System of the United States. April 1787," in Marvin Meyers, ed., *The Mind of the Founder: Sources of the Political Thought of James Madison* (Hanover, N.H., 1981), 57–65 (quotes on 58–59); Wood, *Creation of Republic*, 409–13. For the views of the rulers see Kornblith and Murrin, "Making and Unmaking."

57. For a recent analysis of ideological and economic divisions among the delegates to the Constitutional Convention, see Forrest McDonald, *Novus Ordo Seclorum: The Intellectual Origins of the Constitution* (Lawrence, Kans., 1985), chap. 6; for the impact of the people-out-of-doors on the Constitution, see Alfred F. Young, "Conservatives, the Constitution, and the 'Spirit of Accommodation,'" in Robert A. Goldwin and William A. Schambra, eds., *How Democratic Is the Constitution?* (Washington, D.C., 1980), 117–47, especially 130–38, and Young's afterword. Kornblith and Murrin, "Making and Unmaking," quote Madison on agrarian legislation.

58. Lee Soltow, *Wealth and Income in the United States in 1798* (Pittsburgh, 1989), chap. 10, uses wealth voting profiles of delegates to ratifying conventions to simulate voting on the Constitution. For votes in the conventions see Jackson Turner Main, *The Antifederalists: Critics of the Constitution, 1781–1788* (Chapel Hill, N.C., 1961), 285–88.

59. For an example see "Speeches by Melancton Smith," in Herbert J. Storing, ed., *The Complete Anti-Federalist* (Chicago, 1981), vol. 6, *New York and Conclusion,* 158–59.

60. *Independent Gazetteer* (Philadelphia), 29 Oct. 1787, reprinted in Merrill Jensen, ed., *The Documentary History of the Ratification of the Constitution* (Madison, Wis., 1975–), vol. 2, *Ratification of the Constitution by the States: Pennsylvania,* 205–6.

61. "Melancton Smith," 6: 158–59; Alfred F. Young, ed., *The Debate over the Constitution, 1787–1789* (Chicago, 1965), 23.

62. Jonathan Elliot, ed., *The Debates in the Several State Conventions on the Adoption of the Federal Constitution,* 2nd ed. (1888; New York), 2:101–4. I am indebted to Alfred Young for this reference.

63. Ronald P. Formisano, "Deferential-Participant Politics: The Early Republic's Political Culture, 1789–1840," *American Political Science Review* 68(1974): 473–87, sees more deference than suggested here.

64. Alan Taylor, "Land and Liberty on the Post-Revolutionary Frontier," in David T. Konig, ed., *The Possession of Liberty in the Early American Republic* (Stanford, Calif., 1993), for first quote; Reginald Horsman, "The Image of the Indian in the Age of the American Revolution," in Francis P. Jennings, ed., *The Indian and the American Revolution,* The Newberry Library Center for the History of the American Indian, Occasional Papers Series, No. 6 (Chicago, 1983), 1–11; James H. Merrell, "Declarations of Independence: Indian-White Relations in the New Nation," in Jack P. Greene, ed., *The American Revolution: Its Character and Limits* (New York, 1987), 197–223; Merrell, *Indian's New World,* chaps. 6–7; and White,

Middle Ground, chaps. 9–11 (second quote on 416). This, of course, ignores the Indian side of the story. As Gary Nash has pointed out to me, "yeomen, from the Indian point of view were the intruding agents of a commercial, land-hungry tidal wave of Euro-Americans" (Nash, private communication).

65. See Kulikoff, *Agrarian Origins,* chap. 3, for issues of class language; and consult Taylor, "Agrarian Independence"; Bogin, "New Moral Economy," 391–425, but especially 404–7, 422–25; Samuel Eliot Morison, ed., *"Key to Libberty," WMQ* 13 (1956): 215–19; Michael Merrill and Sean Wilentz, " 'The Key to Libberty': William Manning and Plebeian Democracy," this volume; and Vickers, "Competency and Competition," 3–29, for preliminary confirmation.

66. Michael Merrill, "The Political Economy of Agrarian America" (Ph.D. diss., Columbia University, 1985), chap. 5, coined the term *agrarian realism* in a brilliant evocation of John Adams, Thomas Jefferson, and Adam Smith. See also Richard K. Matthews, *The Radical Politics of Thomas Jefferson: A Revisionist View* (Lawrence, Kans., 1984), chaps. 2–3.

67. Winifred Rothenberg, in "Market and Farmers," 283–314; and "The Emergence of a Capital Market in Rural Massachusetts, 1730–1838," *Journal of Economic History* 45(1985): 781–808, presents the best description of commercial farmers, but see Clemens and Simler, "Rural Labor and Farm Household"; Kulikoff, "Transition to Capitalism"; and Doerflinger, "Farmers and Dry Goods" for alternative viewpoints.

68. Simon Baatz, *"Venerate the Plogh": A History of the Philadelphia Society for Promoting Agriculture, 1785–1985* (Philadelphia, 1985), chap. 1, 109–11; George Morgan, "An Essay, exhibiting a plan for a FARM-YARD, and method of conducting the same . . . ," *Columbian Magazine* 1(1786): 76–82.

69. See Kerber, *Women of Republic,* chaps. 4, 9; Gregory Evans Dowd, "Declarations of Independence: War and Inequality in Revolutionary New Jersey," *New Jersey History* 103(1984): 53–58 (quote on 57); Ruth H. Bloch, "American Feminine Ideals in Transition: The Rise of the Moral Mother, 1785–1815," *Feminist Studies* 4(June 1978): 101–26; and Joan Jensen, *Loosening the Bonds: Mid-Atlantic Farm Women, 1750–1850* (New Haven, 1986), especially chaps. 5–7. Susan Branson, "Politics and Gender: The Political Consciousness of Philadelphia Women, 1790–1815," (Ph.D. diss., Northern Illinois University, 1992) documents that wealthy women expressed private (and more rarely public) political opinions.

70. See Young, *Democratic Republicans,* 258–61; Peter D. McClelland and Richard J. Zeckhauser, *Demographic Dimensions of the*

New Nation: American Interregional Migration, Vital Statistics, and Manumissions, 1800–1860 (Cambridge, England, 1982), 138–39. J. Franklin Jameson, *The American Revolution Considered as a Social Movement* (Princeton, 1926), chap. 2, long ago captured the democratic impact of the Revolution on land.

71. See Dowd, "Declarations of Independence," 53–58; John Mack Faragher, *Women and Men on the Overland Trail* (New Haven, 1979), chaps. 2, 6.

72. Peter S. Onuf, "Liberty, Development, and Union: Vision of the West in the 1780s," *WMQ* 43(1986): 179–213; and Kulikoff, *Agrarian Origins,* chap. 3 explicate the ideological conflicts. For struggles over land policy, see Paul Wallace Gates, *History of Public Land Law Development* (Washington, D.C., 1968), chaps. 4, 7–11.

Liberty for Whom?

"To Secure the Blessings of Liberty"

Language, the Revolution, and American Capitalism

EDWARD COUNTRYMAN

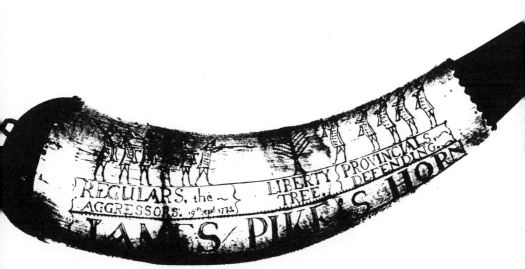

James Pike, a militiaman from a Massachusetts town, carved The Liberty Tree on his powderhorn, depicting the Battle of Lexington. He portrayed six British soldiers, at the left, as "Regulars, the Aggressors, 19th April 1775" with five militiamen, to the right, as "Provincials Defending." At first, a symbol of the traditional rights of Englishmen, the popular Tree of Liberty came to stand for the natural rights of everyone.

Courtesy Chicago Historical Society.

"Liberty is a word which in vulgar use is of very indeterminate signification, and, like so many of the moral kind, few people have *even nearly* the same ideas affixed to it."

Anonymous British writer, 1776[1]

"The question is," said Alice, "whether you can make words mean so many different things."

"The question is," said Humpty Dumpty, "which is to be master—that's all."

Lewis Carroll[2]

T RETHINKING OUR REVOLUTION

he era of independence brought enormous changes in American life. In the realm of public power colonial and British institutions collapsed, new people claimed voices in public affairs, and state and national institutions had to struggle for legitimacy. At the level of high thought and ideology the "Whig science of politics" of the late colonial years gave way to a radically different "American science of politics" during the first years of independence. In terms of both political experience and political conceptualization, the American Revolution was genuinely revolutionary.[3]

These were not the only revolutionary dimensions of the era, for changes of equal magnitude were underway in the conduct of economic life. Both before and after independence, people were thoroughly committed to the principle of private property. But the ways that they thought about their property and put it to use shifted radically. The War of Independence itself created a national American market and endowed that market with a legitimacy that transcended local interests. After the war two new social classes began to take shape. The members of each were free. But one was made up of people who owned commercially valuable property and who began now to use it in innovative, transforming ways. The other comprised people who owned little more than their own capacity to labor. The emergence of these classes continued the transformation of market relations that the war had begun. What had been a simple sequence of mere events, "the exchange of goods in a market 'place,' " now became "an increasingly prevalent *process* that involved the conscious and active mobilization of labor 'time.' " In a very real sense, the Revolution and its immediate aftermath marked "the transition to capitalism in America."[4]

What bound all these processes of political, ideological, and economic innovation together is a subject that preoccupies more and more historians. But it is still poorly understood.[5] This essay will approach that problem by exploring how the revolutionaries used and developed their central ideological symbol, the concept of liberty.

In the broadest terms the notion of liberty, or freedom, is the central value of all Western civilization. When the revolutionary generation of Americans invoked it, they were calling up a tradition that reached as far back as ancient Greece. But the tradition is not straightforward. From the age of Homer, Sophocles, and Plato, through the Age of Washington, Franklin, and Jefferson, to our own time, the transcendent idea of liberty has been bound up closely with the gritty reality of unfreedom. The terms have varied, but the fact of that unending interplay has not. No more than any other great figures in the history of Western liberty did American revolutionaries escape from its bitter dialectic. The idea of freedom has always been polyvalent as well, open to a wide range of interpretation and emphasis. The revolutionary generation knew about that, too.[6]

It is the openness of the concept of liberty that provides the standpoint for this study. Although the word, the arbitrary signifier, remained the same, usage and meaning, what the word signified, did not. Changes took place in usage and in meaning because people were trying to understand their own changing situations. By understanding change, they also were seeking to control it. Liberty became a "keyword," a "contested truth." To establish its definition in a way that others would accept during such a time of tumult was to acquire enormous power for oneself to shape that tumult's eventual outcome.[7]

In broad terms the argument of the essay is this. The ancient "British liberties" that colonials set out to defend comprised a bundle of *specific* characteristics that people enjoyed because of their *specific* social situations. Liberty was good, everyone agreed. But there was no supposition that one person's liberty had to be the same as another's. As the revolutionaries abandoned their British identity, they also abandoned this uneven complexity and substituted the idea of natural, undifferentiated liberty whose praises were sung by Jefferson and Paine. But the revolutionaries themselves were not an undifferentiated people. Rich and poor, urban and rural, famous and obscure, male and female, free and "held to service," white and of color, they were a mixed, heterogeneous lot.

The traditional ideology of British liberty had allowed most of these groups to claim the limited, specific freedoms that went with their own situations. Slaves formed the only group completely excluded from British liberty's American variant, but the liberty of no two other groups was the same. The new ideology of American liberty

. allowed everyone, even slaves, to make at least a claim to equal freedom for themselves, commensurate to that enjoyed by everyone else. That is why one person, one group, after another now began declaring the "true definition" of "the liberty we seek."[8] Even loyalists joined the debate at first, and except for the loyalists all the debaters were becoming "Americans." They were numbering themselves among "the people of the United States" who in 1787 did "ordain and establish the United States Constitution "in order . . . to secure the blessings of liberty to ourselves and our posterity."

The Constitution, however, is precisely where developments in the realm of political thought and practice and developments in the realm of economics and social relations converge. In addition to securing "the blessings of liberty" the Constitution had the purpose of forming "a more perfect union." One of that union's most salient aspects was the creation of a common market on an enormous scale. The interstate commerce clause, the contract clause, the requirement of legal reciprocity among the states, the powers to control weights and measures and to grant patents and copyrights, the supremacy clause, the denial to the states of the power to create their own money and to interfere in contractual obligations: these formed that common market's sinews. With these clauses the framers were establishing conditions immensely beneficial to the capitalist social transformation that was already well under way.

But this was not at all what most people wanted at the beginning of the Revolution or during most of its course. To put changing political language changing political institutions, and a changing society into one picture, we need to begin with what the Revolution left behind.

"PARTICULAR CUSTOMS" AND
"THE CUSTOM OF THE KINGDOM"

Britain's American colonies lay on the far periphery of a world whose metropolis was an ocean away. They displayed most of the elements that made up that world, but none of them in pure form. To use Fernand Braudel's words, they were "like a mosaic with a hundred different colours: modern, archaic, primitive, or curious mixtures of all these."[9]

The desire for gain formed one of the prime forces that drove English people to America. In that sense, "capitalism came in the first ships" in two different ways.[10] One way manifested itself in the commerce and culture of the developing northern ports, which acquired most of the qualities of their English counterparts.[11] The other way, much more important to the larger imperial economy, appeared from

Chesapeake Bay southward. People there learned that the greatest gains would come from using unfree labor to produce tropical and warm-weather crops that England could not grow, under conditions that would not be tolerated in England itself. The results were a truly colonial economy that was wholly subordinated to Britain and a truly colonial society that was wholly unlike it. The staple-crop plantation, with its basis in servitude and later in slavery, was never an American version of the English manor. It was a New World institution, in spite of all the pretensions of Chesapeake planters to the style of English gentlemen. Its emergence in the Chesapeake, the Carolinas, and the Caribbean signified their emplacement in the larger mercantile capitalism of the era.

Capitalism was not all that came. North of the Chesapeake, especially, people re-created a good deal of the social complexity of England itself. We know well enough how colonial assemblymen imitated the House of Commons.[12] But what people re-created was often archaic rather than modern. Puritan villagers rebuilt their lives in traditional English ways.[13] The imagined world of English witchcraft and the social order that supported it reappeared in many instances besides the famous outbreak at Salem.[14] Remnants of feudalism flourished in the Hudson Valley and appeared in many other places.[15] There were echoes of European charivari (or "rough music" or "skimmington") whenever crowds harassed violators of community norms. Crowds themselves enjoyed a legitimacy that no modern rioting could have. As the Massachusetts politician Thomas Hutchinson put it in 1768, "mobs, a sort of them at least, are constitutional."[16]

These are among the pieces that make up Braudel's American mosaic. Taken by itself, any single instance might mean little.[17] But taken together, they shaped a way of life very unlike ours. The isolated early American event or pattern displays its full meaning only as part of the whole picture of class relations and culture in the seventeenth-and-eighteenth-century European world.

One value of Braudel's metaphor is that it lets us appreciate the power of custom and of the small community in early American life. Then as now, groups and places had their own ways, which their members understood. But in pre-revolutionary America, custom often enjoyed a status in law and public affairs that it does not have today. Notions of "positive" enacted law were only beginning to take form. Parliament and the colonial assemblies did legislate in the modern sense, declaring the will of the highest authority. But a major purpose of both was to decide and announce what had "always" been right.[18] Parliament itself existed because of custom that reached back to the Middle Ages. So did the English "Liberties

Privileges Franchises and Immunities" which the colonists claimed for themselves. "The People here, as every where else, retain a great Fondness for their old Customs and Usages," said the Stamp Act Congress of 1765 in its petition to the House of Commons.[19]

Custom was often intensely local. "Constitutional" mobs in both America and England operated on the belief that the small community ought to regulate itself, as the primary unit of both production and consumption.[20] There were times when long-distance trade was legitimate; there were also times when the community should cut itself off, whether by a government embargo or by the action of a crowd. Such "persistent localism"[21] could spill into formal legal practice. The legal historians Morton Horwitz and William Nelson have argued that before the Revolution courts acted in terms of the interests and perceptions of local communities, not in terms of any "supreme law of the land." Almost certainly, Horwitz and Nelson overstate their case. Courts enforced the informal *lex mercatoria,* which meant the recognized customs of the long-distance trading community, as well as the customs of the locality. English common law itself may have rested on custom and precedent. But it applied to the whole realm.[22] Moreover, other legal historians have shown colonial law responding dynamically to increasing commercialization and social complexity.[23]

Nonetheless, as late as 1786, "A Citizen" in Albany, New York, felt free to protest against a rise in local mill tolls in the name of "immemorial custom. . . . a law not written, established by long usage and consent." "Particular customs," he wrote, "are always to be taken for law" even if they were "against the general custom of the Kingdom and the maxims of [written] law."[24] Another Albanian immediately ridiculed the "Citizen" by pointing out that he allowed for no change at all. Nonetheless, Horwitz argues that for prerevolutionary Americans the most privileged form of property was productive land, and that its ideal use was "quiet enjoyment" without disturbance to the rights of heirs or neighbors. Ownership meant having a badge of community membership, not a commodity for trade.[25] Trade itself often meant exchange among neighbors, carried on to satisfy mutual needs. Community meant local networks of obligation, and the "public good" meant keeping those networks in repair.[26]

Commerce was the lifeblood of early America, and private property was its material basis; in that sense, the colonials' world was like our own. But commerce was subordinate to social well-being, usually defined in terms of the interests of small communities. If the colonials were "conservative," they were conserving a way of life, not the prospect of unlimited gain. The revolutionary pamphleteer John Dickinson caught the point perfectly at the end of 1767, when he chose the phrase "this I call an innovation" to condemn British policy. His reference was constitutional for he, like most in his time, regarded any interference with the delicate fabric of the unwritten, customary British Constitution as dangerous. But his resonance was social, in a world that valued continuity rather than change.[27]

But as we will see, the federal Constitution opened the whole republic to commercial and eventually industrial development. It delegitimized the customary right of states and small communities to close their economies against the outside world. In larger terms, it insisted that particular customs not prevail against the general law of the republic. The change was cultural as well as institutional. By 1809 Tench Coxe could write without fear of contradiction that Americans "have not suffered a blind veneration for antiquity, for custom or for names." In Robert Gross's words, "the age of progress had begun."[28]

The ways that people used and explained the concept of liberty during the Revolution show one aspect of how this change happened. At the Revolution's beginning, people were using it in ways that fit with the world they inhabited and wanted to preserve. By its end, the framers of the Constitution and their supporters at least were using it in a way that fit with the world they were beginning to build. The word was as potent an ideological symbol in 1787 as it had been in 1765. But its social and political import had changed dramatically.

"YOUR DEAR-BOUGHT LIBERTY"

The British liberty enjoyed by colonial Americans, was a "multifaceted concept,"[29] an intellectual mosaic to match colonial society itself. To use Orlando Patterson's term, Western ideas of freedom have always been *chordal*. They resonated together to form one grand value. But they also resonated in different ways at the levels of the individual (personal freedom), the participatory community (civic freedom), and the "power to act as one pleases, regardless of the wishes of others" (sovereignal freedom).[30]

For colonial Americans the classical republicanism of the great thinkers of the Italian Renaissance and the English Commonwealth taught that liberty was the freedom of a community to govern itself. In Thomas Hobbes's words, "although the word liberty may . . . be written over the gates of any city . . . yet is it not meant the subject's but the city's liberty."[31] To Montesquieu, observing from the outside, British freedom was the country's balanced institutions: the Crown, the House of Lords, and the House of Commons. At a lower literary level, dissenting eighteenth-century English writers endlessly bemoaned their country's "corruption" and its liberty's decline. All of these themes enjoyed wide influence among colonials.[32]

Protestant colonials, especially New Englanders, were sure that their religion made them free. In mainstream puritan thought this meant "not the liberty of unrestrained freedom, but 'gospel liberty' harnessed to the duties and dictates of God's Word as understood by the congregations and their ministers."[33] Preaching the Connecticut election sermon in 1759, the Reverend James Lockwood described New Englanders' "full liberty to do all the good we can in our Power and to serve GOD . . . but we have no right or liberty to do wrong." "God's Word" could have a secular resonance as well as a sacred one. Lockwood contrasted "the light of freedom and liberty" among the Protestant English and the "dark view" of the Papal States. Under the Papacy, he said, "the people" had to "deliver all the grain they had . . . at half price" to the Pope's agents and then buy it back as bread "at more than double the price."[34] The popular belief that Catholicism went together with the wooden shoes of poverty-stricken mainland European peasants made the same point.

Liberty could be a technical legal term. The Connecticut minister Jared Eliot declared in 1738 that "a legal free Government is when . . . arbitrary and sovereign Power puts itself under Restraints. . . . under such a government only is there true Liberty."[35] In the words of one common-law dictionary, a liberty was a particular "privilege held by grant of prescription, whereby men enjoy some benefit or favour beyond the ordinary subject." One corporate body, such as the city of New York, might enjoy the " benefit of ye market" that gave it control over its own commerce.[36] Another, such as the College of William and Mary might have the "privilege . . . by grant of prescription" of direct institutional representation in the Virginia House of Burgesses. The Burgesses as a whole enjoyed the liberty of being the only body that could tax Virginians. All white Virginians enjoyed the "benefit or favour" of owning slaves. Taken in this way, they had no reason to see the contradiction between freedom and slavery in their lives that is so painfully obvious to us now. Indeed, their own liberty and the slavery of others went together.

"English liberty" also included a long history of direct popular action. The winning of the Magna Carta; the peasant rebellion of 1381; the overthrow of Charles I in 1647; the memory of Oliver Cromwell and the English Commonwealth; religious movements from medieval Lollardy to eighteenth-century evangelicalism: all these told Britons that they owed their freedom to the efforts of their own ancestors.[37] "If we are English men let us show we have English spirits & not tamely submit to the yoak just ready to be fastened about our necks"—these are words not of Bostonians or New Yorkers protesting the Stamp Act but of Londoners protesting the Gin Excise in 1736.[38] Colonials, too, could be roused to rhetorical heights by taxes on drink; in 1754 a move to tax Massachusetts liquor imports was called "the most pernicious attack upon *English Liberty* that ever was attempted."[39]

The "official" position that Americans adopted during the imperial crisis was more simple, and Virginia's House of Burgesses put it succinctly: "The Taxation of the People by themselves, or by Persons chosen by themselves to represent them . . . is the only security against a burthensome Taxation, and the distinguishing Characteristick of *British* freedom." Again and again this theme would echo. Here is a Philadelphia broadside the same year: "No people can be *free,* but where taxes are imposed on them *with their own consent.*" Here is John Dickinson's "Liberty Song" of 1768: "Our purses are ready; Steady, Friends, Steady! Not as slaves but as freemen our money we'll give." Here is a Massachusetts town meeting almost a decade later: "as free men and Englishmen we have a right to the disposal of wt is our own, are certain there is no property in wt another can take from us."[40] Americans did not have and did not want representation in Parliament; therefore they could be taxed only by their own institutions.

To some, this was the limit of legitimate protest. Virginia, New York, South Carolina, and Pennsylvania: each was a corporate body with its own liberties, its "grants of privilege." One of these was the liberty of self-taxation, and when that seemed reassured with the failure of the Stamp Act, all was well. In the words of a doggerel poem called "Joyful News to America," published on the act's repeal:

> Your dear-bought LIBERTY is safe . . .
> Kind Heaven and Pitt we thank for it.
> Ye Sons of LIBERTY rejoice!
> For George and Pitt's our Friends . . .
> Of George our king and Pitt we'll sing.
> Immortal PITT! To thee
> The sons of freedom justly owe
> Their all, their Liberty.[41]

But others understood that neither King George nor sympathetic British statesmen like William Pitt had saved American liberty. The colonials had done it themselves. The Stamp Act failed intellectually because colonial writers destroyed its rationale.[42] It failed politically because people took to the streets, forcing stamp distributors to resign their posts and keeping the paper from being distributed. By the end of the crisis some colonials were starting to identify their liberty with what they themselves had just achieved.

Preaching to his congregation in Haverhill, Massachusetts, the Reverend Edward Barnard gave the Stamp Act resistance a heroic pedigree. He likened it to the struggle for the Magna Carta, to the original puritan flight to New England, and to the overthrow of Sir Edmund Andros, the seventeenth-century New England governor whose "reign" had been as infamous as it was short-lived.[43] Others also placed the resistance in the large context of British history. One pamphleteer recalled how, in the days of King John, the "common people" had learned "that nothing but resolution was required to obtain a reasonable share of freedom." A scribbled note left outside the meeting room of the New York provincial assembly told the members: "Be not conceited as to say or think that other people kno noting about government . . . oppressions of your make gentlemen make us Sons of Liberty think you are not for the public liberty."[44] "Rusticus" in South Carolina called on his fellows: "Arise ye COLONISTS, my sons arise! The servile threats of lawless force despise." John Dickinson's "Liberty Song" invited colonials to "join hand in hand, brave Americans all, and rouse your bold hearts at fair LIBERTY's call."[45] For all of these what counted was self assertion. That had always had a place in colonials' understanding of English liberty. Now it was becoming paramount. But in the Revolution's first stage it remained self-assertion in defence of traditional rights.

"LIBERTY AND THE PURSUIT OF HAPPINESS"

Between 1765 and 1776 the revolutionary movement became an arena for the formation of new political consciousness. People stopped dwelling on the problem of their British past and identity, a change caught perfectly by Thomas Jefferson in the Declaration of Independence. Gone were British liberties; gone was the medieval sense of "privileges held by grant of prescription." "All men" owed their "unalienable" right to "Life, Liberty and the pursuit of Happiness" to "Nature and Nature's God."

Different kinds of Americans began to decide that American liberty had to mean something for them, directly. Among these were the two groups that the old order had excluded most completely: white women and enslaved black people. We know from the scholarship of Mary Beth Norton, Linda Kerber, Ira Berlin, and others that the Revolution did make a difference to both of these groups.[46] "Why should I not have liberty," asked a New Jersey woman of her husband in 1776, "whilst you strive for liberty." "The *God* of nature gave them life and freedom," and "private or public tyranny are alike detestable," proclaimed black people in New Hampshire who were seeking an end to their own bondage.[47]

However much the consciousness of white women and of black people began to change, it was only a beginning.[48] The realities of their world kept them subordinate. For white male artisans and farmers the Revolution offered greater opportunity for self-assertion, in good part because of their own direct importance to the process of breaking the British tie and building republican America. Artisans provided much of the driving force for direct colonial resistance, from the Stamp Act in 1765 to the Boston Tea Party in 1773. Artisans and farmers joined in turning resistance into revolution during 1774 and 1775. Without them the Revolution could not have happened as it did.

The people who resisted the Stamp Act in 1765 and 1766 used blanket labels like "brave colonists," or "free men and Englishmen," or "Sons of Liberty" to describe themselves. But during the nonimportation movement of the late 1760s against the Townshend taxes, urban workingmen began to think and speak of themselves separately and to raise issues of their own.[49] They tied the change to the whole notion of liberty.

New York artisans joined their "neighbours the merchants . . . in the common cause." The "principal Mechanicks" in Charleston gathered to consecrate a liberty tree, to nominate their own candidates for public office, and to sing "the celebrated liberty song." A "Tradesman" asked the *New York Journal* to publish less foreign news and more about the city's own "distressed situation. . . . Is Money grown more plenty? Have our Tradesmen full employment? Is Grain cheaper? Are our importations less?" Sons of Liberty in Providence listened to a patriotic orator condemn men "whose religion is trade and whose god is gain. . . . it is indifferent to them whether we are freemen or slaves, so that they can pluck our feathers."[50]

For men like these, nonimportation proved a "great Benefit." The Stamp Act and the Townshend taxes coincided with a severe depression in the port cities. By closing American commerce, nonimportation increased the market for domestic goods; it was, in fact, the traditional response to economic distress, undertaken now on an intercolonial scale. Merchants, however, survived by oceangoing trade, and for them the boycott meant privation. In 1770, when Parliament repealed four of the five Townshend duties, nonimportation began to collapse and merchants and artisans broke into open conflict over who should have a say in deciding to end it.

Merchants maintained that the choice was theirs alone: they were the ones whose businesses were suffering. But to "Brutus" in New York it seemed "flagrantly wrong" for "our mercantile dons" to say "that the mechanics have no right to give their sentiments." To a Philadelphia "tradesman" the "consent of the majority of the tradesmen, farmers and other freemen . . . should have been obtained." To a "lover of liberty and a mechanic's friend" American liberty was the proper concern of "all ye who glory in the names of FARMER and MECHANIC." A "good mechanic," he wrote, was "one of the most serviceable, one of the most valuable members of society," but merchants were only "weak and babbling boys—clerks of yesterday." "Brother Chip" asked Philadelphia artisans whether they did not have "an equal right of electing or being elected. . . . Are there no . . . men well acquainted with the constitution and laws of their country among the tradesmen and mechanics?"[51] In one sense, nothing new was being said: liberty meant the community's well-being. But in another sense, these workingmen were claiming equal public liberty for themselves.

When the old colonial governments toppled in 1774, 1775, and 1776, ideas of reformed, popular, open governments flourished. "Tent makers, cobblers and common tradesmen composed the Legislature at Athens," said the anonymous pamphlet called "The People the Best Governors." Both farmers in the Berkshire hills of western Massachusetts and artisans in New York City demanded that their states' new constitutions be submitted for public ratification. The town of Ashfield, Massachusetts, proposed that there be only the "Goviner of the univarse" above the voters of the commonwealth. In Anne Arundel County, Maryland, militiamen demanded that there be a broad electorate for all offices, that the governor lose his veto on laws, and that taxes be apportioned according to "a fair and equal assessment in proportion to every person's estate."[52]

The separate dimensions of "civic liberty," now defined as the artisans' and farmers' claim to equal political rights, and "sovereignal liberty," still defined for purposes of exchange in terms of traditional market controls, came together at the end of the 1770s. War, inflation, and absolute shortage of necessary goods combined to create the first general economic crisis in American history. The problem was a direct consequence of the emerging national economy, and it transcended state lines. Ultimately it could be resolved only by measures on the same scale as itself. But people responded in the way they knew. They joined in crowds to harass "hoarders" and "monopolizers." They set up popular committees to control prices. They pressed their state governments for price controls on a larger scale, and for embargoes on the export of what they needed. From the point of view of supplying the army for the ongoing struggle with Britain, or from that of people who lived by long-distance trade, the price-control movement was nothing short of pernicious. Pernicious or not, it was certainly hopeless in terms of the large structural changes that were underway. But to the members of small, self-determining communities, the movement grew directly from the rites they had always used to protect themselves against aggrandizing external forces. Moreover, it enjoyed the sanction of the state constitutions, which defined as well as any possible source what the Revolution was about.

That is why "Oppression, a Poem" described in 1777 how "the poor have been abused for to increase estates" and asked "extortioners and Tories, which of them is the worst / One brings us a fair story, the other a blunderbuss." It is why a Massachusetts almanac complained that men who "but a little while ago seemed ready to sacrifice their all to the shrine of liberty" were now "by the vile practice of extortion" making "extravagant demands for what they have to sell."[53] Bostonians linked together "affixing Prices to the Necessaries of Life," "the many happy consequences which have been derived from the appointment of Committees" and "the cause of truth and righteousness, in the defence and establishment of civil and religious Liberty." A public meeting in Philadelphia called public control of the market "the very spirit of liberty."[54]

To these people American liberty meant both the full right to political participation and their heritage of running their own economies to suit their own needs. They had very good reason to believe that local self-control formed a good part of what the Revolution itself was about, because the constitutions of no fewer than five states, South Carolina, North Carolina, Maryland, Pennsylvania, and Vermont, all said so. They each incorporated a clause that permitted "embargoes, to prevent the departure of any shipping, or the exportation of any commodities" in time of need, regardless of contracts that individuals might have made. Other early state governments acted as if they had been granted the same power.[55] But whatever people believed in Boston or Springfield or Albany or Philadelphia, and whatever those state constitutions said, this was very far indeed from the conditions of legality and trade that the federal Constitution would establish only a few years later.

"TO SECURE THE BLESSINGS OF LIBERTY"

His Excellency Jonathan Trumbull, governor of the state of Connecticut, had never liked the price-control movement. By 1780 the movement was failing and Trumbull was glad to proclaim an end to controls within his state. He made it a matter of principle: "all restraints on trade are grievances . . . a free intercourse and trade among the citizens of the United States tendeth to their mutual advantage."[56]

Trumbull had many allies. They included men of the caliber of John Jay of New York and James Wilson of Pennsylvania, both of whom would become justices of the United States Supreme Court. They also included many less prominent people, particularly in the major towns. These would never be governors or justices. But they were coming to understand the imperatives of the emerging national economy. Among them were the tanners, curriers, and cordwainers of the city of Philadelphia. To these leatherworkers, as to Trumbull or Jay or Wilson, "trade should be as free as air, uninterrupted as the tide . . . it will ever return of itself, sufficiently near to a proper level . . . if . . . injudicious attempts to regulate it are not interposed."[57]

When the war ended, such voices gained strength. Preaching the 1784 Massachusetts election sermon, the Reverend Moses Hemmenway said that "the abuse of liberty destroys liberty itself." The merchant Jonathan Jackson of Newburyport, Massachusetts, wrote in 1788 that liberty meant *that every man . . . be certain . . . to enjoy the produce of his own industry and that his own person be also secure.* In 1787 a writer in the *Connecticut Courant* described "true civil liberty" as "being free . . . from the caprice and violence of factious and tumultuous citizens." Noah Webster bluntly summed the new mood up: "mobs and conventions are *devils . . . too much liberty is the worst species of tyranny.*"[58] To all these, as to Trumbull and the Philadelphia leatherworkers, the economic model offered by small self-controlling communities now seemed useless.

By the mid-1780s such people understood that they were taking part in a campaign, not just a debate. The most serious issues were at stake: power, property, perhaps even the American future. The campaign's great political achievement was the Constitution. Its great ideological achievement was to generate a radical change in the meaning of American liberty. The new meaning and the new document were congruent with each other. Both were congruent as well with the large-scale commercial society that was rapidly taking shape.

Although they enjoyed the support of many ex-loyalists, what these people did defies any attempt to apply simple labels like "conservative" or "reactionary." They were thoroughly committed to both independence and active republican citizenship. James Madison, whose role in writing both the Constitution and *The Federalist* gives him the right to be taken most seriously among them, put the point explicitly: "The genius of republican liberty seems to demand . . . not only that all power should be derived from the people, but that those intrusted with it should be kept in dependence on the people."[59]

As these men saw it, the problem was not whether the United States would be independent and republican. It was the rules on which republican society would be organized. They understood that different rules would lead to different social consequences. During the Revolution the men who now formed the leadership group had been congressmen, diplomats, high officials, and ranking Continental officers. They had learned to work together. They knew how reluctant the states had been to supply the Continental Army.[60] They also knew that state and local economic self-control fit badly with the needs of long-distance trade. Some were already thinking that industrializing England offered a model to America. In the aftermath of the war they were busy organizing banks, reestablishing British trade, and exploring the new possibilities their world had to offer. They were nationalists; they were republicans; they were also committed to a firmly capitalist future.

Their political prominence combined with their sense of the kind of place the United States ought to be to give them an enormous strategic advantage.[61] In 1784 Dr. Benjamin Rush of Philadelphia caught the essence of their new thought. Pennsylvania had adopted a strict test law to exclude men who had not supported the Revolution from the suffrage and from holding office. These included many of Philadelphia's great Quaker merchants, who were among the foremost holders of the city's liquid wealth. Defending them, Rush addressed the question of what kind of property was most "productive" and therefore most deserving of the law's special protection. Many another Pennsylvanian might have answered that productive property could only mean land or tools, but to Rush the answer was specie. What he meant was what we now call capital, hard money to be employed as an investor might see fit. Money could make more money in its own right, without goods necessarily being produced or changing hands. Productivity meant simple gain, not the making of objects that people could consume or use.[62]

The contradictory small-community meaning of liberty was not dead yet. Others would invoke it many times during the decades to come, in city and countryside alike. But its context was changing, and during the nineteenth century it would become increasingly archaic.[63] Two of the most important clauses in the Constitution itself make the point. One gives Congress the exclusive power to regulate commerce among the states; the other forbids those same states to interfere with obligations of contract. Both clauses serve unequivocally to protect the liberty of free individuals to trade on equal terms throughout the country, secure against local political interference in their business. "Particular customs" might once have been able to defeat "the custom of the kingdom." The Federalists intended that they would not defeat "the supreme law of the land."

It would not be correct to say that Americans instantly and unequivocally abandoned the older community-based notions of liberty that had helped to drive the Revolution. But the Constitution was more than just another statement in an ongoing debate. It and the jurisprudence that flowed from it were to be authoritative, even hegemonic in American society. For that reason the Constitution's adoption marked a fundamental break, however many groups or individuals continued to disagree with the ideas that it encapsulated.

Two "benefit[s] or favour[s] beyond the ordinary subject" did remain in a state of legal and customary enshrinement. One was the "sovereignal" liberty claimed by most southern whites, and by a still-large group of northern ones, "to own slaves, to buy them, to import them from abroad, to recover them if fugitives in another state, to have them protected as property."[64] The other was the monopoly that free adult men enjoyed on the "civic" liberty of taking direct part in the political process. Both people of color and white women numbered among the "ordinary subjects" of the American Republic, at least in the sense of owing obedience to its laws and of receiving some protection from those laws in return. Some of these, at least, now were claiming full equal liberty in their own right. Their claims went unrecognized by the white adult males who were now defining themselves as the collective American sovereign. Here was the great contradiction of Federalism, and of the American Republic itself.

What did strike an increasing number of those men much more strongly was a congruence between the new senses of personal economic liberty and of civic political liberty that the revolutionary era itself had generated. During the ratification campaign in 1787 and 1788 Federalist writers developed this theme strongly. Again and again they enumerated the reasons different groups should favor the Constitution: merchants, mechanics, farmers, landholders, public creditors, soldiers, lawyers, judges, and clergymen.[65] Like Braudel's colonists, these formed a mosaic, but it was of a different sort. The "archaic," the "primitive," the "curious mixtures" that had defined the colonial social order's unique qualities had no place in the political coalition the Federalists were building.

Here instead was naked, interest-group politics. James Madison addressed the point in *The Federalist,* no. 10. Madison himself was too much a classical republican, too much a believer in public virtue and self-restraint, to simply applaud the new order. But he understood that Americans were and would be a factious people. Short of "destroying the liberty which is essential to its existence," there was no abolishing faction and self-seeking in American economic and political life. Most men who supported the Constitution agreed. Townsmen showed as much with the great processions that they organized to celebrate each state's ratification in 1788. Each took the same form: a pageant of the history that the Americans themselves had made, a representation of the republic, and unit after unit of tradesmen, bearing banners, and sometimes acting out their skills as they went.[66]

This was the new republican community, displaying its sense of what American liberty now meant. One of the new elements was simple pride in the Revolution; that, more than anything else, is what the burgeoning cult of George Washington represented. A second was these men's pride in themselves, both as citizens in a unique republic and as producers, able to make what they and their neighbors and perhaps the whole world wanted. Linked to pride was self-interest. They supported the Constitution just as they had once supported nonimportation and price controls: in the belief that it would benefit themselves. Once, they had expected the benefit to come from the corporate community, able to close itself off in time of necessity. Now, they thought, it would come from a strong free-market national economy. Also linked to their pride was their belief in their own equal rights. Philadelphia's bricklayers scored both points—productive self-assertion and equal rights— with the slogan they bore in their city's great constitutional procession of 4 July 1788: "Both Buildings and Rulers are the Work of Our Hands." Binding all these together was the newly formed reality of a large republic, congruent with the needs and the vision of men whose energies could not be contained within the small communities of the past. The result was both the permanent political structure of the American Republic and the institutional and cultural environment in which American capitalist development proceeded to take place.

Taken in this context, the change in the meaning of American political language was momentous and liberating, even if white males did all they could to restrict its liberating aspects to themselves. The bundle of uneven, specific, community-based "liberties" that most colonials set out to defend against the British onslaught was radically different from the "blessings" of undifferentiated political and economic "liberty" that the Constitution proposed to secure for "the people of the United States" and their "posterity" in 1787. Appreciating the difference helps us to understand how very much was new in the Constitution itself. It also helps us to see how both the Constitution and the class relations and political culture that surrounded it proved so compatible with the needs of the large-scale capitalist American social order that was appearing, even though that social order was not at all what people had thought they wanted during most of the Revolution's course.

NOTES

ACKNOWLEDGMENTS: This essay has been very long in gestation and more people and institutions have helped than I could possibly name. I owe special thanks to the University of Warwick, New York University, the British Academy, and the American Antiquarian Society for supporting my research, and to Alfred Young for his bottomless pool of encouragement and his generous editing. I gave preliminary versions at the Milan symposium on early American history in 1982, at the Organization of American Historians, Los Angeles, 1984, at the American Historical Association, Chicago, 1984, and as a Scott-Hawkins Lecture at Southern Methodist University, January 1990. I want to give special thanks to my Yale graduate students who made cogent comments on the next-to-final draft during my visit there in 1989, and to Evonne von Heussen-Countryman, who has discussed the problem of American liberty with me for years.

1. *Monthly Review* (London) 55(1776): 218. I owe this and a number of other citations to the courtesy of John Philip Reid. See his book *The Concept of Liberty in the Age of the American Revolution* (Chicago, 1988).

2. Lewis Carroll, *The Annotated Alice,* ed. Martin Gardner (Cleveland, 1963), 269.

3. For a measure of the difference compare the interpretations in Edmund S. Morgan, *The Birth of the Republic* (Chicago, 1961) and Edward Countryman, *The American Revolution* (New York, 1985). For the changing language of high politics see Gordon S. Wood, *The Creation of the American Republic, 1776–1787* (Chapel Hill, N.C., 1969), 3–45, 593–615.

4. See Edward Countryman, "The Uses of Capital in Revolutionary America: The Case of the New York Loyalist Merchants," *William and Mary Quarterly,* 3d series 39 (1992): 3–28; in this volume, Allan Kulikoff, "The American Revolution, Capitalism, and the Formation of the Yeoman Classes," and Gary J. Kornblith and John M. Murrin, "The Making and Unmaking of the American Ruling Class"; and James A. Henretta, "The Transition to Capitalism in America," in

Henretta et al., eds., *The Transformation of Early American History: Society, Authority, and Ideology* (New York, 1991), 218–38. Quotation is from Henretta, 219.

5. I have been influenced in posing these questions by Michael Merrill, "The Anti-Capitalist Origins of the United States," *Review: The Journal of the Fernand Braudel Center* (forthcoming); and by Allan Kulikoff, "Was the American Revolution a Bourgeois Revolution?" paper presented at the conference "The Transforming Hand of Revolution": Reconsidering the American Revolution as a Social Movement, Washington, D.C., 15–16 March 1989. I agree with Kulikoff, but have learned much from Merrill. I have also gained from intense discussions with Carol Berkin, Robert Gross, and a group of fifty schoolteachers at the De Witt Wallace–Reader's Digest Foundation Institute on American History, Princeton, N.J., in July 1989.

6. See Orlando Patterson, *Freedom: Freedom in the Making of Western Culture* (New York, 1991).

7. See Raymond Williams, *Keywords: A Vocabulary of Culture and Society,* rev. ed. (New York, 1985); and Daniel T. Rodgers, *Contested Truths: Keywords in American Politics since Independence* (New York, 1987).

8. See Janice Potter, *The Liberty We Seek: Loyalist Ideology in Colonial New York and Massachusetts* (Cambridge, Mass., 1983).

9. Fernand Braudel, *The Perspective of the World,* vol. 3, *Capitalism and Civilization, 15th–18th Centuries,* trans. Siân Reynolds (London, 1985), 426.

10. Carl Degler, *Out of Our Past: The Forces That Shaped Modern America,* 3d ed., (New York, 1984), 2.

11. See Gary B. Nash, *The Urban Crucible: Social Change, Political Consciousness, and the Origins of the American Revolution* (Cambridge, Mass., 1979).

12. See Jack P. Greene, "Political Mimesis: A Consideration of the Historical and Cultural Roots of Legislative Behavior in the British Colonies in the Eighteenth Century," *American Historical Review* 75(1969–70): 337–60; and Charles S. Sydnor, *American Revolutionaries in the Making: Political Practices in Washington's Virginia* (New York, 1965; originally published as *Gentlemen Freeholders,* 1952).

13. See David Grayson Allen, *"In English Ways": The Movement of Societies and the Transfer of English Local Law and Custom to Massachusetts Bay in the Seventeenth Century* (Chapel Hill, N.C., 1981).

14. See Paul Boyer and Stephen Nissenbaum, *Salem Possessed: The Social Origins of Witchcraft* (Cambridge, Mass., 1974); John Putnam Demos, *Entertaining Satan: Witchcraft and the Culture of*

Early New England (New York, 1982); and Kenneth Silverman, *The Life and Times of Cotton Mather* (New York, 1985), chap. 4.

15. See Rowland Berthoff and John M. Murrin, "Feudalism, Communalism, and the Yeoman Freeholder: The American Revolution Considered as a Social Accident," in Stephen G. Kurtz and James H. Hutson, eds., *Essays on the American Revolution* (Chapel Hill, N.C., and New York, 1973), 256–88.

16. Compare Dirk Hoerder, *Crowd Action in Revolutionary Massachusetts, 1765–1780* (New York, 1977), chap. 1; and Natalie Zemon Davis, "The Reasons of Misrule" in her *Society and Culture in Early Modern France* (London, 1975). Hutchinson quoted in Pauline Maier, *From Resistance to Revolution: Colonial Radicals and the Development of American Opposition to Britain, 1765–1776* (New York, 1972), 24.

17. Edmund S. Morgan makes this point in David T. Courtwright, "Fifty Years of American History: An Interview with Edmund S. Morgan," *William and Mary Quarterly* 44(1987): 355.

18. See Greene, "Political Mimesis," which notes the impact in the colonies of George Petyt's seventeenth-century *Lex Parliamentaria*. Petyt stressed that Parliament could "declare rights *and* define doubtful rights *and* create new rights." I wish to thank Edward Ballesin, both for pointing this out and for the formulation I have quoted.

19. "Maryland Revolves," 28 September 1765, and *Proceedings of the Congress at New York,* repr. in Edmund S. Morgan, ed., *Prologue to Revolution: Sources and Documents on the Stamp Act Crisis, 1764–1766* (Chapel Hill, N.C., 1959), 52–53, 66–69.

20. E. P. Thompson, "The Moral Economy of the English Crowd in the Eighteenth Century," *Past & Present* 50(February 1971): 76–136.

21. T. H. Breen, "Persistent Localism: English Social Change and the Shaping of New England Institutions," in Breen, *Puritans and Adventurers: Change and Persistence in Early America* (New York, 1980), 1–24.

22. See Morton J. Horwitz, *The Transformation of American Law, 1780–1860* (Cambridge, Mass., 1977); and William E. Nelson, *Americanization of the Common Law: The Impact of Legal Change on Massachusetts Society, 1760–1870* (Cambridge, Mass., 1975). For trenchant criticism of the Horwitz-Nelson argument see Stanley N. Katz, "The Problem of a Colonial Legal History," in Jack P. Greene and J. R. Pole, eds., *Colonial British America: Essays in the New History of the Early Modern Era* (Baltimore, 1984), 457–89.

23. See Bruce H. Mann, *Neighbors and Strangers: Law and*

Community in Early Connecticut (Chapel Hill, N.C., 1987).

24. "A Citizen," *Albany Gazette,* 14 December 1786; see also Gary Kulik, "Dams, Fish, and Farmers: Defense of Public Rights in Eighteenth-Century Rhode Island," in Steven Hahn and Jonathan Prude, eds., *The Countryside in the Age of Capitalist Transformation* (Chapel Hill, N.C., 1985), 42.

25. "An Old Citizen," *Albany Gazette,* 21 December 1786; Horwitz, *Transformation of American Law,* 31–62. For all the criticism that has been made of Horwitz's argument about early American law, his contention is supported by a number of empirical studies. See Christopher M. Jedrey, *The World of John Cleaveland* (New York, 1979), chap. 3; Robert A. Gross, *The Minuteman and Their World* (New York, 1976), chaps. 1 and 4; and Edward Countryman, *A People in Revolution: The American Revolution and Political Society in New York, 1760–1790* (Baltimore, 1981), chaps. 1 and 4.

26. See Michael Merrill, "Cash is Good to Eat: Self-Sufficiency and Exchange in the Rural Economy of the United States," *Radical History Review* 3(1977): 42–71; James A. Henretta, "Families and Farms: *Mentalité* in Pre-Industrial America," *WMQ* 35(1978): 3–32; and Christopher Clark, "The Household Economy, Market Exchange and the Rise of Capitalism in the Connecticut Valley, 1800–1860," *Journal of Social History* 13(1979): 169–89. One of the best synthetic statements is Fred Anderson, *A People's Army: Massachusetts Soldiers and Society in the Seven Years' War* (Chapel Hill, N.C., 1984), chap. 2.

27. John Dickinson, "Letters from a Farmer in Pennsylvania to the Inhabitants of the British Colonies," in Merrill Jensen, ed., *Tracts of the American Revolution, 1763–1776* (Indianapolis, 1967), 135.

28. Tench Coxe, "America" [1809], quoted in Steven Watts, *The Republic Reborn: War and the Making of Liberal America, 1790–1820* (Baltimore, 1987), 251; Gross, 191.

29. My thanks to Richard Ross for this formulation.

30. Patterson, *Freedom,* 3–4.

31. Thomas Hobbes, *English Works,* ed. Sir William Molesworth, 11 vols. (London, 1839–45), 2: 134–35. See also J. G. A. Pocock, *The Machiavellian Moment: Florentine Political Thought and the Atlantic Republican Tradition* (Princeton, 1975).

32. See Bernard Bailyn, *The Ideological Origins of the American Revolution* (Cambridge, Mass., 1967) and Staughton Lynd, "Beard, Jefferson and the Tree of Liberty," in his *Class Conflict, Slavery and the United States Constitution: Ten Essays* (Indianapolis, 1967).

33. Harry S. Stout, *The New England Soul: Preaching and*

Religious Culture in Colonial New England (New York, 1986), 15.

34. James Lockwood, *The Worth and Excellence of Civil Freedom and Liberty* (New Haven, 1759), 16–17, 25–26.

35. Jared Eliot, *Give Cesar His Due* [Connecticut Election Sermon, 1738] (New London, 1738; Evans no. 4241).

36. James Cowell and Thomas Manly, *The Interpreter,* 2d ed. (London, 1684, unpaginated; microfilm ed., Ann Arbor, Mich., 1961–), reel 913, no. 8; entries for the years 1683 and 1684 in I. N. P. Stokes, ed., *The Iconography of Manhattan Island,* 6 vols. (New York, 1915–28) 4: 327, 961; Cadwallader Colden to Sir William Johnson, *The Papers of Sir William Johnson,* 14 vols. (Albany, N.Y., 1921–65) 12:699.

37. See Christopher Hill, "The Norman Yoke," in his *Puritanism and Revolution: Studies in Interpretation of the English Revolution of the 17th Century* (London, 1962), 50–122; and Alfred F. Young, "English Plebeian Culture and Eighteenth-Century American Radicalism," in Margaret Jacob and James Jacob, eds., *The Origins of Anglo-American Radicalism* (London, 1984), 185–212.

38. Quoted in George Rudé, *Paris and London in the 18th Century: Studies in Popular Protest* (London, 1970), 215.

39. James Lovell, *Freedom, the First of Blessings* (Boston, 1754), quoted in J. E. Crowley, *This Sheba, Self: The Conceptualization of Economic Life in Eighteenth-Century America* (Baltimore, 1974), 118.

40. Virginia Resolutions, April 1765, repr. in Morgan, ed., *Prologue to Revolution,* 47–48; "Friends and Countrymen," broadside (Philadelphia, 1766; Evans no. 9949); [John Dickinson], "A New Song, to the Tune of Hearts of Oak," (Philadelphia, 1768; Evans no. 10880); Colrain, Mass., resolution, 31 January 1774, U.S. Revolution Collection, American Antiquarian Society, Worcester, Mass.

41. Thomas Plant, "Joyful News to America," (Philadelphia, 1766; Evans no. 10465).

42. The foremost was the Marylander Daniel Dulany. See his "Considerations on the Propriety of Imposing Taxes on the British Colonies, for the Purpose of Raising a Revenue, by Act of Parliament" (1765), repr. In Bernard Bailyn, ed. *Pamphlets of the American Revolution, 1750–1776,* (Cambridge, Mass., 1965), 598–658; see also Edmund S. Morgan and Helen M. Morgan, *The Stamp Act Crisis: Prologue to Revolution* (Chapel Hill, N.C., 1953), chap. 6.

43. Edward Barnard, "Sermon Preached on Psalm 122:1–6," [1766], quoted in Stout, *The New England Soul,* 267.

44. "Considerations upon the Rights of the Colonists to the Privileges of British Subjects" (New York, 1766; Evans no. 10273), 2–3; *New York Assembly Journal,* 20 November 1765, H. M. Public Records Office, London, Colonial Office Papers, series 5, vol. 1217;

see also "Liberty, Property, and No Excise: A Poem," broadside, American Antiquarian Society (Boston, 1765; Evans no. 41555).

45. "Liberty, A Poem, by Rusticus," (Charleston, S.C., 1770; Evans no. 11844); and [Dickinson], "New Song." See also "Liberty, and Property, and No Stamps," broadside, (New York, 1765, Evans no. 10041; [Isaac Skillman], "An Oration on the Beauties of Liberty," (Boston, 1773; Evans no. 13015) and *The Constitutional Courant*, 21 September 1765 (Evans no. 9941).

46. Mary Beth Norton, *Liberty's Daughters: The Revolutionary Experience of American Women, 1750–1800* (Boston, 1980); Linda K. Kerber, *Women of the Republic: Intellect and Ideology in Revolutionary America* (Chapel Hill, N.C., 1980); and Ira Berlin and Ronald Hoffman, eds., *Slavery and Freedom in the Age of the American Revolution* (Charlottesville, Va., 1983).

47. Mary Wollstonecraft, *A Vindication of the Rights of Woman*, ed. Miriam Brody Kramnick (Harmondsworth, Eng., 1975); Norton, *Liberty's Daughters*, 252–55; David Brion Davis, "American Slavery and the American Revolution," in Berlin and Hoffman, eds., *Slavery and Freedom*, 276; Mary Hay Burn to John Hay Burn, 17 October 1776, in Peter Force, comp., *American Archives*, 9 vols. in 2 series (Washington, D.C., 1835–53), 5th series, 2:1094; New Hampshire slaves quoted in Winthrop D. Jordan, *White Over Black: American Attitudes Toward the Negro, 1550–1812* (Chapel Hill, N.C., 1968), 291.

48. See, in this volume, Cathy N. Davidson, "The Novel as Subversive Activity: Women Reading, Women Writing": and Peter H. Wood, " 'Liberty Is Sweet': African American Freedom Struggles in the Years before White Independence."

49. There was, of course, ample precedent in the colonial press for using pseudonyms like "a tradesman," or "a workingman" or "a farmer," and most scholars agree that these generally concealed the actual authorship of a gentleman. John Dickinson's "Letters from a Farmer in Pennsylvania" provides the most notable example. The difference during the Townshend taxes resistance is that the writers in question were not just calling themselves workingmen; they were arguing for workingmen's interests from workingmen's positions.

50. *Boston Gazette*, 19 September and 7 November 1768; *New York Journal*, 17 December 1767; *A Discourse Addressed to the Sons of Liberty* (Providence, R.I., 1766; Evans no. 10286), 6.

51. "To the Free and Loyal Inhabitants of the City and Colony of New York," broadside (New York; Evans no. 11588); "To the Tradesmen, Farmers and other Inhabitants of the City and County of Philadelphia," broadside (Philadelphia, 24 September 1770; Evans no. 11892); "To the Free and Patriotic Inhabitants," broadside

(Philadelphia, 1770; Evans no. 11882).

52. *The People the Best Governors; or, A Plan of Government Founded on the Just Principles of Natural Freedom* (n.p., 1776; Evans no. 43134); "The Respectful Address of the Mechanics in Union . . .", Force, comp., *American Archives*, 4th series, 6:895-98; Ashfield, Mass., constitutional proposals cited in Dirk Hoerder, "Socio-Political Structures and Popular Ideology, 1750s–1780s," in Erich Angermann et al., eds., *New Wine in Old Skins: A Comparative View of Socio-Political Structures and Values Affecting the American Revolution* (Stuttgart, 1976), 41–65; Ronald Hoffman, *A Spirit of Dissension:Economics, Politics and the Revolution in Maryland* (Baltimore, 1973), 173; and *Pennsylvania Gazette,* 27 September 1770.

53. "Oppression, A Poem," broadside (Boston, 1777; Evans no. 10114); "An Address to the People on the Subject of Monopoly and Extortion," in Nathanael Low, *Astronomical Diary or Almanack for 1778* (Boston, 1777);

54. "Boston Circular Letter," broadside, American Antiquarian Society (Boston, 1777; Evans no. 43027); "Proceedings of the Town Meeting," broadside (Philadelphia, 1779; Evans no. 16472). See also "The Address of the Committee of the City and Liberties of Philadelphia," broadside (Philadelphia, 1779; Evans no. 16462); Roxbury resolves, 12 July 1779, Massachusetts Collection, American Antiquarian Society; Lexington Town Records, entries for 12 January 1778 and 5 July 1779, American Antiquarian Society; "The Real Farmer," *New-York Journal*, 18 January–15 February 1779; "A Poem Against Oppression" in *Poems upon Several Occasions* (Boston, 1779; Evans no. 16479); "Come on Warmly" broadside (Philadelphia, 1779).

55. See Countryman, *People in Revolution*, chaps. 5 and 6, and Eric Foner, *Tom Paine and Revolutionary America* (New York, 1976).

56. Proclamation of Governor Trumbull, 25 August 1780, broadside, American Antiquarian Society (New London, Conn., 1780).

57. "Tanners, Curriers, and Cordwainers to the Inhabitants of Pennsylvania," broadside (Philadelphia, 1779; Evans no. 16547). For others taking a free-market position during the economic crisis, see Countryman, *People in Revolution*, chaps. 6 and 7; and Richard Alan Ryerson, "Republican Theory and Partisan Reality in Revolutionary Pennsylvania: Toward a New View of the Constitutionalist Party," in Ronald Hoffman and Peter J. Albert, eds., *Sovereign States in an Age of Uncertainty* (Charlottesville, Va., 1981), 95–133.

58. Moses Hemmenway, *A Sermon Preached Before His Excellency John Hancock* (Boston, 1784), 31; Jonathan Jackson, *Thoughts upon the Political Situation* (Worcester, Mass., 1788; Evans no. 21173), 134; "The Republican, No. II," *Connecticut Courant,* 12 Feb-

ruary 1787; [Noah Webster], "The Devil Is in You," *Pennsylvania Gazette,* 16 May 1787.

59. *The Federalist Papers,* ed. Clinton Rossiter (New York, 1961), 227.

60. See E. Wayne Carp, *To Starve the Army at Pleasure: Continental Army Administration and American Political Culture, 1775–1783* (Chapel Hill, N.C., 1984).

61. One might call this a process of bourgeois class formation. For discussions of two key states see Thomas M. Doerflinger, *A Vigorous Spirit of Enterprise: Merchants and Economic Development in Revolutionary Philadelphia* (Chapel Hill, N.C., 1986); and Countryman, *People in Revolution,* chap. 9. Compare E. P. Thompson's observation that "class happens when some men, as a result of common experiences (inherited or shared), feel and articulate the identity of their interests as between themselves, and as against other men whose interests are different from (and usually opposed to) theirs." Thompson, *The Making of the English Working Class,* paperback ed. (New York, 1966), 7. My argument here is not intended to contradict my assertion in *The American Revolution* that the Revolutionary political process must be understood in terms of coalitions. The coalition nature of the Federalists of 1787 is exemplified both in the close collaboration of the southern planter James Madison and the northern commercial lawyer Alexander Hamilton in the drive for the Constitution and in their subsequent split. Nonetheless, it is apparent that Madison and the other leaders of what would become the Democratic Republican party developed a bourgeois national vision of their own. See Joyce Appleby, *Capitalism and a New Social Order: The Republican Vision of the 1790s* (New York, 1984); and Drew R. McCoy, *The Last of the Fathers: James Madison and the Republican Legacy* (Cambridge, Mass., 1989).

62. [Benjamin Rush], *Considerations upon the Present Test Law of Pennsylvania* (Philadelphia, 1784; Evans no. 18770), 8, 10–11; see also Noah Webster, *Sketches of American Policy* (Hartford, Conn., 1785) and *An Examination into the Leading Principles of the Federal Constitution* (Philadelphia, 1787; Evans no. 20865).

63. Paul A. Gilje, *The Road to Mobocracy: Popular Disorder in New York City, 1763–1834* (Chapel Hill, N.C., 1987).

64. Alfred F. Young, personal communication, 2 September 1989; see also Paul Finkelman, "Slavery and the Constitutional Convention: Making a Covenant with Death," in Beeman et al., eds., *Beyond Confederation: Origins of the Constitution and American National Identity* (Chapel Hill, N.C., 1987), 188–225.

65. For the Federalists' private attitudes see Wood, "Interests

and Disinterestedness"; for examples of Federalist appeals to group interests see *Boston Gazette,* 15 October 1787, 3 December 1787, and 14 January 1788; *Boston Independent Chronicle,* 1 November and 20 December 1787, 28 February 1788; *New York Daily Advertiser,* 22 March and 28 April 1788; *New York Journal,* 26 April 1787, 10 April 1788; *Pennsylvania Gazette,* 29 March and 12 September 1786; 14 March, 30 May, 8–15 August, and 10 October 1787; 6 February and 5 March 1788.

66. For discussions of the parades see Sean Wilentz, "Artisan Republican Festivals and the Rise of Class Conflict in New York City, 1788–1837," in Michael Frisch and Daniel J. Walkowitz, eds., *Working-Class America: Essays on Labor, Community, and American Society* (Urbana, Ill., 1983), 37–77; and Countryman, *The American Revolution,* 214–19. See also the forthcoming Yale doctoral dissertation by David Waldstreicher.

"Liberty Is Sweet"

African-American Freedom Struggles in the Years before White Independence

PETER H. WOOD

S I R,

A S *the Committee of Safety is not fitting,* I *take the Liberty to enclose you a Copy of the Proclamation iſſued by Lord* Dunmore; *the Deſign and Tendency of which, you will obſerve, is fatal to the publick Safety. An early and unremitting Attention to the Government of the* S L A V E S *may,* I *hope, counteract this dangerous Attempt. Conſtant, and well directed Patrols, ſeem indiſpenſably neceſſary.* I *doubt not of every poſſible Exertion, in your Power, for the publick Good; and have the Honour to be, Sir,*

Your moſt obedient and very humble Servant,

P. H E N R Y.

HEAD QUARTERS, WILLIAMSBURG,
November 20, 1775.

In March 1775 Patrick Henry gave his famous speech, "Give me liberty, or give me death," and later, Virginia patriots made him commander-in-chief of the colony's military forces. On November 17 the Royal Governor, Lord Dunmore, issued a proclamation promising freedom to all slaves, owned by rebels, "Able and willing to bear arms" in the King's cause. On November 20 Henry issued this public broadside denouncing the Proclamation, calling for "unremitting attention to the Government of SLAVES." Circular Letter of 20 November 1775, broadside.

Not long after the outbreak of the American Revolution, a prominent Lutheran minister noted in his journal the sentiments of two black house servants he had encountered near Philadelphia. "They secretly wished that the British army might win," Henry Muhlenberg wrote, "for then all Negro slaves will gain their freedom. It is said that this sentiment is almost universal among the Negroes in America."[1]

Only recently have most Americans again begun to take seriously the deeply held commitment to freedom that existed among African Americans on the eve of the Civil War in the mid-nineteenth century. But we have not yet given enough thought to the obvious question of whether this sentiment was equally widespread among enslaved Americans a century earlier, at the time of the Revolution, as the Reverend Muhlenberg reported. Indeed, who were the persons to whom he referred and about whom most of us know so little?

By 1775, African Americans figured far more prominently in the colonial population than they had a century earlier. On the eve of white Independence nearly 500,000 blacks constituted almost twenty percent of the people in England's mainland colonies. They were not spread out evenly, for the vast majority resided south of Pennsylvania. Indeed, nine of every ten African Americans lived in the South, primarily in the Atlantic coastal regions that produced tobacco, rice, and indigo. The black population of the southern colonies had jumped tenfold in the first thirty years of the eighteenth century, and a generation later, in 1775, black Virginians totaled over 185,000; black Carolinians, North and South, numbered roughly 160,000, and even the fledgling colony of Georgia contained 15,000 black inhabitants.[2] At no other time, before or after, have African Americans constituted such a large proportion of the American populace.

Not only did black persons constitute one of the largest single ethnic groups in the heterogeneous eighteenth-century colonies; in addition, they were singularly and explicitly oppressed. All of these men and women, or their recent ancestors, had been forced to migrate from Africa against their will.[3] And almost all remained inextricably ensnared in the dominant southern system of hereditary racial slavery. Though concentrated in several strategic areas and consigned to live at the very bottom of colonial society, black people were highly visible—often troublingly so—to their white contemporaries. Yet they have proven virtually invisible to subsequent scholars of colonial America, who floated for generations on a placid mainstream oriented geographically toward the northeast, ethnically toward the English, and socially toward the colonial elites.

For the better part of two centuries, therefore, historians have retold the saga of the Revolution and its origins with almost no awareness or acknowledgment of these African Americans. Even in 1992, a leading author in the early American field can still write: "the social conditions that generically are supposed to lie behind all revolutions—poverty and economic deprivation—*were not present in colonial America*. There should no longer be any doubt about it," Gordon Wood continues, shifting the subject somewhat, "the *white* American colonists were not an oppressed people. . . ." (Emphasis added.)[4] What are we to make of such a categorical statement, followed by a qualified observation about the Caucasian majority, dropping African Americans into oblivion in mid-paragraph? Did not the perpetual servitude of hundreds of thousands of individuals—denied any right to the fruits of their own labor or to the offspring of their own families—constitute deprivation? Were their numbers too small, or their skins too dark, to be deemed significant by established historians?

Gradually, over the past generation, some eighteenth-century scholars have begun to restore these absent Americans to their distinctive place in the drama of the country's founding, making it harder, although not yet impossible, to ignore their significant presence. But we still have little sense of what these black members of the revolutionary generation were *thinking*. How firm, how widespread, how varied, and how recent were their "sentiments" regarding freedom, for example? After all, the antislavery movement among whites in Europe and America was still only in its infancy, and hence one might suspect—at least countless intellectual historians have—that thoughts of liberty and independence had not yet "reached" the black population of the American colonies. Indeed, it has become a basic tenet of many who write about the period that the most radical ideas of the American Revolution—especially the core concept of personal liberty—for the most part trickled *downward* through colonial society from the top.

Take, as an example, the two house servants encountered by Muhlenberg. Did they hold such an ardent desire for freedom before the outbreak of war, and if so, did they discuss it with one another? Had they merely picked up ideas about individual liberty through their special status as house servants or their privileged location near the focus of colonial rebellion in Philadelphia? It is indeed true, as Gary Nash has written, that "when the language of protest overflowed its initial boundaries and confronted the relationship between American liberty and domestic slavery, black Philadelphians must have listened intently and talked ardously among themselves."[5] This essay argues that we can go further. It is no longer enough for historians to imply that African Americans finally picked up on "the spillover" from an earlier white debate about freedom, or that they belatedly contracted "the contagion of liberty." On the contrary, I believe the evidence suggests that they had a long and bitter familiarity with the ideas and issues at hand.

While white colonists were evolving through a lengthy and un-planned ideological education, linking them to England's Puritan Revolution of the seventeenth century and to the strain of continuing underground radical thought associated with the "eighteenth-century commonwealthmen," several generations of black Americans were also being educated and politicized in the harsh school provided by slavery and racial discrimination. Like their European counter-parts these Africans struggled to integrate knowledge and beliefs brought over from the Old World into their response to conditions faced in America. But enslavement is an extraordinary crucible, and it may well be that, during the generations preceding 1776, African Americans thought longer and harder than any other sector of the colonial population about the concept of liberty, both as an abstract ideal and as a tangible reality.

"The desire of blacks for freedom did not, of course, originate with the American Revolution," writes historian Benjamin Quarles.[6] For resistance to chattel slavery appeared as soon as that coercive insti-tution had taken firm root in England's mainland colonies during the second half of the seventeenth century. And much of this resistance proved collective and prearranged, despite the overwhelming repres-sion reserved for any hint of organized rebellion. As Herbert Aptheker pointed out long ago, slave plots—both rumored and real—occurred frequently, and they often appeared in waves. Throughout the eighteenth century and beyond, these surges of slave resistance seemed to occur during periods when the white community was dis-tracted. (As we shall see later, one such wave, starting in the 1760s, crested a decade later in the eventful months before the Declaration of Independence.)

Often the slaves themselves used arson to create a temporary dis-traction, but there were other larger conflagrations that could throw the dominant society into relative disarray. Epidemics, for example, frequently disrupted the normal patterns of life among white colo-nists, providing an opportunity for enslaved persons to conspire for freedom. While a virulent smallpox epidemic raged in Massachusetts in 1721, Cotton Mather felt obliged, in a midweek lecture to Boston slaves, to denounce the *Fondness* for *Freedom* in many of you," de-spite living "Comfortably in a very easy Servitude."[7] Widespread yel-low fever was in evidence when blacks near Charlestown (modern

Charleston), South Carolina, initiated the Stono Rebellion in September 1739. The sickness had prompted the colonial assembly to adjourn and the local newspaper to suspend publication. The Stono Uprising came remarkably close to succeeding, and as the ranks of the rebellion swelled, it is significant that participants raised the chant of "Liberty!"—a cry that would be repeated by both blacks and whites in Carolina at the time of the Stamp Act crisis.[8]

Imperial wars could also prompt ideological shifts and economic pressures that slightly improved the terrible odds against revolt. At Stono, for instance, the uprising hinged on a plan to gather large numbers and march to St. Augustine, where Spanish authorities were offering sanctuary at Fort Mose to slave refugees from Carolina. So it is probably not coincidence that the largest slave revolt in the history of the English colonies began on the very weekend when news reached Charlestown that Spain and England were at war. Within a generation, the South Carolina elite, in a familiar pattern, were blaming the uprising on "wantonness" among their black workers and "slackness" among their white overseers.[9] But no matter what colonial leaders wished to believe, this had not been a spontaneous outburst prompted by character weakness or poor oversight. On the contrary, black efforts to obtain freedom in the mid-eighteenth century, like white colonial efforts to gain political freedom in subsequent decades, derived from reasoned interpretation of long sequences of events.

For the legally enslaved blacks, as for those whites who eventually came to feel themselves "enslaved," coordination was important, and local initiatives often hinged upon word of related events in other colonies. So it is not surprising that when efforts were mounted to break the bonds of slavery, they often occurred in more than one place at roughly the same time.[10] In Virginia, where significant challenges to enslavement had occurred around 1730,[11] historian Philip Schwarz has noted that another "cycle of insurrectionary thinking emerged" in the 1750s. In recently settled Brunswick County, authorities were troubled to find ideas of liberty circulating too freely among the enslaved population. In June 1752 three black men were tried for insurrection and conspiracy to commit murder in that southside county. The alleged leader, Peter, was hanged, while Harry Cain and James each received thirty-nine lashes. They were charged with "being privy to an Opinion entertained among many Negroes of their having a Right to their Freedom and not making a Discovery thereof."[12]

When war erupted in North America between Protestant England and Catholic France in 1754, it was again predictable in the English colonies that both the unfree workers and the provincial authorities would sense the lack of internal defenses and the prospects for slave revolt. After the initial defeat of Colonel George Washington at Fort Necessity in July 1754, members of the South Carolina Assembly saw the frontier threat as an opportunity to reinforce the wedge which they had gradually driven between African Americans and native Americans. "If Indian Enemies should appear in our settlements, as they too often do," the assembly advised the council in March 1755, "we thought that it might be necessary to Arm some of the most Trusty of our Slaves to defend their masters' Lives and Property and to destroy such Enemies." Making clear their underlying long-term motive, the assemblymen added: "we thought it good Policy in this way to keep up and increase that natural aversion which happily subsists between Negroes and Indians."[13]

Such aversions, of course, were hardly natural; they had been cultivated by colonial authorities at great expense.[14] But efforts to set red against black still could not address the fact so troublesome to white settlers: when conflict flared on the frontier, the prospects mounted for insurrection at home. In particular, reports of possible slave violence increased when the English suffered reversals in the field. During the French and Indian War this occurred most dramatically with General Edward Braddock's defeat at Fort Duquesne in early July 1755.[15] When word of this setback reached Governor Horatio Sharpe of Maryland, he sent out "Circulatory Letters to have the Slaves, Convicts &c well observed & watched," while giving orders for Maryland militia units "to be prepared to quell it in case any Insurrection should be occasioned by this Stroke."[16]

Similarly, in Virginia Lieutenant Governor Robert Dinwiddie received reports after Braddock's loss that groups of black workers were asserting themselves. He wrote to the Earl of Halifax that the defeat in the Ohio country had prompted local slaves to become "very audacious. . . . These poor Creatures imagine the Fr. will give them their Freedom. We have too many here, but I hope we shall be able to defeat the Designs of our Enemies and keep these Slaves in proper Subject'n."[17] In South Carolina it is no coincidence that the engineer beginning work on a new fort at Charlestown in July 1755, to secure the city "against a sudden Surprize from the Sea," also proposed a fortification six miles west of town as a defense against slave revolt. William De Brahm sent to Governor Glen detailed plans for an 11,600-foot canal connecting the Ashley and Cooper Rivers, so that Charlestown Neck would become an island, "protected against an Insurrection of the Negroes or Indian War by the fortified Canal."[18]

By 1760 the South Carolina port of Charlestown had a greater number of blacks and a larger proportion of enslaved residents than any community in North America. "The City is inhabited by about 12,000 Souls," reported engineer De Brahm; "more than half are Negroes and Mulattoes."[19] Moreover, the town was located in the mainland colony with the harshest slave codes and the highest concentration of African workers. (The black majority was approaching 58,000 persons, in contrast to fewer than 39,000 whites; in other words, six of every ten South Carolinians were black during the third quarter of the eighteenth century.) So it should come as no surprise that enslaved men and women again gave signs of testing their chains in 1759–60, when a war erupted with the Cherokees and a smallpox epidemic descended upon the city.

One other powerful factor was also at work, for repercussions of the powerful Christian revival known as the Great Awakening were still being felt throughout the region. Early in 1759 the Reverend Richard Clarke, the influential Anglican rector of St. Philips Church in Charlestown, began preaching—as had earlier millenarians in England—that the world would end during the 1760s.[20] Governor Lyttleton related that "at length his Enthusiasm rose to such a height that he let his beard grow and ran about the streets crying Repent, Repent, for the Kingdom of Heaven is at hand." Fearing civil unrest, authorities made note of Clarke's "overheated" imagination and wasted no time in forcing his resignation and sending him back to England.[21] But Clarke, who would continue his career as a religious radical in England over four more decades, had already aroused the attention of nonwhite Carolinians.

Not long after Clarke's departure in March 1759, a free mulatto or black identified variously in the colonial records as Philip John or Philip Jones was arrested, tried, whipped, and branded for allegedly endeavoring to stir up sedition among blacks. He had apparently been turned in by "two Negroes named Tom and Trane," to whom he had secretly entrusted "a written paper and charged them to carry it to all the Negroes and show it them." At first a date in June "was fixed upon for killing the Buckras," or white people, but later "it was agreed to wait," especially since "the Justice before whom he had been had taken his paper from him." John vowed revenge upon Tom and Trane "for telling the designs" and surrendering his important paper, but he insisted that "he did not care if the devil had it for he had another and would go to Charles Town with it and would do the work God Almighty had set him about," adding that within six months all the buckras "would be killed."

Despite punishment, John persisted with his plan, apparently telling several blacks that "Mr Broadbelt's Caesar is to be the Head man, I am to be the next to him." He then retreated briefly into the backcountry, returning with the claim that "God Almighty had been with him in the woods." He claimed "that he had seen a vision, in which it was reveal'd to him, that in the month of September the White People shou'd be underground,that the Sword shou'd go thru' the Land, and it should shine with their blood." John argued powerfully, in the tradition of a utopian Leveller, "that there should be no more White King's Governor or great men, but the Negroes should live happily and have Laws of their own." Governor Lyttleton, alert to reports of unrest among black Carolinians, recorded that "a spirit of cabal began to shew itself among them" just as he was beginning to plan a campaign against the Cherokee Indians.

On 20 July 1759 the Royal Council issued a warrant for the arrest of Philip John, along with Caesar and a free mulatto named John Pendarvis, who had apparently offered to put up funds for the revolt. After the plot had been foiled, Governor Lyttleton reported from Charlestown that "their scheme was to have seized some arms and ammunition that were in a storehouse in the country belonging to a merchant, and then with what force they could collect to have marched to this town." Like any suspected leader of an unsuccessful rebellion, Philip John was put to death, while Pendarvis, a free man "reputed to be a person of credit and property," was charged with buying guns and ammunition to support the insurrection. The events surrounding Clarke, John, and Pendarvis would have been fresh memories at the time of the Stamp Act Crisis six years later, and their names were no doubt still remembered locally in 1775, when a free black pilot, Thomas Jeremiah, faced similar charges and punishment.

*I*t was in the wake of the Stamp Act in 1765 that large numbers of newly politicized whites began to feel oppressed enough to engage in vociferous debate and public action. For the first time, therefore, the emerging Whig ideology of radical dissent appeared in the streets alongside the well-established black "fondness for freedom." Much has been made of the Stamp Act demonstrations in Boston, which so agitated a whole generation of young provincials, but events in South Carolina's port city remain somewhat less familiar.[22] There, as Donna Spindell has written, "the fear of a slave insurrection, which dominated the thoughts and actions of many Charlestonians, was decidedly the most significant factor in shaping the evolution of the Stamp Act crisis."[23]

Any black South Carolinian who had sympathized with Philip John's opposition to "the white king's governor and great men" in 1759 surely realized six years later that prospects for a successful slave uprising were notably enhanced when the Stamp Act crisis divided Charlestown's white minority. Thousands of black residents must have seen and heard "the very extraordinary and universal commotions" which began on 18 October 1765 with the arrival of a ship rumored to be carrying the stamped paper which Parliament had ordered for the implementation of the Stamp Act. By the next morning a gallows had been erected at the corner of Broad and Church Streets, and a stamp collector had been hanged in effigy above the words, "Liberty and no Stamp Act."[24] Several days later sixty to eighty Sons of Liberty, many with their faces blackened under the "thickest disguise of Soot," staged a march upon the house of the wealthy merchant and slave trader Henry Laurens. Knowing that Laurens was a prospective stamp officer and hoping to confiscate the dreaded paper which they suspected was hidden in his residence, the noisy but orderly crowd visited the Laurens home at midnight chanting, *"Liberty, Liberty & Stamp'd Paper."*[25]

Several days later the town celebrated the resignation of its stamp officers with the largest demonstration in local history, led by Christopher Gadsden's triumphant Sons of Liberty, who unfurled a British flag in the streets with the word LIBERTY emblazoned across it.[26] Soon afterward, further conflict was evident, fomented by some of the 1,400 sailors whose ships were being held in port by confusion over the Stamp Act. A letter written from Charlestown in early December stated, "At present everything is quiet here; our Liberty Boys being content to keep out the stamps, do not injure, but protect, the Town; for some time ago a Parcel of Sailors, having a mind to make the most of this suspension of law, formed a Mob, to collect Money of the People in the Streets; but these Sons of Liberty suppressed them instantly, and committed the Ringleaders to Gaol."[27] Inevitably, these public displays were watched closely by blacks in Charlestown, giving them clear evidence of dissension—and therefore potential weakness—in the dominant power structure.

Racial tensions during the fall of 1765 already seemed more strained than they had been at any time in the quarter century since Stono. In September the noted naturalist John Bartram, exploring the region south of Charlestown, recorded seeing "two negroes Jibited alive for poisoning their Master."[28] In mid-October, two days before the ship bearing stamped paper arrived, the grand jury handed down an unusually long list of presentments, many of which concerned the regulation of blacks in both town and country. They argued "that slaves in Charles-Town are not under a good regulation, and that they at all times in the night go about streets rioting." These same black South Carolinians, the grand jury protested, "do often gather in great numbers on the sabbath day and make riots, where it is not in the power of the small number of watchmen to suppress them, which hereafter may, without any precaution, prove of the utmost ill consequence to this province." The grand jury also noted "the too frequent liberty given to negroes in the country" and "the great neglect of the militia law, the people in the country not mustering often."[29]

Worried that matters were spinning out of control, the legislature took the drastic action of imposing a three-year embargo on further importation of slaves, to take effect 1 January 1766. Ironically, the initial result of this law was a flurry of activity in the Charlestown slave market in anticipation of the closing of the African trade.[30] As the deadline approached and the sudden influx of African newcomers reached record proportions, the prospects for violent challenges to the status quo increased sharply. On 17 December Lieutenant Governor William Bull, Jr., convened the Royal Council to inform them that the wife of Isaac Huger, a white merchant, had overheard from the balcony of her home a conversation between two slaves suggesting that an insurrection was being planned for Christmas Eve.[31]

After the council agreed that these two men should be sent for and questioned, Bull went on to express his apprehension "that a pernicious Custom had lately prevailed of private people Firing Guns by way of rejoycing on Christmas Eve, which would this year be attended with this further Consequence as firing gunns was the method by which an alarm was to be published and therefore if continued might either raise false alarm or prevent a True one being attended to." The council issued a proclamation strictly prohibiting such practices in the future. It also recommended that a party of one hundred militiamen be deployed to mount a guard in Charlestown during the holidays, and it suggested to Bull that sailors from the unusually numerous ships in the harbor might be of great service to authorities in case of a slave uprising.[32]

Christmas Eve passed without major incident, and the council, highly apprehensive, met again on Christmas Day. Lieutenant Governor Bull reported that the ship captains had indicated a "great readyness" to provide assistance, and he offered an elaborate plan for making use of their men. To captains who applied to him, he would make available "a Hundred Stand of arms to be distributed amongst the discretist of their people." When Bull recommended to the council that "it would greatly tend to defeat any attempts of the Negroes if they could hunt out the runaways now in the Woods and destroy their several camps," he received quick approval of a measure calling upon Catawba Indian allies in the backcountry for assistance.[33] "This place has been in an uproar for twelve days past, in consequence of a report which prevailed, that the Negroes had agreed to begin a general insurrection throughout the province," wrote one resident on 29 December. "Every company in town mount guard day and night, and the severest orders given which has prevented it hitherto."[34]

In early January 1766, only weeks after the initial scare, some blacks in Charlestown reportedly took up the shout of "Liberty." The unprecedented display, undertaken at a time of heightened white vigilance, seemed a brazen echo of the earlier Stamp Act demonstrations, and it galvanized authorities to impose even tighter controls. The entire town was placed under martial law for a week, and for ten to fourteen days mounted messengers were dispatched throughout the colony.[35] Moreover, in a message to the Commons House of Assembly on 14 January 1766, Bull stated with precision that he "had received accounts that One Hundred and Seven Negroes had left their plantations soon after the Intended Insurrection had been discovered and joined a large number of runaways in Colleton County which increase to a formidible Body." An account of the episode published in the *Virginia Gazette* stated that "the strictest search" had been made "to find out the ringleaders; that circumstances appeared very strong against them, many fire arms being found concealed; and at several plantations in the country, the house arms were found to have their touchholes plugged up."[36]

By late January, Bull could write to London with assurance: "I have the pleasure to acquaint your Lordships that the apprehensions of a Negro Insurrection last December happily proved abortive."[37] But at the same time he exhorted the provincial legislators to be more mindful of the potential for coordinated resistance within the black community. Satisfied that "the late wicked Machinations are now happily disappointed, and seem to be at an end," he reminded the assemblymen "not to suffer a present appearance of tranquillity to lull you into a dangerous neglect" of internal security. "The cause of our danger is domestic," he cautioned, "and interwoven with almost all the Employments of our lives and so ought to be our attention to the remedy."[38] Despite all that transpired during the subsequent decade, Bull's observation would still hold true in the mid-1770s. What he thought of as domestic dangers and wicked machinations, and what black Americans looked upon as necessary assertions and unprecedented opportunities, grew ever more apparent along the Atlantic seaboard.

*E*ight eventful years later, when the First Continental Congress convened in Philadelphia in the fall of 1774, South Carolina was not the only colony rife with rumors of insurrection. Over the previous decade black challenges to white domination had increased in frequency up and down the Atlantic coast.[39] "There has been a conspiracy of the negroes," a New England woman wrote to her husband in September. "At present it is kept pretty private, and was discovered by one who attempted to dissuade them from it," she informed her spouse, away on business. With the aid of an Irishman, they had prepared "a petition to the Governor, telling him they would fight for him provided he would arm them and engage to liberate them if he conquered" the local rebels. "I wish most sincerely there was not a slave in the province," she added. "It always appeared a most iniquitous scheme to me—to fight ourselves for what we are daily robbing and plundering from those who have as good a right to freedom as we have."[40] The province was Massachusetts, and the author was Abigail Adams, writing to her husband John in Philadelphia.

Throughout the colonies the population of enslaved Africans was growing rapidly, due to importation and natural increase, and expectations of possible change were spreading through the black community. No group had less formal power, or a larger potential interest in the unraveling of established social relationships, than African Americans. Although most were confined to the gulags of southern plantations, hemmed in by legal and physical constraints, they still represented a crucial force in the overall political equation, for their numbers were great, their situation seemed desperate, and their detachment from the niceties of the imperial debate was considerable. Among whites, meanwhile, the gap was widening between popular Whigs on one hand and their Loyalist opposition on the other. Soon all three of these diverse constituencies would find themselves embroiled with one another, as the stakes grew higher for all concerned.

As 1774 changed into 1775, printer William Bradford of Philadelphia received a letter from young James Madison in Virginia. "If America & Britain should come to a hostile rupture I am afraid an Insurrection among the slaves may and will be promoted," wrote Madison, a member of the Committee on Public Safety for Orange County.

> In one of our Counties lately a few of those unhappy wretches met together and chose a leader who was to conduct them when the English troops should arrive—which they foolishly thought would be very soon and that by revolting to them they should be rewarded with their freedom. Their intentions were soon discovered and the proper precautions taken to prevent the Infection.[41]

In early January Bradford replied, "Your fear with regard to an insurrection being excited among the slaves seems too well founded."

The Philadelphian informed Madison that, "A letter from a Gentleman in England was read yesterday in the Coffee-house, which mentioned the design of [the] administration to pass an act (in case of rupture) declaring ['] all Slaves & Servants free that would take arms against the Americans.' "[42]

As the prospects for insurrectionary acts improved and the anxiety of white patriots grew, the frequency and harshness of punishments increased, and the rate of slave executions seems to have risen. In the fall of 1774 two Georgia blacks accused of arson and poisoning had been burned alive on Savannah's Common, and in December several more slaves were "taken and burnt" for leading an uprising in nearby St. Andrew's Parish that killed four people and wounded others.[43] Significantly, not all white colonists responded to prospects of black rebellion with acts of reprisal, due to a blend of religious scruples, ideological consistency, and strategic necessity. On 12 January 1775, for example, a group of Scottish parishioners in Georgia, meeting at Darien, adopted a resolution that slavery was an "unnatural practice . . . founded in injustice and cruelty, and highly dangerous to our liberties, (as well as lives), debasing part of our fellow-creatures below men, and corrupting the virtues and morals of the rest." Slavery's existence, they asserted, "is laying the basis of that liberty we contend for . . . upon a very wrong foundation," and they pledged to work for the manumission of Georgia slaves.[44]

Another immigrant expressed similar sentiments. In early March 1775 Thomas Paine, using the pen name "Humanus," published his first article, three months after reaching Philadelphia. His essay in the *Pennsylvania Journal and Local Advertiser* was entitled "African Slavery in America," and it pointed out that blacks had been "industrious farmers" who "lived quietly" in Africa before "Europeans debauched them with liquors" and brought them to the New World. Paine reminded white colonists that because they had "enslaved multitudes, and shed much innocent blood in doing it," the Lord might balance the scales by allowing England to "enslave" whites. To avoid such retribution and give greater consistency to the patriot cause, "Humanus" urged the abolition of slavery and suggested that freed Negroes be given land in the West to support themselves, where they might "form useful settlements on the frontiers. Thus they may become interested in the public welfare, and assist in promoting it; instead of being dangerous as now they are, should any enemy promise them a better condition."[45]

Paine, as a newcomer to Pennsylvania, may actually have been picking up on an idea regarding western lands that had been in the air for several years, there and elsewhere, among whites and blacks searching for an effective way to end race slavery. In Philadelphia in 1773 the Quaker abolitionist Anthony Benezet had suggested that freed slaves might be settled with whites in new communities beyond the Alleghenies.[46] In Boston, meanwhile, a group of enslaved blacks had submitted a petition to Governor Thomas Hutchinson and the provincial legislators in June 1773 "in behalf of all those, who by divine permission are held in a state of SLAVERY, within the bowels of a FREE country." Arguing forcefully for freedom on religious, legal, and humanitarian grounds, they acknowledged the fact that "if we should be liberated and made free-men of this community, and allowed by law to demand pay for our past services, our masters and their families would by that means be greatly damnified, if not ruined: But we claim no rigid justice," the authors added magnanimously. Instead, with humility and a touch of Old Testament poetry, they only asked the authorities to provide full legal freedom and, in addition, to "grant us some part of the unimproved land, belonging to the province, for a settlement, that each of us may there quietly sit down under his own fig-tree, and enjoy the fruits of his own labour."[47]

During the spring of 1775, even as Paine wrote, the interlocking struggles of Tories, Whigs, and African Americans intensified. In this phase, as talk of rebellion grew among worried officials, aroused patriots, and hopeful slaves, the issue of who controlled supplies of powder and shot took on central importance. Loyalists charged white radicals with spreading rumors of black worker unrest. "In the beginning of 1775," Thomas Knox Gordon of South Carolina recalled, "the Malecontents being very anxious to have some plausible pretence for arming with great industry propagated a Report that the Negroes were meditating an Insurrection."[48] Patriots, in turn, claimed authorities were prepared to enlist black strength if necessary to quell white dissent. The Committee of Safety for New Bern, North Carolina, announced in a circular letter that "there is much reason to fear, in these Times of General Tumult and Confusion, that the Slaves may be instigated and encouraged by our inveterate Enemies to an Insurrection, which in our present defenseless State might have the most dreadful Consequences." The Committee advised "Detachments to patrol and search the Negro Houses, and . . . to seize all Arms and Ammunition found in their Possession."[49]

Black activists, for their part, sought to capitalize on white divisions in their plans for freedom fully as much as white factions tried to implicate half a million blacks in their political designs. In such a highly charged atmosphere timing could be everything, and premature action was a matter of constant risk, but black Americans had grounds to be particularly "impatient of Oppression," and given the enormous stakes some chose armed rebellion well before their white counterparts.[50] Consider a report from Ulster County, New York, that early in 1775 a farmer had caught part of a conversation between two of his slaves, discussing the powder needed and support available to carry out an uprising. The plot included burning houses and executing slave-owning families as they tried to escape. This organized liberation plan involved blacks from the villages of Kingston, Hurly, Keysereck, and Marbletown, and the twenty persons who were taken into custody had considerable powder and shot in their possession. In addition, rumor had it that these blacks were to be joined in their freedom struggle by five or six hundred native Americans.[51]

*I*n the colonies of the upper South in 1775 the demographic and social situation differed markedly from conditions in the Northeast, for fully two-thirds of the black persons in English North America were concentrated in Maryland, Virginia, and eastern North Carolina. Almost all these Americans remained entrapped in the web of hereditary race slavery, and in the spring of 1775 they, like the more numerous whites around them, were paying close attention to internal dissensions and to news from other provinces. Notice of the plot in Ulster County, New York, for example, appeared in the Virginia papers in mid-March, apparently creating fresh hopes and increased consternation in the already volatile capital of Williamsburg, where the royal supply of gunpowder was housed in a well-guarded magazine on the village green. Within a month, when Governor Dunmore ordered the barrels of gunpowder in the Williamsburg magazine removed to a ship under cover of night, the town's Whig mayor immediately submitted a petition claiming that widespread rumors of a local slave revolt made internal security a crucial matter. News soon reached the capital that irate citizens were coming from the west to reclaim the powder by force.[52]

On 1 May 1775 Governor Dunmore wrote to the Earl of Dartmouth that he intended "to arm all my own Negroes and receive all others that will come to me whom I shall declare free," in expectation that such an armed force would be able to "reduce the refractory people of this colony to obedience."[53] Word quickly spread throughout Williamsburg that Dunmore was fortifying the Governor's Palace and had issued arms to his servants; a physician testified that the governor swore to him "by the living God that he would declare Freedom to the slaves and reduce the City of *Williamsburg* to Ashes" if disorder continued.[54] Hearing this, several blacks presented themselves at the palace to offer their services but were turned away.[55] The governor, quipped the *Virginia Gazette* bitterly on 1 June 1775, "who for some time past has been suspected of acting the part of an incendiary in this colony, is to take the field as generalissimo at the head of the Africans." The editor, protecting himself with blank spaces, added that, "the BLACK LADIES, it is supposed, will be jollily entertained in the p----e [palace]."

Word of Lord Dunmore's rumored threat to liberate and arm black Virginians quickly reached Thomas Gage, the British general serving as governor of Massachusetts. "We hear," he wrote in mid-May, "that a Declaration his Lordship has made, of proclaiming all the Negroes free, who should join him, has Startled the Insurgents." And on 12 June 1775, a week before the disastrous engagement at Bunker Hill which was to cost him his command, Gage wrote to his friend Lord Barrington, "You will have heard of the boldness of the rebels, in surprising Ticonderoga. . . . Things are come to that crisis, that we must avail ourselves of every resource, even to raise the Negroes, in our cause."[56] Two weeks later Dunmore himself observed regarding Virginia's planter elite: "My declaration that I would arm and set free such Slaves as should assist me if I was attacked has stirred up fears in them which cannot easily subside."[57] Within a month he was at work on a secret plan with John Connelly of Fort Pitt to add the threat of an Indian attack on the backcountry to the prospect of slave insurrections.[58]

In Maryland in late April 1775, planters pressured Governor Robert Eden into issuing arms and ammunition to guard against rumored insurrections, though the governor feared their acts "were only going to accelerate the evil they dreaded from their servants and slaves." In May, John Simmons, a white artisan in Dorchester County, refused to attend militia muster, saying "he understood that the gentlemen were intending to make us all fight for their land and negroes, and then said damn them (meaning the gentlemen) if I had a few more white people to join me I could get all the Negroes in the county to back us, and they would do more good in the night than the white people could do in the day." Simmons, a wheelwright, reportedly told James Mullineux "that if all the gentlemen were killed we should have the best of the land to tend and besides could get mony enough while they were about it as they have got all the money in their hands." Mullineux told a grand jury "that the said Simmons appeared to be in earnest and desirous that the negroes should get the better of the white people." Simmons was later tarred, feathered, and banished on the accusation of fomenting a slave insurrection. By fall the Dorchester County Committee of Inspection reported, "The insolence of the Negroes in this county is come to such a height, that we are under a necessity of disarming them which we affected on Saturday last. We took about eighty guns, some bayonets swords, etc."[59]

In North Carolina the black freedom struggle during the summer of 1775 was even more intense. "Every man is in arms and the patroles going thro' all the town, and searching every Negro's house, to see they are all at home by nine at night," wrote Janet Schaw, an English visitor to Wilmington. "My hypothesis," she stated, "is that the Negroes will revolt."[60] Her view was confirmed when a massive uprising in the Tar River area of northeastern North Carolina was revealed just before it was to begin, on the night of 8 July. Scores of blacks were rounded up and brought before Pitt County's Committee of Safety, which "Ordered several to be severely whipt and sentenced several to receive 80 lashes each [and] to have [their] Ears crapd [cropped,] which was executed in the presence of the Committee and a great number of spectators." Colonel John Simpson reported that, "in disarming the negroes we found considerable ammunition" and added: "We keep taking up, examining and scourging more or less every day." According to Simpson, "from whichever part of the County they come they all confess nearly the same thing, viz[t] that they were one and all on the night of the 8th inst to fall on and destroy the family where they lived, then to proceed from House to House (Burning as they went) until they arrived in the Back Country where they were to be received with open arms by a number of Persons there appointed and armed by [the] Government for their Protection, and as a further reward they were to be settled in a free government of their own."[61]

*I*n the deep South colonies, where the relative proportion of blacks was high, the prospects for dramatic change in their condition seemed even brighter during the spring and summer of 1775, as contending British authorities and Whig leaders were well aware. Early in 1775 General Gage had written from Boston to John Stuart, the superintendent of Indian Affairs based in Charlestown, observing that South Carolina's Patriot leaders could hardly afford to promote too much "Serious Opposition" and local unrest, or they might find that "Rice and Indigo will be brought to market by negroes instead of white people."[62] In early May a letter reached local Whigs from Arthur Lee, their attentive correspondent in London, suggesting that a plan had been laid before the British administration for instigating American slaves to revolt.[63]

About the same time a black preacher named David—apparently African-born and English-trained—arrived in Charlestown from the settlement of Bethesda in Georgia, founded by the famous evangelist George Whitefield. He stayed at the home of Patrick Hinds, who had been cited in February by the Grand Jury "for entertaining and admitting Negroe Preachers in his House and on his grounds, where they deliver Doctrines to large numbers of Negroes dangerous to and subversive of the Peace, Safety and Tranquility of this Province."[64] But this earlier presentment did not stop Hinds from inviting David to address "several white People and Negroes, who had collected together to hear him." Whatever his intent, "David in the course of his exhortation, dropped some unguarded Expressions, such as, that he did not doubt; but 'God would send Deliverance to the Negroes, from the power of their Masters, as He freed the Children of Israel from Egyptian Bondage.'" Soon after his talk David made a hasty exit from Charlestown, for in the city's tense atmosphere such remarks were "construed, as tho' he meant to raise rebellion amongst the negroes." According to a letter dated 8 May 1775, "the Gentlemen of this Town are so possessed with an opinion that his Designs are bad, that they are determined to pursue, and hang him, if they can lay hold of him."[65]

Word arrived in Charlestown that same day regarding the bloodshed at Lexington and Concord three weeks earlier, and, as one observer put it, "the people of Carolina were thrown into a great Ferment."[66] If such news had differing meaning for Loyalists, Whigs, and enslaved African Americans, all were challenged by its unknown implications. Ten days later Josiah Smith, Jr., wrote that "our Province at present is in a ticklish Situation, on account of our numerous Domesticks, who have been deluded by some villanous Persons into the notion of being all set free" on the arrival of the new governor, Lord William Campbell. The situation was made still more ticklish by the portion of a letter from England that appeared in the local paper at the end of May. The correspondent, apparently linking a regular annual shipment of trade guns for the Indians with the heightened prospect of violence in the colonies, had reported on 10 February that "there is gone down to Sheerness, seventy-eight thousand guns and bayonets, to be sent to America, to put into the hands of N-----s [Negroes], the Roman Catholics, the Indians, and the Canadians; and all the means on earth used to subdue the colonies." Writing again in mid-June, Josiah Smith, Jr., noted that the rumor of freedom among the slaves "is their common Talk throughout the Province, and has occasioned impertinent behaviour in many of them, insomuch that our Provincial Congress now sitting hath voted the immediate raising of Two Thousand Men Horse and food, to keep those mistaken creatures in awe, as well as to oppose any Troops that may be sent among us with coercive Orders."[67]

In early July Charlestown's Council of Safety received word from the Chehaw District south of Edisto River that "Several Slaves in the neighborhood were exciting & endeavouring to bring abt a General Insurrection." For several years a Scotsman named John Burnet had apparently been holding frequent "Nocturnal Meetings" with local blacks, and a slave named Jemmy told the planters "that at these assemblies he had heard of an Insurrection intended," in which slaves were "to take the Country by Killing the Whites, but that John Burnet was to be Saved as their Preacher." Besides Burnet, Jemmy proceeded to name fifteen black men and women on six plantations who "are Preachers, & have (many of them) been preaching for two Years last past to Great crouds of Negroes in the Neighborhood of Chyhaw, very frequently, which he himself has attended." Indeed, Jemmy had heard one of these preachers, a man named George from the plantation of Francis Smith, "say that the old King had reced a Book from our Lord by which he was to Alter the World (meaning to set the Negroes free) but for his not doing so, was now gone to Hell, & in Punishmt That the Young King, meaning our Present One, came up with the Book, & was about to alter the World, & set the Negroes Free."[68]

When Governor Campbell arrived in Charlestown, he found the story circulating that the "Ministry had in agitation not only to bring down the Indians on the Inhabitants of this province, but also to instigate, and encourage an insurrection amongst the Slaves. It was also reported, and universally believed," Campbell stated, "that to effect this plan 14,000 Stand of Arms were actually on board the Scorpion, the Sloop of War I came out in. Words, I am told, cannot express the flame that this occasion'd amongst all ranks and degrees, the cruelty and savage barbarity of the scheme was the conversation of all Companies." A free black pilot named Thomas Jeremiah, who "had often piloted in Men of War" as they entered the harbor, was jailed on charges of being in contact with the British Navy and seeking to distribute arms.[69]

One black witness for the prosecution testified that in April 1775 along the docks Jeremiah had asked him, "Sambo, do you hear anything of the war that is coming?" The pilot had assured the witness that "there is a great war coming soon," advising him to be ready to "join the soldiers—that the war was come to help the poor Negroes." Another slave named Jemmy, the pilot's brother-in-law, claimed that in early April Jeremiah had asked him "to take a few Guns" to a runaway named Dewar, "to be placed in Negroes hands to fight against the Inhabitants of this Province." His relative told him further, Jemmy testified, "that he Jeremiah was to have the Chief Command of the said Negroes," and that while "he believed he had Powder enough already," he "wanted more arms" and "would try to get as many as he could."[70] Although sentenced to hang as a co-conspirator, Jemmy obtained a reprieve through his testimony on 17 August. Jeremiah was publicly hanged and burned in Charlestown on the following afternoon. Governor Campbell reported he had been warned that if he intervened with a pardon, "it would raise a flame all the water in Cooper River would not extinguish."[71]

The situation in Georgia was scarcely different, as John Adams learned through a discussion with several other delegates to the Continental Congress in Philadelphia. "In the evening," Adams wrote on 24 September, "two gentlemen from Georgia, came into my room [and] gave a melancholy account of the State of Georgia and South Carolina. They say that if one thousand regular troops should land in Georgia, and their commander be provided with arms and clothes enough, and proclaim freedom to all the negroes who would join his camp, twenty thousand negroes would join it from the two Provinces in a fortnight." According to Adams, the two Georgians observed "their only security is this; that all the king's friends, and tools of government, have large plantations and property in negroes; so that the slaves of the Tories would be lost, as well as those of the Whigs."[72] Needless to say, human property lost by a Whig or Tory could mean freedom gained by an African American.

Clearly the stakes were mounting for all concerned by the fall of 1775, and the three-way tug-of-war was becoming ever more intense. In the British House of Commons on 26 October, William Henry Lyttleton reminded his colleagues that the southern colonies were weak "on account of the number of negroes in them." Lyttleton, the former governor of South Carolina and Jamaica, prompted a bitter debate when he suggested "a proposal for encouraging the negroes in that part of America to rise against their masters, and for sending some regiments to support and encourage them, in carrying the design into execution." He, for one, believed confidently that "the negroes would rise, and embrue their hands in the blood of their masters."[73]

To many, Virginia seemed particularly vulnerable, for it contained far more blacks than any other mainland colony, and almost all of them remained enslaved. Moreover, although the colony's black population of nearly 190,000 was outnumbered by some 280,000 whites, many of the latter now lived in the backcountry, and all were increasingly divided along partisan lines between Whigs and Tories. By autumn Governor Dunmore, who had retreated from Williamsburg to the safety of a British ship, was preparing to use the desperate card he had threatened to play, and perhaps should have played, six months earlier. When his marines raided a printing office in Norfolk in September, they were joined by cheering blacks.[74] During October he continued to conduct raids and to remove slaves to British naval vessels via small sloops and cutters as he had been doing for months. "Lord Dunmore," charged the Committee of Safety in Williamsburg on 21 October 1775, "not contented with . . . inciting an insurrection of our slaves, hath lately, in conjunction with the officers of the navy, proceeded to commence hostilities against his Majesty's peaceable subjects in the town and neighborhood of Norfolk; captivated many, and seized the property of others, particularly slaves, who are detained from the owners."[75] "Lord Dunmore sails up and down the river," a Norfolk resident wrote to London the following week; "where he finds a defenseless place he lands, plunders the plantation and carries off the negroes."[76]

Edmund Pendleton estimated in early November that perhaps fewer than one hundred slaves had taken refuge with Dunmore, but the situation changed drastically on 14 November, when the governor's forces won a skirmish at Kemp's Landing. Dunmore capitalized on this small victory in two ways. First, he sent off John Connelly toward Detroit with secret orders approved by Gage to return to Virginia with Indian troops, seize Alexandria, and await forces from the coast.[77] Second, Dunmore used the occasion to publish the less-than-sweeping proclamation he had drawn up and signed the week before, emancipating any servants or slaves of the opposition faction who would come serve in his army. It read in part, "I do hereby further declare all indented servants, negroes, and others (appertaining to Rebels) free, that are able and willing to bear arms, they joining his Majesty's Troops, as soon as may be, for the more speedily reducing this Colony to a proper sense of their duty."[78]

Connelly was soon captured, but the proclamation had its intended effect.[79] "Letters mention that slaves flock to him in abundance," Pendleton wrote to Richard Henry Lee at the end of the month, "but I hope it magnified."[80] "Whoever considers well the meaning of the word Rebel," stated a white resident of Williamsburg, "will discover that the author of the Proclamation is now himself in actual rebellion, having armed our slaves against us and having excited them to an insurrection." He added, in a line reminiscent of Patrick Henry, "there is a treason against the State, for which such men as Lord Dunmore, and even Kings, have lost their heads."[81]

Since it ultimately failed from both the British and the black vantage points, there is a tendency to minimize the combined initiative of the months following November 1775.[82] But at the time these events in Virginia had enormous potential significance for blacks and whites throughout the colonies. Word of Dunmore's proclamation must have reached Charlestown by early December, for blacks initiated a work stoppage on harbor fortifications, and many slaves gathered on Sullivan's Island in hopes of boarding a British ship.[83] In Philadelphia, a newspaper related on 14 December that a "gentlewoman" walking near Christ Church had been "insulted" by an African American, who remained near the wall on the narrow sidewalk, refusing to step off into the muddy street as expected. When she reprimanded him, he replied, according to the report, "Stay, you d——d white bitch, till Lord Dunmore and his black regiment come, and then we will see who is to take the wall."[84]

That same day George Washington urged Congress "to Dispossess Lord Dunmore of his hold in Virginia" as soon as possible. In repeated letters the planter-general stressed that "the fate of America a good deal depends on his being obliged to evacuate Norfolk this winter." Washington spelled out his fears to Richard Henry Lee on 26 December 1775: "If my dear Sir, that man is not crushed before spring, he will become the most formidable enemy America has; his strength will increase as a snow ball by rolling; and faster, if some expedient cannot be hit upon to convince the slaves and servants of the impotency of his designs."[85] The general had personal reasons to fear such a snowball. A note written 3 December from Mount Vernon had informed him that Dunmore's proclamation was well known to his own bondsmen. It appeared, wrote Lund Washington, that "there is not a man of them but would leave us if they believed they could make their escape," even though Mount Vernon's workers had "no fault to find" with their master specifically, his reported contended. Nevertheless, Lund Washington concluded, the slaves all seemed to share one universal idea that shaped their discontented frame of mind, namely: "liberty is sweet."[86]

All across the South, planters, who—like George Washington—had committed themselves to the desperate alternative of violent revolution, were growing more apprehensive than ever about the prospect of armed revolt among the enslaved. In February 1776 Richard Bennehan, founder of one of North Carolina's largest slaveholding dynasties, left instructions for his overseer near Hillsborough before setting out to join patriot forces for the battle of Cross Creek: "It is said the negroes have some thoughts of freedom. Pray make Scrub sleep in the house every night and [see] that the overseer keep in Tom."[87] Predictably, such planters blamed Lord Dunmore for kindling a belief in freedom among those being held in bondage. But in reality Dunmore was merely fanning embers of liberation that had been glowing in the black community for generations.

Reports from the Chesapeake southward after Dunmore's proclamation are suggestive of the events surrounding Abraham Lincoln's Emancipation Proclamation of 1863.[88] With the prospect of freedom at hand, flight became the logical form of rebellion, and along the coast hundreds took direct action despite terrible odds. The newspapers told of "boatloads of slaves" seeking out British ships, not always successfully.[89] Seven men and two women from Maryland "who had been endeavouring to get to Norfolk in an open boat" were apprehended near Point Comfort.[90] Three blacks who boarded a Virginia boat that they mistakenly took to be a British vessel were only "undeceived" after they had openly "declared their resolution to spend the last drop of their blood in Lord Dunmore's service."[91] Although perhaps more than a thousand reached Dunmore's ships safely, an outbreak of smallpox among the refugees the next spring reduced their numbers and discouraged others from following. If it had "not been for this horrid disorder," Dunmore wrote to the secretary of state on 26 June 1776, "I should have had two thousand blacks; with whom I should have had no doubt of penetrating into the heart of this Colony."[92]

A great deal had changed in the year since Tom Paine had advocated emancipation and western resettlement. The British had co-opted these ideas and used them to their own advantage, capitalizing on slave aspirations for freedom and swinging black hopes decidedly toward the loyalist position with the carrot of emancipation. Dunmore's proclamation gave public substance to this stance, and the planter elite viewed such a threat to their property as a compelling argument for independence—just as their grandchildren would more than four score years later. Patriot opinion had solidified around the notion that the freedom struggles of enslaved Africans were a liability rather than an asset. When Paine's *Common Sense* first appeared on 9 January 1776, it spoke of the British as barbarous and hellish agitators and of native Americans and African Americans as brutal and destructive enemies. Soon Thomas Jefferson would weave similar sentiments into his drafts for the Declaration of Independence and the preamble to the Virginia constitution.[93]

Preoccupied with imperial misrule and prejudiced from the start against members of another class and a different race, colonial leaders were unable to acknowledge accurately (or perhaps even perceive) the nature of the struggle for liberation that was being waged passionately around them. Unable to acknowledge the strength of the opposition from below, they preferred to believe that outside agitators had been at work, unsuccessfully, among passive and anonymous victims of enslavement. By relying on their persuasive and partisan words, we ourselves have been largely blinded for two centuries to a major factor in the turmoil leading up to the white War of Independence. We have failed to recognize an important chapter in the history of worker and artisan unrest, and we have omitted a significant strand in the ideological origins of the American commitment to freedom.

NOTES

PUBLISHING NOTE: This essay expands and provides additional documentation for an argument presented earlier in Peter H. Wood, " 'Impatient of Oppression': Black Freedom Struggles on the Eve of White Independence," *Southern Exposure* 12 (November-December 1984): 10–16 and in Peter H. Wood, " 'The Dream Deferred': Black Freedom Struggles on the Eve of White Independence," in Gary K. Okihiro, ed., *In Resistance: Studies in African, Caribbean and Afro-American History* (Amherst, Mass., 1986), 166–87.

1. *The Journal of Henry Melchior Muhlenberg,* trans. Theodore G. Tappert and John W. Doberstein, 3 vols. (Philadelphia, 1942–58), 3:78.

2. In contrast, during the 1770s a total of only 15,000 blacks resided in the four northeastern colonies of New Hampshire, Massachusetts, Rhode Island, and Connecticut, making up only three percent of New England's population. William D. Piersen, *Black Yankees: The Development of an Afro-American Subculture in Eighteenth-Century New England* (Amherst, Mass., 1988), table 6, 168–69. On the shifting distribution and relative numbers of blacks, whites, and Indians across the entire South during the eighteenth century, see my demographic survey, "The Changing Population of the Colonial South: An Overview by Race and Region, 1685–1790," in Peter H. Wood, Gregory A. Waselkov, H. Thomas Hatley, eds., *Powhatan's Mantle: Indians in the Colonial Southeast* (Lincoln, Neb., 1989), 35–103.

3. It is important for a variety of reasons to remember that, overall, North American victims of the Middle Passage made up scarcely five percent of the entire slave trade from Africa to the Americas. See Philip D. Curtin, *The Atlantic Slave Trade: A Census*

(Madison, Wis., 1969).

4. Gordon S. Wood, *The Radicalism of the American Revolution* (New York, 1992), 4. This process is not unusual. More than 80,000 African migrants are set aside at the outset of another important recent book by a distinguished colonial scholar. See Bernard Bailyn, *Voyagers to the West: A Passage in the Peopling of America on the Eve of the Revolution* (New York, 1986), 17–19.

5. Gary B. Nash, *Forging Freedom: The Formation of Philadelphia's Black Community, 1720–1840* (Cambridge, Mass., 1988), 39. For the clearest and most influential formulation of this trickle-down theory, see Bernard Bailyn, *The Ideological Origins of the American Revolution* (Cambridge, Mass., 1967), chap. 6.

6. Benjamin Quarles, "The Revolutionary War as a Black Declaration of Independence," in Ira Berlin and Ronald Hoffman, eds., *Slavery and Freedom in the Age of the American Revolution* (Charlottesville, Va., 1983), 285. Quarles's pioneer volume, *The Negro in the American Revolution* (Chapel Hill, N.C., 1961) remains basic to this field. Among many recent contributions, see particularly Jacqueline Jones, "Race, Sex, and Self-Evident Truths: The Status of Slave Women during the Era of the American Revolution," in Ronald Hoffman and Peter J. Albert, eds., *Women in the Age of the American Revolution* (Charlottesville, Va., 1989), 293–337; Robert A. Olwell, " 'Domestick Enemies': Slavery and Political Independence in South Carolina, May 1775–March 1776," *Journal of Southern History* 55 (1989): 21–48; and Sylvia R. Frey, *Water from the Rock: Black Resistance in a Revolutionary Age* (Princeton, 1991).

7. Quarles, "Revolutionary War," 285. Mather is quoted in Lawrence W. Towner, " 'A Fondness for Freedom': Servant Protest in Puritan Society," *William and Mary Quarterly*, 3d series, 19 (1962): 201. Also see Daniel K. Richter, " 'It Is God Who Has Caused Them to Be Servants': Cotton Mather and Afro-American Slavery in New England," *Bulletin of the Congregational Library* 30 (Spring-Summer 1979): 4–13.

8. Peter H. Wood, *Black Majority: Negroes in Colonial South Carolina from 1670 through the Stono Rebellion* (New York, 1974), 312–17. Regarding subsequent black initiatives immediately after Stono, see ibid., 318–23.

9. According to William Bull, Jr., son of the lieutenant governor at the time of the revolt, the Stono Rebellion had taken "its rise from the wantonness, and not oppression of our Slaves, for too great a number had been very indiscreetly assembled and encamped together for several nights, to do a large work on the public road; with a slack inspection." Letter of 30 November 1770, British Public

Record Office Transcripts (hereafter cited as BPROT), 35 vols., located in the South Carolina Department of Archives and History, Columbia, S.C. (hereafter cited as SCDAH) 32:381–83. On Fort Mose, see Jane Landers, "Spanish Sanctuary: Fugitives in Florida 1687–1790," *Florida Historical Quarterly* 62 (January 1984): 296–313; and Larry W. Kruger and Robert Hall, "Fort Mose: A Black Fort in Spanish Florida," *The Griot* (Southern Conference on Afro-American Studies) 6, no. 1 (Spring 1987): 39–48. While war between Great Britain and Spain was not declared formally until October 1739, in July Admiral Edward Vernon was ordered to the Caribbean with a British squadron to "commit all sorts of hostilities against the Spaniards," and word of this pending aggression reached Charlestown in September. Orders cited in Geoffrey J. Walker, *Spanish Politics and Imperial Trade, 1700–1789* (Bloomington, Ind., 1979), 207.

10. At the time of Stono, in late 1739, for example, there was also a reported conspiracy in Prince George's County, Maryland; whites in that heavily Catholic province faced internal divisions during Great Britain's war against Spain (1739–48)—a development which slaves could not have ignored. Aubrey C. Land, ed., *Bases of Plantation Society* (Columbia, S.C., 1969), 228–30; Jeffrey R. Brackett, *The Negro in Maryland* (Baltimore, 1889), 93–94. Similarly in New York City, where some 2,000 enslaved blacks made up one sixth of the port's population, accusations that Catholic agents were encouraging slave unrest figured in the lengthy trials and extensive prosecutions that followed New York's suspected conspiracy of 1741. See T. J. Davis, ed., *The New York Conspiracy by Thomas J. Horsmanden* (Boston, 1971); Davis, *A Rumour of Revolt* (New York, 1985).

11. The return of former Governor Spotswood from England in 1730 sparked rumors that he was carrying an order from the King to liberate Virginia's Christian slaves. Governor Gooch mobilized the militia, and "by Imprisonment and severe whipping of the most Suspected, this Disturbance was very soon Quashed." Soon after, when several hundred enslaved blacks in Princess Anne and Norfolk counties gathered on a Sunday morning to choose officers to lead a revolt, four of the most prominent participants were publicly executed. Thad W. Tate, *The Negro in Eighteenth-Century Williamsburg* (Charlottesville, Va., 1965), 205–7.

12. During the next ten months other black Virginians, in Surry County and in the capital of Williamsburg, were also punished for engaging in such rebellious talk. Philip J. Schwarz, *Twice Condemned: Slaves and the Criminal Laws of Virginia, 1705–1865* (Baton Rouge, La., 1988), 171–74. Schwarz notes that in September 1750 a free black man in Northampton County was charged with "suspicion of

his combining with sundry Negroes in a Conspiracy against the white People of this County." He was sentenced by the county court to thirty-nine lashes and forced to post a bond of £100 for good behavior. Two months later the same court condemned an enslaved man to twenty lashes for the same offense.

13. Parish Transcripts relating to South Carolina, in the New-York Historical Society, New York City (hereafter cited as Parish Trans.), 7 March 1755. Compare William S. Willis, "Divide and Rule: Red, White, and Black in the Southeast," *Journal of Negro History* 48 (July 1963): 157–76.

14. When South Carolina's governor agreed to "Articles of Friendship and Commerce" with Creek Indian leaders in 1721, for example, the headmen promised "to apprehend and secure any Negro or other Slave which shall run away from any English Settlements to our Nation." They would be paid in guns and blankets for returning captured runaways alive, "And in Case we or our People should kill any such Slaves . . . in apprehending them, then we are to be paid one Blanket for his Head by any Trader we shall carry such Slave's Head unto." South Carolina Commons House Journals (hereafter cited as SCCHJ), 1736–39, 110, SCDAH. Articles dated 8 July 1721. For a similar clause in a treaty with the Cherokees signed in London in September 1730, see BPROT 14:21–22, SCDAH.

15. Mark J. Stegmaier, "Maryland's Fear of Insurrection at the Time of Braddock's Defeat," *Maryland Historical Magazine* 71 (Winter 1976): 467–83.

16. Sharpe to Calvert, 15 July 1755, *Archives of Maryland,* ed. William H. Browne, 71 vols. (Baltimore, 1883–) 6:251.

17. Dinwiddie to Secretary Halifax, 23 July 1755, Virginia Historical Society, *Collections,* new series, vol. 4, *The Official Records of Robert Dinwiddie, Lieutenant-Governor of Virginia, 1751–1758,* 2 vols. (Richmond, 1884) 2:114. Also see Dinwiddie to Charles Carter, 18 July 1755, ibid. 2:102, responding to Colonel Carter's report of slave unrest in Lancaster County: "The Villainy of the Negroes in an Emergency of Gov't is w't I always fear'd. I greatly approve of your send'g the Sheriffs with proper Strength to take up those y't appear'd in a Body at Y'r Son's House, and if found Guilty of the Expression mention'd I expect You will send for a Com'o. to try them, and an example of one or two at first may prevent those Creatures enter'g into Combinat'[ion]s and wicked Designs ag'st the Subjects." Apparently worried about using blacks as combatants (as he would again worry two decades later), George Washington advised his subordinate "to detain both Mulatto's and negroes in your Company; and employ them as Pioneers and Hatchetmen." Letter from Washington to Capt.

Peter Hogg, 27 December 1755, John C. Fitzpatrick, ed., *The Writings of George Washington from the Original Manuscript Sources, 1745–1799*, 39 vols. (Washington, D.C., 1931–40) 1:259.

18. Louis De Vorsey, Jr., ed., *De Brahm's Report of the General Survey in the Southern District of North America* (Columbia, S.C., 1971), 91; compare 17 and plate 3.

19. Ibid., 90.

20. The minister publicized his views in a pamphlet, and he predicted a great calamity for South Carolina in September (which was, not incidentally, the twentieth anniversary of Stono). Richard Clarke, *The Prophetic Numbers of Daniel and John Calculated; In Order to Show the Time, when the Day of Judgement for the First Age of the Gospel Is to be Expected; and the Setting Up of the Millenial Kingdom of Jehovah and His Christ* (Charlestown, S.C., 1759), advertised in the *South Carolina Gazette*, 3 March 1759.

21. Evidence here and in the next three paragraphs is from Parish Trans., 9 July 1759 and 1 September 1759. Also see David Zornow, "A Troublesome Community: Blacks in Revolutionary Charles Town, 1765–1775," (undergraduate honors thesis, Harvard College, 1976), and the forthcoming book of John Scott Strickland on "millenial visions and visible congregations" among South Carolina slaves.

22. See Robert M. Weir, " 'Liberty and Property, and No Stamps': South Carolina and the Stamp Act Crisis" (Ph.D. diss., Western Reserve University, 1966); Maurice A. Crouse, "Cautious Rebellion: South Carolina's Opposition to the Stamp Act," *South Carolina Historical Magazine* 73 (April 1972): 59–72.

23. Donna J. Spindell, "The Stamp Act Riots" (Ph.D. diss., Duke University, 1975), 204; compare Pauline Maier, "The Charleston Mob and the Evolution of Popular Politics in Revolutionary South Carolina, 1765–1784," *Perspectives in American History* 4 (1970): 176.

24. Richard Walsh, *Charleston's Sons of Liberty: A Study of the Artisans, 1763–1789* (Columbia, S.C., 1959), 36–37.

25. Henry Laurens to Joseph Brown, 28 October 1765, Philip M. Hamer, George C. Rogers, Jr., David R. Chesnutt, eds., *The Papers of Henry Laurens*, 11 volumes to date (Columbia, S.C., 1968–), 5:29–31; compare 37–40.

26. David Duncan Wallace, *The Life of Henry Laurens* (New York, 1915), 118–20. For a note regarding the slave Equiano's possible description of this celebration, see Peter H. Wood, " 'Taking Care of Business' in Revolutionary South Carolina: Republicanism and the Slave Society," in Jeffrey J. Crow and Larry E. Tise, eds., *The Southern Experience in the American Revolution* (Chapel Hill, N.C., 1978), 289, n. 23.

27. *Boston Gazette,* Supplement, 27 January 1766.

28. John Bartram, "Diary," *Transactions of the American Philosophical Society,* new series, 33 (December 1942): 22.

29. No doubt recalling that the Stono revolt of 1739 had occurred on a Sunday morning, the jurors went on to "complain of the neglect of not carrying arms to church and other places of worship, and against the bad custom of delivering their arms to negroes or other slaves, to keep while they are at devine service." *South Carolina Gazette,* 2 June 1766. Two further items listed by the grand jury read as follows:

VII. We present as a general grievance through the province, the want of a patrol duty being duly done, and submit it to the legislature, whether a provincial or parochial tax to support the expense of a standing patrol, to be constantly on duty, would not better answer the intentions of apprehending fugitive slaves; and that all fugitives after so many months absence should be deemed out laws and subject to death without sentence or expense to the province.

VIII. We present it as a grievance, the too frequent abuse of the law relative to the keeping of a proper number of white men on plantations, according to the number of blacks.

30. The number of enslaved Africans imported into South Carolina in 1765 jumped drastically over previous years, to well above 7,000 persons—more than the entire resident black population, or the white population, of Charlestown at the time. George C. Rogers, Jr., *Charleston in the Age of the Pinckneys* (Norman, Okla., 1969), 42; Elizabeth Donnan, *Documents Illustrative of the Slave Trade to America,* 4 vols. (Washington: D.C., 1930–35) 4:411–13.

31. Mr. Huger told Bull that at first he had doubted the validity of his wife's information, but that "on some other circumstances happening he thought it proper to be so far attended as to communicate it to him as it gave uneasiness to many people." Bull added that he had since received further confirmation of the intended plot through the "friendship to the White People" of two black informers on Johns Island, bordering the Stono River south of Charlestown. BPROT, Council Journal, 17 December 1765.

32. Ibid.

33. BPROT, Council Journal, 25 December 1765. Bull later explained candidly that he had "thought it very Advisable to call down some of the Catawbas, as Indians Strike Terrour into the Negroes, and the Indian manner of hunting render them more sagacious in tracking and expert in finding out the hidden recesses where the runaways conceal themselves from the usual searches of the En-

glish." SCCHJ, 14 January 1766.

34. Extract from a letter from South Carolina dated 29 December 1765, in the *Newport Mercury,* 10 February 1766.

35. Henry Laurens to John Lewis Gervais, 29 January 1766, *Laurens Papers* 5:53–54.

36. *Virginia Gazette,* 7 March 1766. Of more than 100 persons suspected of going into hiding, only 7 were apprehended, even though the Assembly paid out more than £380 in compensation to those who searched. SCCHJ, Audit of Public Accounts, 2 April 1767. When the South Carolina Assembly published its list of public accounts for the year, one entry showed that £277 had been alotted to an "ordnance storekeeper for cleaning the muskets and bayonets and for twelve days work of a white man and two Negroes fixing Bayonets to 599 gunns and Flinting 980 muskets in the late alarm." SCCHJ, 17 January 1766.

37. BPROT, Council Journal, 25 January 1766. "The vigorous execution of our Militia and Patrol Laws for 14 days before and after Christmas Day," Bull told his superiors, "prevented the festivity and the assembling of Negroes usual at that time, and disconcerted their schemes."

38. SCCHJ, 14 January 1766. "I earnestly recommend to you," Bull concluded, "to revise the Militia and Town Watch Acts for better governing Negroes" to assure "not only a punctual but a continued observance of their salutary injunctions." Several years later, a report from Charlestown dated 16 August 1768 mentioned a battle with maroons, "a numerous collection of outcast mulattoes, mustees, and free negroes." *Boston Chronicle,* 3–10 October 1768.

39. For a brief description of those intervening years, see Peter H. Wood, " 'Impatient of Oppression': Black Freedom Struggles on the Eve of White Independence," *Southern Exposure* 12 (November-December 1984): 11–12.

40. Charles Francis Adams, ed., *Familiar Letters of John Adams and His Wife Abigail Adams* (New York, 1876), 41–42.

41. James Madison, letter of 26 November 1774, William T. Hutchinson and William M. E. Rachal, eds., *The Papers of James Madison* (Chicago, 1962) 1:129–30. "It is prudent," Madison reminded the printer, that "such attempts should be concealed as well as suppressed."

42. "By this," Bradford concluded, "you see such a scheme is thought on and talked of; but I cannot believe the Spirit of the English would ever allow them publically to adopt so slavish a way of Conquering." William Bradford to James Madison, Philadelphia, 4 January 1775, Hutchinson and Rachal, eds., *Madison Papers* 1:132.

43. *Georgia Gazette,* 14 and 21 September, 7 December 1774; Herbert Aptheker, *The American Revolution, 1763–1783* (New York, 1960), 220; Herbert Aptheker, *Negro Slave Revolts* (New York, 1943), 201.

44. Harvey H. Jackson, " 'American Slavery, American Freedom' and the Revolution in the Lower South: The Case of Lachlan McIntosh," *Southern Studies* 19 (Spring 1980): 81; Betty Wood, *Slavery in Colonial Georgia: 1730–1775* (Athens, Ga., 1984), 202–3. Also see Kenneth Coleman, *The American Revolution in Georgia, 1763–1789,* (Athens, Ga., 1958), 45–46.

45. Philip S. Foner, ed., *The Complete Writings of Thomas Paine,* 2 vols. (New York, 1945), 2:19. Paine's essay "is said to have inspired the American Anti-Slavery Society, founded on April 14." Wylie Sypher, *Guinea's Captive Kings: British Anti-Slavery Literature of the XVIIIth Century* (Chapel Hill, N.C., 1942; repr. 1969), 61.

46. See Ellen Gibson Wilson, *The Loyal Blacks* (New York, 1976), 15–16; Nash, *Forging Freedom,* 40–46.

47. *The Massachusetts Spy* (Boston), 29 July 1773.

48. This loyalist claims memorial, filed in London, n.d., is in Audit Office 12, vol. 51, f. 289. Gordon goes on, ff. 290–91, to explain how he tried to quiet these fears. The claims memorial of Thomas Irving, another South Carolina official (vol. 51, ff. 306–7), also addresses this matter. I am indebted to Prof. Mary Beth Norton for these references.

49. 31 May 1775, Adelaide L. Fries, ed., *Records of the Moravians of North Carolina,* 2 vols. (Raleigh, N.C., 1968) 2:847, 928–30.

50. The phrase is from a justly famous letter of 11 February 1774 from black poet Phillis Wheatley to Indian minister Samson Occom. Herbert Aptheker, ed., *A Documentary History of the Negro People in the United States,* 2 vols. (New York, 1951) 1:8–9. On Wheatley, see Sidney Kaplan and Emma Nogrady Kaplan, *The Black Presence in the Era of the American Revolution,* rev. ed. (Amherst, Mass., 1989), 170–91; Charles W. Akers, " 'Our Modern Egyptians': Phillis Wheatley and the Whig Campaign against Slavery in Revolutionary Boston," *Journal of Negro History* 60 (July 1975): 405–6. For a fascinating discussion and references to recent scholarship on Wheatley, see David Grimsted, "Anglo-American Racism and Phillis Wheatley's 'Sable Veil,' 'Length'ned Chain,' and 'Knitted Heart,' " in Hoffman and Albert, eds., *Women in Revolution,* 338–444.

51. *Virginia Gazette* (Dixon and Hunter), 18 March 1775.

52. In nearby Norfolk two enslaved workers were arrested for plotting and swiftly condemned to hang. On 29 April, a special supplement of the *Virginia Gazette* reported that the two bondsmen had

been sentenced to death "for being concerned in a conspiracy to raise an insurrection in that town." *Virginia Gazette* (Dixon and Hunter), Supplement, 29 April 1775; Schwarz, *Twice Condemned,* 184, 187. For a discussion of Virginia events during this month, see Ivor Noel Hume, *1775: Another Part of the Field* (New York, 1966), chap. 4. On continuing unrest in Norfolk and Williamsburg during the summer of 1775, see Sylvia R. Frey, "Between Slavery and Freedom: Virginia Blacks in the American Revolution," *Journal of Southern History* 49 (1983): 377–78.

53. Dunmore to Dartmouth, 1 May 1775, CO5/1373, Public Record Office.

54. "Deposition of Dr. William Pasteur," *Virginia Magazine of History & Biography,* 13 (July 1905): 48–49. Compare "Deposition of John Randolph" in ibid. 15 (October, 1907): 150.

55. *Virginia Gazette* (Pickney), 4 May 1775.

56. Gage to Dartmouth, Boston, 15 May 1775, quoted in Quarles, *Negro in the Revolution,* 21–22; Gage to Barrington, Boston, 12 June 1775, in Howard H. Peckham, ed., *Sources of American Independence: Selected Manuscripts from the Collections of the William L. Clements Library,* 2 vols. (Chicago, 1978) 1:133.

57. Dunmore to Secretary of State, 25 June 1775, CO 5/1353, quoted in Wilson, *Loyal Blacks,* 25.

58. Hume, *1775,* 328ff. Connelly had played an important role in Dunmore's war against the Shawnee Indians the previous autumn, ending with the peace settlement at Camp Charlotte.

59. The items in this paragraph are quoted in Ronald Hoffman, *A Spirit of Dissension: Economics, Politics, and the Revolution in Maryland* (Baltimore, 1973), 147–48. See Pauline Maier, *From Resistance to Revolution: Colonial Radicals and the Development of American Opposition to Britain, 1765–1776* (New York, 1972), 284, where the leader is listed as James Simmons.

60. Evangeline Walker Andrews and Charles M. Andrews, eds., *Janet Schaw, Journal of a Lady of Quality . . .* (New Haven, 1921), 200–201.

61. William L. Saunders et al., eds., *The Colonial Records of North Carolina* (Raleigh, 1886–90), 10:94–95. See Aptheker, *Negro Slave Revolts,* 202–3; Jeffrey J. Crow, "Slave Rebelliousness and Social Conflict in North Carolina, 1775–1802," *William and Mary Quarterly,* 3d series 37(1980): 82–86; and Alan D. Watson, "Impulse toward Independence: Resistance and Rebellion among North Carolina Slaves, 1750–1775," *Journal of Negro History* 63 (1978): 317–28.

62. John R. Alden, "John Stuart Accuses William Bull," *William and Mary Quarterly,* 3d series, 2 (July 1945): 318.

63. Communication by D. D. Wallace, *South Carolina Historical and Genealogical Magazine* 47 (July 1946): 191.

64. Court of General Sessions, Grand Jury Presentments, 21 February 1775, South Carolina Archives, Columbia.

65. Letter of 11 May from James Habersham in Savannah to Robert Keen in London, Georgia Historical Society *Collections* 6 (Savannah, 1904): 243–44. After quoting the 8 May report from Mr. Piercy in Charlestown, the disgruntled Habersham (one of Georgia's largest slaveholders) criticizes David for preaching "temporal" rather than "Spiritual Deliverance" for slaves and arranges his passage (return?) to London. "I must say it's a pity, that any of these People should ever put their feet in England, where they get totally spoiled and ruined both in Body and Soul, through a mistaken kind of compassion because they are black."

66. Alden, "Stuart Accuses Bull," 318.

67. Letters of Josiah Smith, Jr., to James Poyas, 18 May 1775, and to George Appleby, 16 June 1775, as cited in Crow, "Slave Rebelliousness," 84–85n; *South Carolina Gazette*, 29 May 1775.

68. Thomas Hutchinson of St. Bartholomew parish to Council of Safety, 5 July 1775, *Laurens Papers* 10:206–8.

69. BPROT 35:192–93, 196. On the strategic importance of black pilots, see P. H. Wood, *Black Majority*, 204–5; and Quarles, *Negro in the Revolution*, 152. For evidence of discussions regarding the tactical significance of ships in Charlestown Harbor, see B. D. Bargar, "Charles Town Loyalism in 1775; The Secret Reports of Alexander Innes," *South Carolina Historical Magazine* 63 (July 1962): 126–28.

70. BPROT 35:215–16.

71. Ibid. 35:198–99. For further references, see Wood, " 'Taking Care of Business'," pp. 284–87; Robert M. Weir, *Colonial South Carolina—A History* (Millwood, N.Y., 1983), 200–203; Philip D. Morgan, "Black Life in Eighteenth-Century Charleston," *Perspectives in American History,* new series 1 (1984): 212.

72. Charles Francis Adams, ed., *The Works of John Adams . . .* 2 (Boston, 1850): 428. The New Englander explained that, "The negroes have a wonderful art of communicating intelligence among themselves; it will run several hundreds of miles in a week or fortnight."

73. William Cobbett and T. C. Hansard, eds., *Parliamentary History of England from the Earliest Period to 1803,* 36 vols. (London, 1806–20) 18:733.

74. *Virginia Gazette,* 7 October 1775; and *Constitutional Gazette,* 21 October, 1775.

75. *Maryland Gazette,* 9 November 1775.

76. *Morning Chronicle and London Advertiser,* 22 December 1775, quoted in Quarles, *Negro in the Revolution,* 22.

77. Quarles, *Negro in the Revolution,* 23; Hume, *1775,* 389.

78. Francis L. Berkeley, Jr., *Dunmore's Proclamation of Emancipation,* (Charlottesville, Va., 1941), 11–12.

79. For an illustration of both the prejudices of our historical heritage and the linking of these two events, see the stilted turn-of-the-century account of Cuyler Smith, "The American Negro," *Frank Leslie's Popular Monthly* (September 1902).

80. Edmund Pendleton, letter of 27 November 1775, quoted in Quarles, *Negro in the Revolution,* 23. Sylvia R. Frey, "Between Slavery and Freedom," 387, reminds us: "Despite his ambitious plans to organize a black army and to use it to discipline the rebellious Virginians, Dunmore was no champion of emancipation. A slaveowner himself, he persistently invited slave defections without, however, freeing his own slaves or unleashing the black violence feared by the horror-stricken proprietor class—a fact that escaped neither the Patriot press nor Virginia slaves."

81. 30 November 1775, Peter Force, ed., *American Archives . . . A Documentary History of . . . the American Colonies,* 4th series, 6 vols. (Washington, 1837–53) 3:1387–88.

82. For example, Gerald W. Mullin, *Flight and Rebellion: Slave Resistance in Eighteenth-Century Virginia* (New York, 1972), 124, observes candidly, "The royal governor's 'Black Regiment,' little more than a group of fugitives temporarily welded together to perform a desperate holding action, was largely a creation of the planters' imagination and their newspaper press."

83. For an account of the ruthless search-and-destroy mission to prevent their departure, and a similar campaign against blacks at Tybee Island, Georgia, see Peter H. Wood, " 'The Dream Deferred': Black Freedom Struggles on the Eve of White Independence," in Gary Y. Okihiro, ed., *In Resistance: Studies in African, Caribbean and Afro-American History* (Amherst, Mass., 1986), 178–80, 185–87; and Gov. James Wright to Lord Germain, 20 March 1776, Georgia Historical Society *Collections* 3 (Savannah, 1873): 241.

84. *Pennsylvania Evening Post,* 14 December 1775. I am grateful to Steven Rosswurm for this reference.

85. Fitzpatrick, ed., *Washington Writings* 4:161, 172, 186, quoted in Noel Hume, *1775,* 417. For additional reactions, see Frey, "The British and the Black: A New Perspective," *Historian* 38 (1976): 227; and Hoffman, *Spirit of Dissension,* 148.

86. Lund Washington to George Washington, 3 December 1775. Letters of Lund Washington (1767–1790), Mount Vernon Library,

Mount Vernon, Va. A month earlier, on the night of 7 November (the very date that Dunmore signed his proclamation aboard the ship *William* in Norfolk harbor), "a negro man named CHARLES, who is a very shrewd, sensible fellow, and can both read and write," disappeared from the Stafford County plantation of Robert Brent. According to Brent's notice in the *Virginia Gazette,* 16 November 1775: "From many circumstances, there is reason to believe he intends to attempt to get to lord Dunmore; and as I have reason to believe *his design of going off was long premeditated,* and that he has gone off with some accomplice, I am apprehensive he may prove daring and resolute, if endeavoured to be taken. His elopement was from no cause of complaint, or dread of whipping (for he has always been remarkably indulged, indeed too much so) but from *a determined resolution to get liberty,* as he conceived, by flying to lord Dunmore." (Emphasis added.)

87. Richard Bennehan, letter of 15 February 1776 to James Martin at Snow Hill Plantation, Little River, in the Cameron Papers, Southern Historical Collection, University of North Carolina, Chapel Hill.

89. An African-born slave near Georgetown, S.C., recalled intense nighttime meetings to discuss the first rumors of secession and the prospect "dat if dey gwo to war de brack man will be FREE!" "Edward Kirke" [James Robert Gilmore], *Among the Pines; Or, The South in Secession Time* (New York, 1862), 48. Charles Joyner, *Down by the Riverside: A South Carolina Slave Community* (Urbana, Ill., 1984), p. 168, notes that blacks near Georgetown were thrown in jail for singing "We'll soon be free" and "We'll fight for liberty." Also see Leon F. Litwack, *Been in the Storm So Long: The Aftermath of Slavery* (New York, 1979).

89. *Virginia Gazette* (Pickney), 30 November 1775.

90. *Maryland Gazette,* 14 December 1775. This issue carried a report from Williamsburg, dated 2 December, which read: "Since Lord Dunmore's proclamation made its appearance here, it is said he has recruited his army, in the counties of Princess Anne and Norfolk, to the amount of about 2000 men, including his black regiment, which is thought to be a considerable part, with this inscription on their breasts:—'Liberty to slaves.'—However, as the rivers will henceforth be strictly watched, and every possible precaution taken, it is hoped others will be effectually prevented from joining those his lordship has already collected."

91. *Virginia Gazette* (Purdie), 29 March 1776. "It is important that the only time before 1785 that slave courts whose records have survived held a trial of slaves for running away was in March, 1776,

when the oyer and terminer court of Northampton County tried and convicted eleven slaves for running away and for stealing the schooner they used to do so. The judges sentenced four of them to hang and inflicted thirty-nine lashes on each of the rest." Schwarz, *Twice Condemned*, 135.

92. Quoted in Mullin, *Flight and Rebellion*, 132. On 28 June 1776, when nearby Maryland's provincial convention voted for independence, they also approved sending troops to the eastern shore, where poor whites, Negroes, and loyalists were reportedly fostering rebellion against the new leadership. Merrill Jensen, "The American People and the American Revolution," *Journal of American History* 57 (1970): 29–32. A month later in Bucks County, Pennsylvania, a slave named Samson "said he would burn houses of Associators and kill their women and children when they left" to go on active duty. His owner, Jeremiah Dugan, Jr., was obliged to post a bond of £100 for his good behavior. Minutes of Bucks County Committee of Safety, 29 July 1776, *Pennsylvania Archives*, 2d series, 15:368. Three days later Henry Wynkoop requested powder from the local Committee of Safety because numerous whites were "somewhat alarmed with fears about Negroes & disaffected people injuring their families when they are out in the service." Wynkoop letter, 31 July 1776, *Pennsylvania Archives*, 1st series, 4:792. I am indebted to Prof. Steven Rosswurm for these last two citations.

93. Garry Wills, *Inventing America: Jefferson's Declaration of Independence* (Garden City, N.Y., 1978), 71–75.

"I Thought I Should Liberate Myself from the Thraldom of Others"

Apprentices, Masters, and the Revolution

W. J. RORABAUGH

Ebenezer Fox, apprentice to a Boston-area barber, went off to sea on a privateering vessel with the approval of his master. Years later he wrote about his adventures. In this illustration from his book, he and a fellow apprentice are being questioned outside of an inn by townsmen, who assumed they were runaways. From *The Adventures of Ebenezer Fox in the Revolutionary War* (Boston, 1848).

Courtesy Chicago Historical Society.

The American Revolution upset much of the political, social, and economic order of colonial society. Among the many institutions profoundly shaken was apprenticeship in skilled trades. The Revolution disrupted youthful service in two distinct ways. Wartime chaos all but destroyed the staid traditional relationship between master and apprentice, while revolutionary ideology led young Americans to assert themselves in ways that drastically weakened this age-old institution. Although a rising republican ideology did not destroy apprenticeship, new ideas did lead Americans to embrace liberty and look with suspicion upon any institution rooted in the arbitrary exercise of authority. Throughout the last quarter of the eighteenth century apprentices and their masters grappled with the problem of reconciling the ideal of liberty with the restrictions of apprenticeship. The young largely redefined the institution in republican terms, and yet, as we shall see, that new definition contained within it enough contradictions to doom bound service in the nineteenth century even before the emergence of the Industrial Revolution.

Let me begin with a comment on evidence concerning apprentices. In an ideal world the historian would sample from lists of apprentices and then use a rich cache of quantitative and literary data to build theses. In the real world the historian must use scanty information in as creative way as possible. Although lists of indented apprentices would, at first glance, seem to be a starting point, Americans rarely kept such records, and after 1800 many apprentices were never indented. Furthermore, indentures tell us little about the lives, working conditions, behavior, and attitudes—in short, the *mentalité*—of novice craftsmen. So I have turned to literary sources and especially apprentices' diaries, letters, and memoirs. These sources are naturally biased toward literate New England printers and include many men who subsequently became famous. However, as apprentices, these youths were not the important men they later became. Literate apprentices did offer insights into the institution within which they lived and worked, and such insights are ultimately more valuable than the diary of a more typical apprentice who merely noted after each entry "work." What follows, then, is a study using biographical sources to suggest an overall pattern of apprentice life during and after the American Revolution.[1]

Colonial apprentices, subordinate to their masters both in theory and in practice, had more or less fixed and stable roles in society. It is true that Benjamin Franklin, as a last resort, had run away from a bad apprenticeship to his brother, but Franklin retained his faith in the institution by taking numerous apprentices, including his brother's son and a runaway son of an English friend. In Franklin's day a particular master or apprentice might cause trouble, but no one condemned the institution or sought to change either its structure or practices. Yet apprenticeship in colonial America had never been robust. It had been imported from England in a weakened and modified form, and American conditions discouraged its full development. For one thing, the colonies lacked the English craft guilds that barred those without certificates showing completion of apprenticeship from obtaining skilled jobs. For another, as Franklin's own case proved, an American apprentice could easily move from one colony to another and thereby escape legal penalties. The institution's lack of vigor made it peculiarly susceptible to radical change during the American Revolution.[2]

For centuries apprenticeship had given a master craftsman reliable, cheap skilled labor, had provided a youth with the skills that would enable him to work as an adult, and had created a structure of authority within which the master and his apprentice conducted themselves. The institution, above all, operated to maintain authority. Both master and novice signed a legal contract, the indenture, which set forth precise terms under which the youth would live and work. This document expressed the notion of reciprocity inherent in the concept of a bargain between two parties. The master promised both to teach the apprentice a trade and to care for the youth, while the learner promised to serve the craftsman faithfully for a fixed period of time, which could be as long as seven years. The apprentice's first years cost the master money, since the youth could do little valuable work but required food, clothes, and shelter. During later years, the apprentice's unpaid labor gave his master a profit. At the moment of indenture both the master and the apprentice hoped for a future return. While a youth might be tempted to run away after he had learned his trade's fundamentals, social pressure kept him in the shop. A colonial apprentice esteemed his master, deferred to the craftsman's authority, and accepted society's view that the system provided good order.[3]

Although rooted in moral values, apprenticeship was fragile, and its success depended upon political, moral, and economic stability. The master risked a loss if the apprentice failed to perform his duties or ran away, and such failure led the craftsman to seek legal enforcement of the indenture. Similarly, the apprentice risked exploitation by an unscrupulous master who beat the youth, starved him, or failed to teach him a trade, and he also depended upon the law to enforce his rights. While both master and apprentice had recourse to the law, public opinion usually determined how apprenticeship was conducted.

It is instructive to note that John Fitch, trapped into two exploitative apprenticeships in the late colonial period, never went to court. Young Fitch persuaded his first master, who had kept the youth at farm labor in violation of the indenture, to assign him to the master's brother. Fitch's joy was short-lived, however, for this watchmaker kept Fitch busy at repetitive tasks and jealously prevented him from learning the trade. Finally, the desperate Fitch borrowed money from a brother to buy the remainder of his indented time. Contemporaries would have conceded that Fitch had suffered two disastrous apprenticeships, but few would have urged young Fitch to go to court or to run away. The colonists held a master's authority, even when abused, to be nearly absolute. To challenge such authority was to threaten the social order upon which the stability of society was perceived to lie.[4]

Economic stability also helped maintain apprenticeship. Although business cycles, foreign competition, and the vagaries of the market buffeted master craftsmen in the cities, most colonial artisans lived and worked in relatively stable rural areas. A shoemaker, for example, made shoes for his local customers, year in and year out, and he could predict both expenses and income. Rural Americans often passed trades from father to son; the Lane family of New Hampshire tanned leather and made shoes for four generations. When such a master took an apprentice, the artisan could calculate both the value of the apprentice's labor and how much it would cost to clothe, feed, and house the youth. Many masters, like the Lanes, combined crafts with farming. A farmer-craftsman could maintain an apprentice at low cost and probably without cash expenses. In such a stable but static economy, the apprentice also knew that after he had learned his trade, unless he was the master's son, he would have to journey around to find work. To prepare for this ordeal, it was important to learn his trade well.[5]

The American Revolution brought chaos both to the country and to apprenticeship. The economy sagged as the British blockaded and then seized the major seaports, large numbers of farmers and craftsmen entered military service, rival armies clamored for war materiel, and the Continental Congress paid for the patriot cause with inflationary paper currency. The loss of foreign trade hindered craftsmen who depended upon imported raw materials, while creating a boom for those whose products normally had competed with imports. British occupation of Boston, New York, Philadelphia, and Charleston for much of the war cut those cities off from their hinterlands. While backcountry residents clamored for goods unavailable through normal trading channels, craftsmen in the cities turned to supplying the British troops stationed there. For example, the New York sail maker James Leonard did a fine business outfitting Tory privateers and supplying bread bags to the British commissary. As Leonard's business grew, so did the number of his apprentices. Both Stephen Allen and his brother William worked for Leonard, but neither was indented, because the war had created uncertainty, and Leonard knew that his British ties discouraged running away more than any indenture. An apprentice who ran away from Leonard, if caught, would be impressed into the British Navy. None of Leonard's boys tried to run away.[6]

Some details about the Allen brothers are worthwhile, because their lives were typical—and Spartan. The two youths, along with another apprentice, slept at Leonard's sail loft. They took meals in the cellar at the master's house, always breakfasting on cocoa and bread and usually dining on a stew made of potatoes, onions, and coarse beef. The stew was cooked in a large pot and reheated until it was consumed. "I have known a single cooking last for a week," recalled Stephen Allen, "which by continued warming up became bitter, being burnt over the fire and sour from age and fermentation. No complaints were made however, at least none within the hearing of the family, except by looks and gestures and they were little minded or attended to by any one." No one took an apprentice's grumblings seriously, and if the complaints were serious, then the apprentice risked offending the master's dignity and position. For supper these apprentices always ate two slices of the ends of the baker's bread smeared with butter, either in a shed in the backyard, where the family's chickens were roasted, or as they walked down the street from the master's house to the sail loft. After supper the youths passed an hour or two in idle conversation before retiring.[7]

Leonard clothed his apprentices by outfitting them annually at a 'slop shop,' which sold cheap secondhand clothes. Over these clothes in winter the youths wore canvas trousers; in summer, wool trousers. Clean check shirts were issued once each week. In winter the master provided wool stockings. The apprentices bought their own hats and neckerchiefs. Leonard was supposed to supply shoes, but he did so only when the old shoes had totally disintegrated, and the boys often had bare feet. One time Stephen's mother complained to Leonard about her sons' clothes, and the apprentices were sent to a tailor to get new clothes. It was the only time Leonard provided new clothes.[8]

Several encounters with the British military indicate the dangerous and uncertain situation within which the Allen brothers lived and worked. Once Stephen and another apprentice went into the woods to gather berries and suddenly found themselves surrounded by British soldiers. The officer in charge said, "Here boys is a couple of rebels. Let's hang them up on this tree." The soldiers taunted and scared the two apprentices, and then laughingly escorted both boys home. On another occasion Stephen, along with several apprentices and journeymen from Leonard's loft, had sailed from Manhattan to Coney Island, where they were captured by Hessian soldiers who mistook these artisans for the ragtag American military. After a great deal of difficulty in finding a bilingual officer, the sail makers were finally released, but not before the Hessians had eaten the group's picnic provisions.[9]

British press-gangs constantly harassed Leonard's apprentices because they wore the seaman's costume of naval canvas trousers and a short jacket. Frequently the press men seized one or another of the youths and held him overnight, but the victim was always released in the morning, when Leonard appeared to claim his apprentice for the Tory sail loft. On one occasion a member of a press-gang had chased Stephen into his mother's bedroom, but the two Allens clung to each other so tightly that the press man realized he would have to take both of them and left. The naval gangs turned Stephen and his brother into staunch patriots, and when the British evacuated New York at the end of the war, both remained behind when Leonard sailed for Nova Scotia. Stephen Allen, age fifteen, was "turned loose upon the world to seek [his] fortune, with nothing to commence but a good constitution, and a scanty wardrobe."[10]

Patriotic fervor also disrupted apprenticeship. In 1775 Peter Edes was a nineteen-year-old apprentice to his father, the publisher of the *Boston Gazette*. Although Benjamin Edes was a staunch patriot, he prudently kept quiet so as not to attract the attention of the British authorities. Peter, on the other hand, was youthfully rash and boasted to friends that, if war came, the Americans would defeat the British troops. Although the British learned of Peter's boasts, they ignored the boy, who might have remained safely in his father's shop. Instead, Peter raced out to watch the battle of Bunker Hill and made the mistake of standing within the British lines on Copp's Hill while shouting encouragement to the Americans. Unfortunately for young Edes, a British officer recognized him, and two days later British troops burst into the family printing office, seized the apprentice, and hauled him to jail. Peter was charged with concealing firearms in the house, a capital offense. Some British officers wanted him tried by a military court and shot as a rebel, but the British civil authorities, seeking to win popular support, did not want the son of a newspaper publisher for a martyr and resisted holding a military trial. Detained for months while his fate remained in doubt, Peter became a hostage; the British authorities used his confinement to put pressure on the *Boston Gazette*. In the end he was released.[11]

Many apprentices saw in the war a chance both to attain glory and to prove manhood. In 1776 news of the Declaration of Independence had been read to the Worcester, Massachusetts, populace by the patriot printer Isaiah Thomas, who not long before had fled with his press from Boston to Worcester in the middle of the night. A crowd had gathered to hear the Declaration, and they soon adjourned to the local tavern to celebrate. Independence had stirred deep feelings often manifested as exhilaration masking fear of the unknown. It was those feelings as much as the fact of independence that engaged the celebrants inside the Worcester tavern. They got drunk. And in the exhilaration, the pride, and the joy mixed with apprehension, a goodly number became so enthralled that they enlisted in the Continental Army.

Among the enlistees was Thomas's apprentice, Ben Russell. The next morning, when Thomas learned what had happened, he set out to have the enlistment revoked. Thomas could not keep his shop open without Russell, and Russell's father, an old friend, had brought his son to Thomas explicitly to keep the boy away from the army and the war. The master believed that he must carry out the father's wishes and, indeed, stand in a fatherly relation to the apprentice. When Thomas and Russell appeared before the local Justice of the Peace, the master looked for an argument certain to win in court. Although an apprentice could not enlist without his master's consent, Thomas knew that the desperate condition of the American military might persuade the judge to overlook that provision and let the zealous young Russell enter the army. Then Thomas discovered that Russell's enlistment was void because the youth was under the age of sixteen. After Thomas presented this evidence to the court, the judge called Russell to the stand and asked the boy his age. Although Russell did not wish to commit perjury, he wanted to join the army, so he swore that he did not know his own age, since he had no recollection of his birth. The judge found this remark more clever than convincing and remanded Russell to Thomas's custody.[12]

Russell, however, remained restless and discontented. He watched as a wartime boom, fueled by plentiful paper money, led to labor shortages. Friends who were journeymen demanded and received high wages, while Russell saw himself perform the same labor just for room and board. Then, one day in 1780, Thomas learned that he had been drafted. Russell's master became despondent, because he had a wife and seven children to support, and he feared losing his business if he left town to serve in the army. Unable to afford a substitute, the printer despaired, until young Russell offered to go in his master's stead without compensation. Russell served in the army only a few months and never saw a battle. After Russell's unit was disbanded, he returned to Worcester and demanded that Thomas yield up the indentures, since the apprentice had risked his life in the war on Thomas's behalf. Although the master was reluctant to give up his valuable apprentice, Thomas recognized that Russell's claims, which might not be valid in a court of law, were overwhelming in the court of public opinion. Twenty-year-old Russell became a journeyman and, after a short time, used savings from his high wages to set up his own printing shop in Boston. Although the war had disrupted Russell's life, he had benefited.[13]

On the other hand, not everyone had gained. John Bosson, a Boston barber and wig maker, found that after the British troops had departed, the population of the town was so small that it would not support his usual trade. Yet Bosson was stuck with two apprentices, who ate as much as ever. In 1779 the Massachusetts militia drafted Bosson for duty in New York. He became distressed, since he could not afford to hire a substitute, and he paced the shop, sharpening razors that were already sharp. Finally, he glared at his two apprentices and said, "Hard times—don't need two apprentices any more than a toad needs a tail." Then he added, by a way of a dare, "If either of you had the spunk of a louse, you would offer to go for me." Bosson then left the shop. The two apprentices discussed the situation, and the older one, who feared being coerced by Bosson into the militia, encouraged Ebenezer Fox, who had not yet turned sixteen, to become Bosson's substitute. The youth had found the work in the shop boring, and the spirit of adventure called. So Ebenezer volunteered, a relieved Bosson generously outfitted his apprentice with clothes and arms, and young Fox made his debut with the Boston militia in a parade on the Common. After two months' service in New York, Fox returned to Boston with sore feet and swore that he would never be a substitute again.[14]

Bosson's business did not improve, and Fox became restless. The youth stood in the street and heard a naval recruiter sing:

> All you that have bad masters,
> And cannot get your due;
> Come, come, my brave boys,
> And join with our ship's crew.

When Fox asked Bosson for permission to quit the shop and join a privateer, the master consented. However, he drove a hard bargain.

The youth had to promise to give half of his sea wages and half of any prize money he earned to his master. After a series of adventures Fox did return to Boston and displayed his $80 of prize money, which Bosson, contrary to their agreement, claimed and seized as a master's lawful property. The paper currency, however, turned out to be worthless.[15]

Bounties promised to soldiers enticed many youths out of apprenticeship and into military service. To a young man who had already learned his trade but perhaps lacked the tools or money to set up his own shop, a bounty promised postwar success in return for military service that might prove no more onerous than the apprentice's remaining service to his master. The expectation of profit certainly had lured Ebenezer Fox into privateering. His master's insistence upon half his naval earnings was typical, and such exploitation of apprentices became so common that the Continental Congress finally outlawed the practice. Whether apprentices could be drafted, and if so, under what conditions, produced controversy throughout the war. The Congress, facing a chronic shortage of both money and soldiers, refused either to compensate masters whose apprentices enlisted or to prohibit such enrollments. These policies unintentionally undermined apprenticeship, since masters resisted taking apprentices who might join the army, and apprentices concluded that patriotic duty overrode legal contracts.[16]

The states vacillated in their policies, too. Those states that found it difficult to meet military quotas allowed apprentices to volunteer. Rhode Island, for example, gave apprentice enlistees the right to keep large bounties but insisted that masters were entitled to half the soldiers' modest pay. Amid the chaos of the war, law was less important than actual practice. Angry masters watched as their charges, having supped at the masters' tables while ignorant and shiftless boys, went to war as soon as they were old enough and large enough to carry muskets.[17]

Irate masters, vacillating governments, tempting bounties, and the fortunes and misfortunes of war all played a role in disrupting apprenticeship. The chaos of war created both opportunity and adversity that led some apprentices to early success and others to premature death. Like a lottery, the war dished up winners and losers willy-nilly. Some apprentices begged and cajoled their masters for permission to enlist, signed up for lucrative bounties, and died of camp fever with their new riches unspent. Other apprentices stayed home, worked, married their masters' daughters, inherited shops, and prospered. Still others enlisted, survived the war, and returned home to take up the old trades again, sometimes with success, sometimes without. As the lives of Stephen Allen, Peter Edes, Benjamin Russell, and Ebenezer Fox suggest, apprentice experiences during the Revolution were varied, yet the variety expresses a common theme of wartime upheaval, uncertainty, and chaos. The predictability upon which the institution of apprenticeship had been based was swept away by circumstances and conditions that no one could have foreseen.

In the postwar years, as the polity stabilized with the adoption of the Constitution, as the economy gradually improved after 1790, and as society regained some sense of order and balance, the institution of apprenticeship might have been expected to regain its prewar stability. It did not. Although many reasons, including economic ones, prevented the institution's reestablishment on a stable basis, one of the most important was the ideology of the American Revolution and especially, as we shall see, its effect upon the young.

The Revolution's most profound effect upon apprenticeship was ideological. As early as 1776, American apprentices had been quick to compare themselves to the colonists, and their masters to King George III. Like Abigail Adams the apprentices even threatened to make a revolution of their own. This revolutionary ideology is expressed most vividly in the recollections of Ebenezer Fox, who wrote:

> I, and other boys situated similarly to myself, thought we had wrongs to be redressed; rights to be maintained; and, as no one appeared disposed to act the part of a redresser, it was our duty and our privilege to assert our own rights. We made a direct application of the doctrines we daily heard, in relation to the oppression of the mother country, to our own circumstances; and thought that we were more oppressed than our fathers were. I thought that I was doing myself great injustice by remaining in bondage, when I ought to go free; and that the time was come, when I should liberate myself from the thraldom of others, and set up a government of my own; or, in other words, do what was right in the sight of my own eyes.[18]

Apprentices acquired their revolutionary ideology from the masters and journeymen with whom they lived and worked. Craftsmen, especially in the cities, formed an important core of support for the Revolution and its ideology. Artisan restlessness, which may have been rooted in poor economic conditions that threatened both the status and well-being of mechanics, was expressed through vigorous participation in politics, such as the Sons of Liberty, in political action, such as the Boston Tea Party, and in the war itself. The Revolution produced artisan heroes like Roger Sherman, a onetime farmer-shoemaker; Paul Revere, silversmith; Gen. Henry Knox, bookseller; and Gen. Nathanael Greene, blacksmith. These men rose from artisan origins into the ranks of a political and military elite long dominated by men from mercantile, planter, or professional backgrounds. Their rise did not mean that craftsmen would govern the new country, but it did mean that such men could help govern it. Mechanics envisioned more direct, personal political participation for themselves. To assert such political rights in a society in which authority and subordination had prevailed was to demand essential equality. As craftsmen developed a republican ideology based on liberty and equality, apprentices naturally followed their masters. And yet apprentices could clearly see that masters, while seeking to elevate mechanics in society, did not intend to elevate apprentices. Youths caught up in the chaos of the war were not likely to let this contradiction pass without notice.[19]

Revolutionary ideals cannot be viewed as merely the thoughts of urban youths, for the new ideals even reached into the conservative religious community of the Moravians at Salem, North Carolina. "Members are beginning to feel the spirit of freedom in the land," noted the Salem church authorities, "and to think that as soon as the children attain their majority they are at liberty to do as they please. . . ." There was a trace of alarm in this remark. The community's leaders had not minded when a local man from outside the church had placed his son as an apprentice to the Moravians to save the boy from conscription; that act, after all, was good for business. But in 1778 the Moravian apprentices, jealous of the high wages paid to journeymen, and infected with the new revolutionary ideology, had actually dared to invoke the notion of liberty and strike for wages. Church authorities were terrified.[20]

Revolutionary ideology must be understood as an attack upon traditional authority. To be freed from the psychological bonds that had tied the colonists both to the mother country and to the father figure of King George III, Americans now asserted that they were no longer children. This idea was expressed brilliantly in Thomas Paine's *Common Sense* and more subtly, but with equal effect, in the Declaration of Independence's indictment of the king as the bad father against whom sons might properly rebel. Yet the revolutionists knew that the psychic bonds that had tied America to Great Britain had to be replaced with new ideas. Americans were no longer the sons of a king but the Sons of Liberty. The idea of liberty became a main theme in American life. Boston had its Liberty Tree, all across the land people erected liberty poles in public places, and the Declaration proclaimed, "Life, Liberty, and the Pursuit of Happiness." Of the Declaration's three concepts, liberty was the one most closely identified with independence from Great Britain, the one most easily imagined as a pure ideal, and the most radical. Liberty, at least in some quarters, did not mean merely political independence but the positive freedom for Americans to act as they pleased. It was this second kind of liberty, the liberty of the person rather than of the state, that posed a potential threat to the social order, since the personal pursuit of liberty could easily degenerate into an attack upon authority and a justification for freewheeling vice.[21]

Considerable evidence suggests that this problem was not just theoretical. After the war many conservatives, especially ministers, concluded that vice had triumphed among the young, who had been most affected by the war and revolutionary ideals. Conservatives denounced the shift in popular values. Rev. Samuel Mather blamed the absence of authority for leading young people "to speak and act in a loose, unrestrained, and licentious manner. . . ." Rev. Jeremy Belknap complained, "How melancholy to think that a great part of the rising generation is likely to be ignorant & unprincipled." He gloomily concluded, "Too many already go by no other rule than their own wills." The self had triumphed, as the Revolution had undermined all authority, including the authority within the family known as family government. "Family devotion, and parental instruction and discipline," said Rev. Nathanael Emmons, "are very generally neglected and despised." The ministers urged parents and masters to reassert authority over children, servants, and apprentices.[22]

The Revolution had eroded authority based on distinctions of rank, position, or status. Because such authority clashed with both liberty and equality, Americans now distrusted any kind of authority rooted in tradition. The Virginia minister Rev. Devereux Jarrett elaborated upon this reaction against authority. "In our high *republican times,*" he wrote sarcastically, "there is more *levelling* than ought to be, consistent with good government. I have as little notion of oppression and tyranny as any man, but a due subordination is essentially requisite in every government." Older conservatives, almost frightened by revolutionary ideals, stressed "subordination to just and prudent regulations," the need for conducting oneself in the "proper spheres," or that society was "a chain of many links." They emphasized not decorum, manners, or propriety but the need to maintain hierarchical authority. An old-fashioned advice book declared, "It pleases divine Providence to dispose of persons into various stations and relations in this world." Revolutionists rejected that idea. Or as one foreign visitor put it, the "loss of subordination in society" caused youths to "assume the airs of full-grown coxcombs." As Americans, and especially master craftsmen, generally embraced republican ideology, masters still sought to control apprentices, but maintaining such subordination was unlikely in a society in which artisans held liberty to be a paramount value.[23]

Both the decline of authority and fear of chaos had led many Americans to define liberty not as the pursuit of personal will but as the freedom to act responsibly for oneself within society's common mores. Liberty, said Rev. Moses Hemmenway, "consists in a person's being allowed to hold, use and enjoy all his faculties, advantages, and rights, according to his own judgment and pleasure, in such ways as are consistent with the rights of others, and the duty we owe to our maker and our fellow creatures." The key word in this formulation is "duty," which acts to restrain liberty, and conservatives increasingly portrayed duty as a counterweight to liberty necessary for the good of society. Americans, however, found duty less appealing than liberty. Before the war, noted David Daggett, ministers had dominated New England society, and aristocracy had curbed liberty. But the Revolution had weakened the clergy's influence, and the ideal of liberty had grown more powerful after political independence. "We flattered ourselves," he said, "that independence was liberty—was affluence—was government—was every thing. . . ." That kind of euphoria made it difficult to restrict liberty, and swollen liberty in all its self-serving variations threatened all forms of authority. It seemed doubtful that apprenticeship could survive in a "world turned upside down."[24]

Since the institution had rested so heavily upon the apprentice's willing acceptance of the master's just authority, the destruction of the polity's symbolic familial authority had grave implications for apprenticeship. A master who simply stood on tradition, like Robert Aitken of Philadelphia, risked being misunderstood and defied. In 1783 Rev. Jeremy Belknap had sent his fourteen-year-old son Joseph from Dover, New Hampshire, to Philadelphia to be an apprentice in Aitken's printing office. Although Aitken, a Scots immigrant, had a high reputation for technical proficiency, the minister probably placed his son with Aitken because he was printing a book for Belknap. Neither father nor son had met Aitken, and Belknap charged a friend, Ebenezer Hazard, with keeping "the watchful eye of a father" on the boy. There was trouble almost from the beginning. The youth from New Hampshire must have impressed Aitken as unsophisticated, bumpkinish, and, frankly, spoiled. Jo, for his part, did not cotton to the barbed accusations, sarcasms, and blue words that sprang from the mouth of the stiff and overbearing Mr. Aitken. Young Belknap was not prepared to subordinate himself to a sour Scot.[25]

By 1787 Rev. Belknap recognized that this apprenticeship had

failed. "I find the breach is grown so wide," he wrote, "that they *both*
desire a separation. A., by *his own* account, has made a very free use
of 'the fist' and the 'knotted cord,' both very bad instruments of reformation in the hands of a perfervid Caledonian." The minister described one incident in which his son had skipped Sunday afternoon
and evening religious services. Aitken viewed this omission as doubly
serious because it mixed defiance of the master's authority with contempt for religion, but the youth explained to his father that he could
not attend services because of a black eye that his master had given
him at dinner that day. The master accused his apprentice of neglect-
ing business and keeping the company of "*bad* boys." Whatever the
truth of that charge, there is no doubt that the streets of Philadelphia could be remarkably fascinating. The minister was troubled by
his son's claim that only one of Aitken's six apprentices had ever
served out his time, and that that one bore the "marks of the old
man's cruelty." This dispute may have been nothing more than a
clash between a rigid master and a lazy apprentice, but one senses
that Aitken, cast in the traditional mold, at least in part badgered
young Belknap because of the youth's boldness. Was not this insolence encouraged if not created by the republican ideology in the air?
After the minister and the master called in arbitrators, who agreed
that there was "no prospect of an hearty reconciliation," the indentures were cancelled.[26]

The father recognized the danger: the apprentice had triumphed
over his master. This was a bad precedent, for it gave eighteen-year-
old Jo unrealistic expectations about maneuvering himself through
the ordinary difficulties of life. Rev. Belknap next indented his son to
William Mycall of Newburyport, Massachusetts. Before agreeing to
the indentures, his father satisfied himself that Mycall was a republican. The spirited apprentice continued to cause trouble. One morning Jo and Mycall's other two apprentices were scolded for wasting
time in the cellar. The youths prudently said little to their master,
but half an hour later, while breakfasting among themselves, they reflected upon their ill treatment. The oldest boasted, "It is only one
year more I have got to live in this situation." The youngest added
that "though he had more than one, yet *he* had only two years to stay
and that was not quite so much as seven which he once had." Jo
Belknap noted that he had to serve only fifteen more months. At this
point Mycall, who had eavesdropped on the conversation, flew into
the room in a rage. Belknap reported that his master resembled "a
mad boar." Mycall said that "he did not wish any body to live with
him who was not contented" and that all three might go just as soon
as they pleased. Note the contrast with Aitken. Mycall did not box

ears or threaten to beat the apprentices. In Mycall's world a master did not have the right to control his apprentices absolutely, but if a master and apprentice had different views, then the apprenticeship should be dissolved. When the youths indicated that they could do better for themselves elsewhere, Mycall invited them to tear up their indentures. In the end, none of the apprentices left.[27]

Although Joseph Belknap continued to urge his father to cancel the apprenticeship, the Rev. Belknap declined to interfere. As the son's term of service drew to a close, he suspected that he was being harassed by Mycall for a devious purpose. Under the terms of Belknap's indenture, he was to be paid a substantial sum of cash (his 'freedom dues') at the end of his service, but if Mycall could provoke the apprentice into running away, the payment would be forfeited. The apprentice, however, wondered if it would not be better just to leave the apprenticeship, since he believed the master would not pay the freedom dues. The minister counseled, "Your time with Mycall is indeed short & I hope you will perform your duty with *fidelity* to the last (if you cannot without reluctance) for a faithful discharge of duty on your part is the foundation on which you may expect & *demand* a fulfillment of the contract on his part. —It is a matter of no consequence what his *intentions* are, for if he cannot *prove* that you have forfeited your right to the conditions on which he took you, it will not be in his power to withold payment—Therefore you have only to look at your own conduct & if that be such as will justify you before impartial judges you have nothing to fear." The minister's advice to his son was rooted in his belief in law and contract, in his faith in Mycall as a sound republican, and in the fear that if Joseph Belknap were allowed to leave a second apprenticeship without completing it, that the youth might slip from republican virtue into self-indulging licentiousness.[28]

Some conflict between masters and apprentices in the years after the Revolution resulted from the fact that artisans had not imbibed revolutionary ideology in exactly the same way as had their charges. The older generation, having grown up in an earlier time with different values, remained fearful of the effect of the new attitudes on the character development of the youth. This point is illustrated by an incident in 1792 that took place in the printing shop of Thomas Adams, publisher of the Boston *Independent Chronicle*. Adams's four apprentices liked their master but, in the words of one of them, found Mrs. Adams "not very sweet composed." The youths, who boarded with the master, found the food wretched. John Prentiss recalled, "Our breakfast was usually a bowl of *thin* chocolate, with brown bread. With often a poor cook, the bread was *doughy* and sometimes too old. On one occasion we talked *out loud loud* about it, and this brought forward the mistress of the house, indignant at our expressed [dis]satisfaction. The other boys did not defend, but I, the youngest took a coarse piece of our bread and brake it in her presence, making the mouldy strings very visible, and she said no more!" It is instructive to compare Prentiss's boldness with the meekness of the poorly fed Allen brothers during the Revolution. The encounter with Mrs. Adams, however, did not end the moldy bread. Sometime later, after the apprentices had been given another bad half loaf, Bill Cowan humiliated the Adamses by tossing the loaf over a high fence into a neighbor's yard. Unfortunately for the apprentice, someone in the Adams house watching from an upper window had seen the act, and the neighbor was asked to send the bread home. Adams considered the incident a high misdemeanor, and he called in each of his apprentices in turn for an interview. Cowan so justified his conduct without apology that he either left of his own account or was dismissed. The other apprentices were allowed to remain. Had Cowan's attempted self-defense overstepped the bounds of propriety? The apprentices saw Cowan's justification of his conduct as that of a youth asserting his rights, but the master considered the matter as an offensive defiance of authority.[29]

During the economic depression of the 1780s apprentices had little reason to run away to join the ranks of the unemployed, but the economic recovery of the 1790s encouraged apprentices to improve their fortunes either by overturning their indentures in court or by running away to pass themselves off as journeymen. During the 1790s the number of court cases involving apprentices increased dramatically, state legislation against runaways proliferated, and the number of advertisements of runaways in the newspapers soared. In addition, the adoption of the new Constitution was seen as a way to create a national framework for curbing the excesses of youth. Simeon Baldwin advocated the Constitution's ratification "to lop off the libertinism of juvenile independence." During the 1790s masters created artisan organizations that, at least in part, were designed to curtail runaways. The erosion of the master's traditional authority and the republican concept of the need for personal responsibility combined to push apprentices toward acting, as Adam Smith would have put it, in their own perceived self-interest, rather than continuing in a disadvantageous contractual relationship. The contrast with the colonial apprentice John Fitch is instructive. That meek youth had been counseled to accept, and had in fact accepted, an unfair situation. By the 1790s one looks in vain for a similar case, as apprentices often are urged to act, and do act, to promote their own interests.[30]

The pursuit of self-interest brought an aggressive style. When fourteen-year-old Millard Fillmore, an apprentice cloth dresser, found himself constantly chopping wood, he rebelled. The youth boldly told his master that he had not come to the shop merely to chop wood and added that he was not disposed to submit. The master insisted upon obedience to his orders. Millard bridled, "Yes, if they are right; otherwise I will not; and I have submitted to this injustice long enough." The master said, "I will chastise you for your disobedience." As the master stepped closer, the apprentice raised his axe and said, "You will not chastise me. If you approach me I will split you down." The master wisely walked away.[31]

Another sturdy young republican was James Horton, an apprentice machinist to the textile mill pioneer Samuel Slater. In 1797 Horton ran away from Slater, returned, got a local girl pregnant, and then ran away again. In 1799 Slater's partners, Almy and Brown, tried to get young Horton to return by advising the youth's relatives that they would help him settle his "difficulty" concerning the pregnant girl. They also promised the youth a place in the business upon completion of the apprenticeship. Horton offered an insolent reply. "If Mr. Slater had tought me to work . . . all the different branches I should have ben with you now," he wrote, "but instead . . . he ceepe me always at one thing and I might have stade there until this time and never new nothing. I don't think it probable that I shall return . . . for the business I follow now I think is much more bennefisheal to my interest Except you wanted to give me a Thousand Dollars a year then—I expect I might come and resume my former business. Concerning the Difficulty with Mis Cole that is for me and them to Settle. . . ."[32]

Saucy boys were prepared to make their own way in the world. Benjamin Franklin's life offered a model, and the popularity of Franklin's autobiography encouraged apprentices to ponder its lessons. Parts of the autobiography were published in American magazines in 1790. Between 1794 and 1799 the autobiography went through seven American editions and was included in another ten editions of Franklin's works. Franklin's story could be read on two levels. As a self-proclaimed guide to morals, it was the sort of book that a master might give to his apprentice for guidance, but as a biography, the book left the apprentice with a completely different view about Franklin and his worldly success. Although Franklin had described his running away from the apprenticeship with his brother as one of his life's major errors, no reader of the autobiography could be convinced that this was so. Running away, in fact, had been Franklin's first step on his path to fortune, fame, and success. It may have been difficult

for an apprentice to imagine himself to be another Franklin, but it
was not so difficult to imagine that one could profit from leaving a
confined and constricted situation to explore the world by striking
out on one's own. After E. S. Thomas had grown disenchanted with
his Uncle Isaiah's printing business in Worcester and Boston, the
youth made his way to Charleston to seek his fortune. On the long
sea voyage along the Atlantic coast young Thomas carefully read
Franklin's autobiography.[33]

As apprentices became more defiant and unruly, and as runaways
apparently increased, masters responded by calling for new laws to
enforce the traditional contract laid out in the indentures. Between
1783 and 1799 an unprecedented twelve states enacted, reaffirmed,
or modified statutes concerning apprenticeship. The only states that
did not—North Carolina, Georgia, Tennessee, and Vermont—were
overwhelmingly rural. The new state laws codified practices inherited from the English common law, modified those practices in the
light of post-revolutionary American experience, and dealt with
problems that first arose during the economic boom of the 1790s. One
way in which most of these laws—Virginia was a glaring exception—
bowed to republican ideology was in breaking with English precedent
to prohibit a youth from being indented as a craft apprentice past the
age of twenty-one. At that age all males, except slaves, children born
to slaves under certain conditions, or indentured servants imported
under contract, were to be free to pursue whatever business they
wanted. Although Vermont passed no legislation, the Green Mountain state also expressed this ideal of freedom for all adult males in
its radical 1777 constitution.

The laws also specified more clearly the conditions under which an
apprentice might bring charges against a master for cruelty or neglect, and how such a suit was to be handled. The greater ease with
which an apprentice could lodge a complaint against his master sig-
naled the erosion of the master's authority. The laws, however, concentrated on the problem of runaways. Most states established new,
efficient procedures for the return of such apprentices, and several
states imposed stiff fines for anyone enticing an apprentice to run
away or for harboring a runaway. In New York a runaway who was
caught was required to serve double the time lost, while in New Jersey the master of an absconding apprentice could sue the person any-
time within six years of the runaway's attaining twenty-one. Such
provisions were a sign of a growing social problem related to the decline of the master's authority. There is, however, no evidence that
these penalties were assessed very often, and most apprentices knew
that leaving the state in which they had been indented made them

safe from prosecution.[34]

Court cases from the 1790s, as illustrated by the Philadelphia Mayor's Court, show little sympathy for apprentices. A youth who sought release from his indentures by charging that he had been bruised by his master's fist was remanded to the master's custody. So were two apprentices who complained that they had not been taught their trade. Another apprentice seeking release stated that for three years his master, a hatter, had been too poor to buy any fur to make hats and instead had spent the time fishing. "Perhaps one week he will get as much fur as will keep me in work for that week," said the apprentice, "and then I must be idle five or six." The court declined to revoke the indentures, unless this apprentice could find a new master.[35]

Four other apprentices offered graphic testimony of neglect and abuse. Their master provided poor food, insufficient winter clothes, and bedding composed of "three worn out blankets" and "two old straw beds in an open room on the floor, the straw of which has not been shifted since they were his apprentices." Although the master had promised to teach them to build a spinning wheel, this seemed unlikely, since the master had never made one and lacked the tools to do so. Nor did these apprentices believe that they would receive freedom dues, since "their master has been for some time confined in gaol." Even in this case the court declined to order an immediate revocation of the indentures and merely took the case under advisement until the court's next meeting.[36]

During the prosperous 1790s, when masters were desperate to keep apprentices, the courts routinely declined to overturn indentures except in the most outrageous cases. After 1800, however, the courts' sympathies shifted away from masters toward apprentices. In 1803, for example, one apprentice drove his master to such exasperation that the master finally sent a note to the youth's legal guardian. "I was in hopes you would continue to keep him, when he come home," wrote the master, "but I tell you plainly, that I do not intend to keep him no longer. If you will come and take him away, very well; but if not, I will turn him out o' doors very soon; for I will not have so saucy a boy in my house." But when the guardian tried to remove the boy, the master objected. The youth departed anyway, and the master then sued the guardian for enticing the apprentice. The Connecticut appeals court ruled against the master because of the master's letter, which the court saw as an invitation to the guardian to remove the apprentice.[37]

In Massachusetts the master of an apprentice who had run away in 1806 sued the apprentice's guardian, who argued that his consent to the indenture had been worded in such a way that he did not guarantee the apprentice's good behavior. The master's attorney warned that if this position were upheld, "every apprentice in the commonwealth, as soon as he has become master of the trade which he is to learn, may leave his master's service, and the master is without remedy." Despite this warning, the Massachusetts appeals court sided with the guardian. In 1811 the same court held that a master could not sell an apprentice's services to another artisan. Such an assignment, declared the judge, gave the master "monstrous" authority. Given the frequency with which Americans entered and left business, the inability to assign an indenture to a successor had significant consequences. What gave the courts the greatest difficulty was the conflict between the new apprentice statutes and the common-law principle of a father's right to the services of his minor child. A father could hire out his underage son as a laborer and pocket the money, but the apprentice statutes generally provided that any consideration paid when a father indented his son as an apprentice had to be paid to the youth. The courts tried to strike a balance, and as they did so, they became inundated with new cases. The possibility of court revocation of indentures encouraged apprentice suits, while the same fact led masters to avoid indentures.[38]

The new century brought other changes. For one thing, after 1810 the use of indentures declined markedly. For example, in largely rural Frederick County, Maryland, from the 1790s to 1810 about one-fifth of all white males aged fifteen through twenty had been indented; by 1820 the proportion had fallen to one-tenth. The legally enforceable contract became the first casualty of the new republican age, and although apprenticeship continued into the 1820s, it was an institution lacking the solemnity of a contract, the guarantee of law, or the moral weight of the master's authority that had prevailed for centuries. Another change was the disappearance of the *Conductor Generalis,* a legal guide for justices of the peace first published in the colonies in 1711. Generations of justices, who heard most apprentice disputes, had used this book for guidance, and the last American edition was published in 1801. Also disappearing was *A Present for an Apprentice,* a mid-eighteenth-century advice book written by a lord mayor of London. Between 1747 and 1804 this volume, which stressed the master's authority, went through eight American editions; it then lost its appeal. In 1822 the conservative Quakers who ran the Philadelphia Apprentices Library published the last edition. While this volume faded into obscurity, Benjamin Franklin's autobiography, with a distinctly more modern appeal, continued to attract an apprentice audience.[39]

The master had to learn to cultivate his apprentice on a republican basis. If "all men [were] created equal," that did not mean that the apprentice was equal to his master, since the master was older, richer, and more knowledgeable, even if not wiser. But it did mean that the apprentice expected that upon completion of his service he would be treated with respect based upon republican equality. Perhaps the new attitude had its most profound effect upon the way in which a master conducted everyday business. If a master merely asserted his authority and commanded his apprentice on the old basis that the master's word was law, he faced the kind of rebellion that had plagued Robert Aitken. Instead, the master had to treat the apprentice with respect, the way Joseph Cushing, publisher of the Amherst *Farmer's Cabinet,* treated Isaac Hill. Never indented, this apprentice always accepted his master's "reasonable demands" and stayed on until he turned twenty-one. After Hill had acquired his own newspaper, the Concord *American Patriot,* he followed Cushing's policy toward his own apprentices.[40]

Although Hill treated his charges with respect, he still exhibited paternalism, and paternalism clashed with the rising spirit of liberty. Since an apprentice could not attain equality, he emphasized liberty. Liberty became a rallying word to attack not only a master's abuse of his apprentices but the very nature of the institution itself: the master was in some sense expected to control the apprentice, to curb the youth's liberty. Certainly William Mycall as well as Robert Aitken had considered such responsibility for young Joseph Belknap to be a part of their duty. Traditionally, the master's moral authority had been so great that he had dictated not only the work habits of his apprentice but also the youth's life-style: where he lived, what he ate, when he rose and went to bed, how he dressed, when and where he worshipped, and with whom he associated during his leisure hours. Yet much of this regulation had been beyond the strict legal bargain contained in the indentures. The contract had spoken nobly but nebulously of the master's authority over the apprentice's morals; it had spoken more concretely about the education and training of the apprentice and the work that the youth was to perform. The master's fatherly role was open to interpretation and to questioning, and even if a generous master, such as Isaac Hill, asserted his fatherly concern, there was no guarantee that the apprentice would accept that concern.

The republican apprentice subverted the arrangement in an insidious way. He knew that the legal contract left much vague or unmentioned, and he knew that the master's real interest in him was in his labor and not in his person. And so the apprentice came to strike a new sort of bargain with his master, whereby the apprentice would submit himself to the master's authority at work according to the strict legal definition of the indenture, but would not submit to the general proposition that the master had the right to control the apprentice's person, leisure activities, or companions. By the 1790s American cities and towns were clogged with surly apprentices asserting their rights on the streets in illicit ball games, snowball fights, and general rowdiness. Denouncing these activities, the older generation passed local ordinances demanding that masters control their apprentices. In Newburyport, Massachusetts, for example, a disturber of the peace was subject to a fine up to $2, and if the offender was underage, the parent or master was obliged to pay. In Albany, New York, a similar violator had to pay a fine, and if the master responsible for the fine of his apprentice refused to pay, his apprentice was sent to jail. In Georgetown, Maryland, an apprentice who obtained liquor illegally could be whipped up to thirty-nine stripes or imprisoned twenty days. In 1799 the New York Common Council ordered 2,000 handbills warning citizens to stay away from nightly gatherings of "Crowds of Apprentices and other disorderly Persons." Masters were specifically instructed to restrain their apprentices.[41]

The truth, however, was that apprentices were beyond their masters' control. The mayor of New York, Cadwallader Colden, acting in his capacity as a judge of the Mayor's Court, warned, "It is the duty of the apprentice to submit in all things to his master. . . ." But this admonition fell on deaf ears, and the defiance continued. In the end masters found it convenient to give up the idea that they controlled their apprentices. After the master Joseph O. Bogart had been fined $100 for his apprentice's interference with a New York official, Bogart appealed his fine to the Common Council. Two aldermen investigated and concluded that Bogart's apprentice was "not the best inclined." Indeed, the master had "endeavoured to get rid of him by giving up his indentures but his parents refused to take them." Nor would the apprentice accept the master's offer to give the apprentice his time. The council, recognizing the master's inability to control his apprentice, remitted the fine. As a group, apprentices were simply asserting their liberties—their right to conduct their own affairs outside of the shop and outside of working hours. A master might grumble, but if his apprentice performed his work well, and good apprentices were hard to get and keep, then the wise master was grateful that the apprentice did not run away and simply endured the insult of a youth who went about his own business.[42]

The master and the apprentice had rearranged what had been a personal relationship based on the master's authority into an economic relationship based increasingly upon the needs of a capitalist society. It is instructive to note the way in which Benjamin Coopwood, a stonemason, offered an apprenticeship to his stepson, Robert Bailey. "Robert I will make a man of you, and learn you a trade," said Coopwood. "I now have a job that comes to $1000, and I can earn it in six months." Coopwood's lure was the promise of a lucrative craft. To Robert, however, the promise was less important than Coopwood's savage beatings, and in the end Robert decided, like a good republican, to make his own way in the world and ran away. If the apprentice demanded and received more freedom in the noneconomic realm, then the master perhaps asserted more control than ever over the apprentice's work. The runaway Robert Bailey apprenticed himself to Robert Brooken, a Virginia house carpenter. For a time young Bailey worked hard and learned much of the trade, but then Brooken's business fell off, and the youth was put to work grinding meal in a mill. The vagaries of the market had ended Bailey's apprenticeship in carpentry. Bailey ran away.

Because the probability for running away was very high, the master was inclined not to teach the apprentice the whole of the trade until the apprenticeship was nearing an end. The high degree of risk and the consequent low rate of return on a master's investment in an apprentice meant that a master was unwilling to take a young boy and insisted upon getting valuable work out of a youth from the beginning of an apprenticeship. The familial nature of the institution had begun to be transformed into exploited child labor.[43]

Apprenticeship on a republican basis would not last beyond the 1820s. As the master's noneconomic authority eroded, the institution began to disintegrate. After all, if the relationship between master and apprentice depended strictly upon work, what was the difference between an apprentice and a journeyman employed for wages? In the end apprentices demanded and got cash wages and, in the process, ceased to be apprentices. Although the disintegration of apprenticeship had many causes, including important economic ones, the institution had begun its decline with the turmoil of the American Revolution. Not only had wartime chaos disrupted apprenticeship in myriad ways, but revolutionary ideology threatened the institution. There was, in fact, a fundamental contradiction between the authoritarian nature of apprenticeship and republican values. In the postwar years conservatives yearned to reestablish the structure of traditional authority, including apprenticeship, that had prevailed before the war, while those Americans most committed to revolutionary ideals sought to build a society based on liberty and equality. Artisans committed to republican values tried to build apprenticeship

as a republican institution, and they favored the new laws that provided a republican framework for apprenticeship. But the laws
failed, and artisans found themselves constantly forced to yield to
the demands of their apprentices for more and more rights. In the
end both the master and the apprentice, for economic as well as ide-
alistic reasons, abandoned indentures. As indenturing fell into dis-
use, apprenticeship was doomed to become a shadowy vestige of its
former self.

NOTES

PUBLISHING NOTE: Expanded and adapted from *The Craft Apprentice:
From Franklin to the Machine Age in America* by W. J. Rorabaugh.
© 1986 by Oxford University Press, Inc. Used with permission.

1. Once an apprenticeship was completed, indentures had no
value and were often destroyed. A few jurisdictions did require the
registration of indentures for minors indented by the courts. Boston's
poor-law indentures have been studied by Lawrence W. Towner, "A
Good Master Well Served: A Social History of Servitude in Massachusetts, 1620–1750" (Ph.D. diss., Northwestern University, 1955);
and W. Graham Millar, "The Poor Apprentices of Boston: Indentures
of Poor Children Bound Out Apprentice by the Overseers of the Poor
of Boston, 1734–1776" (M.A. thesis, College of William and Mary,
1958). Towner's work was continued in "The Indentures of Boston's
Poor Apprentices: 1734–1805," *Publications of the Colonial Society of
Massachusetts* 43(1966): 417–68. Philadelphia indentures for 1771–
73, many of which pertain to indentured servants, have been published in *Proceedings of the Pennsylvania-German Society* 16 (1907).
Others are in manuscript at the Philadelphia Archives. Although
Philadelphia required the registration of all indentures in the early
nineteenth century, the extant records indicate that this require-
ment was ignored. See Ian M. G. Quimby, *Apprenticeship in Colonial
Philadelphia* (New York, 1985; originally M.A. thesis, University of
Delaware, 1963). New York City indentures for 1695–1707 and 1718–
27 have been published in the *Collections of the New-York Historical
Society* 18 (1885): 565–622, and 42 (1910): 111–99. Others are loose at
the Society. Quebec City's excellent records have been studied by
David T. Ruddel, "Apprenticeship in Early Nineteenth Century
Quebec, 1793–1815" (M.A. thesis, University of Laval, 1969), trans-
lated into French and published in Jean P. Hardy and David T. Ruddel, *Les apprentis artisans à Québec, 1660–1815* (Montreal, 1977).
Paul Lachance has been studying New Orleans records, which are at
the New Orleans Public Library. On Maryland records see W. J.

Rorabaugh, *The Craft Apprentice: From Franklin to the Machine Age* (New York, 1986), 211. Phinehas S. Bradley Diary, 1813–1816, Manuscript Collection, Yale University.

2. Benjamin Franklin (1706–90), son of Boston candlemaker Josiah Franklin, was apprentice to his brother James in Boston ca. 1718–23; he ran away to Philadelphia. Benjamin Franklin, *The Autobiography and Other Writings,* ed. L. Jesse Lemisch (New York, 1961), especially 34. Benjamin Franklin, *The Papers of Benjamin Franklin,* ed. Leonard W. Labaree, (New Haven, 1959–) 2:232, 261–63, 388; 5:440; 10:343–45, 347; 11:418; 13:476, 493; 17:131. On England see Olive J. Dunlop, *English Apprenticeship and Child Labour* (New York, 1912); Margaret G. Davies, *The Enforcement of English Apprenticeship: A Study in Applied Mercantilism, 1563–1642* (Cambridge, Mass., 1956); and K. D. M. Snell, *Annals of the Labouring Poor: Social Change and Agrarian England, 1660–1900* (Cambridge, Eng., 1985).

3. On colonial apprentices, in addition to the sources in note 1, see Stanley R. Keyser, "The Apprenticeship System in North Carolina to 1840" (M.A. thesis, Duke University, 1950). For a general discussion of crafts in colonial society see Carl Bridenbaugh, *The Colonial Craftsman* (New York, 1950); Peter C. Marzio, "Carpentry in the Southern Colonies during the Eighteenth Century with Emphasis on Maryland and Virginia," *Winterthur Portfolio* 7 (1972): 229–50; Richard B. Morris, *Government and Labor in Early America* (New York, 1946), especially 364–89; and Ian M. G. Quimby, ed., *The Craftsman in Early America* (New York, 1984).

4. John Fitch (1744–98), son of a poor Connecticut farmer, was apprentice clock maker to Benjamin Cheney and apprentice brass founder to Timothy Cheney; he became an inventor. John Fitch, *The Autobiography of John Fitch,* ed. Frank D. Prager (Philadelphia, 1976), 37–42. For other rural apprentices in colonial America see Thomas B. Hazard, *Nailer Tom's Diary,* ed. Caroline Hazard (Boston, 1930); Charles S. Sellers, *Charles Willson Peale* (Philadelphia, 1947), 1–2, 23–24, 35–44. For an early ironworks see Edward N. Hartley, *Ironworks on the Saugus* (Norman, Okla., 1957). On printing see William L. Joyce et al., eds., *Printing and Society in Early America* (Worcester, Mass., 1983); Stephen W. Botein, "Reluctant Partisans: The Role of Printers in Eighteenth-Century American Politics" (Ph.D. diss., Harvard University, 1970); Alan Dyer, *A Biography of James Parker, Colonial Printer* (Troy, N.Y., 1982); Hugh Gaine, *The Journals of Hugh Gaine Printer,* ed. Paul L. Ford (New York, 1902); and Ward L. Miner, *William Goddard, Newspaperman* (Durham, N.C., 1962).

5. On urban crafts see Allan Kulikoff, "The Progress of Inequality in Revolutionary Boston," *William and Mary Quarterly* 3d series 28 (1971): 375–412; Jackson T. Main, *The Social Structure of Revolutionary America* (Princeton, 1965), 66–67, 75–82, 186; Gary B. Nash, *The Urban Crucible: Social Change, Political Consciousness, and the Origins of the American Revolution* (Cambridge, Mass., 1979), 13–20, 59–63, 104, 114, 117–18, 120–22, 124; Billy G. Smith, *The "Lower Sort": Philadelphia's Laboring People, 1750–1800* (Ithaca, N.Y., 1990), especially 63–149; Alfred F. Young, "George Robert Twelve Hewes (1742–1840): A Boston Shoemaker and the Memory of the American Revolution," *William and Mary Quarterly* 3d series 38 (Oct. 1981): especially 561–62. Joshua Lane (1696–1766) was a Hampton, N.H., tanner-shoemaker; Isaiah Lane (1730–1815), son of Joshua, was a Hampton farmer-shoemaker; Samuel Lane (1718–1806), eldest son of Joshua, was a Stratham, N.H., shoemaker, tanner, and surveyor; Jabez Lane (1760–1810), youngest son of Samuel, was a tanner-shoemaker; Charles Lane (1796–1884), son of Jabez, was a tanner-shoemaker; he became a merchant. For genealogy see Samuel Lane, *A Journal for the Years 1739–1803,* ed. Charles L. Hanson (Concord, N.H., 1937), 1–2. See also contracts dated 29 Dec. 1746; 15 May 1755; 10 June 1777; Joshua Lane to Samuel Lane, 22 Mar. 1797; and genealogy, all in Lane Family Papers, New Hampshire Historical Society, Concord. For other examples see Charles S. Parsons, "The Dunlaps of New Hampshire and Their Furniture," in *Country Cabinetwork and Simple City Furniture,* ed. John D. Morse (Charlottesville, Va., 1970), 109–50; Charles F. Hummel, *With Hammer in Hand* (Charlottesville, Va., 1968). In general see Quimby, *Craftsman;* Bernard Farber, *Guardians of Virtue, Salem Families in 1800* (New York, 1972), especially 48–50, 96–98, 102–5. See also Main, *Social Structure,* 11–32, 51–53, 132–33, 182–85.

6. Stephen Allen (1767–1852), youngest son of a New York carpenter who died ca. 1769, was apprentice sail maker to James Leonard, 1779–83; he became a merchant and mayor of New York. Stephen Allen, "The Memoirs of Stephen Allen (1767–1852)," typescript, 15–21, New-York Historical Society. See also Samuel McKee, Jr., *Labor in Colonial New York, 1664–1776* (New York, 1935), 175; Morris, *Government and Labor,* 291–94; Charles G. Steffen, *The Mechanics of Baltimore* (Urbana, Ill., 1984). 53–80.

7. Allen, "Memoirs," 22.

8. Ibid., 29–30.

9. Ibid., 13–14 (quote at 14), 25–27.

10. Ibid., 23, 37 (quote).

11. Peter Edes (1756–1840), son of Boston printer Benjamin

Edes, was apprentice to his father; he became a Maine printer. Samuel L. Boardman, *Peter Edes* (Bangor, Me., 1901), especially 15–16. A brief sketch of Edes's career in Maine is in Joseph Griffin, ed., *History of the Press of Maine* (Brunswick, Me., 1872), 87–88.

12. Benjamin Russell (1761–1845), son of Boston stonemason John Russell, was apprentice printer to Isaiah Thomas at Worcester, Mass., 1775–81; he became the publisher of the Boston *Massachusetts Centinel* in 1784. Joseph T. Buckingham, *Specimens of Newspaper Literature: With Personal Memoirs, Anecdotes, and Reminiscences* (Boston, 1850) 2:1–13, especially 6; Francis Baylies, *Eulogy on the Hon. Benjamin Russell* (Boston, 1845); Isaiah Thomas, "The Diary of Isaiah Thomas, 1805–1828," ed. Benjamin T. Hill, *Transactions and Collections of the American Antiquarian Society* 9 (1909): 90n–91n. Isaiah Thomas (1749–1831), a Bostonian whose father disappeared in the South, was apprentice printer by the Overseers of the Poor to Zechariah Fowle, 1756–65; he ran away to Nova Scotia but returned to Boston in 1770 to publish the *Massachusetts Spy,* which he moved to Worcester in 1775. Isaiah Thomas, *Three Autobiographical Fragments* (Worcester, Mass., 1962); Annie R. Marble, *From 'Prentice to Patron: The Life Story of Isaiah Thomas* (New York, 1935), especially 104; Clifford K. Shipton, *Isaiah Thomas: Printer, Patriot and Philanthropist, 1749–1831* (Rochester, N.Y., 1948); Benjamin F. Thomas, *Memoir of Isaiah Thomas* (Boston, 1874); Ebenezer S. Thomas, *Reminiscences of the Last Sixty-Five Years* (Hartford, Conn., 1840) 2:3–30.

13. Buckingham, *Specimens* 2:9–13; Baylies, *Russell,* 13–14. See also Benjamin Russell to Isaiah Thomas, 29 Sept. 1780, Richmond Autograph Collection, Massachusetts Historical Society.

14. Ebenezer Fox (1763–1843), son of a poor tailor of Roxbury, Mass., was apprentice barber and wig maker to John Bosson in Boston, 1775–80; he was a seaman, 1780–83, then a Boston barber. Ebenezer Fox, *The Adventures of Ebenezer Fox* (Boston, 1848), 44–49, 55 (quotes at 47).

15. Ibid., 56, 58 (quote), 232n.

16. Worthington C. Ford, ed., *Journals of the Continental Congress, 1774–1789* (Washington, D.C., 1906) 4:103–4; 7:369; Richard Smith Diary, 1776, in Paul H. Smith, ed., *Letters of Delegates to Congress, 1774–1789* (Washington, D.C., 1976–) 3:157, 161, 167, 172, 175, 257; Thomas Burke to Richard Caswell, 15 April 1777, in ibid., 6:581; John Adams to Abigail Adams, 8–11 April 1777, in L. H. Butterfield, ed., *Adams Family Correspondence* (Cambridge, Mass., 1963) 2:204.

17. John R. Bartlett, ed., *Records of the Colony of Rhode Island* (Providence, R.I., 1862) 7:319; William W. Hening, ed., *The Statutes*

at Large (Richmond, Va., 1822) 10:335–36; James T. Mitchell and *Henry Flanders, eds., The Statutes at Large of Pennsylvania from 1682 to 1801* (Harrisburg, Pa., 1896–1911), 7:360–63; 9:216–17; *Pennsylvania Packet, or the General Advertiser,* 6 May 1777. A concise summary is in Morris, *Government and Labor,* 291–94. For an apprentice who enlisted see Johnson Green, *The Life and Confession of Johnson Green* (Worcester, Mass., 1786), broadside.

18. Fox, *Adventures,* 17–18. Paul Gilje has gently chided me for making so much of this example, which was recorded in the mid-nineteenth century. I plead both the poverty of other sources and the brilliant illumination offered by this particular one. It seems reasonable to me that many young Americans shared Fox's feelings. Revolutionary values also led women to question their place in society. Abigail Adams to John Adams, 31 Mar. 1776, in Abigail S. Adams, *The Book of Abigail and John: Selected Letters of the Adams Family, 1762–1784,* ed. L. H. Butterfield, et al. (Cambridge, Mass, 1975), 121; Mary B. Norton, *Liberty's Daughters: The Revolutionary Experience of American Women, 1750–1800* (Boston, 1980), especially 223–24; and Linda K. Kerber, *Women of the Republic: Intellect and Ideology in Revolutionary America* (Chapel Hill, N.C., 1980).

19. On the cities see Dirk Hoerder, *Crowd Action in Revolutionary Massachusetts, 1765–1780* (New York, 1977); Charles S. Olton, *Artisans for Independence: Philadelphia Mechanics and the American Revolution* (Syracuse, N.Y., 1975); Alfred F. Young, *The Democratic Republicans of New York: The Origins, 1763–1797* (Chapel Hill, N.C., 1967); Young, "Hewes"; Nash, *Urban Crucible;* Nash, "Artisans and Politics in Eighteenth-Century Philadelphia," in his *Race, Class, and Politics: Essays on American Colonial and Revolutionary Society* (Urbana, Ill., 1986), 243–67; and Eric Foner, *Tom Paine and Revolutionary America* (New York, 1976). On artisan heroes see Roger S. Boardman, *Roger Sherman* (Philadelphia, 1938); Esther Forbes, *Paul Revere and the World He Lived in* (Boston, 1942); C. Donald Dallas, *The Spirit of Paul Revere* (Princeton, 1944); Noah Brooks, *Henry Knox: A Soldier of the Revolution* (New York, 1900); North Callahan, *Henry Knox: General Washington's General* (New York, 1958); Francis S. Drake, *Life and Correspondence of Henry Knox* (Boston, 1873); Theodore Thayer, *Nathanael Greene: Strategist of the American Revolution* (New York, 1960); Francis V. Greene, *General Greene* (New York, 1898); William Johnson, *Sketches of the Life and Correspondence of Nathanael Greene* (Charleston, S.C., 1822); and William G. Simms, *The Life of Nathanael Greene* (New York, 1849).

20. Salem Boards Minutes, 14 Nov. 1780, in Adelaide L. Fries et al., eds., *Records of the Moravians in North Carolina,* 11 vols. (Ra-

leigh, N.C., 1922–69) 4:1609. On the draft dodger see ibid., 4:1801. The strike is in Jerry L. Surratt, *Gottlieb Schober of Salem* (Macon, Ga., 1983), 22–23. The Moravian records at the church headquarters in Winston–Salem, N.C., are one of the richest and least known sources for social history in the United States. Fries translated and published only five to ten percent of the records.

21. In general see Edwin G. Burrows and Michael Wallace, "The American Revolution," *Perspectives in American History* 6 (1972): 287–89; Winthrop D. Jordan, "Familial Politics: Thomas Paine and the Killing of the King, 1776," *Journal of American History* 60 (1973): 294–308; Jay Fliegelman, *Prodigals and Pilgrims* (New York, 1982); and Garry Wills, *Inventing America: Jefferson's Declaration of Independence* (New York, 1978).

22. [Samuel Mather], *A Serious Letter to the Young People of Boston* (Boston, 1783), 5, 7 (quote); Jeremy Belknap, *An Election Sermon* (Portsmouth, N.H., 1785), 16 (quote), 18–19 (quote); and Nathanael Emmons, *A Discourse, Delivered November 3, 1790, at the Particular Request . . .* (Providence, R.I., [1790]), 19. See also Henry T. Channing, *God Admonishing His People of Their Present Duty, as Parents and Masters* (New London, Conn., 1787), especially 21.

23. Devereux Jarrett, "Autobiography," *William and Mary Quarterly* 3d series, 9 (1952): 361; Aaron Kinne, *A New-Year's Gift, Presented Especially to the Young People . . .* (New London, Conn., 1788), 6; Samuel Haven, *An Election Sermon Preached before the General Court, of New-Hampshire, at Concord, June 8, 1786* (Portsmouth, N.H., 1786), 10; William Arthur, *Family Religion Recommended* (Philadelphia, 1794), 13; *A Parent's Advice for His Family* (New London, Conn., 1792), 18; Charles W. Janson, *The Stranger in America, 1793–1806* (1807; New York, 1935), 304. See also Joseph Huntington, *God Ruling the Nations for the Most Glorious End* (Hartford, Conn., 1784), 26; Joseph Lyman, *A Sermon, Preached before His Excellency James Bowdoin, Esq., Governour* (Boston, 1787), 8–9; [Francis Hopkinson], *Account of the Grand Federal Procession, Philadelphia, July 4, 1788* (Philadelphia, 1788), 20. The generational nature of conservative opposition to revolutionary ideals needs to be explored; the passing of a generation may explain why the Jeffersonian revolution of 1800 took place when it did. For suggestive comments see Robert H. Wiebe, *The Opening of American Society: From the Adoption of the Constitution to the Eve of Disunion* (New York, 1984). For a speculative theory see William Strauss and Neil Howe, *Generations: The History of America's Future, 1584 to 2069* (New York, 1991).

24. Moses Hemmenway, *A Sermon, Preached before His Excellency*

John Hancock, Esq. . . . (Boston, 1784), 12; David Daggett, *An Oration, Pronounced in the Brick Meeting-House, in the City of New-Haven, on the Fourth of July, A.D. 1787* (New Haven, Conn., 1787), 6, 9 (quote). See also John Murray, *Jerubbaal, or Tyranny's Grove Destroyed, and the Altar of Liberty Finished* (Newburyport, Mass., 1784).

25. Joseph Belknap (1769–1800), son of Rev. Jeremy Belknap of Dover, N.H., was apprentice printer to Robert Aitken in Philadelphia, 1783–87, and to William Mycall in Newburyport, Mass., 1787–90; he became a printer in Boston. Jeremy Belknap to Ebenezer Hazard, 10 June, 14 July, 1, 20, 29 Sept., 12, 27, 31 Oct., 7, 11 Nov. 1783; 11 Feb., 16 Apr. [misdated 1784] 1785; 18 May 1787, in Jeremy Belknap, "Belknap Papers," *Collections of the Massachusetts Historical Society* 5th series 2:215, 230–32, 244–46, 250, 257, 262, 269–70, 270–71, 271–73, 274–75 (quote at 275), 412–13, 331, 478–80; replies, 24 Sept., 8 Oct., 30 Nov., 13–17 Dec. 1783; 23 Oct., 6 Nov. 1784; 24 Mar. 1785, in ibid., 2:256, 260–261, 286, 286, 403–4, 404–5, 419; William McCulloch to Isaiah Thomas, 1 Sept. 1812, Isaiah Thomas Papers, American Antiquarian Society; Jeremy Belknap Travel Diary, 1785, Belknap Papers, Massachusetts Historical Society; Jeremy Belknap to his wife, Oct. 1785, quoted in [Jane Marcou], *Life of Jeremy Belknap, D.D.* (New York, 1847), 115. In general see ibid., especially 102, 107, 115, 116, 120–21, 139; "Jeremy Belknap," *Dictionary of American Biography* 2:147; "Belknap Papers," 5th series, vols. 2–3; 6th series, vol. 4; and Belknap Papers at Massachusetts Historical Society and New Hampshire Historical Society.

26. Jeremy Belknap to Ebenezer Hazard, 29 Apr., 18 May 1787, in "Belknap Papers," 5th series 2:473, 478–79 (quotes at 478–79, 479, 479); reply, 5 May 1787, in ibid., 2:476. Jeremy Belknap to Ebenezer Hazard, 23 June 1787, Belknap Papers, Massachusetts Historical Society, quotes the arbitrators' findings.

27. Jeremy Belknap Travel Diary, 20 Sept. 1785, Belknap Papers, Massachusetts Historical Society; Jeremy Belknap to Ebenezer Hazard, 14 July 1787, Belknap Papers, Massachusetts Historical Society; Jeremy Belknap to Joseph Belknap, 29 Sept. 1787, Belknap Papers, New Hampshire Historical Society; reply, 30 Aug. 1789, Belknap Papers, New Hampshire Historical Society (quotes).

28. Joseph Belknap to Jeremy Belknap, 30 Aug. 1789; 6 Oct. 1790 (quote), Belknap Papers, New Hampshire Historical Society.

29. John Prentiss (1778–1873), fifth of thirteen children of Rev. Caleb Prentiss of Reading, Mass., was apprentice printer to Thomas Adams in Boston, 1792–95; then journeyman to his brother Charles in Leominster, Mass., 1795–99; he became the publisher of the Keene *N.H. Sentinel.* John Prentiss, "Autobiography" (n.d.), 36–40 (quotes

at 38, 39), American Antiquarian Society. This is one of four manuscript memoirs bound in one volume. For a shrewd insight into generational differences, see Bryant's remarks in David J. Hill, *William Cullen Bryant* (New York, 1879), 26–27. Recent studies of mechanics in the early republic include Steffen, *Mechanics;* Gary J. Kornblith, "From Artisans to Businessmen: Master Mechanics in New England, 1789–1850" (Ph.D. diss., Princeton University, 1983); Gary B. Kulik, "The Beginnings of the Industrial Revolution in America: Pawtucket, Rhode Island, 1672–1829" (Ph.D. diss., Brown University, 1980); Mark A. Lause, *Some Degree of Power: From Hired Hand to Union Craftsman in the Preindustrial American Printing Trades, 1778–1815* (Fayetteville, Ark., 1991); Howard B. Rock, *Artisans of the New Republic: The Tradesmen of New York City in the Age of Jefferson* (New York, 1979); Deborah D. Waters, " 'The Workmanship of an American Artist:' Philadelphia's Precious Metals Trades and Craftsmen, 1788–1832" (Ph.D. diss., University of Delaware, 1981); Sean Wilentz, *Chants Democratic, New York City and the Rise of the American Working Class* (New York, 1984).

30. On early industry see Thomas C. Cochran, *Frontiers of Change* (New York, 1981). On the economy see B. G. Smith, *"Lower Sort"*, especially 101–2, 108, 110–11, 114, 116, 118, 121; Smith, "The Material Lives of Laboring Philadelphians, 1750 to 1800," *William and Mary Quarterly* 3d series 38 (Apr. 1981): 184, 195–201; Waters, "Workmanship," 134, 140. Legal issues are covered below. On advertisements of runaways see Rita S. Gottesman, "The Arts and Crafts in New York, 1726–1804," *Collections of the New-York Historical Society* 69 (1938); 81 (1954); 82 (1965). The quote is from Simeon Baldwin, *An Oration Pronounced before the Citizens of New-Haven, July 4th, 1788* (New Haven, 1788), 13. On masters' organizations see Young, *Democratic Republicans.* A list of craft organizations is in Rorabaugh, *Craft Apprentice,* 230–31. For a revealing pamphlet see Matthew Clarkson, *An Address to the Citizens of Philadelphia, Respecting the Better Government of Youth* (Philadelphia, 1795).

31. Millard Fillmore, "Autobiography," *Publications of the Buffalo Historical Society* 10 (1907): 6–8 (quote at 7).

32. James Horton to Almy & Brown, 25 Nov. 1799, box 23A, Almy, Brown, & Slater Papers, Rhode Island Historical Society, as quoted in Kulik, "Beginnings," 235. For another example of surly apprentices see Salem Board Minutes, 7 Nov. 1793, in Fries et al., eds., *Records,* 6:2482–83.

33. Publication data were compiled from the Evans bibliography. A complete publication history is in Benjamin Franklin, *The Autobiography of Benjamin Franklin: A Genetic Text,* ed. J. A. Leo

Lemay and P. M. Zall (Knoxville, Tenn., 1981), xlviii–lviii. See Rorabaugh, *Craft Apprentice,* 3–15, 216 n. 17. Ebenezer Smith Thomas (1775–1845), son of a farmer in Lancaster, Mass., was apprentice printer to his Uncle Isaiah Thomas in Worcester, 1788–92; he learned bookbinding in Boston, 1792–94, worked in a dry goods store, 1794–95; he became a merchant and publisher in Charleston, S.C., and Cincinnati. E. S. Thomas, *Reminiscences,* 2:30–31.

34. These conclusions are based on an examination of state session laws and codes. Laws were enacted in New Hampshire, 1792; Massachusetts, 1794; Rhode Island, 1798; Connecticut, 1784; New York, 1788; New Jersey, 1798; Pennsylvania, 1799; Delaware, 1797; Maryland, 1793; Virginia, 1785, 1792; South Carolina, 1783; and Kentucky, 1797. For a recent discussion see Robert J. Steinfeld, *The Invention of Free Labor: The Employment Relation in English & American Law and Culture, 1350–1870* (Chapel Hill, N.C., 1991), especially 130–34. Unfortunately, this book appeared too late to inform my thinking more generally.

35. Petition of Robert Simpson, 2 Apr. 1790; Petition of Christopher Cronnenberger and Robert Miller, Dec. 1791; Petition of James Killigan, Sept. 1790, in Philadelphia Mayor's Court Docket, 1789–1792, bound MS vol., Philadelphia Municipal Archives, 225–26, 336–37, 208–9 (quote at 208).

36. Petition of Adam Doland, Peter Ledinbourgh, Daniel Perkins, and John Lackey, 23 Dec. 1789, in ibid., 113–14 (quotes at 113, 114). For a similar example from another jurisdiction see Petition of Robert Edging to Frederick County Maryland Court, 28 Mar. 1794, in Paul H. Downing Coach and Carriage Papers, Colonial Williamsburg, Inc.

37. On economic trends see Donald R. Adams, Jr., "Wage Rates in the Early National Period: Philadelphia, 1785–1830," *Journal of Economic History* 28 (1968): 404–26; Adams, "Some Evidence on English and American Wage Rates, 1790–1830," ibid. 30 (1970): 499–520. For Connecticut cases see Paddock v. Higgins, 1795; Hewit v. Morgan, 1796; and Clement v. Wheeler, 1796, all in 2 Root 316, 363, 466. Lewis v. Wildman, 1803, in 1 Day 153 (quote at 154).

38. Blunt v. Melcher, 2 Mass. Rep. 228 (quote at 230); Davis v. Coburn, 8 Mass. Rep. 299 (quote); Day v. Everett, 7 Mass. Rep. 145; Pennsylvania Chief Justice Edward Shippen, Opinion, 27 Jan. 1793, Edward Shippen Manuscript in Shippen folder, Miscellaneous Collections, Historical Society of Pennsylvania.

39. On the decline in indentures see Rorabaugh, *Craft Apprentice,* 211. For comparable data from Baltimore see Steffen, *Mechanics,* 4, 29. Information on the *Conductor Generalis,* which

was published eleven times in America, 1711–1801, was compiled from the Evans and Shaw-Shoemaker bibliographies. The same bibliographies were used for [Sir John Barnard], *A Present for an Apprentice*.

40. Isaac Hill (1788–1851) was the eldest of nine children of Isaac Hill of Cambridge, Mass.; the father went insane, 1794, and the mother moved the family to a farm in Ashburnham, Mass., 1798; Isaac was apprentice printer to Joseph Cushing in Amherst, Mass., 1802–09; he became publisher of the Concord *New Hampshire Patriot* and U.S. Senator. [Cyrus P. Bradley], *Biography of Isaac Hill* (Concord, N.H., 1835), 13–17 (quote at 15); Isaac Hill to [?], 5 Mar. 1814, quoted in Rollo G. Silver, *The American Printer, 1787–1825* (Charlottesville, Va., 1967), 2. On Cushing see Joseph T. Buckingham, *Personal Memoirs and Recollections of Editorial Life* (Boston, 1852) 1:45. For other examples see Jonathan Roberts Memoirs, Historical Society of Pennsylvania; William Morgan, "William Morgan's Autobiography and Diary: Life in Sussex County, 1780–1857," ed. Harold B. Hancock, *Delaware History* 19 (1980): 39–52, 106–26.

41. Newburyport, Mass., *Bye-Laws of Newburyport* (Newburyport, Mass., 1797), broadside; Albany, N.Y., *Laws and Ordinances, Ordained and Established* (Albany, N.Y., 1791), 79–80, 91–95, 107; Georgetown, D.C., *Ordinances of the Corporation of Georgetown* (Georgetown, D.C., 1811), 62–63; New York (City) Common Council, *Minutes of the Common Council of the City of New York, 1784–1831* (New York, 1917) 2:560.

42. People v. William P. Connelly, 1820, in Barent Gardenier, *The New-York Reporter* (New York, 1820), 12–13 (quote at 13); Petition, 1818, New York (City) Common Council, *Minutes*, 10:75, 91–92 (quotes at 91, 91–92).

43. Robert Bailey (1773–?), son of a Pennsylvania officer killed in the Revolution, was apprentice stonemason to his stepfather, Benjamin Coopwood, in Maryland; he ran away to Virginia, where he learned carpentry from Robert Brooken; he became a professional gambler. Robert Bailey, *The Life and Adventures of Robert Bailey* (Richmond, Va., 1822), 13–19, 26–33 (quote at 18). For another example see Samuel Seabury, *Moneygripe's Apprentice: The Personal Narrative of Samuel Seabury III*, ed. Robert B. Mullin (New Haven, 1989).

In Victory and Defeat

Agrarian Independence

Northern Land Rioters after the Revolution

ALAN TAYLOR

This drawing, very likely by a settler in western Pennsylvania, depicts "An Exciseman (center) carrying off two kegs of whiskey," who is "pursued by two farmers (to the left), intending to tar and feather him." According to the hand-lettered caption, the exciseman is pulled by the devil to a gallows (left), "where he is immediately hanged," whereupon "the people puts a barrel of whiskey under him, sets fire to it, burns and blows him up." The writer condemns excisemen as "burdensome drones" in league with "Squire Vultures."

Courtesy Atwater-Kent Museum.

Shortly before midnight 26 June 1788, armed men broke down the bedroom door of Col. Timothy Pickering's house in Wilkes-Barre, Pennsylvania. This was a daring affront, for Pickering was his frontier county's judge, court clerk, register of probate, recorder of deeds, a proprietor of 10,000 acres, and an agent for several other Pennsylvania land speculators. Pickering's alarmed wife lit a candle to reveal that their bedroom was filled with fifteen men armed with muskets and hatchets and disguised as Indians: faces blackened and handkerchiefs tied round their heads. The "Indians" seized the colonel, tied his hands, and led him outdoors, through the sleeping village, and up the Susquehanna into the sparsely settled hinterland, where they held Pickering for nearly a month. Known as "Wild Yankees," Pickering's captors were new settlers from New England who had staked homestead claims with the connivance of "the Susquehanna Company," Connecticut land speculators who hoped to wrest the upper Susquehanna country from Pennsylvania and that state's competing proprietors. By freely granting portions of their vast claim to actual settlers, the Susquehanna Company's leaders gambled that they could seize and hold the entire northern third of Pennsylvania, and reap great profits from future sales to later settlers. So, they recruited, in Pickering's words, "men destitute of property, who could be tempted by the gratuitous offer of lands; on the single condition that they should enter upon them *armed,* 'to man their rights,' in the cant phrase of those people." The violent contest between competing speculators of competing states created an opportunity for landless men willing to fight for free homesteads.[1]

On 27 October 1791 Cornelius Hogeboom, sheriff of New York's Columbia County, and two assistants rode into Hillsdale, a hill-country town beside the Massachusetts border. They meant to arrest several "Anti-Renters," tenant farmers who had suspended payments to their landlord Philip Schuyler, a Federalist United States senator and a revolutionary war general. Convinced that their farms should be freeholds, the Anti-Renters hated tenancy as "tending to degrade your Petitioners from the Rank the God of Nature destined all Mankind to move in, to be SLAVES and VASSALS." The area's settlers had resisted their landlords intermittently since the 1750s. When the sheriff's party reached Jonathan Arnold's farm, seventeen armed men, disguised as Indians, burst from the barn and fired their muskets and pistols in the air. One Anti-Renter rode up to the sheriff and fired, killing him instantly.[2]

On the morning of 18 July 1800 in Lincoln Plantation (now Thorndike), Maine, seven surveyors stumbled into an ambush laid by armed men "blacked and disguised like Indians." Bullets ripped into the surprised surveyors' ranks. They retreated to the coast, bearing their three wounded. The surveyors worked for Gen. Henry Knox, George Washington's artillery commander during the Revolutionary War and the new nation's first secretary of war. He was also one of the "Great Proprietors," wealthy land speculators who claimed legal title to most of mid-Maine, the frontier region between the Androscoggin River, on the west, and the Penobscot River, to the east (until 1820 Maine belonged to Massachusetts). Determined to build his fortune by retailing homesteads to settlers, General Knox sent the surveyors into the backcountry to subdivide his claim into townships and lots. But the backcountry settlers were squatters who wanted neither to pay for their new homesteads nor have neighbors who would. In June 1801 Knox sent another survey party into the backcountry, but they, too, fell into an ambush that sent them reeling back to the coast with one badly wounded man. Knox's land agents reported. "Our defeat occasioned exultation among the greater part of the people in the suspected regions. . . ."[3]

To discover the backcountry settlers' motives, the general sent two emissaries into the hostile region in August 1801. They found self-styled "Liberty-Men," defending their notion of the American Revolution against betrayal by the Great Proprietors. The two men reported:

> Instead of reasoning they resort to harangue. All old & young, husbands & wives, mothers & sons have gotten the same story by rote & two or three demagogues in & about Sheepscott Pond Settlement deliver it with a great deal of impassioned & boisterous eloquence. "We fought for land & liberty & it is hard if we can't enjoy either. We once defended this land at the point of the bayonet & if drove to the necessity are now equally united, ready & zealous to defend it again in the same way. It is as good to die by the sword as by the famine & we shall prefer the [former]. Who can have a better right to the land than we who have fought for it, subdued it & made it valuable which if we had not done no proprietor would ever have enquired after it. God gave the earth to the children. We own no other proprietor. Wild land ought to

be as free as common air. These lands once belonged to King George. He lost them by the American Revolution & they became the property of the people who defended & won them. The General Court did wrong & what they had no right to do when they granted them in such large quantities to certain companies & individuals & the bad acts of government are not binding on the subject. . . ."

The harangue summarized three propositions at the heart of the agrarianism prevalent in the American backcountry, among the Wild Yankees of Pennsylvania, the Anti-Renters of New York, and the Liberty-Men of Maine: that laboring men had a God-given right to claim and improve wilderness land, that the American Revolution had been a collective enterprise to secure the natural right, and that communities must resist laws that traduced the Revolution's meaning. This was not what General Knox wanted to read.[4]

W hat can we make of these incidents of Indian-disguised agrarians resisting the land claims of Federalist grandees? In this essay I will argue that, instead of concluding with the 1783 Treaty of Paris that ended the war with Great Britain, the American Revolution persisted in an attenuated, internal form in parts of the backcountry during the subsequent three decades. During this last phase of the Revolution gentlemen and yeomen who had cooperated against British rule fell out over the nature of property, whether power should be diffused locally or consolidated centrally, and whether extralegal crowds retained any legitimacy in the new republic.[5]

Two competing visions of America's future came into conflict in the Pickering, Schuyler, and Knox incidents. Both visions identified the frontier as the cutting edge of America's future, the point where the process of white expansion westward recurrently created new property, new communities. Both sides shared a devout commitment to private property as the foundation for family independence and social order—although the *agrarians* stressed the first and *proprietors* the second. But the two groups clashed over how property was legitimately created and properly defended, and so over whose property was at stake and who was the aggressor. As holders of large speculative land grants, the Federalist proprietors insisted that property in wilderness land *began* when the domain's sovereign (whether English king or Federal government, colonial or state legislature, or Indian sachem) issued documentary "title" to a specified tract, but the agrarians countered that their improving labor *created* legitimate, private property in the previously common forest. So Henry Knox's land agents were only half right when they charged that "banditti" had formed "a settlement of men in opposition to the rights of property and the utter subversion of all laws relative thereto." For, far from seeking to eliminate "the rights of property," the agrarians meant to defend their own.[6]

As gentlemen of property and standing, Timothy Pickering, Philip Schuyler, and Henry Knox fought a war for national independence, a war intended to place America's government in their own hands and to safeguard their extensive property from arbitrary parliamentary taxation. They expected the new order to safeguard prerevolutionary legal contracts, especially large land grants. Unwilling to entrust ordinary folks with the political decisions affecting great property, Federalist gentlemen sought to consolidate political power as much as possible: in counties rather than towns, in states rather than counties, in a new federal government rather than the states. They hoped that centralization would permit the discerning gentlemen of the commercial centers to govern independently of popular pressure between elections (when they expected the electorate to choose between gentlemen). Otherwise, they feared that the Revolution would spin out of control and humbler men intoxicated with ill-understood liberty would plunder their betters. Consequently, gentlemen regarded extralegal resistance to constituted authority as presaging a collapse into anarchy. Urging the Pennsylvania legislature to send militia to suppress the Wild Yankees, Thomas Fitzsimons insisted, "if the frontiers are suffered to insult your government, the contagion spreads more and more wide, by the accession of all the disselute and idle, until it may reach the centre, and all be anarchy, confusion and total ruin." Safeguarding the gentry's limited Revolution required parrying the "popular license" of backcountry agrarians.[7]

But those agrarians perceived Pickering, Schuyler, and Knox as de facto Tories, greedy betrayers of the American Revolution's proper meaning. The Wild Yankees, Anti-Renters, and Liberty-Men believed in a different American Revolution, one meant to liberate small producers from the moneyed parasites who did not live by their own labor but, instead, preyed on the many who did. They dreaded any prolonged economic dependence as tenant or wageworker as the path to "slavery." So, they sought an American Revolution that maximized their access to, and secured their possession of, freehold land upon which they could realize their labor as their own private property. This meant minimizing the levies of the "great men": taxes, rents, land payments, and legal fees. Convinced that the republic could not endure (except as an exploitative sham) unless property was widely and equitably distributed among adult white males, agrarians regarded free access to frontier land as essential to liberty's survival. Otherwise, they feared, America would ultimately replicate Europe's oppressive regimes where arrogant aristocrats lorded over impoverished peasants.[8]

Agrarians distrusted any translocal establishment, religious or political, as the natural preserve of parasitical great men ever bent on expanding their power and property at the expense of the many. To protect their farms for transmission to their children, agrarians insisted on the right of local communities forcefully to nullify new exactions. In 1771 a land agent explained to New York landlord James Duane why the Yankee settlers on his manor resisted tenancy: "Their whole fear was drawing their Posterity into Bondage. Silly People!" Dispersed over a rough landscape, possessing only limited means, and hindered by their farms' chronic demands on their labor, the agrarians pursued a strategy that was, of necessity, limited and defensive. They organized their own militia companies to prevent the service of legal writs, disrupt surveys, intimidate local opponents, and forcibly liberate imprisoned compatriots. They meant to obstruct particular laws until their rulers could amend them; that done, the yeomen meant to return to their farms, leaving governance to the gentlemen until the next moment that they transgressed their proper bounds.[9]

EXTENT AND BOUNDS

The Pickering, Schuyler, and Knox episodes belonged to an extensive pattern of backcountry resistance. From the mid-eighteenth century to the mid-nineteenth century, frontier settlement and political interest building frequently clashed, as yeomen seeking free farms confronted gentlemen who exploited their connections to secure large land grants. Yeomen were small producers living by family labor, while the gentlemen were mercantile capitalists intent on extracting a surplus, either as rent, land payments, or legal and judicial fees. Moreover, yeomen and gentlemen moved in distinct circles and possessed starkly different self-conceptions; yeomen sought economic independence while pursuing an evangelical faith that insisted upon man's utter dependence on God; conversely, the gentry were well-educated, well-connected, and outwardly self-confident paternalists determined to guide the common folk and usually contemptuous of evangelical "superstition." Conflict between the two groups was simultaneously and inseparably material and cultural.[10]

In at least eleven areas, settlers fought proprietors to obtain free or cheap access to wilderness land. In New Jersey during the 1740s and 1750s yeomen resisted land laws that favored their proprietors. During the 1750s and early 1760s some settlers in South Carolina's Rocky Mount district violently obstructed surveyors working for non-resident speculators. At the same time settlers in North Carolina's Granville District rioted against unscrupulous land speculators. Beginning in the 1750s and recurring intermittently until about 1860, tenants in east-central New York rebelled against their landlords. Between 1760 and 1815 mid-Maine's "Liberty-Men" resisted their Great Proprietors. From 1762 to 1808, "Wild Yankees" in northeastern Pennsylvania challenged the state's proprietors. Beginning in 1764 and persisting through the revolutionary war, western Vermont's "Green Mountain Boys" rebelled against their New York landlords. In the 1770s settlers around Pittsburgh with cheap Virginia land titles violently resisted Pennsylvania's jurisdiction and land speculators. During the 1780s Ohio squatters evaded federal land laws and federal troops. From 1795 through 1810 squatters in northwestern Pennsylvania waged gang warfare against land speculators' hired hands. Finally, during 1835–36 settlers in western New York's Holland Purchase rioted against the land company that held their burdensome mortgages.[11]

The costs and mode of administering justice represented a second focal point of conflict over the surplus produced by common farmers. Heavy taxes, burdensome debts, excessive judicial fees—or the legal establishment's failure to protect farmers from marauding outlaws and Indians—threatened to impoverish freeholders, raising the dreaded specter of tenancy. In ten "rebellions" rural folk organized to protect their "liberty" (equated with secure and egalitarian possession of freehold property) against apparent extortions or indifference by outside "great men." In 1763 and 1764 central Pennsylvania's "Paxton Boys" massacred government-protected Indians and started (but did not complete) a march on Philadelphia. Beginning in 1764, North Carolina's "Regulators" challenged their rulers until crushed at the Battle of Alamance in 1771. During the late 1760s South Carolina's "Regulators" defied their colony by establishing vigilante justice in the backcountry. During the same decade New Jersey's "Liberty Boys" rioted against their county courts. Similarly, from 1770 through 1775 rioters in eastern Vermont frequently closed their courts. From 1774 until ratification of a new state constitution in 1780, western Massachusetts's "Berkshire Constitutionalists" kept their courts from sitting. In 1782 "Ely's Rebellion" rallied yeomen in parts of western Massachusetts and northern Connecticut against their judges. Four and five years later the New England Regulation (or "Shays's Rebellion" as dubbed by its foes) shut down the courts and hindered tax collection in Massachusetts's hinterland and in parts of Vermont, New Hampshire, and Connecticut. In much of the West, and especially western Pennsylvania, "Whiskey Rebels" defied federal excise taxes during the 1790s. And in 1799, farmers in central Pennsylvania mounted "Fries's Rebellion" against a new federal land tax.[12]

Although widespread, backcountry resistance was localized and episodic rather than universal and perpetual. A dangerous gamble that could cost losers their farms and perhaps their lives, resistance was not embarked upon lightly. Consequently, settlers usually confined their resentments to grumbling, chronically laggard land payments, and plundering the standing timber on unsold lots. To proceed further to armed resistance, settlers needed a strong community solidarity, a mutual confidence that all would stand together against the formidable legal pressure that the "great men" could bring to bear, a shared conviction that they deserved to prevail and would certainly succeed. Agrarians insisted that all must cooperate to sustain the aggregate, collective value of the property created by their particular, individual labor applied to the wilderness, and that individuals should not, heeding fears and pursuing self-interest, seek a separate peace with their proprietor.[13]

Sugar Creek, a Wild Yankee settlement on the upper Susquehanna, constructed the necessary solidarity. Maj. Nathaniel Allen, a leading man in the community, reported:

> There is a perfect union with the people & Settlers here, though without Law except the dictates of Consceance which in so good a Cause is Sufficieant to keep peace and order. . . . The Minds of the people are much agetated at the proceeding of the [Pennsylvania] Legislative land jobers, but are firm in the good old cause and are better united than they have been Since I have ben in the Country & are determined that Agents, Surveyors & Such Imesaryes Shal not infest our peaceful abodes. There has ben two Meetings of the Settlers on the Creek which was to try the minds of the people which they Manefested to be firm & Stedfast. And determined to share an equal fate.

Recognizing the importance of breaking Sugar Creek's solidarity, Dr. Robert H. Rose, the Pennsylvania Proprietors' land agent, traveled from cabin to cabin during the summer of 1803, dealing with the settlers as individuals to preach self-interest and to sow doubts about their neighbors. He proudly reported to his employers, "I found that my attempt to make a division among them had not been unsuccessful, & that suspicions of each others' proceedings existed among those who formerly prided themselves on their being the strongest union among the Settlers on Sugar Creek & that they would all stand or fall together." When reproached by Major Allen for "underhanded proceedings," Rose coolly retorted "that I thought it right for every man to consult his own interest, & not to seek his ruin because his neighbours wished it." Timothy Beach, another Sugar Creek leading man, rebuked Rose:

> Sir, a long & unhappy dispute has existed in this Country in respect to the land which affords subsistence for ourselves, our wives, and our children. The title of these lands we have honestly purchased, & sincerely believe we can trace a regular chain of title from the God of Nature. Still, Sir, there is power vested in a certain portion of our fellow mortals to harness & depress us. . . . You have with unwearied pains traversed every part of our settlement, endeavouring, as far as in your power, to practise on us the vilest imposition, & to destroy that harmony which unites us like a band of brothers engaged in the cause of justice. . . .

Weathering Rose's challenge, in June–July 1804 Sugar Creek's settlers donned 'Indian' attire to capture and expel an invading posse after "a good deal of hard work," and to attack and rout the Pennsylvania proprietors' surveyors.[14]

To sustain the critical solidarity, confidence, and conviction, settlers needed the allegiance of their settlements' *leading men:* political and economic mediators between their communities and the wider world. Men like Nathaniel Allen and Timothy Beach comprised the pivotal, intermediate group in the conflict between gentlemen and the yeomanry. In every protracted resistance the yeomen enjoyed leadership from the substantial farmers and prosperous millers in their midst. A luckless deputy who ventured into Maine's backcountry knew he was in for a long day when the confident locals could boast "that they had all the town to join them, that they had *the first men* in town & were determined that no property should be attached . . . & [they] would defend it at the expense of their lives. Their language was very abusive & threatening." The deputy returned home with his unserved writs.[15]

Consequently, the agrarian conflicts pivoted around the contest for the allegiance of each settlement's leading men, a contest between community and class notions of duty. The leading men possessed more property and, often, wider ambitions than their yeomen neighbors, but lacked the social graces, family connections, and literary education necessary for acceptance among the new nation's genteel establishment. Such men lay at the conflicts' balance point: a risky, high-stakes position rife with cloudy choices, hidden dangers, and promising opportunities. On the one hand, the leading man felt the pull of his community's expectation that he must protect the people's liberty and property from the encroaching, cosmopolitan "great men." On the other hand, the Federalist gentry wooed or cajoled backcountry leading men to prove their worthiness as fellow gentlemen by converting their neighbors to the "good principles" of orderly submission to the law.[16]

Leading men needed to tread a fine line—for fear of arson, fence-toppling, and livestock mutilation at home or of legal retribution by external authorities. The leading man who misplayed his balancing act could lose his property to a proprietor's lawsuit or to a neighbors' hot coal, placed at night beneath his barn. Conversely, an especially ambitious leading man could reap extensive speculative possession claims by exploiting his neighbors' resistance, as did Vermont's Ethan Allen, despite his masterful denunciations of New York's absentee landlords. As a leading man in Wyalusing, a Wild Yankee settlement, John Ingham had to proceed carefully to retain both his community preeminence and his external standing as a state legislator. In 1806 Pennsylvania's proprietors sent a surveyor to run lines through the settlement. The settlers turned to Ingham for advice. He knew he could channel but not obstruct his neighbors' resistance. "I told them to make any kind of opposition they pleased, only to kill and hurt nobody, nor let anybody appear in arms. When this surveyor came a great many of the inhabitants collected, some in the woods shooting [in the air], others around the surveyor threatening him. I was afraid some worse mischief would happen, so I ordered some one to break the [surveyor's] compass or I would. Upon this one of the company broke the compass and the surveyor went away."[17]

Three interrelated characteristics distinguished those districts where settlers secured the critical allegiance of their leading men in favor of resistance. These characteristics simultaneously increased the agrarians' ability to pressure their leading men, and their leaders' readiness to respond to that pressure. First, resistance districts were contested: conflicting titles and jurisdictional disputes cast doubt on proprietary claims and on authorities' legitimacy, providing pretexts for resistance. Mid-Maine was a welter of conflicting, overlapping Indian and Crown titles, a confusion that encouraged settlers to justify improving possession as ownership's only true font. Anti-Renters turned first to Massachusetts, then to the Stockbridge Indians for free or cheap titles to justify resisting New York's landlords. Similarly, the Green Mountain Boys favored legally suspect but dirt-cheap New Hampshire titles as a means of evading higher land prices or dreaded rents to New York's landlords. The Wild Yankees endorsed the Susquehanna Company's free grants to avoid paying the Pennsylvania proprietors' price.[18]

Second, resistance emerged in the economically marginal districts where settlers could ill-afford the burdens of rents or land payments. Rough, hilly districts with inferior land and poor access to market attracted only especially poor newcomers and prolonged their marginality. Vermont, New York's Yankee borderlands, mid-Maine's backcountry, and the upper Susquehanna all fit this description. Dr. Robert H. Rose reported of the Wild Yankees, "They can not pay at present. They are a very industrious set of people, & such as make the best first settlers in a country like this; but the difficulty of clearing the land is so great that some years expire before a man can raise a subsistence for his family from it." Least able to pay for their lands, these settlers had the most to gain from resistance, and the least to lose from possible defeat. Chronically anxious over their tenuous hold on the "liberty" of independent producers, they were sensitive to any exaction on their limited means. And with little reason to anticipate a boom in local land values, the settlers in marginal districts were less susceptible to the prospect that tomorrow they could profit by reselling what their proprietor sold them today, a prospect that corroded agrarian solidarity in more fertile areas. Moreover, the leading men in marginal districts were few and closer to their neighbors' circumstances and culture than was the case in more promising districts. More loyal to their neighbors and less likely to receive proprietary patronage, marginal districts' rougher-edged leading men were quicker to commit themselves to community solidarity.[19]

Third, resistance districts enjoyed a crucial degree of isolation that afforded some cultural autonomy. The same rough terrain and isolation that prolonged the settlers' marginality also provided a common identity in opposition to the more prosperous outside world. Shared hardships and cultural adaptations drew yeomen and leading men together against the liens placed on their labor by wealthy outsiders who knew none of their difficulties. A sense of their remoteness increased the settlers' confidence in their capacity to repel external authority. Finally, it meant sufficient distance from authority's presence for yeomen to nurture their agrarian ideas through the fragile, initial stage of experimentation, honing their notions into the local consensus and conviction essential to solidarity against external authority. Agrarians initially adopted native American costumes simply to disguise their identities, but over time they elaborated their mock-Indian identity. They adopted more garish costumes, and cultivated the myth of a benevolent Indian king come to the settlers' rescue, in the words of one Maine settler, "to Cut down all poopery [Popery] and kill the Devil and give the world of mankind some piece by stopping the progres of Rogues and Deceivers and helping every man to his right and privilidges and libertys: the same as our indian nation injoys. . . ." With their elaborate costumes and rituals they pointedly set themselves apart from the outside world that harbored their proprietary foes. This strengthened group identity and loyalty in opposition to those not privy to the resistance's culture, encouraging the participants to stand together against external authority's laws.[20]

The ideas upholding resistance emerged from the combination of (partial) internal autonomy with external threats to the yeomen's tenuous economic autonomy. The agrarian vision advanced by backcountry rebels was not the ordinary, day-to-day intellectual possession of all American yeomen; rather, it was the distinct elaboration of previously inchoate notions, an elaboration rendered necessary and possible in specific situations of external threat and internal autonomy. Men who did not need a full-fledged agrarian ideology to protect their interests, or who did not live where resistance seemed possible, simply did not develop one.[21]

EXPANSION

Backcountry resistance increased in the wake of the American revolutionary war with the dramatic expansion of the bounds of the contested, marginal, and (relatively) autonomous districts where yeomen and leading men drew together against external gentlemen. Accelerating migration inland away from the Atlantic seaboard multiplied the settled backcountry. During the period 1760–1800 frontier migration redistributed most of the population increase in the United States to new counties virtually unpopulated by whites in 1760. In 1790, counties virtually unpopulated thirty years before claimed one-third of the nation's population; ten years later that share exceeded two-fifths. During the 1790s the post-1760 frontier region's population grew five times faster than the longer-settled seaboard. Except for the first colonists in the early seventeenth century, never before nor since has such a high proportion of America's white population lived in newly settled communities.[22]

This frontier migration occurred at the same moment that the Revolution discredited received authority and legitimated confronting rulers who imperiled "natural rights." As in the English Revolution of the 1640s depicted by Christopher Hill, the American Revolution encouraged a creative, cultural ferment among ordinary men and women seeking to bypass a learned clergy to attain direct contact with divinity. The Revolution's dramatic unpredictability encouraged millennial anticipation. The thoughts of common folk were alive with new possibilities. On 30 December 1781 Jonathan Sayward of York, Maine wrote in his diary, "In the present struggle every body's imagination is exercised, and hath produced new disorders. Distraction is become . . . common, new kinds of sicknesses, new sectaries in religion, various opinions: yes I do not know but there must be new heavens and new earth before all these things shall be finished. I had almost forgot to add we have new pollitions and new polliticks, almost as strange as the other disorders." Sayward concluded that the people were "remarkably unsettled in religious as well as political principles." Seven years later, William Frost, a conservative merchant from York, worried, "There is nothing but tumult & noise & free thinkers, prognosticators, & the Deavil knows what stiring about now a days, but I hope the time is near at hand when every lowsey fellow shall not be a law maker." Settlers carried this ferment with them into the many new backcountry settlements formed immediately after the Revolution.[23]

In every agrarian resistance or rebellion antiauthoritarian evangelical preachers encouraged, clarified, spread, and invested with divine meaning their settler neighbors' agrarian notions. Baptist preacher James Finn was one of the Wild Yankees' leaders, moderating a 20 July 1786 meeting that declared, "an equal distribution of property, and not engrossing large domains, is the basis of free and equal government, founded on republican principles. . . . the labours bestowed in subduing a rugged wilderness were our own, and can never be wrested from us without infringing the eternal rules of right." Rev. Jacob Johnson, a New Light Congregationalist who preached among the Wild Yankees, told Timothy Pickering that the Susquehanna "lands belonged to the Con[necticu]t people, by the laws of God & nature; but that the laws of Penn[sylvani]a would take them from them: that laws contrary to the laws of God & Nature were not to be obeyed." Ethan Allen's idiosyncratic deism was either irrelevant to, or at odds with, his enormous personal popularity in Vermont; indeed, ultraevangelical "Antinomians" (who sought to bypass a learned clergy in pursuit of direct spiritual encounters) played important roles in mobilizing Vermont's resistance. A New York supporter reported:

Another Kind of People who have Contributed much to the Continuing the People in their state of outlawry is a religious order that have lately sprang up. One Reuben Jones is the Father of this Sect and one

> Alijah Lovejoy is a Fellow Labourer and preacher of the Same—this pious order profess the Greatest Reverence for the Holy Word of God and declare it is the Law of a perfect Law-giver, and contains in it all Laws necessary for the Well Ruling ordering and Governing all Kingdoms and Counties on the Earth that it is Blasphemy against the g_d given [law] for anybody or bodies of men to make any Laws or ordonances and Sinful to obey such Laws and ordonances when made . . . that in the Holy book of God there is not so much as Magna Charta, Habeas Corpus Act, Writs of Habeas Corpus, Supervisors, Sheriffs, Constables, Grand-jurors or pettit Jurys, . . . and that therefore these words names etc ought to be Treated with a Holy Contempt as becometh Saints, these two Reformers have had Considerable success not having been on their Mission more than a year.

Mid-Maine's agrarian leaders all wrote or spoke in a religious vein, and all claimed religious authority. Prominent in both the North Carolina Regulation and western Pennsylvania's Whiskey Rebellion, Herman Husband was a mystical visionary, itinerant preacher, and prolific religious pamphleteer, who espoused "Antinomian" principles identical to those found in Maine and Vermont, and who also invoked those principles to justify resisting political elites. Husband was also a rare Pennsylvania assemblyman to support the Susquehanna Yankees' homestead claims.[24]

Federalist gentlemen worried that migration to the frontier compounded the destabilizing potential of evangelical religion and recent revolution by removing thousands from older districts where social and political authority combined in the same traditionally recognized and respected families. While touring mid-Maine, Timothy Dwight, arch-Federalist and president of Yale College, observed, "In most new settlements a considerable proportion of the adventurers will, almost of course consist of roving, disorderly, vicious men. In the regular, established society in which they were born, they were awed and restrained. On the new grounds to which they resort, they are set loose, and usually break out into open licentiousness of principle and conduct." In this view, the timing of that migration could not have been worse, for it occurred at the very moment when common folk, newly agitated by the Revolution's exertions and the evangelicals' preaching, most needed elite counsel to calm their expectations and to recognize the proper limits on their "liberty."[25]

Timothy Pickering agreed that frontier "anarchy" ramified "the natural instability of the common people." He, like the other Federalist grandees, saw a civilizing mission as well as potential profits in his frontier lands. He observed of the Susquehanna's settlers, "their [agri]culture is ordinary and often of the most slovenly kind but the hovels they dwell in are beyond description. They are generally built with logs, but in the very worst manner. In a great part of them there is no chimney, but a hole is left in the roof, thro' which the smoke escapes. The children [are] often very ragged & the whole family very dirty. Indeed, I did not imagine such general apparent wretchedness could be found in the United States." Blaming the settlers' poverty on their supposed indolence, Pickering concluded: "I shall have it in my inclination, as it will be not a little in my power, to introduce such means of education as will prevent their degenerating to a savage state, to which they have been verging."[26]

In September 1787 a Connecticut newspaper warned, "a dangerous combination of villains, composed of runaway debtors, criminals, adherents of Shays, &c is now actually forming on the river Susquehanna." The newspaper concluded, "we see *banditties* rising up against law and good order in all quarters of our country." But, although correct in seeing Anti-Renters, Shaysites, Wild Yankees, and Liberty-Men as of a piece, gentlemen grossly overestimated the degree of collusion between them; indeed, the agrarians' defiant localism precluded interregional cooperation, contributing to the eventual frustration of their visions.[27]

CONTRACTION

Agrarian resistance peaked during the two decades following the American Revolution. But, the social collapse into disunion, civil war, and anarchy that many observers forecast in the 1790s on the basis of agrarian discontent, sectional rivalry, political partisanship, and urban rioting was averted in the succeeding decade by the Jeffersonians' sweeping political triumph. America's more astute, more pragmatic, and more ambitious gentlemen saw Federalist intransigence toward popular discontent as both a national danger and a political opportunity. Confident in their ability to conduct republican governance in a manner that channeled and mollified popular grievances, these more flexible gentlemen rallied around Thomas Jefferson to shatter the Federalists' political predominance.[28]

Determined to accumulate property and power, the Jeffersonians were loath to undermine the legal defenses surrounding great property. Characteristically, Jeffersonian politicians simultaneously legislated against extralegal resistance while establishing institutional mechanisms to set compromise prices, whereby the settlers would pay *something* to their proprietors for the land. In 1801 Pennsylvania's Jeffersonian legislature appointed commissioners, headed by Thomas Cooper, to liberally apply a 1799 "Compromise Act," allowing most of the Susquehanna's Yankee settlers (those with claims pre-dating 1783) to secure up to 300 acres at an average of about thirty-two cents an acre. The state government drew upon these payments and additional state funds to compensate Pennsylvania's affected proprietors. Also in 1801, the legislature stiffened the 1795 "Intrusion Act," providing draconian penalties against new squatters and the leading men who abetted them.[29]

Upon capturing Massachusetts's executive and legislative branches in 1807 (the life-term judiciary remained solidly and stolidly Federalist, restricting the relief that the Jeffersonians could extend), the Jeffersonians responded to mid-Maine's agrarian unrest with a program similar to Pennsylvania's. In 1808 the Massachusetts legislature passed the "Betterment Act," allowing juries to set compromise prices that settler defendants in ejectment cases should pay to their proprietor plaintiffs. A handful of jury decisions per community usually sufficed to set the prevailing price that most settlers paid their proprietors: generally two to three dollars per acre. In 1810 the legislature passed a bill intended to crush remaining resistance by authorizing the use of militia against insurgents, and by levying stiff new fines and prison sentences for wearing Indian disguise, resisting deputy sheriffs, or obstructing surveys. In both Maine and northeastern Pennsylvania, agrarian resistance faded as the leading men endorsed the Jeffersonians' program. Because New York's manor lords insisted on renting their land—refusing to sell—the Jeffersonians could not solve the Anti-Renter agitation. When the Anti-Renters surged to unprecedented strength in the 1840s, most Democrats staunchly defended the landlords, obliging the farmers to find limited support among the Whigs.[30]

Jeffersonianism sapped resistance by winning over the leading men. The Jeffersonians' message and approach offered the leading men a path out of the protracted conflicts in a manner that preserved their prosperity and local influence. Wary and weary of their humbler neighbors' armed capacity to attack anyone who violated their notions of community solidarity, most backcountry leading men appreciated the Jeffersonians' promise that, once cleansed of Federalist privilege, republican institutions could peacefully and equitably mediate social conflicts. The Jeffersonians' triumph offered leading men compelling arguments for persuading their neighbors that further resistance was counterproductive, that their new friends in office offered all the relief that was possible. Moreover, the Jeffersonians' liberal social vision made sense to the backcountry's leading men. They had garnered property by hard work and market shrewdness, but could not obtain a full measure of respect and acceptance among the Federalist gentry. Consequently, leading men readily identified with the Jeffersonians' promise to secure a perfectly equitable economy, polity, and society, by allowing the free market and voluntary association—rather than political privilege and social elitism—to allocate wealth, power, and status. In sum, the Jeffersonians' liberal vision offered the leading men an escape from their uncomfortable middle position in the land conflicts, an escape in a manner that promised to complete their drive to respectability in the eyes of the wider world. Over time, the social mobility of a strategic few shrank the contested, marginal, autonomous districts that had temporarily expanded after the Revolution.[31]

CONCLUSION

During the two decades after the Revolution, the settlers in certain locales found the social space from authority necessary to organize efforts to defend their new freeholds: the property that enabled them to live free from another man's dominion. In the process, the settlers defended their version of the American Revolution. The settlers' resistance helped topple the Federalist regime and inaugurate a more liberal social order guided by Jeffersonian politicians. By defending their values and their lands, these settlers contributed to the preservation, for another generation, of the republic of small producers living in agrarian independence from the domination of would-be landlords.

NOTES

ACKNOWLEDGMENTS: I am grateful to the late Stephen Botein, and to Robert A. Gross, Michael McGiffert, Peter Mancall, and Alfred F. Young for comments and suggestions that greatly improved this essay.

PUBLISHING NOTE: By exploring agrarian resistance in New York and Pennsylvania—as well as in Maine—this essay extends the analysis in *Liberty Men and Great Proprietors: The Revolutionary Settlement on the Maine Frontier, 1760–1820* (Chapel Hill, N.C., 1990). Excerpts used with permission of the University of North Carolina Press.

1. Octavius Pickering and Charles W. Upham, eds., *The Life of Timothy Pickering*, 2 vols. (Salem, Mass., 1829) 2:297–98 (quote), 381–97.

2. For Hillsdale's rough terrain and history see Franklin Ellis, *History of Columbia County, New York* (Philadelphia, 1878), 368–70. On the earlier tenant uprisings see Sung Bok Kim, *Landlord and Tenant in Colonial New York: Manorial Society, 1664–1775* (Chapel

Hill, N.C., 1978), 281–345. For the sheriff's party see Alfred F. Young, *The Democratic Republicans of New York: The Origins, 1763–1797* (Chapel Hill, N.C., 1967), 203–5; and David Maldwyn Ellis, *Landlords and Farmers in the Hudson-Mohawk Region, 1790–1850* (Ithaca, N.Y., 1946), 34–35. For Schuyler and the Yankees see David J. Goodall, "New Light on the Border: New England Squatter Settlements in New York During the American Revolution" (Ph.D. diss., State University of New York at Albany, 1984), 177–84. The protest petition quoted is Petrus Pulver et al. to the New York legislature, 7 January 1795, in Edmund Bailey O'Callaghan, *The Documentary History of the State of New York,* 4 vols. (Albany, 1851) 3:834–41.

    3. Henry Knox's notice, 26 May 1800, Henry Knox Papers (hereafter cited as HKP) 52:79. Massachusetts Historical Society (hereafter cited as MHS); North Callahan, *Henry Knox, General Washington's General* (New York, 1958), 338–64; Robert Houston's deposition, 14 August 1800, Bradstreet Wiggins' deposition, 15 August 1800, and George Ulmer to Henry Knox, 23 July 1800, in the related papers of the resolve of 15 November 1800, Massachusetts Archives; and George Ulmer et al., deposition, 31 October 1801, HKP, Box 6, Maine Historical Society (hereafter cited as MeHS).

    4. Henry Knox to George Ulmer, 11 July 1801, HKP 44:25, MHS; Thurston Whiting and Benjamin Brackett to Henry Knox, 7 September 1801, HKP 52:87, MHS.

    5. On the Revolution's backcountry dimension persisting after the "statehouse" dimension was concluded, see Elisha P. Douglass, "A Three-Fold American Revolution," in John Parker and Carol Urness, eds., *The American Revolution: A Heritage of Change* (Minneapolis, 1975), 69–83; Richard E. Ellis, *The Jeffersonian Crisis: Courts and Politics in the Young Republic* (New York, 1971), 250–84; and, especially, Richard Maxwell Brown, "Back Country Rebellions and the Homestead Ethic in America, 1740–1799," in Brown and Don E. Fehrenbacher, eds., *Tradition, Conflict, and Modernization: Perspectives on the American Revolution* (New York, 1977), 79–82.

    6. Robert Houston and George Ulmer to Gov. Caleb Strong, 12 August 1800, in the related papers of the resolve of 15 November 1800, Massachusetts Archives (quote). For the differing notions of property see Alan Taylor, " 'A Kind of Warr': The Contest for Land on the Northeastern Frontier, 1750–1820," *The William and Mary Quarterly,* 3d series (hereafter cited as *WMQ*), 46 (January 1989): 3–26. On labor as the source of property see Ethan Allen, *A Brief Narrative of the Proceedings of the Government of New York . . .* (Hartford, Conn., 1774; Evans no. 13102), 135–38.

    7. Thomas Fitzsimons in the "Debate on the Supplement to the

Confirming Act," 16 November 1787, *Susquehannah Company Papers* 9:188, 278. See also Thomas P. Slaughter, *The Whiskey Rebellion: Frontier Epilogue to the American Revolution,* (New York, 1986), 134; Gordon S. Wood, *The Creation of the American Republic* (Chapel Hill, N.C., 1969), 396–413; and Alan Taylor, *Liberty Men and Great Proprietors: The Revolutionary Settlement on the Maine Frontier, 1760– 1820* (Chapel Hill, N.C., 1990), 31–59.

8. For the yeomanry's pursuit of family independence see Jack P. Greene, "Independence, Improvement, and Authority: Toward a Framework for Understanding the Histories of the Southern Backcountry during the Era of the American Revolution," in Ronald Hoffman, Thad W. Tate, and Peter J. Albert, eds., *An Uncivil War: the Southern Backcountry during the American Revolution* (Charlottesville, Va., 1985), 11–12; Randall A. Roth, " 'Whence This Strange Fire'?: Religious and Reform Movements in the Connecticut River Valley of Vermont, 1791–1843," (Ph.D. diss., Yale University, 1981), 3; and Slaughter, *Whiskey Rebellion,* 112. For dread of tenancy see Ethan Allen, *A Vindication of the Opposition of the Inhabitants of Vermont to the Government of New York* (Dresden, Vt., 1779), repr. in E. P. Walton, ed., *Records of the Council of Safety* 1:462, 465; Gregory H. Nobles, *"Divisions throughout the Whole": Politics and Society in Hampshire County, Massachusetts, 1740–1775* (New York, 1983), 124; Edward Countryman, *A People in Revolution: The American Revolution and Political Society in New York, 1760–1790* (Baltimore, 1981), 48–49; Mark H. Jones, "Herman Husband: Millenarian, Carolina Regulator, and Whiskey Rebel," (Ph.D. diss., Northern Illinois University, 1982), 68–72; and, especially, Richard L. Bushman, "Massachusetts Farmers and the Revolution," in Bushman et al., *Society, Freedom and Conscience; the American Revolution in Virginia, Massachusetts, and New York* (New York, 1976), 77–124.

9. John McFarland to James Duane, 21 December 1771, quoted in Patricia U. Bonomi, *A Factious People: Politics and Society in Colonial New York* (New York, 1971), 203n. For the pursuit of extreme local autonomy see Jackson Turner Main, *Political Parties before the Constitution* (Chapel Hill, N.C., 1973), 395, 403; Slaughter, *Whiskey Rebellion,* 72; and R. E. Ellis, *Jeffersonian Crisis,* 250–65. For fear of "great men" see Nobles, *"Divisions,"* 185–86; Ruth Bogin, "New Jersey's True Policy: the Radical Republican Vision of Abraham Clark," *WMQ* 35 (1978), 105–6; and Edward Countryman, " 'Out of the Bounds of the Law': Northern Land Rioters in the Eighteenth Century," in Alfred F. Young, ed. *The American Revolution: Explorations in the History of American Radicalism* (Dekalb, Ill., 1976), 49. On the right to resist laws that threatened the yeomanry's property see

Allen, *Brief Narrative*, 57, 169. For the limited strategy see Thomas
L. Purvis, "Origins and Patterns of Agrarian Unrest in New Jersey,
1735–1754," *WMQ* 39 (October 1982): 623–25. Allen, *Brief Narrative*,
42, insisted the Green Mountain Boys carefully refrained from inter-
fering with writs of executions for debt, and in breaking jails, did not
liberate debtors; in *Liberty and Property without Oppression: As Is
Set Forth in Sundry LETTERS Directed to the PUBLIC of the County
of Monmouth, in the Province of New Jersey* (n.p., 1769; Evans no.
41951), 12–13, New Jersey's "Liberty-Boys" pledged not to interfere
with the criminal trials that were essential to "the Peace of Society,
and good Order of Government," and promised to return home as
soon as their "Regulation" succeeded. For agrarians calling on gentlemen to renounce land speculation, and confine themselves to commerce and governance, see James Shurtleff, *A Concise Review of the
Spirit Which Seemed to Govern in the Time of the American War,
Compared with the Spirit Which Now Prevails* . . . (Augusta, Me.,
1978; Evans no. 34548), 27.

10. Frederick Jackson Turner, "Contributions of the West to
American Democracy," *Atlantic Monthly*, 91 (January 1903): 91;
Brown, "Back Country Rebellions," 79–82; Edmund S. Morgan, "Con-
flict and Consensus in the American Revolution," in Stephen G.
Kurtz and James H. Hutson, eds., *Essays on the American Revolution*
(Chapel Hill, N.C., 1973), 298–301. On political fortune building and
land grants see Kim, *Landlord and Tenant*, 3–43. For the fundamen-
tal distinction between gentlemen and other Americans, see Jackson
Turner Main, *The Antifederalists: Critics of the Constitution, 1781–
1788* (Chapel Hill, N.C., 1961), 3; and Robert Mutch, "Yeoman and
Merchant in Pre-industrial America: Eighteenth Century Massachusetts as a Case Study," *Societas* 7 (1977): 279–302.

11. On New Jersey see Gary S. Horowitz, "New Jersey Land Riots, 1745–1755," (Ph.D. diss., Ohio State University, 1966); and Purvis, "Origins and Patterns," 600–627. On Rocky Mount see Robert L.
Meriwether, *The Expansion of South Carolina, 1729–1765* (Kings-
port, Tenn., 1940), 95–96, 107. On New York see Irving Mark, *Agrarian Conflicts in Colonial New York, 1711–1775* (New York, 1940);
Staughton Lynd, *Anti-Federalism in Dutchess County, New York* (Chicago, 1962); Countryman, *People in Revolution*, 46–54; Kim, *Landlord and Tenant*, 281–415; and Eldridge Honaker Pendleton, "The
New York Anti-Rent Controversy, 1830–1860," (Ph.D. diss., University of Virginia, 1974). On Granville District see A. Roger Ekirch,
*'Poor Caroline': Politics and Society in Colonial North Carolina,
1729–1776* (Chapel Hill, N.C., 1981), 132–47; and William S. Powell,
et al., eds., *The Regulators in North Carolina: A Documentary His-*

tory, 1759–1776 (Raleigh, N.C., 1971), 4–12. On Susquehanna see Peter S. Onuf, *The Origins of the Federal Republic: Jurisdictional Controversies in the United States* (Philadelphia, 1983), 49–73. On Maine see Gordon E. Kershaw, *The Kennebeck Proprietors, 1749–1775* (Portland, Me., 1975), 150–81; and Thomas A. Jeffrey, "The Malta War," (M.A. thesis, University of Maine, 1976). On Vermont see Countryman, "Out of Bounds," 39–61. On the land conflicts around Pittsburgh see Dorothy Fennell, "From Rebelliousness to Insurrection: A Social History of the Whiskey Rebellion, 1765–1802," (Ph.D. diss., University of Pittsburgh, 1981), 25–37. On the Ohio squatters see Robert L. Brunhouse, *The Counter-Revolution in Pennsylvania, 1776–1790* (Harrisburg, Pa., 1942), 127–28; and Randolph C. Downes, "Ohio's Squatter Governor: William Hogland of Hoglandstown," in Ohio State Archaelogical and Historical Society, *Quarterly* 43 (1934): 273–82. On northwest Pennsylvania see Elizabeth K. Henderson, "The Northwestern Lands of Pennsylvania, 1790–1812," *Pennsylvania Magazine of History and Biography* 40 (1936): 131–60. On the Holland Purchase see Paul Demond Evans, *The Holland Land Company* (Buffalo, N.Y., 1924), 397–427.

12. On Paxton see George William Franz, "Paxton: A Study of Community Structure and Mobility in the Colonial Pennsylvania Backcountry," (Ph.D. dissertation, Rutgers University, 1974). On North Carolina see Marvin L. Michael Kay, "The North Carolina Regulation, 1766–1776: A Class Conflict," in Young, *American Revolution,* 73–106; James P. Whittenberg, "Planters, Merchants, and Lawyers: Social Change and the Origins of the North Carolina Regulation," *WMQ* 34 (March 1977): 215–38; and Ekirch, *'Poor Caroline'* 161–210. For South Carolina see Rachel N. Klein, "Ordering the Backcountry: The South Carolina Regulation", *WMQ* 38 (October 1981): 661–80; and Richard Maxwell Brown, *The South Carolina Regulators* (Cambridge, Mass., 1963). On the "Liberty-Boys" see Larry R. Gerlach, *Prologue to Independence: New Jersey in the Coming of the American Revolution* (New Brunswick, N.J., 1976), 185–92. On eastern Vermont see Matt B. Jones, *Vermont in the Making, 1750–1777* (Cambridge, Mass., 1939), 255–75. For the Berkshire Constitutionalists see Robert J. Taylor, *Western Massachusetts in the Revolution* (Providence, R.I., 1954), 75–101. For Ely's Rebellion see ibid., 104–24; and Robert E. Moody, "Samuel Ely: Forerunner of Daniel Shays," *The New England Quarterly* 5 (1932): 105–34. For Shaysism see David P. Szatmary, *Shays' Rebellion: The Making of an Agrarian Insurrection* (Amherst, Mass., 1980). On the Whiskey and Fries rebellions see Slaughter, *Whiskey Rebellion;* and Barbara Karsky, "Agrarian Radicalism in the Late Revolutionary Period,

1780–1795," in Erich Angermann et al., eds., *New Wine in Old Skins: A Comparative View of Socio-Political Structures and Values Affecting the American Revolution* (Stuttgart, 1976), 87–114.

13. Brown, "Back Country Rebellions," 76–77, 85–90; Horowitz, "Land Riots," 70; Purvis, "Origins and Patterns," 614–16, 624–25.

14. Nathanial Allen to Col. John Jenkins, 25 June 1804 quoted in Louise Welles Murray, *A History of Old Tioga Point and Early Athens* (Athens, Pa., 1907), 420; Robert H. Rose to Samuel Hodgdon, 28 July 1803, and Timothy Beach to Robert H. Rose, 1 August 1803, in *The Susquehannah Company Papers* 11:399, 401–2; David Craft, *History of Bradford County, Pennsylvania* (Philadelphia, 1878), 49.

15. Artemas Kimball's deposition, 23 June 1820, Maine Executive Council Files, box 1, folder 10, Maine State Archives (quote). On leading men as "mediators" see Stephen Innes, *Labor in a New Land: Economy and Society in Seventeenth-Century Springfield* (Princeton, 1983), 17–42.

16. Brown, "Back Country Rebellions," 76–77, 85–90; Horowitz, "Land Riots," 70; Thomas L. Purvis, "Disaffection along the Millstone: the Petition of Dollens Heggeman and Anti-Proprietary Sentiment in Eighteenth-Century New Jersey," *New Jersey History* 100 (Fall-Winter 1983): 62; and Purvis, "Origins and Patterns," 614–16, 624–25).

17. Charles A. Jellison, *Ethan Allen: Frontier Rebel* (Syracuse, N.Y., 1969), 320–22; Brown, "Back Country Rebellions," 90; Ingham quoted in Craft, *Bradford County,* 443.

18. Oscar Handlin, "The Eastern Frontier of New York," *New York History* 18 (January 1937): 54–66, 75; Goodall, "Light on Border," 16–17; Thomas Young, *Some Reflections on the Dispute Between New-York, New-Hampshire, and Col. John Henry Lydius of Albany* (New Haven, Conn., 1764; Evans no. 9889), 14–15; F. Ellis, *Columbia County,* 40.

19. Robert H. Rose to Samuel Hodgdon, 28 July 1803 (quote), and Rose to Henry Drinker, 28 July 1803, in *The Susquehannah Company Papers* 11:401, 418. For quantitative evidence for the more egalitarian distribution of property amidst relative poverty in New York's Yankee borderland, see Goodall, "Light on the Border," 118–21. For similar evidence for mid-Maine see A. Taylor, *Liberty Men,* 61–87.

20. See Nobles, *Divisions,* 125, on "the settlers' perception of a shared disadvantage" giving them "a sense of their common attitudes and common identity." On Indian disguise and identity see Samuel Gardenier's deposition, 21 September 1771, in O'Callaghan, *History of New York,* 4:442–43; Pendleton, "Anti-Rent Controversy," 36–40;

Slaughter, *Whiskey Rebellion,* 113, 115, 188, 208–11; and Alan Taylor, " 'Stopping the Progres of Rogues and Deceivers': A White Indian Recruiting Notice of 1808," *WMQ* 42 (January 1985): 90–103, quote on 102. On the "producers' ideology" see Bogin, "True Policy," 104–6; Samuel Eliot Morison, ed., "William Manning's 'The Key of Libberty,' " *WMQ* 13 (1956): 202–54; and Paul G. Faler, *Mechanics and Manufacturers in the Early Industrial Revolution: Lynn, Massachusetts, 1780–1860* (Albany, N.Y., 1981), 31–33.

21. Alan Taylor, " 'The Seedplot of Sedition': The Struggle for the Waldo Patent Backlands, 1800–1801," in Geoff Eley and William Hunt, eds., *Reviving the English Revolution: Reflections and Elaborations on the Work of Christopher Hill* (London, 1988), 251–76.

22. On America's non-Indian population in 1760 see J. Potter, "The Growth of Population in America, 1700–1860," in D. V. Glass and D. E. C. Eversley, eds., *Population in History: Essays in Historic Demography* (Chicago, 1965), 638. On the location of the frontier in 1760 see Lester J. Cappon, ed., *Atlas of Early American History, the Revolutionary Era, 1760–1790* (Princeton, 1976), 22. For county-by-county population totals in 1790 see Evarts B. Greene and Virginia D. Harrington, *American Population Before the Federal Census of 1790* (Gloucester, Mass., 1966). For county-by-county population totals in 1800 see *Return of the Whole Number of Persons within the Several Districts of the United States* (Washington, D.C., 1802; Shaw-Shoemaker no. 3442). In 1800 the pre-1760 settled area had a population of 3,045,784 (57.4% of the nation's total, a 14.6% growth over that area's 1790 population) and the post-1760 settled areas had a population of 2,262,999 (42.6% of the nation's total, a 77.7% growth over its 1790 population). In 1760 the colonies' non-Indian population equalled 1,610,000. By 1800 the areas that had been setttled prior to 1760 increased their population by 1,435,484—less than the 2,262,999 residents in areas settled after 1760.

23. Stephen A. Marini, *Radical Sects of Revolutionary New England* (Cambridge, Mass., 1982); Christopher Hill, *The World Turned Upside Down: Radical Ideas During the English Revolution* (New York, 1972); Sayward quoted in J. H. Cary, " 'The Juditious are Intirely Neglected': the Fate of a Tory," *The New England Historic and Genealogical Register* 124 (1980): 113; William Frost to George Thatcher, 7 February 1788, George Thatcher Papers, Boston Public Library.

24. Minutes of a settlers' meeting, 20 July 1786; and Johnson quoted in Timothy Pickering's Journal, 25 January 1787, *Susquehannah Company Papers* 8:371; 9:51; Chilton Williamson, *Vermont in Quandary: 1763–1825* (Monpelier, Vt., 1949), 21 (Phelps' quote), 56

(on Jones's and Lovejoy's important roles in Vermont's independence movement). For the salience of "experimental religion" among New York's eastern border Yankees, see Goodall, "Light on the Border," 9–10, 275–79. For mid-Maine see A. Taylor, *Liberty Men*, 123–53. For Husband see M. H. Jones, "Herman Husband," especially 87–89, 94–96, 154–56, 339. On preachers' important role among New Jersey's land rioters see Horowitz, "Land Riots," 70–72, 87, 169. When it suited his propaganda purposes, Ethan Allen could adopt religious rhetoric. See [Ethan Allen], "The Vision of Junus, the Benningtonite," *Collections of the Vermont Historical Society* 1:105–8.

25. Timothy Dwight, *Travels in New England and New York*, 4 vols. (1821; Cambridge, Mass., 1969) 2:162; Peter S. Onuf, "Liberty, Development, and Union: Visions of the West in the 1780s," *WMQ* 43 (April 1986): 179–92. Some daring frontier ideologues made exactly the sort of connection between Revolutionary precedent and migration west that eastern gentlemen most dreaded. In the 1780s and 1790s Herman Husband expounded his visions of a "New Jerusalem" of independent farmers and artisans in the west who would secede from the eastern state governments controlled by "great men." Eastern gentlemen were not surprised to find Husband prominent in the Whiskey Rebellion of 1794. See M. H. Jones, "Herman Husband."

26. Timothy Pickering to George Clymer, 1 November 1787, *The Susquehannah Company Papers* 9:256 ("anarchy"); Timothy Pickering's Journal, 18 August 1786, *Susquehannah Company Papers* 8:384 ("slovenly"); Pickering to Rev. John Clark, 11 October 1786 ("inclination"), in Pickering and Upham, eds., *Timothy Pickering* 2:192–93. Years later, when obliged by declining fortunes to supervise clearing land for a farm in northeastern Pennsylvania, Timothy Pickering reconsidered: "Clearing land I find much more laborious, tedious, and expensive than I supposed, and yet the first settlers here had to encounter many more difficulties than I have met with." See Pickering to his wife, 2 November 1800, in ibid. 4:16.

27. Extract from the *Connecticut Courant*, 10 September 1787, *Susquehannah Company Papers* 9:188. On the weakness of interregional agrarian ties see, for example, Jellison, *Ethan Allen*, 314–21; and Purvis, "Origins and Patterns," 621–22.

28. Slaughter, *Whiskey Rebellion*, 105. For the Jeffersonians' liberal values see Joyce Appleby, "Commercial Farming and the Agrarian Myth in the Early Republic," *Journal of American History* 68 (1982): 833–49; Appleby, "Republicanism in Old and New Contexts," *WMQ* 43 (January 1986): 24–34.

29. Robert J. Taylor, ed., "Introduction," *The Susquehannah Company Papers* vol. 11, 1801–08 (Ithaca, N.Y., 1971), xv–xxviii.

30. Ronald F. Banks, *Maine Becomes a State: The Movement to Separate Maine from Massachusetts, 1785–1820* (Middletown, Conn., 1970), 55–56; Act 122 (6 March 1810), in *Laws of the Commonwealth of Massachusetts, Passed by the General Court* . . . (Boston, 1810; Shaw-Shoemaker no. 23309), 218–21; Pendleton, "Anti-Rent Controversy," 30–32, 64–66. The Pennsylvania Jeffersonians tried to defend the interests of northwestern Pennsylvania's squatters but the federal judiciary, specifically an 1805 ruling by Chief Justice John Marshall, secured the proprietors' complete triumph there; see Henderson, "Northwestern Lands," 152–53.

31. For the consequences of social mobility on agrarian solidarity, see Morgan, "Conflict and Consensus," 292; Greene, "Independence, Improvement, and Authority," 17–20; and James T. Lemon, "Early Americans and their Social Environment," *Journal of Historical Geography* 6 (1980): 115–31.

"The Key of Libberty"

William Manning and Plebeian Democracy
1747–1814

MICHAEL MERRILL

AND

SEAN WILENTZ

The first page of William Manning's unpublished "Constitution of the Labouring Society," appearing at the conclusion of the 1798 draft of his essay, "The Key of Libberty." The second paragraph of the introduction states his fundamental principle: "As Labour is the Soul parrant of all property by which all are seported, therefore the Cauling ought to be honourable and the Labourer Respected." Article 1 opens the Society to "all the free male persons that are twenty one years of age, who Labour for a Living."

"You shall see men you never heard of before, whose names you don't know, . . . rude and sturdy, experienced and wise men, keeping their castles, or teaming up their summer's wood, or chopping alone in the woods; men fuller of talk and rare adventure in the sun and wind and rain, than a chestnut is of meat; who were out not only in '75 and 1812, but have been out every day of their lives; greater men than Homer, or Chaucer, or Shakespeare, only they never got time to say so; they never took to the way of writing. Look at their fields, and imagine what they might write, if ever they should put pen to paper."

—Henry David Thoreau,
A Week on the Concord and Merrimack Rivers (1849)

William Manning was one of those "rude and sturdy, experienced and wise men" whose idealized memory haunted Henry Thoreau. A farmer and tavernkeeper in Billerica, Massachusetts, until his death in 1814, Manning answered the patriot call to arms in 1775 and fought at the battle of Concord. After the Revolution, he took an active interest in Shays's Rebellion, the debates over Alexander Hamilton's fiscal program, and the other momentous events that shaped the postwar era. But unlike the thousands of other Middlesex farmers, living and dead, whom Thoreau called to mind, Manning actually did become a writer.[1]

The results of Manning's labors, dating from the 1790s, were not literary masterpieces: He was no Homer, Chaucer, or Shakespeare. Nor did his writings have any discernible impact on his time, for they were only published more than a century after his death. Nevertheless, they are remarkable documents. Although framed as attacks on Federalist policies, his two main essays ranged much wider, to consider what Manning viewed as an eternal struggle between moneyed men and the laboring majority over free government. And in his most important work, "The Key of Libberty," he issued the first known call for a national organization of American laboring men and their political allies.

Manning was hardly the only plebeian democratic writer to take up the issues he did; indeed, the more that historians delve into the popular intellectual history of the early republic, the more it seems that Manning's basic outlook was widely shared, perhaps by a majority of the citizenry.[2] But none of the other popular writers yet discovered surpassed Manning in his tough-minded, realistic, ambitious appraisal of class and politics in postrevolutionary America. None revealed quite so much about the intellectual origins and self-making of a plebeian political thinker. None had nearly as much to say about how the laboring majority might ultimately secure the democratic rights it had fought for in the Revolution.

More broadly, Manning's essays raise serious questions about prevailing approaches to the ideas and ideologies of the revolutionary era—especially those that would render democratic thinking as a by-product of either classical republicanism, capitalist liberalism, or some admixture of the two. The main thrust of Manning's arguments hardly ran along classical republican lines. Although he believed that virtue had its place, he remained firm in his realistic conviction that politics mainly rested on self-interest, as did all human affairs—an idea he derived from the Bible. Unlike some Country ideologues, Manning never cultivated a disdain for profitable commerce; quite the reverse. Nor did he think primarily in terms of preserving local privileges against a corrupt, centralized, tyrannical state.[3]

At the same time, Manning never imagined that the key of liberty lay in unleashing private interests in an unfettered marketplace. Although he heartily endorsed honorable trade and money-making as a means to human happiness, he refused to elevate the pursuit of personal self-interest to a good in itself. As he understood humankind, the allure of profits would always pose a threat to the achievement and preservation of a democratic polity. Believing that the chief aim of government was "the protection of the life, liberty, and property of individuals," he remained mindful, above all, of how great concentrations of wealth and power in the hands of "the Few" could injure the well-being of "the Many"—what Manning called "the benefit of the community."[4] A man of commerce himself, he well understood the uses of banks and other financial institutions in facilitating the circulation of money and the expansion of trade—but he had no use for the emerging system that the world would come to know as capitalism.[5] Nor did Manning foresee an American economy that would operate as an inherently self-regulating, "classless" system which the government would do well to leave alone—according to some historians, the central belief of postrevolutionary democratic thought.[6] On the contrary, he insisted, without the constant political vigilance of the laboring majority, the moneyed minority would always rig the marketplace in its own favor.

Manning, in short, had no truck with the republicanism of either a country squire or a countinghouse capitalist. His was the democratic republicanism of a Calvinist yeoman and petty trader, outraged at how the postwar era augured the triumph of a new American system of exploitation. It was a way of thinking—forward-looking, expansive, optimistic about the potential blessings of a genuinely democratic commerce—that was foreign to any fanciful depictions of early America as a communitarian pastorale. But it was equally a way of thinking that was deeply suspicious of moneyed men—not simply the traditional, hierarchical gentry, but all those who lived without performing productive labor. And if Manning is any indication, it was a way of thinking that helped greatly to inspire the early democratization of American politics.

Manning's writings carried the strong imprints of his country background and of his political awakening during the Revolution. He was born in Billerica, a farming community about eight miles north of Concord, on 21 May 1747, the eldest son of William Manning, senior, a small farmer and tavernkeeper. We know little about his youth, except that he had only about six months of formal schooling. One episode, however, stands out in local records. In March 1769, when only 22 years old and still living in his father's household, William married Sarah Heywood, also 22, of nearby Woburn. Six months later Sarah gave birth to their first child.[7]

The elder William Manning left no direct statement about the circumstances of his son's marriage, but there are signs of disapproval and strain in the Manning household over the next few years. William *père* provided the couple with some livestock, but failed to sell or deed over any land to his eldest son during his own lifetime. In 1775 his neighbors elected the younger William (now aged 27) as the town's highway surveyor, a recognition of his impending coming-of-age; three years earlier, however, the father had quietly voided his will and drawn up a new one, stipulating that the land be shared after his death by his wife and all his children. When the older man finally died in 1776, William contested the will and gave way only when his siblings agreed to sell their shares for £40 each (a deal he apparently financed by selling 40 acres of his allotment to a neighbor).[8]

Thus the headstrong, resourceful William Manning consolidated his place in the town as the head of the household. Like many young men in the long-settled, land-hungry Massachusetts countryside, he had struggled against the traditional, patriarchal constraints imposed by his father—in the end, buying out his siblings to ensure that the farm he inherited was a viable property. Yet given his boyhood, and his location, he could hardly have foreseen any marked change in his way of life. Historians have accurately caught the tempo of late-eighteenth-century Billerica in their passing descriptions of the place as a sleepy, "secondary country town."[9] A network of simple country roads had always linked the town to its neighboring communities; by the middle of the eighteenth century, a nearby secondary highway facilitated travel to and from Boston, nearly 20 miles to the southeast. Most of the district's farming families (including the Mannings) produced a marketable surplus of grain each year, some of which found its way to Concord, Boston, and elsewhere. But Billerica's commercial contacts were only of secondary or tertiary importance to the local economy. In 1771, the proportion of Billerica farms that practiced mixed husbandry and produced enough foodstuffs to be self-sufficient was greater than the statewide average for Massachusetts towns.[10]

Like most other New Englanders young Manning found himself at the intersection of different sets of economic relations, traditional and modern, communal and commercial. A Manning tavern account book spells out in detail his simultaneous connections with local barter networks and with commercial markets—a vantage point that would help shape his views about national political affairs.[11] If he never stopped serving what he called "the erivarsable sentance of Heaven on Man . . . to hard Labour dureing life," he did have the promise of a secure living in return.[12] Having seized his personal independency in 1776, he might well have quietly lived out his life within the familiar environs of his farm, his tavern, and his town. Upon this prospect, however, had already broken the uncertain storms of war and revolution.

Billericans played their part in the events leading up to the battle at Concord and the eventual rupture between the colonies and Great Britain. By the mid-1770s the town was among the most radical in the Massachusetts countryside, one of a handful willing to join the Solemn League and Covenant organized by Boston militants in 1774 in response to the Coercive Acts.[13] The Crown and Parliament, Billericans agreed on that occasion, were attempting to "dragoon us into slavery because we disdain patiently to take the yoke upon our neck," and their official protest ominously recalled "the unlimited Prerogative, contended for by those arbitrary & misguided Princes, *Charles* the First & *James* the Second, for which the One lost his Life, & the Other his Kingdom."[14] In April 1775, when the royal governor, Gen. Thomas Gage, issued his fateful order that sent a detachment of 700 British troops against the military stores at Concord, Billericans quickly rallied to the cause. The town's militia arrived in Concord in time for a bloody skirmish with the British at Merriam's Corner, and many of them then joined in hot pursuit of the retreating redcoats. Among them was Sgt. William Manning.[15]

Years later, in "The Key of Libberty," Manning described how the sight of the dead and dying caused "serious sencations" in his mind and led him to be "highly taken up with Liberty & a free government." Many others involved in the early fighting found their dedication to the cause similarly strengthened by their experience. As it happened, Manning saw only a ten-day tour of duty, which was not unusual for men with aged parents and a growing brood of young children to care for at home. But no matter the brevity of his stint, he was a changed man. From then on, he reported, even with the distractions of a working farm and a wayside tavern, he made it his business to pay close attention to public events.[16]

To judge from his later writings, the political controversies that followed the Revolution had an equally powerful effect on his intellectual outlook and loyalties. During the 1780s he served the town in a variety of official capacities, culminating in his election to the post of selectman in 1786 and 1787. Although still a man of moderate means, he seemed poised to become one of the leading figures of the town—until the Massachusetts Regulation of 1786–87 derailed his political career.[17]

Manning's account of "the Shais Affair" is one of the more dramatic sections in "The Key of Libberty." At the close of the Revolution, Manning reported, "the peopel ware drove to the gratest extremity." Merchants shipped off "lode after load" of hard money "untill their was but little left." Massachusetts taxes, payable only in specie, were the highest in the land. The situation rapidly worsened in the mid-1780s. Creditors, obeying the unforgiving conventions of high commerce, began calling in old debts but refused to receive payment in paper money. Those who had hard money to lend demanded "30, 40, & some 50 pursent interest." Fee officers garnished "double, thribble, & some 4 times so much as the law alowed them." Property sold at less than half its value. The jails became filled with debtors. Even worse, Manning continued, the people, "being ignorant that all their help lay in being fully and fairly represented in the Legeslature," refrained from voting. By 1785 "the few ondly ware Represented at cort, with an Aristocratical Bodoin"—conservative Governor James Bowdoin—"at their head."[18]

Under Bowdoin's direction the legislature refused to pass any measures to relieve the fiscal pressure on the state's debtors, and instead aggravated the situation with a series of hard-money policies. Several towns centered in the western counties (but also including some in northern Middlesex) called popular conventions and issued public remonstrances, condemning the government and calling for reforms. But their protests had no effect, and in frustration "some countyes ware so follish as to stop the Corts of Justis by force of arms"—insurgencies that "shook the government to its foundation."

All told, an estimated one-quarter of the Massachusetts population took an active part in the uprisings. A large number of others sympathized with the Regulators and refused to support the government's effort to suppress them. Even the legislature hesitated before the movement, rejecting Bowdoin's request that it declare the existence of a state of rebellion and place the western counties under martial law; instead, the legislature settled for a combination of police measures and mild reforms. Bowdoin had to act on his own to raise troops to crush the uprisings—and he managed to do so only with great difficulty and after considerable delay.[19]

For William Manning, the entire affair had reverberating implications. As a selectman, he found himself in a highly exposed position. Although two dozen or so Billericans joined the force that marched against the Regulators, most of his townsmen—judging from the large number of them who refused to vote for Bowdoin in the next election—seem to have abhorred the repression.[20] A decade later, in "The Key," Manning would present himself as one of this latter group—opposed to the government's policies and sympathetic to the debtor's plight but unable to support the Regulator's tactics.[21] In fact, however, he was not the neutral bystander he later claimed to be—for according to a receipt in the Massachusetts Archives, he spent five days with other town officials helping supply the army sent westward through Billerica in January 1787 to suppress the Regulation.[22]

Manning's activities might seem treacherous in view of his subsequent opinions. One does not expect friends of "the Many" to give aid and comfort to the armies of "the Few"—especially when those armies are directed against endebted small farmers. And Manning himself, it seems, took no pride in his participation—if his misleading account of his role in "The Key" is any indication.[23] At the same time, it is crucial to recognize that his actions were consistent both with his official position in the town, and with his subsequent political writings. As a town selectman, he had responsibilities to uphold the law. Moreover, having fought in the Revolution, Manning could not countenance taking up arms against the revolutionary governments it had produced, or supporting those who did so. Citizens, he would later observe, ought "always be riady to seporte the Constituted Athorityes" in the suppression of insurrections.[24] Nor did Manning doubt that the newly established governments provided enough safeguards for popular sovereignty to obviate any form of uprising. The Declaration of Rights in the Massachusetts Constitution of 1780 provided explicitly that "all power lays in the peopel," he later wrote; were it ever violated, the people had the right to deliberate and, if need be, to "reforme, alter & totally change their Constitution."[25]

The ultimate outcome of the Regulation only confirmed to Manning the legitimacy of the Commonwealth's constitutional government. After Bowdoin suppressed the armed demonstrations of the Regulators, the citizenry undertook what Manning later called "the most zelous sarches after a remidy for their greviences." These led them at last to seize upon their electoral rights and sweep the governor and his offending legislative majority out of office. In the end, "everything appeared like the clear & plesant sunshine after a most tremendious storme . . . a streiking demonstration of the advantages of a free elective government."[26] In short, the Regulation underscored Manning's abiding attachment to constitutional procedures, even as it dramatized what he would soon be describing as an overarching struggle between "the Few" and "the Many."

The uprising's effect on Manning personally was more clouded. At the town elections in March 1787 two of the most prominent progovernment men, Josiah Bowers and Edward Farmer, were not returned to office—a signal of the town's displeasure with the government's measures. Manning, too, was passed over as selectman, and was instead named the town constable and tax collector. One year later he was not elected anything.[27] Did he salvage a political post in 1787, only to be shunned by his townsmen later on? Or did he simply tire of town politics? There is no way to tell from the existing evidence. What is clear is that after 1787 he would never again hold a major position in town government.

In one respect, though, the politics of the mid-1780s did have an unmistakable personal impact. If the American Revolution made Manning a reader, then the Massachusetts Regulation and its aftermath made him a writer. His public career may have been over in 1787, but his political passions were far from spent. Soon thereafter, more interested than ever in public affairs, he started writing out his complaints about the policies of the first administration to serve under the new federal Constitution.[28] These complaints grew directly from his acute awareness of the sorts of controversies that had racked Massachusetts over the previous ten years.

Manning wrote his first essay in February 1790, and gave it the cumbersome title, "Some Proposals for Makeing Restitution to the Original Creditors of Government & to Helpe the Continant to a Mediam of Trade." At its heart was Manning's contention that Alexander Hamilton's fiscal program, announced just the month before, amounted to a kind of robbery. The plan, Manning argued, would reward those wealthy men who had bought up government paper for a song, and leave the original creditors (mainly men of modest means) with nothing but new tax burdens to help pay off the energetic speculators. Deriding the strictly commercial logic proffered by Hamilton—that the speculators had bought their notes fair and square—Manning rehearsed a different sense of justice, more akin to the ethic common to local barter networks, which emphasized the government's continuing obligation to the original creditors. To fulfill that obligation, Manning called for a different repayment scheme, favoring the original creditors and tied to issuances of paper money, with the necessary financing to be drawn from a sinking fund secured by taxes "Equelly assessed."[29]

But he did not stop there. In the essay's rhetorical high points, Manning laid out some general observations about money, class and justice. In all governments, he asserted, there had been a "grate Dividing Line . . . betwen those that Labour for a Living & those who git one without or as they are generally tarmed the few & the Many."[30] The Few, he specified, were those whose property consisted chiefly of "Rents—Money at Interest—Sallaryes & fees," but also included merchants, bankers, and speculating "sharpers." This small group of men always looked to "alterations of Money affares" secured through government to maximize their advantages over the Many, and consequently their profits. If left alone, he concluded, the American Few would "purchis hole townships at a time & bring us in to Lordships"—conjuring up an old popular fear of provincial days that the entire colony would be signed over to some royal favorite as their proprietary.[31]

Here, then, was the first literary effort of a self-educated farmer, groping toward a deeper understanding of the forces driving American politics. His basic concern was with class and injustice—and with how moneyed men perverted honorable commerce to oppress the laboring majority. Having come this far, however, Manning apparently could go no further. At the beginning of the essay he had promised to sketch out "the Moste prudent & Likely way" to get his plan adopted—but when the moment came, his inspiration flagged.[32] He never completed the manuscript, and the Massachusetts legislator to whom it had been addressed probably never received it. Manning, it seems, could not yet see how the Many might, by constitutional means alone, check the ambitions of the Few. Only over the next several years did he sort things out. He did so using all of the intellectual and spiritual resources at his command—from tavern badinage to the word of God.

In the 1790s, Manning's home town seemed about to open itself up to the region's accelerating commercial and cultural life. The most dramatic improvement involved the planning and construction of the Middlesex Canal, begun in 1795 and completed in 1803—a route that promised to connect Billerica's farmers to eastern markets as never before. A regular stagecoach line linking Billerica to Boston and New Hampshire began service in 1795; two years later the town received its first post office. The town's Social Library, founded in 1773, enjoyed so much success that a second lending library had to be opened in 1807.[33]

An enterprising soul, Manning contributed to the town's improvements. One local source claims that his tavern gained a lively business from the additional stagecoach traffic. Without question, Manning performed contract work digging the new canal; he also bought and sold land in and around Billerica, transactions from which, overall, he took in slightly more than he spent.[34] Yet the decade was not without its headaches—and Manning was unable to escape persistent economic difficulties. The precise reasons for his troubles are unclear. He once mentioned the difficulties of supporting "a large family"—he and his wife had thirteen children—by hard labor on a small landed estate.[35] What is certain is that he was perpetually in need of cash. Several times, in 1787, 1792, and 1793, he mortgaged his property to raise funds (on one occasion from a friendly Boston bank); several times more he had to secure personal loans from neighbors and kin.[36] His continuing scramble for money no doubt contributed to Manning's sense of the perils as well as the promises attached to Billerica's widening commercial contacts.

In the midst of these cross-currents—and during the ferocious debate instigated by the ratification of Jay's Treaty—Manning began to compose "The Key of Libberty."[37] He completed one draft in March 1797, and planned to send it to the editors of his favorite newspaper *The Independent Chronicle* of Boston. (Whether he actually did so is unknown.) Over the following winter he composed a second, longer draft, which arrived at the *Chronicle* in April 1798. By then, however, the storm of criticism set off by Jay's Treaty had passed, and the political climate was becoming increasingly hostile to writers with such strong democratic views. The "self-created" Democratic societies, on the wane since 1795, had all but disappeared; war with France loomed on the horizon; the XYZ affair was breaking; in June and July 1798 Congress would respond to criticism of the Adams administration with the Alien and Sedition Acts; the editors of well-known opposition papers—including *The Independent Chronicle*—were beginning to feel the heat of repression. Not surprisingly, the *Chronicle*'s editor, Thomas Adams, declined to publish Manning's piece, pleading ill health and lack of time to read it. (As things stood,

Adams had enough trouble on his hands. Both he and his brother, Abijah, the *Chronicle*'s bookkeeper, would eventually be arraigned for seditious libel; Thomas died before his trial began, but his brother was duly convicted and served thirty days.) Manning, undeterred, proceeded to revise the original, with a letter bidding the *Chronicle* to publish the new version to help ensure "the Republican printers would not be personal sufferers by any prosicutions what ever."[38]

It is easy to understand Manning's tenacity. His manuscript amounted to a summa of years of reading and thinking about a wide range of material and issues. In making his argument, he referred effortlessly to the Massachusetts constitution of 1780, the federal Constitution, Washington's neutrality proclamation of 1793, and Jay's Treaty—documents he had obviously examined closely. Cited alongside numerous biblical and theological references were the essays on government by "Free Republican" (Benjamin Lincoln, Jr.) that had appeared in the *Chronicle* in 1785–86, and which had influenced several passages in "Some Proposals." His observations also drew on the pamphlet literature about Franco-American relations.[39] Although Manning claimed he was not much of a reader of "antiant history," he had a good working knowledge of Dutch and British history from the seventeenth century onward, gleaned largely from the *Chronicle*. He certainly subscribed to the weekly paper; judging from "The Key," he seems to have assembled a small archive of clippings that he referred to over and over again. He also used the Billerica Social Library.[40]

None of this made Manning all that unusual, for plebeian autodidacticism was widespread in the new republic, even if, in his own view, it had not proceeded as far as he hoped, or with the kinds of ideas he favored. The 1790s in particular witnessed something of a print revolution—and what one historian of New England has called a "village Enlightenment"—which brought a proliferation of newspapers, periodicals, and inexpensive books to an ever-growing audience.[41] Although the extent and discipline of Manning's reading may have been greater than the norm, it was not so much greater for Manning to lack confidence that his intended plebeian readership could grasp his references and explications.[42]

Manning's reading in turn affected how he wrote "The Key." Although he never commanded the high-toned style of a well-schooled philosopher or political essayist, his manuscript clearly conformed to the learned convictions, right down to the elaborate table of contents. At the same time, he also transformed these conventions to accommodate his own voice. On "The Key" 's title page, for example, the byline read, "A Labourer," with no hint of Manning's actual name.

Superficially, Manning would seem to have been following the form of such writers as John Dickinson ("A Farmer in Pennsylvania"), who adopted anonymous personae to lend their political writings a touch of romanticized rustic virtue. But Manning's opening also subverted the conventional ploy—for he actually *was* a laborer, and his account of rural life was anything but romantic.[43]

Political treatises, meanwhile, were by no means the only influence on Manning's rhetorical patterns. In many respects, "The Key" more closely resembled a lengthy sermon or theological tract. The tripartite structure of the traditional Protestant sermon—text, doctrine and reasons, application or improvement—is clearly visible in its organization. Manning's account of selfish depravity, which may have owed much to the "New Divinity" Calvinism of Samuel Hopkins, formed one of the linchpins of his politics.[44] And his argumentation fully displayed his close familiarity with the Bible and the social thought of pietistic New England Congregationalism. Manning consistently borrowed from Scripture and from numerous strands of popular belief (including, as we shall see, the Methodists). He invoked the stories of Adam and Eve, Joseph, Hazael, and Haman from the Old Testament; he cited Solomon on education; his dire account of current affairs—"Gog and Magog are gathered together," he wrote, "to destroy the Rights of Man & banish Libberty from the world"— borrowed liberally from popular millennial literature and the Book of Revelation.[45]

These explicitly religious passages, so central to his political arguments, were never as simple as they might appear. He did not, for example, choose his biblical references at random. Many were exactly the same ones that Billerica's longtime pastor, Henry Cumings, liked to rehearse in his Sunday pulpit; Manning's reflections on them formed a sort of running commentary, an extension of what must have been a continuing quarrel with the minister. Theologically, Cumings was a liberal Congregationalist with ideas about grace that aligned him with the Arminians of Boston. His politics—turning increasingly conservative and strident over the 1790s—fit in with his social and theological allegiances. Manning, however, was a more orthodox Calvinist, a follower of those whom the Unitarian William Bentley contemptuously referred to as "farmer metaphysicians."[46]

Repeatedly, "The Key of Libberty" picked up Cumings's favorite themes in order to sustain Manning's very different conclusions. Whereas Cumings blamed original sin solely for introducing hate into the world (and with it the need for orderly deference to one's superiors), Manning added—with more scriptural warrant—that Adam's curse sentenced humankind to a life of hard labor.[47] Whereas

Cumings condemned lowly men of "levelling principles," Manning understood the Bible to say that "the higher a Man is raised in stations of honour power and trust the greater are his temtations to do rong."[48] Cumings construed the story of Haman as "a signal display of the wisdom and goodness of Providence," which occasionally used evil to produce good; Manning, however, viewed Haman as an exemplar of the "depravity & pride of the human hart" common even among those who "could boste of the highest preferments" on earth.[49] Cumings, the Arminian Federalist, spoke of the need for "mutual subjugation"; Manning, the orthodox Calvinist democrat, of the need for "mutual assistance."[50]

Manning was not simply scoring debater's points here, either against Cumings or against the larger body of liberal Congregationalist theology. Nor did he deploy biblical phrases merely to strike a popular rhetorical chord. Manning took his religion extremely seriously. Humanity's propensity to sin and its universal, blind devotion to self-interest was, to him, a fundamental article of faith. His beliefs fed an intense suspicion of both the moneyed Few and those among the Many who lapsed into self-satisfied apathy or counseled violent rebellion. Even when guided by bedrock spiritual assumptions, however, Manning's reading of contemporary political problems—and, even more important, his solutions for them—were always secular. And although his writing was beholden to the church, it also had the flavor of a very different, profane milieu—the tavern common room—and of yet another set of devices for holding one's own in an argument.

The tavern, along with the church and the town meeting hall, was a hot spot of community life in the eighteenth-century countryside. The keeper himself was by law expected to be an orderly, honest, temperate person. Commonly, taverns were sites of official and semi-official functions, from electioneering to militia training days; they were also places where newspapers were received and could be read. Not surprisingly, they served as informal debating halls and political lyceums—proving grounds for local political talent. The Manning tavern—a site for several election day carousings and similar gatherings at least through the 1770s—was no exception.[51] If anything, the political importance of the tavern grew after the Revolution, especially in the countryside, as a newer, more rough-and-tumble democratic politics emerged. In the 1790s Federalists particularly complained of "itinerant Jacobins," political "runners," and the "democratic literati," who "harangue[d] the mobs" gathered in local public houses.[52]

"The Key of Libberty" is full of the kinds of rural imagery and

barbed quips familiar to tavern disputes. "The poor man's shilling,"
Manning remarked at one point, "aught to be as much the care of
government as the rich mans pound." Lawyers, for whom he showed
a special contempt, were to Manning "a kind of Mule ordir," holding
neither judicial nor executive responsibilities. Expecting them to
curb the arbitrary rule of judges, he thought, was "like seting the Cat
out to watch the Creem pot." Although Manning admired learning,
he had no use for it as a mere ornament—or instrument—of privilege. There was, he thought, about as much need for most schoolteachers to know "all languages" as there was "for a farmer to have
the marinor's art to hold plow." Uninformed, reflexive supporters of
the government, once challenged with the "true circumstances,"
would initially shrink from their position and, "like lambs that are
dumb after they are sheared, turne away & wish to hear no more
about it." Manning lifted some of these lines from the Bible, and he
may have drawn others from farmer's almanacs, a genre he knew
well. But still other, more vulgar images plainly evoked the ambience
as well as the verbal exchanges of the tavern. There was, for example, Manning's charge that the Federalists had tried to frighten people into believing that without Jay's Treaty, the British would make
war on the United States, and "rouse off a grate gun 3000 miles distance & blow all our brains out if we stept out to piss."[53]

The striking thing about these departures into tavern wit is not so
much their bluntness as the ease with which Manning moved from a
"low" to a "high" style—sometimes within the span of two sentences.
In a discussion of Manning's views on education, the historian Richard Hofstadter misconstrued them as a reflection of an "anti-
intellectualist populism" that contained "a dark and sullen suspicion
of high culture." To the contrary, although Manning plainly abhorred
how the Federalist elite had arrogated learning to itself, his prose
was a blend of plebeian rhetoric and borrowings from learned
tracts—always signalling his deep respect for the latter. His comments on a poor man's shilling, for example, followed a declaration,
straight from John Locke, that the "soul end of Government is the
protection of Life, Liberty & property." In other instances, it is quite
possible that some of Manning's quips and apothegms were, in fact,
inspired by "high" sources, themselves couched in plainspoken
phrases. His observation that lawyers were a "mule ordir" almost
certainly built upon the polemical attack on the profession by the
artisan-turned-politician, Benjamin Austin, published in *The Independent Chronicle* as a reply to "Free Republican" in 1786. One of
his lines about money—that it "will go where it will fetch the most
as naturally as water runs down hill"—may have been a snatch of

country wisdom; alternatively, he could have lifted it out of one of David Hume's essays.[54] There is something immensely attractive about the porousness of this way of writing, with its overtones of Paineite impudence and common sense, combined with an autodidact's fearlessness when wading into learned controversy. Certainly it attracted a man like Manning, who wrote at a time when the hierarchies of learned and low were temporarily out of joint—a self-taught philosopher who, having been caught up by the Revolution, may never have heeded those hierarchies in the first place. It is a self-consciously democratic style.

Throughout, Manning's persistent respect for reason and orderly procedures tempered his demotic irreverence. He took care to qualify his attacks, lest they seem like caricatures. Refusing to share in the ad hominum animus of some plebeian critics of "high flyers," he went out of his way to stress that he did not believe that "any ordirs of men who live with out Labour are intirely needless or that they are chargable with blame."[55] Nor did he romanticize "the Many" as the peculiar possessors of some innate wisdom or virtue. A consistent, postlapsarian Calvinist, he believed all men were fallen; he was not a democrat because of his faith in the virtues of the populace, but because of his lack of faith in the virtues of the elite. Only occasionally did Manning's moderation fail him, as in the case of the Society of the Cincinnati—which he portrayed as a sinister conspiracy.[56] But for the most part, he presented himself as a balanced and realistic man of reason—a champion of constitutionalism and the rule of law, cognizant of the shortcomings of the ignorant and apathetic Many as well as of the potential tyranny of the Few. "Larning" and "knowledge" were keywords for Manning in the late 1790s, to which he returned again and again; only by pursuing "larning" and "knowledge"—including the "knowledge that when laws are once constitutially made, they must be obayed"—could the Many secure their rights and keep the Few from "putting Darkness for Light, & Light for Darkness, falsehood for truth, & truth for falsehood."[57]

In these passages, the many strands of Manning's self-education pulled together as a comprehensive solution to the political dilemmas that had burdened him since the days of the Massachusetts Regulation. How, he had long wondered, could the interests of the Many be secured constitutionally against the manipulations of the Few? His initial impulse was to inquire into the underlying struggles that pitted the moneyed minority against the laboring majority, an inquiry that was well advanced by 1790. But beyond these important matters numerous others remained. How did the Few consistently manage to benefit from the ignorance of the Many? Why, after the experience of the Massachusetts Regulation, had events transpired that only enhanced the power of the nation's moneyed men? And how could a political movement be organized to end these abuses and secure free government once and for all? In pondering these issues, Manning began to generalize from his own experience—through "unweryed study & prayers"—and to regard enlightenment and education as the bulwarks of popular liberty.[58]

On its face, it was not a particularly fiery proposition—but for Manning, the ideal of universal knowledge had radical implications. The Few, he assumed, would not automatically relinquish their monopoly on knowledge; doing so would strip them of one of their most powerful weapons. The Many would have to fight hard to secure their mental independence; once victorious, they would have to institute safeguards to ensure they would never lose what they had won. Their prospects looked unpromising over the winters of 1797 and 1798. In a last-ditch effort Manning offered his collected thoughts and a blueprint for action.

To turn from Manning's earlier writing to "The Key to Libberty" is to see how greatly he had expanded the scope and the force of his arguments during the 1790s. The arcane disquisitions about credit and paper money that had dominated his criticisms of Hamilton's fiscal program gave way, in "The Key," to much more wide-ranging propositions. The eternal struggle between the Few and the Many, portrayed earlier mainly as a fight over monetary policy, now unfolded in a much more comprehensive manner. Although addressed primarily to Manning's fellow Americans, "The Key" took up the concerns of democrats the world over, including the French Revolution and the continuing war in Europe. By the time the manuscript concluded, Manning had utterly confounded what have since become standard categories for describing popular political thought in the early republic. He emerged as a partisan of the Many who was unalterably opposed to popular Regulators; a critic of commercial society who was deeply suspicious of self-interest but nevertheless championed democratic commerce; a tavernkeeper concerned with "strict Justis" in the marketplace who favored defaulting on a portion of the national debt; a plebeian democrat who thought the creation and defense of free government required a better-educated populace and the support of at least a few leading men; a defender of individual rights and of state governments who was also a nationalist (indeed, an internationalist) and a determined "cosmopolitan."[59]

Manning divided the manuscript into three principal sections.

He opened with a few personal remarks about his own background and his motives for writing the tract to follow. The second section (approximately two-thirds of the total) offered "A General Description of the Causes that Ruen Republicks." In the final part Manning detailed the steps the Many could take in order to defend their rights and liberties under a free government.

There is a certain slackness in some of the argumentation within each part. Overall, "The Key" was a thoughtfully planned piece of work, but the whole grew tighter and more polished with each revision.[60] The starting point of its major section was "the grate dividing line" between the Few and the Many. "Labour is the soul parrant of all property," Manning observed (echoing Locke); without labor, "the land yealdeth nothing"; every "nesecary of life . . . is generally esteemed valuable according to the Labour it costs." It followed logically that a man's property ought to stand in some direct proportion to the amount of labor he performed. No one could own property without laboring "unless he git it by force or craft, fraud or fortun out of the earnings of others."[61]

Stated this way, these axioms contained little that was new or controversial. The notion that labor created all property—self-evident to working farmers and artisans—was a commonplace in eighteenth-century America, repeated in folk sayings and learned treatises alike; Manning lifted his own discussion directly from his old standby, the "Free Republican."[62] Consistent with the emphases of his major literary source, Manning was no crude leveller. He did not hold that the root of injustice was inequality, or that the distinctions between the classes could be cured by equalizing property. He explicitly stated that because people were born with a "grate veriety of capacietyes," there would always be "a very unequel distribution of property in the world" even under the best of governments.[63] Nor did Manning condemn commercial markets—or merchants and professionals—out of hand, as preternaturally evil. Befitting a farmer-tavernkeeper, he had only praise for the "commerce & the exchange of the produce of one cuntry for another" as a source of human happiness. "Marchents," as the facilitators of that exchange, performed perfectly useful and honorable functions. So long as merchants, physicians, lawyers and others who got their livings "without bodily labours" charged no more for their services than was consistent with "justis"—i.e., in proportion to the time and property they devoted to preparing themselves in their work—they could honestly expect to earn a handsome income.[64]

The problem, as Manning saw it, lay in an eighteenth-century form of what later critics would call exploitation. Not *all* of the Few, he repeatedly emphasized, were at fault; a small fraction of them virtuously conducted their business honorably, sided with the Many, and favored free government. Nevertheless, he quickly added, most of those who "live without labour," gripped by the self-interest known to all men, sought maximum advantages for themselves, even if these advantages came at others' expense. In "The Key," as in "Some Proposals," the monetary system remained the focus of this "grate skuffel between the few & many." The incomes—and thus the interests—of the Few lay in "haveing mony scarse & the price of labour & produce as low as possible," while the incomes and interests of the many were dependent on money being cheap and plentiful. And although a number of state banks had been established to provide ordinary farmers and laborers with the currency and credit necessary to conduct honest trade, the Few still controlled the financial system. The largest and most important banks, Manning charged, including the one established by Congress at the urging of Alexander Hamilton, had fallen under the control of men who arbitrarily manipulated their remittances and the money supply in order to enrich themselves and their friends and "bring the Many into destress."[65]

Unlike "Some Proposals," however, "The Key" also offered a more general analysis of the instrumentalities of power. In addition to controlling the money supply, the Few also sought to monopolize the creation and dispersion of knowledge. They were always promoting the foundation of "costly colleges, national acadimyes of grammer schools" geared to their own advantage. They "always opposed" any plans to create a universal, public education for both boys and girls, in which "Labour & Larning would be conected together" and "spread amongue the Many."[66] Similarly, the newspapers, once a reliable source of all necessary knowledge, had been "almost ruened of late by the doings of the few." And when these strategies were insufficient to obtain their object, the Few did not shrink from corrupting the electoral process itself.[67]

The social and political ramifications of these tendencies were profound. The Many were being deprived of their right to "injoy the good of [their] Labour," by merchants, bankers, and stockjobbers, as well as members of the various liberal professions—doctors, clergymen, teachers, lawyers—who combined to raise their fees beyond the abilities of poor men to pay.[68] Betraying their trust, former officers in the revolutionary army formed what Manning thought was the most diabolical combination of all—the hereditary, self-perpetuating Society of the Cincinnati. Smitten by a resurgent social snobbery, the Few saw themselves as a leisured class set above the rest of the citizenry. Then, unwilling to be on a level with "the Swinish Multitude" or to submit to the power of a democratically elected legislature, they combined in politics to oppose free government. To that end they used every available tool of subversion. They tried to keep the people ignorant. They undermined the liberty of the press. They favored obscurely written constitutions and laws, and (when necessary) quietly violated constitutional provisions that hindered their power. They encouraged a bellicose spirit among nations in order to justify the raising of standing armies to overawe their own people.[69]

To Manning, the entire political history of the infant American Republic bespoke the tenacious efforts of the Few to erect their new system—and his list of abuses was formidable, beginning with Hamilton's funding program and continuing through to the excise taxes, Jay's Treaty, and the western campaigns against the American Indian (pursued "with out any just provocation" at great cost in lives and treasure).[70] Overall, he allowed, the Few had yet to seize complete control of the government; the great danger, in his eyes, was that in 1797 and after, they seemed on the verge of succeeding. So brazen had the Few become in their unconstitutional chicanery (as evidenced by the adoption of Jay's Treaty), so ignorant and complacent were the Many (their minds beclouded by Federalist propaganda, their spirits numbed by a transitory period of prosperity) that America had begun to resemble an aristocracy or monarchy, "whare the people have nothing better to do in maters of government but to seport the few in luxery & idleness."[71]

The only remedy, to Manning's way of thinking, was for "Republicans to Unite as well as the Roiallist." The former constituted a clear majority of the people. Let them "do as the roiallest do" and organize a mutual association to provide themselves with "knowledge anough to act rationally" on behalf of their common interests and the preservation of free government.[72] And, in the final section of the essay, Manning offered a constitution for such an organization—the Labouring Society.

Manning envisioned a national membership organization, with state, county, town, and neighborhood chapters, whose elected leaders would meet annually (or more often if necessary) to conduct its affairs. The Society's primary purpose would be to provide the laboring majority with "cheep, easy & sure" access to all the "knowledge & larning necessary for a free man"—including everything from a general understanding of human nature to the credentials and views of political candidates.[73] In order to acquire such learning, the Many would need access to "a continued series of publications that can be red with confidence."[74] He therefore proposed that the Labouring Society publish a "Munthly Magazin," to provide the Many with ample information about elections, legislative debates, and their constitutional rights. Additionally, he proposed that the Society establish neighborhood "clases"—a notion he almost certainly adopted from Methodist organizers, then busy all across rural Massachusetts—presided over by a librarian. Class members could "use the Magazein by turnes or meet together & have it red." (For many people, this would be the only affordable way to take the magazine.) At the same time, the classes might serve as a political rallying point. "[I]f their should com on such times as their was in Masachusets in 1786," he observed, "all the many would gladly be at the expense of obtaining such knowledge & the Society would come together like a building well framed & marked."[75]

Manning's ultimate goal, however, was not simply to enlighten the Many. He wished to create a vehicle that would help to turn the Few and their friends out of office and to replace them with "true Republicans." By his calculations, fewer than half of those eligible to vote participated in elections for federal representatives and electors—largely, he believed, because of mass ignorance. But once the Many (thanks to the Labouring Society) possessed the knowledge necessary to make informed decisions, he was certain that most would "vote no person into any office (even not in the towns) but what they are confident are true Republicans." Beyond that, once properly organized, the members of the Labouring Society would also be able to "make a common cause of detecting male administration [i.e., maladministration] & breaches of law by the Juditial & Executive officers," and, if necessary, "make presentments, prosecutions, & manage impeachments" against them.[76] Politicians would then once again feel "the presents of their Constituants & act as servents & not masters."[77]

Manning had no illusions that his plan would win immediate acceptance. He was certain the Few would denounce it as "daingerous to Government," and that they would do all they could to oppose its organization. Others would claim that the project would be too expensive (a notion he refuted with some quick calculations about the actual costs involved). Yet Manning believed such obstacles were surmountable, especially if some of the more virtuous among the Few—"some Influential Carictors or body of men"—would join with the Society and promote it.[78] Let the Labouring Society be established on a strong and lasting foundation, and Congress would have "some reason to boste of our being the most free and inlightned peopel in the world." By convincing the world of the United States' determination to be free, the very existence of the Society would "do more to prevent a war with France" than anything else which might be done. Indeed, were free governments and an international Labouring Society organized throughout the world, all differences might be settled by "sotial corraspondance & mutual consestions" and all wars "bannished from the Earth." Everyone could then look forward to a prosperous future with an expansive economy of commerce, agriculture, and manufacturing, all in accord with the self-evident truth, that a man's "prinsapel hapiness" on earth is to "eat & drink & injoy the good of his Labour."[79]

As far as we know, Manning's proposal for the Labouring Society was the first of its kind in the United States. Combining his many concerns into a single project, it also brought together his democratic convictions, his respect for learning, and his constitutionalist politics. The Society's broadly based membership was intended to reach beyond the propertied to include "all the free male persons who are 21 years of age [and] who Labour for a living in the United States," as well as "all persons of ani other denominations" who paid their dues and subscribed to the society's principles—making it in conception by far the most democratic political organization in the nation. Its institutional structure was similarly democratic. (To head off further Federalist objections to "self-created societies" and to help to ensure that the Society would be seen as "perfectly Constitutional," Manning pointedly and shrewdly based his draft of its constitution on the Society of the Cincinnati's *Institutes*.) The Society's members were expected to live up to the same standards of respect for the law that they would demand from their representatives—and to pledge their respect by signing a "covenant," attached to the constitution, promising to support the government against armed uprisings.[80]

In sum, "The Key" offered Manning's answer to the central question that had long troubled democratic theorists: How could a government remain for long both free and democratic? The "Enemies to Free Government," he later observed, always asserted that there was "not Virtue & knowledge among My brother Laborers to Seport such a government." But those who made such charges had not considered what would happen if the Many received a "means of Knowledge . . . almost without money & without price," as the Labouring Society would do. Then, Manning was certain, "their would always be a large majority that would read, see, think & act for themselves & their own interest & would jealously Seport a free government."[81] During the next few years, his faith would be at least partially vindicated.

*M*anning's reflections were lost to his contemporaries. The editors of *The Independent Chronicle* turned aside his manuscript in 1798, and gave no greater consideration to a third draft he completed a year later. Nor, it seems, did they or anyone else print the additional shorter pieces he composed after 1799.[82] Nevertheless, it is just possible that "The Key of Libberty" may actually have circulated outside Manning's immediate circle—and that the *Chronicle*'s failure to publish it may not have been due to the editorial distraction or inattention. On the contrary, Thomas and Abijah Adams may have been only too familiar with what Manning had to say.

Even as Manning was writing and attempting to publish "The Key of Libberty," another self-described "labouring man," David Brown, was traveling around Massachusetts denouncing Federalist policies, perhaps circulating a petition asking for a redress of the people's grievances, and warning of dire consequences if they were not acted upon favorably. Without question, Brown carried with him a sheaf of writings, reportedly his own, from which he read to all who would listen in the stores, taverns, and private homes he passed along the way.[83] Brown's travels might have gone unnoticed had the residents of Dedham's Clapboardtree Parish—locally notorious as a hotbed of sin and Jacobinism—not erected a liberty pole soon after he passed through the area, to which they attached placards denouncing Federalist policies, calling for the retirement of President Adams, and praising Vice President Jefferson. Even though he had not been present at the pole's erection, Brown was charged with sedition and a warrant was issued for his arrest. The authorities finally caught up with him three months later in Andover, where he was bound over to the Salem jail to await trial.

A picture emerges from the comments elicited by Brown's arrest, and from the testimony at his trial, of an extensive political subculture, centered on the taverns and plebeian meeting places where men like Brown (and presumably Manning, too) propounded their views. By his own account, Brown visited more than eighty towns in the commonwealth. According to a letter by a "gentleman from Andover," which appeared soon after Brown's arrest, this "wandering apostle of sedition" specifically mentioned visiting Concord and Dracut, among other Middlesex towns near Billerica; and witnesses at his trial testified that they heard him reading from the manuscripts in his possession, as well as such other notorious literature as Tom Paine's *Age of Reason,* and discussing them with his listeners. The same Andover gentleman also offered an abbreviated summary of the writings in Brown's possession. According to him, they represented "officers of the government, the Clergy and Lawyers" as "enemies of the people," who had already consumed a large portion of the people's property, and were endeavoring to engross the remainder and reduce them to "abject slavery." Stockholders, bankers, merchants, and other people of property also met with condemnation. The "main object" of these manuscripts, the gentleman insisted, was to "alarm the Farmers, Mechanics and Labourers, with an apprehension that the preservation of liberty and property depends upon a thorough Revolution."[84]

Even through the hostile filter of a high Federalist's testimony, the echoes, if not the actual call, of "The Key of Libberty" are audible. Or do we hear the echoes of what even *The Independent Chronicle* called Brown's "malignant and perverse misrepresentations" in "The Key of Libberty"?[85] Either way, the similarities are suggestive—not only about what the *Chronicle*'s editors viewed as the limits of safe political opinion, but also about the context within which "The Key" was written. There is no evidence that Manning and Brown ever crossed paths. But they clearly came from different corners of the same popular opposition and shared many of the same criticisms of the existing order.

In the frenzied climate of the 1790s, the likes of David Brown and William Manning were being openly courted by members of the Democratic Republican elite. Drawing room agitators like Thomas Jefferson also spoke of a country divided between "anti-republicans" and "true republicans"—the former consisting mostly of returned Tories, merchants, speculators, stockjobbers, and both officeholders and office-seekers ("a numerous and noisy tribe"); the latter of landholders and "the great body of labourers, not being landholders, whether in husbanding or the arts."[86] And they, too, were hard at work preparing for the coming elections by stirring up opposition to the government's measures. The possibility loomed that they might well succeed, by linking up with the less polished insurgents of the lower and middling sort, cutting across lines of wealth, region, and religion.

It was this potential alliance of high and low, of national and local interests, in league against Federalist policies, that most alarmed and enraged the friends of the Adams administration. "We have seen of late, indeed within a single year, an almost total change in the tactics and management of the parties," Fisher Ames, the High Federalist Congressman from eastern Massachusetts, lamented in April 1799. The Republicans—or "Jacobins," as Ames preferred to call them—had begun to organize themselves: "Emissaries are sent to every class of men, even to every individual man that can be gained. Every threshing-floor, every husking, every party at work on a house-frame or raising a building, the very funerals are infected with bawlers and whisperers against government."[87] Ames was far from paranoid—for with precisely these tactics, Republicans in Massachusetts and in other states (with far greater success) built the mobilization that effected the so-called Revolution of 1800 which brought Jefferson to the presidency. Six years later, the same tactics enabled the Democratic Republicans to take power in Massachusetts as well.[88]

In some respects, "The Key to Libberty" can be read as a manifesto for this electoral revolution. Certainly, the Republican leadership sounded many of its themes. Moreover, in several states, including Massachusetts, the party organized itself along lines quite similar to those Manning had suggested. There were statewide committees, consisting of a small number of prominent Republicans, many of whom were members of the state legislatures; beneath them were the county committees, town committees, and parish or precinct committees, responsible for rousing the party's members and arguing its case before the public. Nathaniel Ames, Fisher Ames's "Jacobin" brother and a member of the Norfolk County Committee, would later describe the party's purpose in terms that could have almost been lifted directly from "The Key": "[T]o watch over the Republican interest both in State and National Governments, especially as to elections and appointments—convey intelligence—confute false rumors—confirm the wavering in right principles—prevent delusion of weak brethren—and fight the most formidable enemy of civilized men, political ignorance."[89]

Of course, the Democratic Republican party was hardly the brainchild of William Manning and his friends—although state and local party committeemen may well have learned a great deal from the plebeian political subculture. Nor did the party, as constituted, fulfill all the hopes that Manning had for his Labouring Society. As one historian of the Democratic Republicans described their organization in New England, "subordinate units were strictly accountable to their superiors."[90] The party's leaders were not about to surrender their control to "itinerant Jacobins" like David Brown, nor to country scribblers like William Manning. Neither did Jefferson and his associates have any intention of expanding the power of the party's rank-and-file members over such potentially explosive functions as impeachments. Indeed, shortly after his election Jefferson, reverting to older eighteenth-century notions of virtuous politics, denied the need for further party development, now that the allegedly dangerous High Federalist faction around John Adams had lost control of the national government.[91]

Still, popular and elite opposition politics converged in the years immediately preceding 1800, especially around the need for new sorts of democratic organizations to unite the Many against the Few. Once that convergence occurred, American politics would never be the same. If, in the end, Jefferson's and not Manning's political vision held sway, the Democratic Republicans, unlike their opponents, were prepared to make room for men like Manning. They could afford to do no less. By tapping the sources of popular political ferment, the Virginia slaveholders who headed the party were able to build a national electoral bloc that ruled nearly unchallenged for a generation. As the price of their success, however, the Democratic Republican elite became dependent upon the energies and loyalties of the more plebeian democrats to whom they appealed. In the years following the victory of 1800–01, far from co-opted or absorbed, the rank-and-file of the party continually reminded Democratic Republican leaders of their claim to represent the Many against the Few. The terms of American politics shifted decisively in a more democratic direction, leaving old Federalist notions of deference in tatters, and opening up the machinery of government as never before to continual, legitimate, and peaceful appeals from below. It was not exactly what Manning had in mind. But it is easy to imagine that he was reasonably pleased at the outcome.

William Manning fell seriously ill in 1803. Unable to work his farm, he was cared for by one of his sons, Jephtha. Nevertheless, the old man stubbornly kept at his writing. At least as late as 1807, he was still designing schemes to get "The Key" published and the Labouring Society launched. Finally, in 1814, he died. Thanks to his descendants, his combined house-and-tavern building still stands in Billerica—although over the years authenticity has given way to practicality. (At last report, it housed a Szechuan restaurant). Apart from that, his manuscripts, and his gravestone on a nearby hillside, there is nothing to memorialize the man.[92]

That subsequent generations lost track of Manning and his writings is, however, no reason why we should do so. His life testifies to the extraordinary intellectual ferment that gripped plebeian democrats after the Revolution—exemplifying how what some scholars have called the "democratization of the American mind" proceeded from below (and from the countryside) as well as from the cosmopolitan seaboard centers.[93] And Manning's ideas indicate how the entire history of democratization in the early United States needs to be appreciated afresh, as something more than the outcome of jockeying among divided elites.

As Manning and the other rediscovered writers like him show, the lower and middling sort were also thinking hard about their political grievances well before the rise of a formal opposition in the 1790s. And as Manning's reflections suggest, they did so not so much to enshrine selfless classical virtue or a new capitalist order—in neither of which they placed much faith—as to defend the laboring Many against the moneyed Few. Democratic free government, to a man like Manning, had less to do with free markets—though they were certainly important—than it did with the promise of representative government and popular sovereignty to give the Many an equal say with the Few in the conduct of the public's affairs. In his view, such political equality was necessary to keep the Few from yoking honest commerce to the service of their own selfish ends. Over the past two centuries, it has become all too easy to bury the moral and political claims of this sort of grassroots democracy under the market's abundance, substituting the promise of equal economic opportunity for the equal rights demanded by small farmers and artisans like William Manning, and conflating free government with the laissez faire characteristic of nineteenth-century, liberal capitalism. William Manning's vision of a democracy resists such facile reductions. For that, if for nothing else, he is worth rereading and remembering.

NOTES

ACKNOWLEDGMENTS: We are deeply grateful to Richard and Barbara Manning, now of Saco, Maine, for their help in tracking down sources and for their encouraging words. We owe a special debt to Alfred Young, who read each draft of this essay more than once, and whose prodding made it very much better than it would have been otherwise. We would also like to thank John Murrin, the participants in the Third Biennial Symposium of the Milan Group in Early United States History, and the Social History Colloquium of the Rutgers Department of History for their stimulating comments on an earlier draft.

PUBLISHING NOTE: An extended version of this essay will appear as an introduction to *The Key of Liberty: The Life and Democratic Writings of William Manning, "A Laborer," 1747–1814* (Cambridge, Mass., 1993), and hereafter cited as *Key*.

1. The Manning manuscripts, along with some scattered related material, are located at the Houghton Library, Harvard University. Additional material on Manning and his family is located at the Baker Library, Graduate School of Business Administration,

Harvard University, and at the Manning Family Collection, Martin J. Lyndon Library, University of Massachusetts at Lowell.

The Manning Family Association published the longest essay in the collection in 1921; see William Manning, *The Key of Libberty*, ed. Samuel Eliot Morison (Billerica, Mass., 1921). Thanks to Lawrence Towner, Morison's edition was later reprinted, with corrections, as "William Manning's *The Key of Libberty*," *William and Mary Quarterly* 3d series (hereafter cited as *WMQ*), 13 (1956): 202–54. Manning's other major manuscript, "Some Proposals for Makeing Restitution to the Original Creditors" has recently appeared as Ruth Bogin, " 'Measures So Glaringly Unjust': A Response to Hamilton's Funding Plan by William Manning," *WMQ* 46 (1989): 315–31. Unless otherwise noted, all the citations below will be to the *WMQ* editions (hereafter cited as "The Key" and "Some Proposals").

2. The lives and writings of plebeian democrats are attracting more scholarly attention; see, for example, Ruth Bogin, "New Jersey's True Policy: The Radical Republican Vision of Abraham Clark," *WMQ* 35 (1978): 100–109; Alfred F. Young, "George Robert Twelves Hewes (1742–1840): A Boston Shoemaker and the Memory of the American Revolution," *WMQ* 38 (1981): 561–623; James P. Walsh, " 'Mechanics and Citizens': The Connecticut Artisan Protest of 1792," *WMQ* 42 (1985): 66–89; Alan Taylor, " 'Stopping the Progres of Rogues and Deceivers': A White Indian Recruiting Notice of 1808," *WMQ* 42 (1985): 90–103; and Ruth Bogin, "Petitioning and the New Moral Economy of Post-Revolutionary America," *WMQ* 45 (1988): 391–425.

In addition to these works, a number of biographies and local studies have modified and enriched our understanding of popular democracy during and after the Revolution, including Alfred F. Young, *The Democratic Republicans of New York: The Origins, 1763–1797* (Chapel Hill, N.C., 1967); Ronald Hoffman, *A Spirit of Dissension: Economics, Politics, and the Revolution in Maryland* (Baltimore, 1973); Eric Foner, *Tom Paine and Revolutionary America* (New York, 1976); Edward Countryman, *A People in Revolution: The American Revolution and Political Society in New York, 1760–1790* (Baltimore, 1981); Randolph Roth *The Democratic Dilemma: Religion, Reform, and the Social Order in the Connecticut River Valley of Vermont* (New York, 1987); and Alan Taylor, *Liberty Men and Great Proprietors: The Revolutionary Settlement on the Maine Frontier, 1776–1820* (Chapel Hill, N.C., 1990).

3. For the most ambitious early statements linking American political ideology to the classical republican tradition, see J. G. A. Pocock, "Virtue and Commerce in the Eighteenth Century," *Journal of*

Interdisciplinary History 3 (1972): 119–34; and Pocock, *The Machia-vellian Moment: Florentine Political Thought and the Atlantic Repub-lican Tradition* (Princeton, 1975). For elaborations and refinements see John Murrin, "The Great Inversion; or, Court versus Country; A Comparison of the Revolutionary Settlements in England (1688–1721) and America (1776–1816)," in J. G. A. Pocock, ed., *Three British Revolutions, 1641, 1688, 1776* (Princeton, 1980); and Lance Banning, *The Jeffersonian Persuasion: The Evolution of a Party Ideology* (Ith-aca, N.Y., 1978). For an update see the exchange between Banning and Joyce Appleby in *WMQ* 43 (1986): 3–34.

4. William Manning, "The Key of Libberty," [1798–99 version], Houghton Library, Harvard University. These remarks come from the last of three drafts of "The Key," which appears in modernized form in *Key*.

5. There is considerable confusion among historians over just what one can or ought to mean by "capitalism"—a confusion that has long clouded discussions of economics and politics in the early Re-public. The term was coined by Karl Marx in an anonymous circular letter of the International Workingman's Association in 1870, and rarely, if ever, appeared in his other writings. In that circular, Marx referred to England as a nation dominated by "capitalism" and "land-lordism"—that is, ruled by both a moneyed and a landed interest. The term then gained currency in the 1880s, when egalitarian working-class radicals in Europe and the United States used it to de-scribe the dominance of the moneyed Few over the laboring Many—in their eyes, a denial of fundamental democratic principles.

Subsequent writers have drained the term of its original em-phasis on the political power of capitalists (that is, moneyed men). These usages run the gamut from latter-day Marxism through main-stream liberalism to free-market libertarianism. All fancifully in-flate the word *capitalist* to cover anyone who is involved in profitable commerce or trade—as if the pursuit of profit, self-interest, or ma-terial improvement is the key distinguishing characteristic of a cap-italist. Approaching American history schematically, all are prone to label any form of non-socialist democratic political thought as inher-ently "capitalist" (or "bourgeois" or "entrepreneurial"), dismissively in the case of Marxists, warmly in the case of others. Most important, common to them all is the notion that any system characterized by private enterprise, freedom of contract, and individual initiative is a species of "capitalism"—regardless of whose interests the system is designed directly to maximize. But that, after all, is the key point. A society run by capitalists, or run as if the whole community's inter-ests are identical to those of capitalists, deserves to be called "capitalist." A society run by or in the interests of ordinary farmers, mechanics, and laborers needs to be called something else. Throughout this essay, we use the term *democratic commerce* to refer to this alternative system—the system William Manning and others thought best suited to the preservation of free government. For more on these matters see Michael Merrill, "The Anti-Capitalist Origins of the United States," *Review* 13 (Fall 1990): 465–97, especially 470–77.

6. Joyce Appleby makes this claim in her *Capitalism and a New Social Order: The Republican Vision of the 1790s* (New York, 1984), especially 25–78, and further confuses matters by calling this "classless system" capitalism. (The core of the argument also appeared in the earlier writings of Richard Hofstadter, David Potter, and Louis Hartz, among many others.) In our view, there are serious problems with this interpretation.

Above all, it rests on the mistaken notion, discussed in note 5 above, that profitable commerce is only compatible with capitalism. This conflation of commerce and capitalism in turn obscures the nature of the differences between the economic policies of the Federalists and those of the Democratic Republicans in the 1790s. The first were designed to enhance the economic power and control of moneyed men. The second were more complicated. Although some Democratic Republicans, especially in the Middle States, may have only been seeking their own opportunities for capitalist money-making, the party's main thrust was designed to minimize the power of moneyed men in the economy, and to enhance the power of farmers, artisans, and other small property holders.

7. Rev. Henry A. Hazen, "Genealogical Register," in Hazen, *History of Billerica, Massachusetts* (Boston, 1883), 93–94, 174. On the Manning homestead and tavern, see also E. F. Bacheller, "Manning House," in Bacheller and C. H. Lawrence, eds., *Colonial Landmarks of the Bay State* (Lynn, Mass., 1896), 15; William H. Manning, "The Manning Homestead," *Massachusetts Magazine* 1 (1908): 42–43; and Myra Manning Koenig, "The Story of the Manning Manse" mimeo in authors' possession (n.p., 1950), 6–7. For a more detailed discussion of the Mannings and their situation in Billerica, see *Key*, 7–14.

8. On the younger William Manning's holdings before his father's death, see the Massachusetts valuations for 1771, Massachusetts Archives, vol. 132 (Billerica), State House, Boston (hereafter cited as MV-B). In April 1776, Manning purchased an additional two acres of land, along with a dwelling house, wood house, and blacksmith shop, from Joseph Osgood of Billerica for £13 6s 8p. Agreement dated 22 April 1776, Manning Family Collection.

On the younger Manning's election, see Billerica Town Records,

Town Hall, Billerica, Massachusetts (hereafter cited as BTR), 6 March 1775.

The details of the disposal of the elder Manning's estate are included in Middlesex County Probate Records, 1st series (1648–1871), file no. 14611, William Manning, 1776 (microfilm). The younger William Manning's purchases of his siblings' land rights are elaborated in the agreement dated 7 May 1777, between William Manning and Jonathan Manning, Timothy Manning, Solomon Manning, and Elizabeth Carlton, Manning Family Collection. Manning's sale of 40 acres to his neighbor is recorded in Middlesex County Registry of Deeds, *Billerica Grantors* (hereafter cited as *Grantors*) 8:380–82, Middlesex County Courthouse, Lowell, Massachusetts.

In 1790, upon his mother's death, Manning bought his sister's and brother-in-law's rights to her widow's third for £12 10p. Two years later he bought Timothy and Solomon's rights, paying them £18 apiece. Agreement dated 20 April 1790, Manning Family Collection; Registry of Deeds, *Grantors* 8:366.

9. Edward Cook, Jr., *Fathers of the Towns: Leadership and Community Structure in Eighteenth-Century New England* (Baltimore, 1976), 167–68, 177–79. See also Van Beck Hall, *Politics without Parties: Massachusetts, 1780–1791* (Pittsburgh, 1972), 3–23. Hall constructed elaborate indices measuring how all Massachusetts towns ranked on various economic and social-cultural scales. By Hall's calculations, Billerica was almost squarely in the middle of all major categories, marking it as neither a frontier village nor a commercialized town. See "Appendices to Van Beck Hall's *Politics without Parties*" (n.p., n.d.) Hillman Library, University of Pittsburgh.

10. Hazen, *History,* 87–102, 278–79, 309; MV-B. In all, 89 percent of Billerica's farms in 1771 (including the Mannings') contained tillage, pasture, and hay land together, compared to 76 percent of the farms which did so in the state as a whole. In addition, 93 percent of these so-called complete farms (again, including the Mannings') produced at least 30 bushels of grain per year, considered by one historian as the absolute minimum requirement to support an average-sized family; the colonywide figure for all complete farms was 81 percent. These proportions suggest a high degree of local self-sufficiency in Billerica, mediated, of course, by an intricate web of barter and commercial exchanges of labor and produce of various kinds. On Massachusetts figures and standards of self-sufficiency, see Bettye Hobbs Pruitt, "Self-Sufficiency and the Agricultural Economy of Eighteenth-Century Massachusetts," *WMQ* 41 (1984), 333–64. Billerica figures computed from MV-B.

11. The account book is in the manuscript collections of the

Baker Library, Graduate School of Business Administration, Harvard University. Unfortunately, like many other accounts of this period, the entries end in 1778, most likely because of the runaway inflation of 1779–80, the looming shadow of which seems to have utterly defeated the best efforts of many otherwise diligent account keepers to record their transactions. At the same time, however, the accounts suggest that Manning closed the tavern in 1778, at least temporarily. For a more exacting look at the Manning accounts and their significance, see *Key*.

12. "The Key," 217–18.

13. BTR, 28 December 1767; 5 February 1773; 6 June 1774; Richard D. Brown, *Revolutionary Politics in Massachusetts: The Boston Committee of Correspondence and the Towns, 1772–1774* (Cambridge, Mass., 1970), 200n.

14. BTR, 6 June 1774.

15. Allen French, *The Day of the Battle of Concord and Lexington* (Boston, 1925), 73, 217–18. Manning officially served with Captain Solomon Pollard's (Billerica) Company and was credited with ten days service beginning April 19. See *Massachusetts Soldiers and Sailors of the Revolutionary War* (Boston, 1902), 10:194–95.

16. "The Key," 211. On the early fighting and the political dedication it inspired, see Charles Royster, *A Revolutionary People at War: The Continental Army and the American Character, 1775–1783* (Chapel Hill, N.C. 1979), 25–53.

17. Manning served on the school committee, the grand jury, and a committee to report on the proper conduct of church singing before being chosen selectman. BTR, 4 March 1782; 1 March, 6 May 1784; 7 March 1785; 6 March 1786; 5 March 1787.

18. "The Key," 242. On the origins and fate of Shays's Rebellion, see especially Hall, *Politics without Parties*. Also see George Richards Minot, *The History of the Insurrection in Massachusetts* 2d ed. (Boston, 1810); Josiah Holland, *History of Western Massachusetts* (Springfield, 1855); C. O. Parmenter, *A History of Pelham, Massachusetts* (Amherst, Mass., 1898), 145–63, 366–402; Marion Starkey, *A Little Rebellion* (New York, 1955); David Szatmary, *Shays' Rebellion: The Anatomy of an Insurrection* (Amherst, Mass., 1980).

19. "The Key," 242–43. According to William Greenleaf in a letter to Governor Bowdoin, the protesters referred to themselves as "regulators." Greenleaf to Bowdoin, n.d., Massachusetts Archives 190:235. The estimate of citizen support for the regulation comes from Szatmary, *Shays' Rebellion*, 59. On the difficulty of raising troops, see ibid., 80. On legislative reluctance, see Hall, *Politics without Parties*, 215–16.

20. BTR, 8 May 1786; 25 February 1788. For more on Billerica and the Massachusetts Regulation, see *Key*, 21–28. On the revulsion against Bowdoin, see Richard D. Brown, "Shays' Rebellion and the Ratification of the Constitution," in Richard Beeman, et al., eds., *Beyond Confederation: Origins of the Constitution and American National Identity* (Chapel Hill, N.C., 1987), 113–27.

21. "The Key," 242.

22. Shays' Rebellion Vouchers, Massachusetts Archives, Boston.

23. Manning's sense of personal accountability also turns up in "Some Proposals," in which he wrote that his motive was "to Clear Myself from the guilt of Consenting or parsively submitting to Measures so Glareingly unjust." "Some Proposals," 302. He was referring to Hamilton's funding program, but he could well have had his late experiences in the Regulation in mind.

24. "The Key," 254.

25. On the conventions of the 1780s, see Hall, *Politics without Parties*. For Manning's views, see "The Key," 215, 233–34.

26. Ibid., 243.

27. BTR, 11 March 1787.

28. Manning's ambivalent views on the Constitution itself—critical of the motivations behind it but convinced of its benefits "by a fair construction"—are discussed more fully in *Key*, 27–28.

29. "Some Proposals," 322. For a lengthier discussion of "Some Proposals," including its connection to the barter ethic, see *Key*, 28–39.

30. "Some Proposals," 329. These were common social categories in the 1790s. Manning borrowed them directly from essays by Benjamin Lincoln, Jr., who writing as "Free Republican" in 1785 had presented a conservative case for why "the few" should control politics. Manning admired "Free Republican" 's scholarship, but used it to reach very different conclusions. For a discussion of Manning and his reliance on "Free Republican," see *Key*, 36, 51.

31. "Some Proposals," 329–31. On rural fear of lordships, see Richard Bushman, *King and People in Provincial Massachusetts* (Chapel Hill, N.C., 1985).

32. "Some Proposals," 321.

33. Hazen, *History*, 257, 273–77, 315; John Farmer, *An Historical Memoir of Billerica* (Amherst, N.H., 1816), 21, 27.

34. Hazen, *History*, 275; Agreement between William Manning and L[oammi] Baldwin, et al., 13 December 1794, box 4, folder 1, Loammi Baldwin Collection, Baker Library, Graduate School of Business Administration, Harvard University.

Land sold by William Manning: 28 acres to David Rogers for

£60, 25 Feb. 1794, *Grantors,* 8:457; 15 acres to Joseph Jacquith for £40, 23 Jan. 1793, ibid., 9:117; 7 acres to David Levenstone for £40, 19 Oct. 1796, ibid., 9:245; 3.5 acres to Timothy Manning for £21, 10 Jan. 1797, ibid., 9:275; about 4 acres to Timothy Sprague for £30.18s., 20 April 1797, ibid., 9:300; about 11 acres to Joseph Jacquith et al. for $268.81, 1 March 1799, ibid. 9:399.

Land purchased by William Manning: 4 acres from John Laws for £8, 17 Nov. 1790, Manning Family Collection; 50 acres from David Levenstone for £50, 20 Jan. 1794, ibid.; 10 acres from Thomas Richardson for $50, 30 April 1796, ibid.

35. Manning, "Key of Libberty," [1798–99].

36. William Manning to Catharine Cummings, 18 July 1787; 27 April 1792, Registry of Deeds, *Grantors,* 8:102, 368; Agreements, William Manning and the Directors of the Union Bank, 30 January 1793; William Manning and Joseph Davis, 6 March 1802; William Manning and Theophilius Manning, 1 December 1808; Manning Family Collection; Jephtha Manning to His Father, William Manning [1804–1811], Manning Account Book, Baker Library.

37. For a detailed treatment of the controversy over Jay's Treaty, see Jerald A. Combs, *The Jay Treaty: Political Battleground of the Founding Fathers* (Berkeley, Calif., 1970); and Banning, *Jeffersonian Persuasion.*

38. William Manning to Thomas Adams, 15 February 1799, Manning Papers, Houghton Library, Harvard University. On the Adamses and the 1798 repression, see James Morton Smith, *Freedom's Fetters: The Alien and Sedition Laws and American Civil Liberties* (Ithaca, N.Y., 1956).

39. "The Key," 247; James Monroe, *A View of the Conduct of the Executive* (Philadelphia, 1797); and Joseph Fauchet, *A Sketch of the Present State* (Philadelphia, 1797).

40. William Manning Probate, 1814, Middlesex County Probate no. 14615, Massachusetts Archives, Boston (microfilm).

41. See David Jaffee, "The Village Enlightenment in New England, 1760–1820," *WMQ* 47 (1990): 327–46; Alfred McClung Lee, *The Daily Newspaper in America: The Evolution of Social Instrument* (New York, 1937), 29, 728, 711; Donald Stewart, *The Opposition Press of the Federalist Period* (Albany, N.Y., 1969), 652; and Appleby, *Capitalism,* 54–55. For a broader look at the circulation of knowledge in the eighteenth-century countryside, see Richard D. Brown, *Knowledge is Power: The Diffusion of Information in Early America, 1700–1865* (New York, 1989), 132–59.

42. "The Key," 211, 220, 238.

43. [John Dickinson], "Letters from a Farmer in Pennsylvania

(1767–1768)," in Paul L. Ford, ed., *Writings of John Dickinson* (Philadelphia, 1895). Ruth Bogin makes a similar point in her commentary on "Some Proposals" in *WMQ* 46 (1989): 315–31.

44. "The Key," 214.

45. Ibid., 245–46. Manning had probably seen the English broadside, "A Remarkable Prophecy" (Exeter, N.H., 1794)—widely circulated in the United States—which predicted, among other things, "There will Gog and Magog that will make war against all the nations in the world." See Ruth Bloch, *Visionary Republic:* Millenial Themes in American Thought (Cambridge, 1985), 162–63. On Manning's religious leanings and their impact on his political views, see *Key*, 42, 52–54.

46. See the entry for Cumings in William B. Sprague, *Annals of the American Pulpit* (New York, 1865) 8:55–64. On the theological differences within New England Congregationalism, see Conrad Wright, *Beginnings of Unitarianism in America* (Boston, 1955); Joseph Conforti, *Samuel Hopkins and the New Divinity Movement* (Grand Rapids, Mich., 1981); and William Breitenbach, "The Consistent Calvinism of the New Divinity Movement," *WMQ* 41 (1984), 241–64. For Bentley on the New Divinity pastors, see *The Diary of William Bentley, D.D.* (Salem, Mass., 1904–14) 1:275. For more on the divisions between Cumings and Manning, and on the importance of Manning's religion to his politics, see *Key*, 39–48.

47. Henry Cumings, *A [Christmas] Sermon . . . at Billerica* (Boston, 1797), 27; "The Key," 217–18.

48. Henry Cumings, *A Sermon Preached before His Honor Thomas Cushing, Esq.* (Boston, 1783), 16; "The Key," 214.

49. Henry Cumings, *A Sermon Preached at Lexington* (Boston, 1781), 12; Cumings, *A [Thanksgiving] Sermon . . . at Billerica* (Boston, 1798), 9; "The Key," 214.

50. Cumings, *Sermon before Cushing*, 7, 18; "The Key," 214.

51. Manning Tavern Accounts, 1753–1777, Baker Library, Harvard Business School, 25, 45–47, 49, 112. For a long time, most writing on early American taverns did not rise above the anecdotal. Two exceptions are John D. R. Platt, *The City Tavern* (Denver, Colo., 1973); and Kym S. Rice, *Early American Taverns: For the Entertainment of Strangers* (Chicago, 1983). More recently, there has been a renewed interest in the subject, open to more exacting cultural analysis. See Peter Thompson, "A Social History of Philadelphia Taverns, 1683–1800," (Ph.D. diss., University of Pennsylvania, 1989); and David Weir Conroy, "The Culture and Politics of Drink in Colonial and Revolutionary Massachusetts, 1681–1790," (Ph.D. diss., University of Connecticut, 1987).

52. *American Mercury,* 31 Dec. 1792; William Plumer to Theodore Foster, 28 June 1790, quoted in William A. Robinson, *Jeffersonian Democracy in New England* (New Haven, 1916), 56; *Connecticut Journal,* 4 April 1799.

53. "Some Proposals," 322, 328, 330; "The Key," 217, 227, 230, 232, 238.

54. Richard Hofstadter, *Anti-Intellectualism in American Life* (New York, 1963), 151–53. "The Key," 217, 219; David Hume, "Balance of Trade," in Eugene F. Miller, ed., *Essays: Moral, Political, Literary* (Indianapolis, 1987), 312–13. Hofstadter's misreading of Manning also led him to ignore "The Key" 's call for the state to maintain colleges that would grant "the highest Degrees of Larning," "The Key," 231. On Austin's polemic, see Sydney Kaplan, " 'Honestus' and the Annihilation of the Lawyers," *South Atlantic Quarterly* 48 (1949):401–20.

55. "The Key," 212; "Some Proposals," 329–30. For a plebeian democrat of the contrasting temperament, see Staughton Lynd, ed., "Abraham Yates's History of the Movement for the United States Constitution," *WMQ* 20 (1963): 223–45; and in general, Cecilia Kenyon, "Men of Little Faith: The Anti-Federalists and the Nature of Representative Government," *WMQ* 12 (1955), 3–43.

56. "The Key," 223–24, 239, 241. For more on Manning and his reaction to the Cincinnati, see *Key.*

57. "The Key," 221–22, 247.

58. Ibid., 211, 221, 233, 247.

59. On "localists" versus "cosmopolitans," see especially Jackson Turner Main, *Political Parties before the Constitution* (Chapel Hill, N.C., 1973).

60. For details on Manning's various drafts and the changes he made, see *Key,* 48–50.

61. "The Key," 218, 251–52.

62. Compare ibid., 218–21, and [Benjamin Lincoln, Jr.], "A Free Republican," *Massachusetts Magazine* (1784), 420–21.

63. "The Key," 218.

64. Ibid., 251, 218–20; compare 225.

65. "The Key," 219, 222, 244–45. Quite clearly, Manning's conception of exploitation (as of much else) was wholly different from that of various nineteenth-century radicals and socialists, including Karl Marx—a point Samuel Eliot Morison obscured in his assessment of "The Key" as "a lonely American whisper" of Marx's writings. If Manning prefigured anything, it was the economic critique elaborated in the equal rights radicalism that ran from the Working Men of the 1820s through the Populist revolt. Unfortunately, this tradi-

tion itself has been misconstrued as "bourgeois" or "entrepreneurial," a legacy of the consensus historians of the 1940s and 1950s. For more on this, see *Key*, 204n. 68. The Morison edition mistranscribes Manning's reference to "the great skuffel" as "the great shuffel."

66. "The Key," 221, 231. Manning was one of the many late-eighteenth-century Massachusetts democrats who called for increased attention to the education of girls. As a result of their efforts, the numbers of schools open to girls expanded greatly in the 1790s. According to Kathryn Kish Sklar, the principal opponents of such schooling were members of the local elites, who pressed for Latin grammar schools intended to prepare their sons for college, and preferred to educate their daughters at private finishing schools. See Sklar, "Sources of Change in the Schooling of Girls in Massachusetts, 1750–1810," (unpublished paper, Department of History, State University of New York, n.d.).

67. "The Key," 219, 220, 221, 222–23, 231–32; compare "Some Proposals," 330.

68. "The Key," 251.

69. Ibid., 218, 220, 238, 221–23, 236–41.

70. Ibid., 236–44.

71. Ibid., 220. On the effects of the prosperity, see ibid., 237; for a fuller discussion, see *Key*.

72. Ibid., 246–48, 250.

73. Ibid., 252, 247.

74. Ibid., 248.

75. Ibid., 249, 252–53; William Manning, Letter fragment, n.d., Houghton Library, Harvard University. For more on Manning and the Methodists, see *Key*.

76. "The Key," 233, 250, 253. This latter provision, especially, can easily be misunderstood. While one might, at first glance, assume that Manning had in mind something akin to people's tribunals, like those that had been the instruments of terror in the French Revolution, he was in fact proposing something far more benign—and, arguably, far more likely to be effective. In the late-eighteenth-century United States, as two recent historians of impeachment have reported, "literally anyone could bring an impeachment by a report or complaint." Peter C. Hoffer and N. E. H. Hull, *Impeachment in America, 1635–1805* (New Haven, 1984), 93. A Labouring Society that "managed impeachments" was not adding to the rights of the people; it was simply, to borrow one of Manning's terms, "improving" upon them.

77. "The Key," 250.

78. Ibid., 248, 249. Manning, "A Proposed Method for Carrying

[The Labouring Society] into Execution . . . ," Houghton Library, Harvard University.

79. "The Key," 250, 251.

80. Ibid., 248, 252, 254.

81. William Manning, "The Key of Libberty, Containing Proposals for Taking a Monthly Magazine to be Stiled the Farmers or Labourers Magazine . . . ," [1800?] Houghton Library, Harvard University.

82. For a complete discussion of these additional writings, see *Key*, 70–72, 77–78.

83. On Brown, see Smith, *Freedom's Fetters*, 257–70; Charles Warren, *Jacobin and Junto; or, Early American Politics as Viewed in the Diary of Dr. Nathaniel Ames, 1788–1822* (Cambridge, Mass., 1931), 106–10; Boston *Independent Chronicle*, 17, 20 June 1799.

84. Boston *Columbian Centinel*, 27 March 1799.

85. *Independent Chronicle*, 17 June 1798.

86. Thomas Jefferson, "Notes on Professor Ebeling's Letter of July 30, 1795," in Merrill Peterson, ed., *Thomas Jefferson Writings* (New York, 1984), 700; see also Jefferson to George Washington, 23 May 1792, ibid., 985–90.

87. Seth Ames, ed., *Works of Fisher Ames*, 2 vols. (Boston, 1854) 2:115. For more on Republican party organization, see Robinson, *Jeffersonian Democracy*, 52–75; and Noble Cunningham, Jr., *The Jefferson Republicans in Power* (Chapel Hill, N.C., 1963), 133–42.

88. See Robinson, *Jeffersonian Democracy;* David Hackett Fischer, *The Revolution of American Conservatism: The Federalist Party in the Era of Jeffersonian Democracy* (New York, 1965); and, James M. Banner, *To the Hartford Convention: The Federalists and the Origins of Party Politics in Massachusetts, 1789–1815* (New York, 1970).

89. Robinson, *Jeffersonian Democracy*, 63–65; Warren, *Jacobin and Junto*, 226.

90. Robinson, *Jeffersonian Democracy*, 63.

91. See Richard Hofstadter, *The Idea of a Party System: The Rise of a Legitimate Opposition in the United States* (Berkeley, Calif., 1969).

92. For details on Manning's later years, see *Key*, 77–80.

93. Gordon S. Wood, "The Democratization of Mind in the American Revolution," in Robert Horowitz, ed., *The Moral Foundations of the American Revolution* (1978; 3rd. ed., Charlottesville, Va., 1986).

The Novel as Subversive Activity

Women Reading, Women Writing

CATHY N. DAVIDSON

A woman reads, while a small child plays nearby and a man identified as "the honest and industrious laborer" tills the field. The illustration, called "The Farmer's Cottage," is the frontispiece in *The Columbian Primer* (1802) by Herman Mann, a novelist, educator, and publisher.

Courtesy American Antiquarian Society.

Is it not a little hard [as Jonathan Swift asked], . . . that not one gentleman's daughter in a thousand should be brought to read or understand her own natural tongue, or be judge of the easiest books that are written in it? . . . If there be any of your acquaintance to whom this passage is applicable, I hope you will recommend the study of Mr. [Noah] *Webster*'s Grammatical Institute, as the best work in our language to facilitate the knowledge of Grammar. I cannot but think Mr. *Webster* intended his valuable book for the benefit of his countrywomen; for while he delivers his *rules* in a pure, precise, and elegant style, he *explains* his meaning by *examples* which are calculated to inspire the female mind with a thirst for emulation, and a desire for virtue.[1]

Although the above quotation reads as if it might come from an early American advice book, pedagogical work, or sermon, it actually appears in William Hill Brown's novel, *The Power of Sympathy* (1789), widely accepted as the "first American novel."[2] Equally surprising, this recommendation for Webster's popular spelling book interrupts a sensational story of the young lovers Harriot and Harrington, who learn, shortly after this lecture on female education, that they have the same father. A wealthy, dissipated lawyer, the Honorable J. Harrington had seduced and subsequently abandoned Harriot's mother, Maria Fawcett, a young woman with no fortune of her own and limited marital prospects. She died in childbirth. A generation later, the daughter of that illicit union, Harriot, dies too, of grief, when she realizes that it would be incestuous to marry the younger Harrington, the man whom she loves. And then that young man also expires, by his own hand, providing a final testimony to the evils of seduction. But a problem remains: What is the relationship between literacy and secret sin, between Webster's speller and Harriot's unfortunate family history?

That question deserves our attention precisely because it would not have been posed by the early American novel reader. *The Power of Sympathy*, like many of the novels written in America between 1789 and 1820, assumes that there is an obvious and causal connection between poor female education and sexual vulnerability. "Of the Letters before us," the author notes in his preface, "it is necessary to remark, that . . . the dangerous Consequences of SEDUCTION are exposed, and the Advantages of FEMALE EDUCATION set forth and recommended."[3] Well over half of the approximately one hundred novels written in America between 1789 and 1820 overtly or covertly assert a similar relationship between women's intellectual and sexual well-being.[4] In the two best-selling novels of the early national period, for example, we have variations on William Hill

Brown's insistence on the need for female education. The poor
fifteen-year-old schoolgirl in Susanna Haswell Rowson's *Charlotte, A
Tale of Truth* (1791; later and popularly known as *Charlotte Temple*),
is seduced by an army officer largely because she is misled by the
false precepts of a lascivious and evil French teacher, Mademoiselle
La Rue. Charlotte herself lacks the knowledge and self-confidence
necessary to discern the duplicity beneath the dubious counsel of La
Rue or inherent in the sentimental (but empty) promises of a handsome young soldier. Similarly, in Hannah Webster Foster's *The Coquette* (1797), an upper middle-class woman, Eliza Wharton, has a
typical genteel, female education which in no way prepares her to support herself but does lead her (rightly) to scorn the idea of marriage
to a dull, pompous minister. Yet still unwed at thirty-seven years of
age, with little income of her own and no suitors on the scene, Eliza
dishearteningly acquiesces to the sexual advances made by Major
Sanford, a dissolute army officer who, we are informed, loves Eliza but
had rejected her in order to marry a wealthier woman. Eliza Wharton
also dies in childbirth—like Maria Fawcett, like Charlotte Temple.

As such rudimentary content analysis attests, these novels acknowledged the economic foundations of matrimony in the early national period and suggested that a solid, worldly education was one
way that a poor woman could protect herself on the marriage market
even though she had little other bargaining power. Had Maria or
Charlotte known more, they might not have been taken in by the se-
ductive arguments of wealthier suitors concerned mostly with their
own pleasure. Had Eliza been prepared by a useful education to support herself, she might not have acquiesced to a man so obviously her
intellectual and moral inferior. The same message is conveyed more
positively in a novella by one of early America's most prominent phi-
losophers and feminists, Judith Sargent Murray. In *Story of Margaretta* (1798), Murray shows how Margaretta Melworth, armed with a
superior education and a strong sense of her own worth, is able to see
through an ominously named suitor and would-be seducer, Sinisterus
Courtland. Margaretta rejects him, then discovers that he is already
married and the father of three children. Her carefully nurtured intelligence and consequent self-assurance prevent a bigamous relationship and later allow her to accept a proposal from the admirable
Edward Hamilton, and to enter into a marriage based upon "mutual
affection." Whether portrayed positively or negatively, the causal
connection between a woman's education and her success in the
world is clear. Nor are these four novels exceptional. Virtually every
novel written in America before 1820 at some point includes either a
discourse on the necessity of improved education (often with special

attention to the need for better female education), a description of
the deplorable state of mass education in America or, at the very
least, a comment on the educational levels and reading habits of the
hero and the heroine.[5]

Again and again the nation's first novelists showed the ways in
which a woman's intellect had to be improved if women were going to
be able to cope with a social situation in which they were clearly at
a disadvantage. To generalize, the novels warn that women need not
just a proper, domestic education, but an education that will allow
them the intellectual independence and the self-confidence necessary to protect themselves against a host of articulate, better-
educated, and invariably wealthier American men (the stock
seducers in early sentimental fiction). The implicit but insistent
point behind this educational agenda is that because women continued to be, for all practical purposes, economically and legally power-
less in post-revolutionary America, they needed all the advantages
of an excellent education in order to survive in the real world. In
short, at a time when many of America's leading citizens boasted of
the glory that was the new nation, the novelists tended to look at the
actual status of women. And because they focused on the plight of
women, the novelists tended to paint a more realistic (because more
inclusive) portrait of early America than did the Founding Fathers.

It is the thesis of this essay that the novel was read—and cherished—by its women readers precisely because it alone, of all the
available literary and cultural forms, was dedicated to the proposition that women's experience was worthy of detailed, sympathetic,
and thoughtful attention. Novels situated the specific events of
women's lives—from childhood education to adolescent sexuality
to adult decision-making, marriage, childbirth, child-rearing, and
death—within a social and political context in which women were
shown to have little power and few rights. Novels also argued that a
practical education (of a kind rarely supplied by the rudimentary female schools of the time) was necessary if women were to survive in
a nation in which they were, for the most part, invisible.

In presenting this thesis I will first discuss the development of an
indigenous fiction in America and the mechanisms by which fiction
came to be available to all but the poorest class of American readers;
second, I will examine some of the reasons for the general popularity
of fiction and more specifically the ways individual novels were regarded by individual readers; third, I will discuss why many social
authorities were alarmed by the increasing popularity of the genre;
fourth, I will show the ways in which many of the critiques of early
women's fiction mirrored women's low social and political status;

fifth, I will show how specific titles offered up a different vision of the potentialities of life for poor readers and especially for females of all classes; and finally, I will suggest some "subversive" functions novels played in the lives of early American women readers. From these early novels the contemporary reader can gain a unique sense of the emotional, intellectual, and social dilemmas confronting women in the early national period.

William Hill Brown wrote *The Power of Sympathy* the same year that General Washington was inaugurated as President Washington. The novel as an indigenous form thus began in America virtually as the nation was working out its identity, its definition of itself.[6] Previously, novels had been imported into America in great quantity from England and Europe, but the twenty-three-year-old Brown, son of a Boston clock maker, is now generally credited as the first American to try his hand at writing one.[7] Brown writes with all the self-consciousness of someone trying to create a new art form for his new nation, and the plot of his novel is continually diverted into democratic discussions of such topics as the evils of class consciousness, the contradiction of slavery in a free land, and as we have seen, the necessity for improved female education. Equally important, in 1789, Isaiah Thomas, one of early America's most prosperous printers, advertised Brown's novel as the "FIRST AMERICAN NOVEL" in a series of newspaper advertisements designed to play off the excitement of Washington's inauguration and to profit from the nationalistic enthusiasms at that exhilarating moment in American history.[8] Many subsequent novels also emphasized their Americanness and their authors often attempted to retool older, European fictional forms to the specific social, political, and geographical situations of the new nation. Like others in the new nation, American novelists attempted to sort out the possibilities and the problems facing the new nation.

Because the American novel as a genre emerged just as America "constituted" itself, these first novels can provide the contemporary historian with a singularly detailed symbolic map of important attitudes and issues in the new nation. The timing was propitious. At precisely the same historical moment that Americans began writing novels, the novel as a genre (both indigenous and imported) was becoming the single most prevalent cultural form in the nation. In short, fiction was to the early national period what television was to the 1950s—a new mode of expression that captured the attention (positive and negative) of an entire society.

The Preface to Royall Tyler's *The Algerine Captive* (1797) describes the change that occurred in America during the seven years in which the novel's protagonist, Updike Underhill, has been held captive in Algiers:

> When he left New England, books of biography, travels, novels, and modern romances were confined to our seaports; or, if known in the country, were read only in the families of clergymen, physicians, and lawyers: while certain funeral discourses, the last words and dying speeches of Bryan Shaheen, and Levi Ames, and some dreary somebody's *Day of doom*, formed the most diverting part of the farmer's library. On his return from captivity, he found a surprising alteration in the public taste. In our inland towns of consequence, social libraries had been instituted, composed of books designed to amuse rather than to instruct; and country booksellers, fostering the new-born taste of the people, had filled the whole land with modern travels and novels almost as incredible.

This wandering son of the New Republic come home again is especially struck by the "extreme avidity with which books of mere amusement were purchased and perused by all ranks."[9]

Numerous literary historians have corroborated the phenomenon that Tyler here describes and have documented an increasing prevalence of fiction among women of all classes as well as among working-class and lower-class readers of both genders.[10] Yet in 1797, when Tyler wrote, owning a novel was still a luxury. Before the invention of the Napier-Hoe cylinder press, the mass production of machine-made paper, and other technological advances brought down the cost of books, ordinary people rarely owned more than a few precious books.[11] A typical early American novel, for example, cost between 75 cents and a dollar in 1790. A day laborer in Massachusetts then earned 50 cents to a dollar a day. A serving girl earned that much in a week. Or a schoolteacher, who might well have had a vocational propensity to read books, often received his or her wages in "country pay," not cash, and when a cash salary was paid, the sum was generally modest and typically more modest for women than for men.[12] Diarist Ethan Allen Greenwood, for example, earned only three dollars a month at his first teaching position, and, at his most lucrative post, only fourteen dollars a month.[13]

How could industrious young men or women, eager to expand their own intellectual horizons, possibly afford novels? *The Power of Sympathy,* for example, cost 89 and ½ cents. For the same amount one could spend an evening at the theater (usually considered an upper-class or upper middle-class entertainment) or could buy a season's worth of the imported French watermarked blue ribbons that signified the height of fashion in Boston in the late 1780s.[14] For the less affluent, the choice might be between *The Power of Sympathy* and a bushel of potatoes and a half bushel of corn, or between Charles Brockden Brown's *Jane Talbot* (1801) and enough homespun to make dresses for a woman and for two or three of her daughters.[15] For most Americans of the time, this was not really a choice at all.

When the fictional Updike Underhill returns in 1797 from seven years' captivity in Algiers, he notes not just a proliferation of books among the poor and in rural communities but also a change in the primary mechanism by which a new group of readers came to peruse books. That mechanism was the lending library, the single most important agency for making books (and especially novels) accessible to all but the very lowest class of Americans. In the 1790s, coincident with the "invention" of an indigenous fiction, lending libraries proliferated at a rate never seen before in America.[16] For six dollars a year, payable in installments, a reader could borrow up to three novels a day from the nearly 1,500 novels that Hocquet Caritat stocked in his Circulating Library in New York.[17] A laborer in Philadelphia, a serving girl in Pelham, Massachusetts, a mechanic in New Haven, a farmhand in the small village of Harwinton, Connecticut, or even a pioneer on the frontier of Belpre, Ohio, could all, thanks to the local lending library, borrow the books they could not afford to buy.[18] As Robert B. Winans has argued, "the increase in the number of circulating libraries was largely the result of the increasing demand for novels; the general growth of the reading public was caused primarily by the novel."[19] Libraries made novels affordable and accessible to a new audience. These new readers identified with the middle-class and even lower-class young men and women who populated such novels as Martha Meredith Read's *Monima, or the Beggar Girl* (1804) or Sarah Savage's *The Factory Girl* (1814), the first novel of factory life in America and one in which the heroine organizes the other factory girls into a study group.[20]

Numerous early American novelists—including Read, Savage, and Tyler, as well as Charles Brockden Brown and Helena Wells—noted that many Americans read no other kinds of books besides novels, read their favorite novels over and over again, and, indeed, relied upon these novels for a kind of education into the world. Novels, numerous novelists asserted, were good for readers. They educated, of course, but they also kept the lower classes away from more disreputable activities such as horse racing or cockfights. Hocquet Caritat, for example, had assembled America's largest circulating library of novels in the first years of the nineteenth century. He published a pamphlet in 1804 in which he both advertised and apologized for his holdings. For Caritat, "the decrease in drunkenness in this country is, perhaps, owing to the introduction of circulating libraries, which may be considered as temples erected by literature to attract the votaries of Bacchus."[21]

Not until the mid-nineteenth century would novels be cheap enough to be purchased by virtually any American citizen. But already in the early national period, through the mechanism of the circulating libraries, novels found their ways into the hands, hearts, and minds of American citizens of diverse backgrounds.

*M*ost of the readers who flocked to the circulating libraries to borrow novels were women, and apparently women of virtually all social classes. From numerous personal accounts we know that the serving maid who was sent out to fetch a novel for her mistress often read it on the way home. Novels were shared among family and friends, read aloud in communal gatherings such as quilting bees or mending sessions, and otherwise incorporated into the round of women's lives. Often operating at a relatively low level of linguistic complexity, novels could have a special appeal to women whose education and literacy levels were still low. Furthermore, not only were novels linguistically and stylistically accessible, they also made a point of addressing a new female audience, implicitly by portraying women characters in a variety of situations and often explicitly. *The Power of Sympathy* is unapologetically dedicated "to the YOUNG LADIES of UNITED COLUMBIA."[22] Susanna Rowson, in *Charlotte Temple,* addresses the "young and unprotected woman in her first entrance into life," while Samuel Relf, in the Advertisement to *Infidelity, or the Victims of Sentiment* (1797), assumes that the "generality" of his readers "will be of 'the mild, the soft and gentle formed of soul.' "[23] Although other forms of republican discourse overwhelmingly posited a male audience, the novel assumed a female one. Quite simply, the majority of early American novels are written about women, for women, and are often by women as well. It is safe to generalize that the early American novel was, for the most part, a female form with an implied female readership.

But just how did individual women (and particularly women who were not well educated) actually read these early novels? Numerous quantitative studies have confirmed that novels were among the most popular books in circulating libraries and women's libraries, but how can one begin to reconstruct the private and personal responses women had to the books they read?[24] One way, of course, is through the occasional diary reference to novel reading. The diary of Patty Rogers of Exeter, New Hampshire, for example, is filled with allusions to the various novels she is reading. Perhaps equally revealing, Rogers's style mimics that of her favorite novelist, Laurence Sterne. Writing in 1785, Rogers notes:

> Read in a sweet novel the D——r brought me. It affected me so, I could hardly read it, and was often obliged to drop the book to suppress my grief!—Went to Bed, Lay, and thot of the Lovely Woodbridge—Shed a *torrent* of tears, at the *Recollection* of past interviews with him! . . . He [Woodbridge] press'd me to his *Bosom* with a *fondness* I thought expressive of approbation, *never never* P——y hesitate a *moment* to let me know if 'tis in my power to make you *happy*! would you would you, no Sir! *said* I, at the same time kissing his Hand with *trembling* Lips![25]

Unfortunately, Miss Rogers should have paid more attention to the sentimental novels she read and imitated. We know, from the rest of her diary, that she was jilted first by "dear Woodbridge," then by Dr. Samuel Tenney, who would go on to marry one of the most popular novelists of the early national period, Tabitha Tenney. Patty Rogers lived alone in Exeter, New Hampshire, to pious old age, where she continued to ply her needle and read her novels.[26]

Unquestionably, novels played an important role in the lives of many readers, but just how extensive that role was is difficult to gauge if we rely only on notably scarce and inconclusive diary or epistolary accounts. To gain a broader sense of how individual readers responded to the books they read, I have examined approximately 1,200 extant copies of early American novels for signs of the readers who originally read, borrowed, or owned them.[27] Obviously, my findings are both preliminary and impressionistic in that there is nothing statistically controlled about the percentage of copies that happens to have survived, nor have I seen every extant copy of every early American novel. Nonetheless, early American readers left their marks. From marginalia, inscriptions, and even the material evidence of book use and repair, one can begin to "see" a novel's first readers and to appreciate how much they cherished their books as prized and vital possessions. Torn pages neatly hand-sewn back into the volume, dog-eared corners carefully trimmed, thumb papers (little tabs of vellum or wallpaper) secured in the spines of books to prevent a reader's fingers from soiling the pages all suggest the care early readers took to preserve even cheap, badly produced novels and, by inference, suggest the ways in which early readers valued their books.

To generalize, the three most prevalent kinds of marks in early American novels can be categorized as possessive, dedicatory, or imitative. In the first category, readers not only inscribed their names but often proclaimed (through underlinings, repeated words, or multiple signatures) that they owned a book (again, it must be emphasized, a relatively rare occurrence in early America). The book, on this level, operates as "cultural capital," to use Pierre Bourdieu's evocative term—as commodity and status symbol, but also, I would insist, as something far more intimate.[28] Readers identified with these novels; in some very real sense, the novels became part of their lives. In the second category, we find books not just as private possessions but as objects of cultural exchange and, judging from the personal nature of many dedications, an exchange that operates on the level of shared ideas and aspirations. A gift is not merely another form of commodity exchange. More than just the monetary value of the book-as-object, the values of the book are passed on from one reader to another. In the third (and most pertinent for the present discussion) category, readers actually copied out on the endleaves or in the blank spaces at the end of chapters favorite passages from the novel. Sometimes the handwriting is crude, the letters ill-formed, the transcriptions inaccurate. Sometimes it is clear that the reader is copying not the content but the actual form of the letters (suggesting the novel's function as copybook and expository model for a reader still at a relatively elementary stage in her or his personal education). Since reading was taught before writing in the schools and many women never progressed beyond elementary reading instruction, these novels indicate that there were some readers who may have been able to read a novel even though they could not yet write at a competent level. Or sometimes words are listed and at times defined on the end pages of early novels. Different copies of the same novel (and, occasionally, even the very same copy) could be used on all these levels. For example, one copy of *Charlotte Temple* might display a beautifully penned dedication (the novel serving as a token of friendship between one affluent reader and another), while the flyleaf of another exhibits beginning penmanship exercises (such as "push-pulls and ovals," to use the terminology of the Palmer handwriting method). Observing such diverse signs, the contemporary historian is reminded that it is often difficult to generalize from a content analysis of a given novel to an implied audience. My survey suggests that the same novel could often be enjoyed by readers of all ages, both sexes, and most social classes—and also by readers who possessed markedly different degrees of literary sophistication.

Yet it does seem safe to assume that the novelists themselves accurately perceived who most of their readers would be when they specifically addressed a female readership. In the copies of early novels I have located, women's signatures outnumber men's by roughly two to one. Considering the restrictions on women's economic power in the eighteenth century and the proscriptions against female novel reading, this is an unusually high number of women readers.[29] Men, however, read and cherished novels, too. Writing in Pittsburgh on 10 March 1872 in a copy of *Charlotte Temple* published in 1824, William T. Dunn noted: "This book was presented to me by my grandmother Dunn, about the year 1830."[30] Sometimes a separate story is itself hidden in the inscriptions. Written on the inside front cover of one copy is "Susan Smith Property Bought October the 9 1806," but on the back we find, "William Smiths Book Bought October the 4 1806," along with two signatures of William Smith. Did she buy it from him (sister from brother? wife from husband?) so that it would be her book, or did he use the back inside cover to claim prior purchase and consequent ownership? We cannot answer that question, but in either case the significance is the same; the two dated declarations attest to the importance of the book as a possession, literally and figuratively an object of identification.

Novels were often bequeathed across generations: different copies of *The Coquette* were given by a mother to her daughter or by a son to his father. Other copies passed between brothers and sisters, wives and husbands, between lovers, among friends. I have found as many as twenty signatures in single copies of early novels, and one copy of *Charlotte Temple* has passed through four generations to the present one, along with the family Bible.[31]

"So true a tale," Sally B[owles?] wrote after the last sentence of her volume of *Charlotte Temple*. Another reader inscribed a brief poem on the endpapers of another edition of the same novel: "The rose will fade / the truth withers / But a virtuous mind / will bloom forever." The verse echoes the "innocent flower" metaphors associated with Charlotte throughout the novel. This same reader also drew a rather crude illustration of a young girl in a long dress, presumably a rendition of the heroine. Similarly moved to poetry by Charlotte's plight, still another reader wrote (with more sincerity than accuracy or clarity): "She was fair and sweet as the Lilly Inosentas [*sic*] / the young lamb folly misled / her love betrayed her misery / Cros'd the awful final ocean / in the twentieth year of her age—so ended the unfortunate Charlotte." Another reader wrote but two words in an otherwise pristine 1809 edition of *Charlotte Temple*: "My Treasure."[32]

What was "treasured" by all of these readers, it must be remembered, was the pathetic story of a schoolgirl without a dowry who was seduced by a young soldier whose father had warned his son severely against marrying "precipitously," for love, instead of carefully, for money. After she is pregnant, Charlotte is then abandoned by Montraville, who marries another woman who is both virtuous and, far more significantly, rich. Rowson's seduction story can thus be read as an allegory of the prerogatives and perils of class and gender. But it could also be read as tragically true, so much so that for over a hundred years readers visited the real grave of the fictitious Charlotte Temple in the Trinity Churchyard in New York City, leaving behind locks of their hair or the ashes of their love letters. Even into the twentieth century, Charlotte's fake grave still received more visitors than did the neighboring graves of Robert Fulton or Alexander Hamilton, a testimony to the unparalleled power that fiction sometimes can exert over "real" life.[33]

The very fact that the novel greatly appealed to lower-class readers and to women readers of all classes suggests why it aroused such fears among elites. Many social authorities believed, to paraphrase a comment repeated often in the local press, that novels would unfit the poor to be good workers, and women to be good wives. As the Reverend Samuel Miller, a Presbyterian minister and a teacher at Princeton, argued:

> Every opportunity is taken [in novels] to attack some principle of morality under the title of a "prejudice;" to ridicule the duties of domestic life, as flowing from "contracted" and "slavish" views; to deny the sober pursuits of upright industry as "dull" and "spiritless;" and, in a word, to frame an apology for suicide, adultery, prostitution, and the indulgence of every propensity for which a corrupt heart can plead an inclination. . . . The author has no hesitation in saying, that, if it were possible, he would wholly prohibit the reading of novels. . . .[34]

The tone of Miller's critique is representative, even if his metaphors are somewhat less lurid than those used in many contemporaneous attacks (which often emphasized seduction, satanic possession, or addiction) against the novel and its readers—especially its women readers.

To generalize from over 200 denunciations of fiction written between 1789 and 1820 and appearing in newspapers, magazines, sermons, advice books, and sometimes in the novels themselves, critics were most concerned that the novel portended a rebalancing of power in a new and sometimes unruly democracy. What did it mean, these critics asked, when a literary form chose ordinary people and often the marginally educated for its audience? Conversely, what did it mean when readers flocked to the local lending libraries to borrow books in which beggar girls, factory girls, emigrants, and orphans (all featured in the titles of sundry early American novels) triumphed against greedy and lascivious plutocrats?[35] For many of early America's most respected political, religious, and social leaders, the novel seemed an innately subversive form that would have deleterious effects on a nation still struggling to define itself. This criticism, moreover, escalated as the novel increased in popularity. For its well-placed critics, the new form represented not only a major shift in American culture, but also the most fearful possibilities of "mobocracy."

Before examining more closely the critiques of fiction advanced in America, we should note that the novel as a literary genre was early and universally deemed subversive. The literary historian and theorist Mikhail Bakhtin has argued that the literary form itself was what was seen to be threatening and was consequently condemned in virtually every Western country into which it was introduced. It was considered subversive of certain class and gender notions of who should and should not be literate; subversive of notions of what is or is not suitable literary subject matter, form, and style; subversive of the term *literature* itself.[36] Because the novel did not rhyme or scan, because it required no prior knowledge of Latin or Greek, it seemed to many elite commentators that anyone could write one and virtually anyone could read one. The form required no intermediation or interpretation by cleric or critic, and neither did it require on the part of its authors or readers any special training or classical erudition since, by definition, the novel was new, "novel." Indeed, formalistically, the novel at once absorbed a host of familiar forms of "street literature" (associated with the lower classes) such as chapbooks, penny histories, and almanacs as well as travel, captivity, and military narratives and social, political, and religious tracts. Not only did it thus blur traditional literary class lines, it also confused the distinction between truth and fiction. How could any one reading a novel sort out salutary truth from misleading lie—especially when so many novels (particularly in America) were often based on lightly fictionalized accounts of local scandals among the highborn, with names only slightly changed to protect (while accusing) the guilty? What social good could be gained from such reading?

Equally perturbing, the novel "fit" into the routines of life by appropriating such nonliterary forms as letters (almost one third of the novels written in America before 1820 were epistolary) or diaries, as well as traditionally oral forms of culture such as local gossip, rumor, hearsay, and folktales. Psychologically, the novel also embraced a new relationship between art and audience, writer and reader, a relationship that replaced the authority of the sermon or the Bible with the unbridled enthusiasms of sentiment, horror, or adventure, all of which relocated response in the individual, reading self. To summarize Bakhtin's complex argument, the novel was feared precisely because it seemed a literary form that, on every level, could not be readily controlled.

While the novel was widely censured in Europe, the criticism was more pervasive and prominent in America. It was most vehement in the years after the Revolution, when, coincidentally, Americans began writing novels of their own and when the circulating libraries increasingly made both imported and indigenous novels available to a wider spectrum of readers than ever before. Here the critique of fiction must be seen within a larger social context. It was a time when significant questions on the limits of liberty and the role of authority were very much at issue in the republic, as especially evidenced in the often acrimonious constitutional debates. It was also a time when polarized party politics fostered bitterness and rivalries, and when political radicalism still residual from the recent revolutionary war seemed, to many of those in authority in post-revolutionary America, to threaten the very foundation of the newly laid republic. "We are fast verging to anarchy and confusion!" the father of the nation, George Washington, worried in the late 1780's after Shays's Rebellion.[37] "This is an age of Folly, Vice, Frenzy, Brutality, Daemons, Buonaparte, Tom Paine, or the Age of the Burning Brand from the Bottomless Pit: or *anything* but the Age of Reason," John Adams fulminated after his presidential defeat.[38] Somewhat more succinctly, Alexander Hamilton spoke for many of the nation's Founding Fathers when he observed, sadly, after the defeat of the Federalists, "this American world was not made for me."[39]

In such a place, at such a historical moment, the novel became, in effect, a cultural scapegoat that many elite Americans could blame for precisely those tendencies they most deplored in the new Republic. Might not the American novel, by addressing an audience hitherto largely excluded from the political process (and especially women), persuade them that they should have a voice in that society? The novel itself thus became the literary equivalent of a Daniel Shays or a Thomas Paine leading its followers to riot and ruin. Many of America's best-educated and most illustrious citizens thought so, and the genre provided a locus for their apprehensions about mobocracy on both the cultural and political level. Timothy Dwight took time out from presiding over Yale, Dr. Benjamin Rush from attending to his medical and philosophical investigations, Noah Webster from writing dictionaries, and Thomas Jefferson and John Adams from presiding over a nation—all to condemn the novel.[40] But even that formulation devalues the seriousness of such attacks by differentiating the censure of fiction from the official duties of these Founding Fathers. Denouncing the novel, they would have insisted, was integral to their civic, religious, or educational mission. "Culture," as Raymond Williams has persuasively argued, was not defined as separate from the larger fabric of Anglo-American society until the middle of the nineteenth century. For the social spokespersons of the new Republic, an aberrant form of literary culture equaled an aberration in the very design of America.[41]

The passage from *The Algerine Captive* quoted earlier sets forth a kind of Gresham's law of texts or reading. Bad new works would supposedly drive out good old ones, so that a print world dominated by the Bible, the *Day of Doom,* sermons, tracts, and sundry other religious works well might be superseded by a new world of predominantly secular reading, of texts designed merely to amuse, not to instruct.[42] Moreover, as the critics of the novel understood, changes in the primary reading of an increasingly greater number of people presaged far more than a faddish new use of leisure time.

The crucial matter was not so much a question of how common citizens invested that time allowed for reading but the question of where the society vested the voice of authority. The censure of fiction represented, then, a retrograde attempt by a still elite minority to retain a self-proclaimed role as the primary shapers and interpreters of American culture. The critics of fiction again and again invoked an earlier idyllic time, when the minister, not the novelist, commanded the public's attention; when the Bible, not *Charlotte Temple,* lay on every bed table. The novel, to many, seemed the unfortunate reverse of that earlier model of patriarchal discourse. Sage oratory, they would have it, should be dispensed from the pulpit to constrain the audience's unruly passions, instead of falsehoods (fictions) being served up by a book to inflame them.[43]

The sermon model of discourse emblemized a hierarchical society in which the minister served as the officially authorized translator of texts, who thereby mediated between the finally unfathomable authority of God and the all-too-human limitations of his audience. As expert witness to the world and the Word, the minister interpreted science, philosophy, and other forms of learning as well as theology for his congregation. Wills and estate inventories show that at least

until late in the eighteenth century, the local minister often possessed the largest (and sometimes the only) personal library in his
community. He typically was the only citizen in a small town or village who had received a classical education at one of the prestige
colleges.[44] As novels became increasingly available to the public
(both because of the form's linguistic simplicity and the new readers'
improved literacy), they were increasingly perceived to be in direct
competition with the local minister for authority within the community, and thus were accused of eroding the pulpit model of erudition
and authority. Moreover, the novel by definition undermines an oli-
garchical and patriarchal model of authority—ministerial or, by extension, political—precisely because it rules out the intermediation
that the preacher was professionally prepared to provide. While
other forms of literature can be paraphrased, novels must be *experienced:* the content or meaning is never the sum total of a novel. On
the contrary, the full impact of novels derives from the private, emotional experience of decoding the plot, and thus cannot be separated
from the act of reading itself. Sitting in a church pew, listening to the
local minister expound certain religious and social truths is ultimately a communal event which supports the values of the community of listeners within the church. In contrast, and in a very real
sense, a novel is no more nor less than the sensations aroused by its
reading, and that reading must finally be private and personal.

The power of fiction to absorb fully the reader's attention and
imagination seemed to many commentators a kind of seduction or
even a satanic possession. The critics of the novel—ministers, edu-
cators, political leaders—strove to dispossess readers of the novel in
order to repossess themselves in their "elect" status and role. The
critic's attempt in striving to perpetuate a posited and essentially
nostalgic myth of a stable social order reinforced the position from
which they believed they spoke, the stance of a superior dismayed by
another's reading habits—but still willing to warn that other of the
grave consequences of his or her unfortunate literary tastes—novel
reading today, licentious riot and senseless revolution tomorrow. Un-
wary readers still might be saved from that unfortunate end through
the generous intermediation of the critic. The critique of fiction thus
emphasized the need for the critic, the need for the very social authority that the novels themselves presumed to question.

Many of the same critics who most denounced fiction as a genre
also read it. Nor would they have seen their actions as hypocritical.
As Gordon S. Wood has shown, most of the Founding Fathers believed discourse worked "situationally." According to the classical
rhetorical models and exercises practiced at the nation's colleges,

one tailored one's style and even content to the understanding (or "susceptibility," to use an eighteenth-century word) of the auditor.[45] For example, Thomas Jefferson was an avid collector and reader of novels. When a young gentleman, Robert Skipwith, wrote to Jefferson for advice on what to purchase for his private library, Jefferson included several novels among the essential titles that should constitute a proper gentleman's library. Yet Jefferson could also vehemently castigate the novel for its effects on women and the poor.[46] In short, he understood that no literary form can be evaluated apart from the reader to whom it is addressed—that the same novel can support or subvert the status quo, depending upon the class or gender expectations of its readers.

Jefferson was most concerned about the potentially deleterious effects of fiction on the female reader. In this respect Jefferson was very much a man of his time. Women were the chief targets in the censure of fiction, just as women were not coincidentally the implied readers of most of the early novels. Ministers and politicians pleaded almost hysterically with women to abandon their fatal attraction to this new genre. The novel, women were told over and over again, could only lead them to ruin, and once they had strayed from virtue's path, the whole Republic would surely fall, too.

The critical preoccupation with the female novel reader must be understood within the much larger political and ideological situation of women in the aftermath of the revolutionary war.[47] Briefly, women had taken an active role in keeping the domestic economy alive during the revolutionary war. Many women, forced in the direst circumstances to maintain a farm or a family business, realized both that they were fully capable of being independent and that the laws of the time made any independence extremely difficult. In most states women could not legally inherit property or businesses. Their names frequently carried no legal weight on documents. Unmarried women were, for all intents and purposes, the property of their fathers and wives of their husbands.[48]

The war pointed up the liabilities—political as well as economic—of coverture. Yet as numerous historians have also shown, in the aftermath of the war, while politicians hammered out both state and national constitutions that would define a new citizenry, the inequitable status of women under British common law was translated virtually intact into an American legal and political system in which women remained, for the most part, invisible. American jurist St. George Tucker pointed out in 1803 that women were, de facto and de jure, victims of "taxation without representation; for they pay taxes without having the liberty of voting for representatives." Although the Revolution freed America from an oppressive colonial status, it had not freed American women from their subservient status. As Tucker summed it up: "I fear that there is little reason for a compliment to our laws for their respect and favour to the female sex."[49]

Even in education, where perhaps the most improvement could be seen, the gains for women were not unequivocal. As Mary Beth Norton has shown, after the Revolution "public education at the elementary level was opened to female as well as male children, and private academies founded in the 1780s and 1790s greatly expanded the curriculum previously offered to girls."[50] Yet, as Norton also indicates, the academies were for the most part restricted to affluent girls and often were less institutions of higher learning than elite "finishing" schools, offering subjects such as embroidery, dancing, drawing, oratory, and other genteel arts. In rural areas and among the poor women's education continued to be rudimentary in the postrevolutionary era, and not surprisingly women's literacy levels (especially advanced reading and writing skills) continued to lag behind those of men.[51]

Educated or uneducated, married or single, women had virtually no rights within society and no place within the political operations of government except as the symbols of that government—Columbia or Minerva or Liberty. In contrast to the "fallen women" of so many early novels (women whose fall reflects their already low status in society), the official female symbols were exalted paragons of virtue, proffered almost as the consolation prize for women's actual invisibility within American legal and political structures. An ideology of republican motherhood and virtue even posited that women need not clamor for legal or political rights, since they were "actually" far more powerful than men.[52] Writing in 1808, the Reverend Samuel Miller could heave a sigh of relief that "Wollstonecraftism" (a common term for the feminist activism of the great British philosopher Mary Wollstonecraft and her American followers) had happily passed away. Women had realized that they were not suited to "the Academic Chair . . . the Senate . . . the Bench of Justice [or] the train of War" but had finally realized that, as virtuous mothers, they were actually the most powerful citizens of the nation (even if the nation did not politically recognize them as citizens).[53]

If numerous social authorities insisted that female virtue was its own reward, and thus was more "powerful" significant than either legal or political reform, what did it mean when myriad novel readers wept over the cruel fate meted out to women who were, according to the usual definition, not virtuous? Clearly the early American novel confused the republican equation. Many authorities argued that the novel subverted female virtue (and the sexual double standard) even more insidiously than did the "new philosophy" (especially as propounded by Wollstonecraft or Paine or William Godwin). One commentator noted, "novels . . . are the most powerful engines with which the seducer attacks the female heart, and if we judge from every day experience, his plots are seldom laid in vain."[54] Still more explicit in its charges and histrionic in its tone is an 1802 jeremiad portentously titled "Novel Reading, a Cause of Female Depravity," in which novels are accused of instilling "poison . . . into the blood" of females and making them "slaves of vice."[55]

In the various critiques of the novel female sexuality was defined in the strictest of terms, and possible offenses against female virtue became public, not private, lapses (crimes, in effect, against the whole nation). A Yale graduate and a Federalist, the Reverend Enos Hitchcock, for example, included within his didactic novel *Memoirs of the Bloomsgrove Family* (1790) a sustained critique of the novel as a genre, and noted that women's education and women's reading had to be carefully monitored lest women take into marriage expectations that are "above the drudgery of learning the necessary parts of domestic duties."[56]

To summarize, the condemnation of fiction scarcely concealed a condemnation of any woman who did not fill her expected domestic role. Woman's aspirations (what she read and what she thought of what she read) had to be controlled so that her sexuality could be curbed—all for the good of the nation. Her reading had to be monitored so that her efficiency as a domestic laborer would not be curtailed; woman's productivity (in the Reverend Timothy Dwight's phrase, her "useful life" as childbearer and household worker) was a national resource, not a matter of individual choice.[57] In the two scenarios most common in the critiques of fiction—engaging in sex or engaging in reading—what might be regarded as an ultimately private, personal experience is publicized and politicized, and is therefore (the main point) subject to social restriction, censorship, and control. To control female minds and feminine sexuality, the novel (its critics unanimously agreed) had to be kept out of women's hands.

What, the contemporary reader well might ask, could possibly be so threatening in novels? How could anyone think a mere work of fiction could in any way destabilize the status quo? To begin to answer those questions let us imagine a hypothetical young woman living in, say, Leicester, Massachusetts, in 1820. She enters a local circulating library, where she has access to the one hundred novels written in her native land. (No library could boast such a collection, it must be emphasized; this example is purely hypothetical.) Our reader has the liberty to browse at will through the volumes on the shelves in order to choose a book or two that might interest her. What might she find?

There are surprising fictive possibilities for her to select from this imaginary library shelf—far more possibilities, it must be noted, than she would be allowed within American society. Our young reader could peruse Herman Mann's *The Female Review; or, Memoirs of an American Young Lady* (1797) or the anonymous *The History of Constantius and Pulchera; or Constancy Rewarded* (1794), each in part the story of a brave woman who dressed like a man to fight in the revolutionary war—a fictively liberating fantasy for a young woman who, under the normal course of events, would move quietly (and always in proper feminine attire) from her father's house to her husband's house, from the role of subservient daughter to the role of feme covert. *The Female Review* would be a particularly inspiring novel for our reader since she would have known the popular story of the real Deborah Sampson who had—like her highly romanticized alter ego—dressed and fought like a man.

The same reader might never in the course of an entire lifetime leave the small village in which she was born. But through picaresque adventure tales such as James Butler's *Fortune's Foot-ball; or, The Adventures of Mercutio* (1797–98), Susanna Haswell Rowson's *Trials of the Human Heart* (1795), or S. S. B. K. Wood's *Ferdinand and Elmira: A Russian Story* (1804), she could travel to exotic places around the globe. Or she might ride along with Captain Farrago in Hugh Henry Brackenridge's *Modern Chivalry* (1792–1815) and thus experience life on the various highways and byways of America. In a somewhat different vein and in Gothic novels such as Charles Brockden Brown's *Wieland* (1798) or Isaac Mitchell's *The Asylum; or, Alonzo and Melissa* (1811), she could imagine herself brave enough to fend off even the most evil (and well-armed) of villains—while yet remaining alluring enough (as in contemporary Gothic romances) to procure for herself a happy marriage at the end of her exotic trials.

More is provided in these novels than mere escape and entertainment. Royall Tyler's *The Algerian Captive*, for example, or the anonymous *Humanity of Algiers; or, The Story of Azem* (1801) would allow her to travel, imaginatively, to North Africa; to experience, vicariously, captivity in another culture; and to understand, in a specific and immediate way, the horrors of slavery—whether practiced by Barbary pirates of North Africa upon captive Americans or by Americans upon captive Africans. Or William Williams's *Mr. Penrose: The Journal of Penrose, Seaman* (published in 1815) would take the reader to Nicaragua, where she would live among the Native Peoples and meet Quammino, a brutalized slave escaped to the Moskito Coast. When Penrose asks Quammino why he has never become a Christian, the slave pointedly replies that those "who say they are Christians are worse than we who know not the books of God as they do." Mr. Penrose sits "silently puffing" after Quammino's speech then quietly responds that he "had Little to answer in behalf of my own colour, but told him that I believed him a much better man than many Thousands who call'd themselves Christians."[58] This implicit and explicit criticism of both Christianity and the American institution of slavery would be heady fare for any young lady of the time, and small wonder many wanted to keep her (protect her?) from such books.

But what might be deemed most subversive in these novels was also what might be, for this hypothetical reader, most mundane and most appealing—the fictional rendering of one crucial aspect of her own life. The implied reader of most American novels is young, unmarried, white, and of New England stock, as is the typical protagonist of an early American novel. Socially, those protagonists range from Martha Meredith Read's beggar girl in *Monima; or, The Beggar Girl* (1802) to the well-educated "coquette" in Hannah Foster's novel, a character modeled after the poet Elizabeth Whitman, a descendant of Connecticut's prominent Stanley family and one of the most learned and respected women of her day. But rich or poor, character and reader still faced the same dilemma. Given woman's lack of social or legal power in early America, her choice of a husband could, quite literally, be a life-or-death decision.

Dozens of early American novels would allow this reader the opportunity to work out, in the safe context of her imagination, just what she wanted from men and from marriage. These fictions dramatize how a woman can protect herself from the deceptions of male suitors, and why she should make sexual and marital decisions based on a rational weighing of all alternatives, rather than based on the passions of the moment or the persuasions of a silver-tongued seducer. Again and again, the novels implicitly or explicitly emphasize woman's powerlessness in America, especially the married woman's status as a feme covert, and the absolute necessity for a woman to take the question of matrimony with extreme seriousness. Lacking political or legal power, the married woman has only her wits to protect her from the various evils men are capable of inflicting in these early novels. To cite one notable example, the plot of Sukey Vickery's

Emily Hamilton, a Novel (1803) is almost exclusively about how a group of young women separately make their marital choices. Women who choose wisely are briefly described and ranged against a contrasting catalogue of women who do not. The most pathetic of the latter, a Mrs. Henderson, is brought to the verge of death by a violent, alcoholic, profligate, and emotionally abusive husband.[59] The early American reader could sympathize with a married woman who, through no fault of her own, endures a life of relentless misery.

In even the first American novel, as we have seen, our hypothetical reader would find lectures on the importance of a sound education and self-esteem, especially for women of the underclasses, who seem constantly at the mercy of men both mercenary and lascivious. This theme reaches something of an apotheosis in Rebecca Rush's powerful novel *Kelroy, a Novel* (1812), in which Mrs. Hammond, widowed with little income and no financial resources except the marital prospects of her two beautiful daughters, deceives the young men of Philadelphia into believing her daughters have excellent financial prospects. Mrs. Hammond even feigns inconsolable grief at her husband's death in order to justify taking herself and her daughters into hiding for several years, where they can all live frugally until the eldest daughter reaches marriageable age. Mrs. Hammond then puts on an elaborate coming-out party for her daughters, at which no expense is spared. Rush's novel is a devastatingly cynical portrait of American manners and mores in early nineteenth-century Philadelphia, a portrait which totally reverses the image of the virtuous "Republican Mother."

Not all of the fiction of the time was so obviously critical of women's second-class status. Our hypothetical female reader, making her way through the circulating library, well might come across novels by two of America's most socially conservative women writers, Helena Wells and S. S. B. K. Wood. Here she would find diatribes against Mary Wollstonecraft's feminist principles, including Wood's assurance, in *Amelia; or, The Influence of Virtue* (1802), that Amelia "was not a disciple or pupil of Mary Woolstonecraft [sic]. . . . She was an old fashioned wife and she meant to obey her husband: she meant to do her duty in the strictest sense of the word. To perform it cheerfully would perhaps be painful, but . . . it would most assuredly be best."[60]

No doubt, the humor in that description of the "old fashioned wife" is unintentional. But, ironically, the socially conservative books present an even darker view of the Cult of Domesticity than overtly feminist novels such as Murray's *Story of Margaretta* which, as suggested earlier, minimizes the hardships women face by showing how one intelligent, well-educated young woman manages to triumph against all odds. Margaretta's reward is an affectionate marriage based on egalitarian principles. In graphic contrast, Mrs. Hayman in Helena Wells's *Constantia Neville; or, The West Indian* (1800), possesses little education, a low self-esteem, and a philosophy of wifely submission. For much of the book the reader must witness the consequences of Mrs. Hayman's commitment to feminine servitude. Her husband is physically and emotionally abusive. She is forced ignominiously to raise his illegitimate offspring (there are apparently several). She lectures the reader on the necessity of being a dutiful wife, but enjoys none of the rewards that are supposed to follow from such virtuous living. Amelia, too, in Mrs. Wood's novel, is virtuous, innocent, patient, perfect—and must stand silently by as her husband continues an extended affair with the woman he loves but could not (for economic and parental reasons) marry. It is hard to imagine that the young woman in the circulating library would ever choose to model her life on the sad circumstances of Amelia or Mrs. Hayman, especially when Murray's novel presents a far more satisfying portrait of a marriage both egalitarian and happy.

This is a crucial point. Given the legal and social restrictions on the life of our hypothetical woman reader, it was virtually impossible to write for her a novel that supported the status quo. Wells and Wood tried, but the very medium of the novel worked against the socially conservative message they wanted to convey. Whereas a tract might extol the virtues of submission in the face of all trials, a novel must create trials, to which the heroine virtuously submits. But those trials fully visualized give us not an inspiring icon of feminine virtue but a perturbing portrait of the republican mother and virtuous wife as perpetual victim. A tract can lecture in the abstract, but the conservative novel, portraying through concrete example, evokes (quite inappropriately for its explicit social purposes) the legal, social, and political status of the average female reader, and that reader is not apt to applaud the tortured image of her own condition. Fictions such as *Amelia* and *Constantia Neville* set forth the appalling truths of many women's lives in the late eighteenth century perhaps even more graphically than the overtly reformist novels, for the simple reason that they depict the essential powerlessness of women in the new republic, a powerlessness that seems even more appalling when glossed by the conventional rhetoric about the omnipotence of feminine virtue.

Clearly, novels were not simply expendable commodities, escapist fantasies that had no bearing on their readers' "real" lives. Given the restrictions on women's mobility and experiences in the early Republic, for many readers a novel could provide the adventure, opportunity, maybe even love that life lacked. Similarly, for many readers these novels provided a kind of education, and perhaps even an education better than the rudimentary one offered to girls in the early national period. More important, the novels in general assured their female readers that writing—and writing well—was a virtue; that an unblemished prose style was as proper to a would-be heroine as a spotless reputation or a winsome smile. In contrast to the numerous contemporaneous attacks against intellectual women and the widespread fear that education would "unsex" females, the novel championed the female intellect and in a very real sense provided, by its own example, a kind of education to its women readers.[61]

"Copy well!" English novelist Hannah More admonished her readers in 1799.[62] Or as Judith Sargent Murray put it, "I have thought that many a complete letter writer has been produced from the school of the novelist."[63] Precisely this kind of informal learning by imitation is what Margáret Smith advises for her younger sister, Susan, in a letter written on 6 June 1797. The older sister notes, "It is by constantly reading elegant writing" that one learns the "rules of grammar" and that "our ear becomes accustomed, to well constructed and well divided sentences. I always find I write much better immediately after reading works of an elegant and correct style."[64]

Sometimes we can even catch, within the covers of an early American novel, a reader working her or his way to improved literacy. To cite just one example, an anonymous reader who paid one dollar for the first edition of Hannah Webster Foster's best-selling novel, *The Coquette*, underlined difficult vocabulary words throughout the text and recorded, in a notably shaky hand, a number of these words on the blank pages at the end. This reader not only vicariously participated in Eliza's cruel betrayal and inevitable death, but also picked up the meaning of such words as "volubility," "satire," and "misanthrope" along the way. We see here, in short, a novel reader aspiring after improved literateness—inspired, perhaps, by Foster's insistence throughout the novel on the unparalleled importance of a sound and sensible education.[65]

Even such rudimentary scribblings should remind the sophisticated historian that these novels were written for the readers of the time and they played a vital (if unquantifiable) role in those readers' lives. These novels were cherished; they were shared among friends and relatives; contended over by brother and sister; or bequeathed across generations.

"To the Young Ladies of Columbia, This volume, intended to inspire the mind with fortitude under the most unparalleled Misfortunes; and to Represent the happy consequences of Virtue and Fidelity, is Inscribed, with Esteem and Sincerity, By their Friends and Humble Servants, The Publishers."[66] Most of America's first novelists wrote for young ladies, and America's young ladies repaid that authorial attention. Miss Susan Heath of Boston, for example, in 1812 repeatedly escaped from the dull round of visitors and suitors brought before her by retreating into the more interesting world of fiction. Feigning fatigue, the affluent young woman "stole upstairs under the pretense of going to bed—when I sat down and read an hour in Temper—at last I heard Mama coming and jumped under the coverlid with my clothes on and she thinking I was asleep took away my light." As Susan Heath continues, in words that could apply to thousands of readers of America's first fiction: "Being this day seventeen years old and feeling fully my own ignorance and the importance of time I am determined to avail myself of every opportunity of improving my mind and if possible not let a day pass without spending a few hours in reading and writing."[67] Ms. Heath's resolution was shared by many women in the first years of the Republic.

Reading these early novels in the latter part of the twentieth century, we can easily overlook the subversive role they played within their society. But one must also remember that the novel took the daring step of addressing women respectfully at a time when this was not the standard mode of discourse. The Constitution had not "remember[ed] the Ladies," as Abigail Adams had asked her husband. On the contrary, the society in general assumed an attitude similar to John's in his response to his wife's request: "Depend upon it, We know better than to repeal our masculine systems."[68]

In contrast to this private dismissal (and its public manifestation in the Constitution), the early American novel took women seriously. Of all the available literary forms, only the novel looked carefully and sympathetically at the issues, problems, and limitations placed upon women's lives in the new Republic. It honored women as decision-makers, warned against the powers of men, and admonished women to make rational life choices based on a clear view of the heinous implications of the "masculine systems" that John Adams so ardently championed. As such, the novel was a subtly subversive form that accorded women a dignity and, perhaps more important, a visibility that they did not possess in the official documents of a nation ostensibly founded on principles of freedom and equality.

NOTES

ACKNOWLEDGMENTS: The author would like to acknowledge the generous support of the American Council of Learned Societies and the

John Simon Guggenheim Memorial Foundation, as well as the excellent editorial suggestions made by Alfred F. Young.

PUBLISHING NOTE: This essay is partly drawn from *Revolution and the Word: The Rise of the Novel in America* (New York, 1986). Used with permission from Oxford University Press.

1. William Hill Brown, *The Power of Sympathy,* ed. William S. Kable (Columbus, Ohio, 1969), 95.
2. Kable discusses his designation in his "Editor's Introduction," ibid., xi–xxxii.
3. Brown, ibid., 5.
4. The exact number of early American novels is difficult to specify for several reasons. First, some authors and printers avoided using the term "novel" before 1800 because the form was not considered respectable; however, since the form was increasingly popular, other publishers and library proprietors applied the same term indiscriminately to virtually any lengthy prose work. Second, the very nature of the genre makes it difficult (and perhaps foolish) to try to demarcate an exact boundary between early novels and, for example, fanciful novelistic "travel books," such as Elkanah Watson's *A Tour of Holland* (1790). I prefer a loose, rather than a strict, definition of the form. Finally, the whole question of national origins (what is American?) is as much ideological as actual. For excellent discussions of this issue see William C. Spengemann, "The Earliest American Novel: Aphra Behn's *Oroonoko,*" *Nineteenth-Century Fiction* 38 (1984): 384–414; and Spengemann, "What Is American Literature?" *Centennial Review* 22 (Spring 1978): 119–38. Although several new titles have come to light since it was compiled, the best bibliography of early American fiction remains Lyle H. Wright, *American Fiction, 1774–1850,* rev. ed. (San Marino, Calif., 1948). See also Henri Petter, *The Early American Novel* (Columbus, Ohio, 1971).
5. Most of the novelists about whom anything is known (over two-thirds of the novels were originally published anonymously and approximately one-third remain anonymous today) also published separately essays, poems, or books on education: Jeremy Belknap, Hugh Henry Brackenridge, Charles Brockden Brown, William Hill Brown, Hannah Webster Foster, Charles Ingersoll, Herman Mann, Isaac Mitchell, Judith Sargent Murray, Susanna Haswell Rowson, Rebecca Rush, Sarah Savage, Benjamin Silliman, Tabitha Tenney, Royall Tyler, Sukey Vickery, and Helena Wells.
6. The first novel written on the North American continent was Frances Brooke's *The History of Emily Montague* (1769), partly set in

Quebec. Other early contenders for the honor of being the "first American novel" are Charlotte Ramsay Lennox's *The Life of Harriot Stuart* (1751), Hugh Henry Brackenridge and Philip Freneau's *Father Bombo's Pilgrimage to Mecca* (1770; first published, 1975), Francis Hopkinson's *A Pretty Story: Written in the Year of Our Lord 1774* (1774), Thomas Atwood Digges's *The Adventures of Alonso* (1775), the anonymous *The Golden Age* (1785), and Peter Markoe's *The Algerine Spy in Pennsylvania* (1787). *The Power of Sympathy* (1789) is the first novel written by a native-born American, set in America, and advertised as the first American novel.

7. For excellent discussions of how novels were imported (and often reprinted in separate editions for readers with different literacy levels), see Jay Fliegelman, *Prodigals and Pilgrims: The American Revolution Against Patriarchal Authority, 1750–1800* (Cambridge, Eng., 1982). See also Robert B. Winans, "Bibliography and the Cultural Historian: Notes on the Eighteenth-Century Novel," in *Printing and Society in Early America,* ed. William L. Joyce et al. (Worcester, Mass., 1983), 174–85.

8. The first advertisement for *The Power of Sympathy* appeared in the *Herald of Freedom* on 16 January 1789, the second on 23 January 1789. The "First American Novel" ads ran in the *Massachusetts Spy, or Worcester Gazette* on 29 January, 5 February, and 12 February 1789; and in the *Massachusetts Centinel* on 28 January 1789.

9. *New York Magazine,* new series 2 (1797): 398.

10. See David Lundberg and Henry F. May, "The Enlightened Reader in America," *American Quarterly* 28 (Summer 1976): 262–71, and appendix; and Robert B. Winans, "The Growth of a Novel-Reading Public in Late-Eighteenth-Century America," *Early American Literature* 9 (Winter 1975): 267–75. For excellent work on reading among working class and poor readers in colonial and Revolutionary America, see Elizabeth Carroll Reilly, in "The Wages of Piety: The Boston Book Trade of Jeremy Condy," in *Printing and Society in Early America,* 83–131; and Reilly's unpublished paper, "Cheap and Popular Books in Mid-Eighteenth-Century New England," which she was kind enough to make available to me. See also Victor E. Neuburg, *Chapbooks: A Bibliography of References to English and American Chapbooks of the Eighteenth and Nineteenth Centuries* (London, 1964); and David Paul Nord, "A Republican Literature: Magazine Reading and Readers in Late-Eighteenth-Century New York," *American Quarterly,* 40, 1 (April 1988).

11. For overviews of the American book industry, see Milton Hamilton, *The Country Printer* (New York, 1936); Hellmut Lehmann-Haupt et al., *The Book in America,* 2d ed. (New York, 1951); Douglas

C. McMurtrie, *The Book: The Story of Printing and Bookmaking* (New York, 1937); Charles Madison, *Book Publishing in America* (New York, 1969); Rollo G. Silver, *The American Printer, 1787–1825* (Charlottesville, Va., 1967); John Tebbel, *A History of Book Publishing in the United States,* 4 vols. (New York, 1972); and Mary Ann Yodelis, "Who Paid the Piper? Publishing Economics in Boston, 1763–1775," *Journalism Monographs* 38 (1975): 1–49. For a comparative analysis of the relationship between book costs and readership, see Richard D. Altick, *The English Common Reader: A Social History of the Mass Reading Public, 1800–1900* (Chicago, 1957); Rolf Engelsing, *Der Burger als Leser: Lesergeschichte in Deutschland, 1500–1800* (Stuttgart, 1974); and Albert Ward, *Book Production, Fiction, and the German Reading Public, 1740–1800* (Oxford, 1974).

12. See Carroll D. Wright, *History of Wages and Prices in Massachusetts: 1752–1883* (Boston, 1885), 63–65; and U.S. Department of Labor, *History of Wages in the United States from Colonial Times to 1928* (Washington, D.C., 1929), 53, 57, 133–34, 137.

13. Diaries of Ethan Allen Greenwood, log at the end of the diary for 30 December 1805 to 9 February 1806, Manuscript Department, American Antiquarian Society (hereafter cited as AAS).

14. Diary of Elizabeth Bancroft, Manuscript Department, AAS.

15. L. H. Wright, *Wages and Prices,* 63–65. For a discussion of the class affiliation of theatergoers, see Kenneth Silverman, *A Cultural History of the American Revolution* (New York, 1976), especially 545–54. It should also be noted that the same novel could be produced for different classes of readers. For example, the anonymous *The History of Constantius and Pulchera* sold for as much as $1.00 when bound in calfskin on relatively good paper and, in a crude edition, for as little as a quarter.

16. See Winans, "Novel-Reading Public"; and Jesse H. Shera, *Foundations of the Public Library* (Chicago, 1949).

17. George Raddin, *An Early New York Library of Fiction, with a Checklist of the Fiction of H. Caritat's Circulating Library, No. 1, City Hotel, Broadway, New York, 1804* (New York, 1940), 14–16.

18. A bookplate listing the bylaws of the Philadelphia Circulating Library is affixed within the covers of the AAS copy of Charles Brockden Brown's *Edgar Huntly* (Philadelphia, 1799). An advertisement in the *Massachusetts Mercury,* 18 April 1797, includes the terms for the Pelham Library. A card advertising the Mechanics Library of New Haven is in the Trade Card Collection (call no. 1975–209), Colonial Williamsburg Research Library. (Special thanks to Alfred Young for supplying me with this reference.) See also, *Records of the Union Harwinton Library,* ed. Terry Belanger (New York,

1977); and for a fascinating description of the first social library in Belpre, Ohio (a town settled in 1788; its library founded in 1796), see William H. Venable, *Beginnings of Literary Culture in the Ohio Valley* (New York, 1891), 135.

19. Winans, "Bibliography," 176.

20. Sarah Savage also wrote *Advice to a Young Woman at Service: In a Letter from a Friend* (New York, 1823), 1–4, in which she recommended that the young woman "reserve one hour a day for reading and writing" and suggested that from the one dollar she earned each week, she would be able to save enough to purchase one book a year and, in time, "get a pretty collection."

21. Raddin, *Early Library*, 24–25.

22. W. H. Brown, *Power of Sympathy*, 3.

23. Susanna Haswell Rowson, *Charlotte Temple*, ed. Cathy N. Davidson (New York, 1986), 5. This edition is based on the first American edition published by Mathew Carey in 1794. Samuel Relf, *Infidelity; or, The Victims of Sentiment* (Philadelphia, 1797).

24. See Lundberg and May, "Enlightened Reader," 262–71, and appendix.

25. Diary of Patty Rogers, 10, 11 January 1785. Manuscript Department, AAS.

26. Charles H. Bell, *History of [the Town of] Exeter, New Hampshire* (1888; Bowie, Md., 1979), 382–84.

27. The only other study I know to make use of the impressionistic evidence of readers in extant copies of old books is Clifton Johnson's delightful *Old-Time Schools and School Books* (1904; New York, 1925), 155–66. Others, however, have recently turned their attention to readers. For example, in the spring of 1984 Roger Stoddard of Houghton Library, Harvard University, mounted an exhibition "Marks in Books." At Michigan State University Jannette Fiore and Anne Tracey have begun to record and identify readers who left inscriptions in the 2,000 volumes of the Pedagogy Collection in the Russel B. Nye Popular Culture Collection. And at AAS the North American Imprints Program (NAIP), a computerized updating of Charles Evans's *American Bibliography* (Chicago, 1903–34), includes citations of inscribers' names in AAS volumes. In his 1987 Wiggins Lecture, "Frenchness in the History of the Book: From the History of Printing to the History of Reading," published in the *Proceedings of the American Antiquarian Society* 97 (October 1987): 299–329, Roger Chartier describes how the field of *l'histoire du livre* is currently preoccupied with the history of reading.

28. Pierre Bourdieu, *Distinction: A Social Critique of the Judgment of Taste*, trans. Richard Nice (Cambridge, Mass., 1984).

29. One indication of how little women exercised discretionary control over family income can be seen in account books such as those of Mathew Carey or Isaiah Thomas in the Manuscript Department, AAS. Carey, for example, recorded seven transactions with the irresponsible William Rowson, none with William's wife, Susanna Haswell Rowson, Carey's single best-selling author. Similarly, of the 1,445 names William J. Gilmore has found in the account books from the Upper Valley district of rural Vermont (recorded between 1755 and 1851), only 21 are female. See Gilmore, "Elementary Literacy on the Eve of the Industrial Revolution: Trends in Rural New England, 1760–1830," *Proceedings of the American Antiquarian Society* 92 (1982): 116. And Mary Silliman, in her diary, notes that her husband, a state's attorney, would not even discuss with her the mounting debts that directly affected her and their children. See Joy Day Buel and Richard Buel, Jr., *The Way of Duty: A Woman and Her Family in Revolutionary America* (New York, 1984), 198–200.

30. William T. Dunn's copy of *Charlotte Temple* (Boston, 1824) is a multiple monument to the social role played by books. It was given to me by another scholar who shares my fascination with America's first best-selling novel.

31. For a more detailed discussion of actual readers of *Charlotte Temple,* see my monograph, *Ideology and Genre: The Rise of the Novel in America* (Worcester, Mass., 1987).

32. The first four copies are at AAS. They were published, respectively, by Samuel A. Burtus (New York, 1814); by Silas Andrus (Hartford, Conn., 1832); by Mathew Carey (Philadelphia, 1812); and by Benjamin Warner (Philadelphia, 1818). The Mathew Carey copy of *Charlotte Temple* (Philadelphia, 1809) was found in a bookstore in New York in 1979.

33. For a full discussion, see Davidson, *Ideology and Genre.*

34. Samuel Miller, *A Brief Retrospect of the Eighteenth Century,* 2 vols. (New York, 1803) 2:179.

35. Novels which feature the underclasses even in their titles include: [Adam Douglass?], *The Irish Emigrant* (1817); [John Finch?], *The Soldier's Orphan* (1812); the anonymous *The Hapless Orphan; or, Innocent Victim of Revenge* (1793); Enos Hitchcock, *The Farmer's Friend, or, The History of Mr. Charles Worthy* (1793); Gilbert Imlay, *The Emigrants, & c.; or, The History of an Expatriated Family* (1793); Martha Meredith Read, *Monima; or, The Beggar Girl* (1802); Susanna Haswell Rowson, *The Fille de Chambre* (1794); and Sarah Savage, *The Factory Girl* (1814).

36. Mikhail M. Bakhtin, "Epic and Novel," in *The Dialogic Imagination: Four Essays,* ed. Michael Holquist and ed. and trans. Caryl

Emerson and Michael Holquist (Austin, Tex., 1981), especially 3–40.

37. George Washington to James Madison, 5 November 1786, in *The Writings of George Washington from the Original Manuscript Sources,* ed. John C. Fitzpatrick, 39 vols. (Washington, D.C., 1931–44) 39:51–52.

38. John Adams to Benjamin Waterhouse, *Selected Writings of John and John Quincy Adams,* ed. Adrienne Koch and William Peden (New York, 1946), 148.

39. Alexander Hamilton, quoted in Bernard Bailyn et al., *The Great Republic* (Boston, 1977), 322, 342.

40. See especially Timothy Dwight, *Travels in New England and New York,* 4 vols. (New Haven, 1821) 1:518; Benjamin Rush, "Plan on the Establishment of the Public Schools" (1786), in Frederick Rudolph, ed., *Essays on Education in the Early Republic* (Cambridge, Mass., 1965); and Noah Webster, "On the Education of Youth in America (1787–88)," in ibid.

41. Raymond Williams, *The Long Revolution* (New York, 1961), especially 41–43.

42. The censure of fiction in America has received extensive attention. See Jean-Marie Bonnet, *La Critique Litteraire aux États-Unis, 1783–1837* (Lyon, 1982), 97–156; William Charvat, *The Origins of American Critical Thought, 1819–1835* (Philadelphia, 1936), especially chaps. 2, 7; Harrison Orians, "Censure of Fiction in American Romances and Magazines, 1789–1810," *PMLA* 52 (1937): 195–214; Ormond E. Palmer, "Some Attitudes Toward Fiction in America to 1870, and a Bit Beyond" (Ph.D. diss., University of Chicago, 1952); and Sergio Perosa, *American Theories of the Novel: 1793–1903* (New York, 1983), 4.

43. See Emory Elliott, *Revolutionary Writers: Literature and Authority in the New Republic, 1725–1810* (New York, 1982), 30–35; Terence Martin, *The Instructed Vision: Scottish Common Sense Philosophy and the Origins of American Fiction* (Bloomington, Ind., 1961).

44. The cultural and social role played by the local minister has been discussed by Christopher M. Jedrey, *The World of John Cleaveland: Family and Community in Eighteenth-Century New England* (New York, 1979); and recently by Harry S. Stout, *New England Soul: Preaching and Religious Culture in Colonial New England* (New York, 1986).

45. Gordon S. Wood, "The Democratization of Mind in the American Revolution," in *The Moral Foundations of the American Republic,* 2d ed., Robert H. Horwitz, ed. (Charlottesville, Va., 1979), 102–28. See also Wilbur Samuel Howell, *Eighteenth-Century British Logic and Rhetoric* (Princeton, 1971); and Warren Guthrie, "The Develop-

ment of Rhetorical Theory in America, 1635–1850," *Speech Mono-graphs* 13 (1946): 14–22.

46. Thomas Jefferson to Robert Skipwith, 3 August 1771, repr. in Gordon S. Wood, *The Rising Glory of America, 1760–1820* (New York, 1971), 170–74. Jefferson was also positive in his letter to novelist Charles Brockden Brown, quoted in David Lee Clark, *Charles Brockden Brown: Pioneer Voice of America* (Durham, N.C., 1952), 164. For a very different evaluation, however, see *The Works of Thomas Jefferson in Twelve Volumes*, ed. Paul Leicester Ford (New York, 1905) 12:91.

47. My discussion of women's status in the eighteenth century is especially indebted to Nancy F. Cott, *The Bonds of Womanhood: "Woman's Sphere" in New England, 1780–1835* (New Haven, 1977); Linda K. Kerber, *Women of the Republic: Intellect and Ideology in Revolutionary America* (Chapel Hill, N.C., 1980); Mary Beth Norton, *Liberty's Daughters: The Revolutionary Experience of American Women, 1750–1800* (Boston, 1980); and Joan Hoff Wilson, "The Illusion of Change: Women and the American Revolution," in *The American Revolution: Explorations in the History of American Radicalism*, ed. Alfred F. Young (DeKalb, Ill., 1976), 383–445.

48. Kerber, *Women of Republic*, 9.

49. St. George Tucker, ed., *Blackstone's Commentaries: With Notes of Reference, to the Constitution and Laws of the Federal Government of the United States; and of the Commonwealth of Virginia*, 5 vols. (Philadelphia, 1803) 2:445.

50. Norton, *Liberty's Daughters*, 256. For different treatments of education in early America, see Samuel Bowles and Herbert Gintis, *Schooling in Capitalist America* (New York, 1976); Michael B. Katz, *Class, Bureaucracy, and Schools: The Illusion of Educational Change in America*, 2d ed. (New York, 1975); Carl F. Kaestle and Maris A. Vinovskis, *Education and Social Change in Nineteenth-Century Massachusetts* (Cambridge, Eng., 1980); Kerber, *Women of Republic*, 189–231; Walter H. Small, "Girls in Colonial Schools," *Education* 22 (1902): 533; Thomas Woody, *A History of Women's Education in the United States*, 2 vols. (New York, 1929); and Michael Zuckerman, *Peaceable Kingdom: New England in the Eighteenth Century* (New York, 1970), especially 72–83. Working on the Salem School Committee in 1790, the Reverend William Bentley noted that "all the girls [are] unprovided for, as upon the Boston establishment." See *The Diary of William Bentley, D.D., Pastor of the East Church, Salem, Mass.*, 4 vols. (Salem, Mass., 1905–14) 1:188; also 2:96.

51. Although most historians agree that women's literacy was lower than men's in colonial America, and did not approach men's

levels until the second portion of the nineteenth century, there are widely different estimates of just how much a discrepancy there was between male and female literacy. See, for example, Linda Auwers, "The Social Meaning of Female Literacy: Windsor, Connecticut, 1660–1775," Newberry Papers in Family and Community History, 77-4A (Chicago, 1977); Ross W. Beales, Jr., "Studying Literacy at the Community Level: A Research Note," *Journal of Interdisciplinary History* 9 (1978): 93–102; Harvey Graff, *The Literacy Myth* (New York, 1979); and Kenneth A. Lockridge, *Literacy in Colonial New England* (New York, 1974), especially 38–42, 57–58. For overviews and interpretations of the various literacy studies, see Cathy N. Davidson, *Revolution and the Word: The Rise of the Novel in America* (New York, 1986), 56–70; David D. Hall, *On Native Ground: From the History of Printing to the History of Book* (Worcester, Mass., 1984); Carl F. Kaestle, "The History of Literacy and the History of Readers," *Review of Research in Education* 12 (1985); and E. Jennifer Monaghan, "Literacy Instruction and Gender in Colonial New England," *American Quarterly,* 40, 1 (April 1988).

52. Norton, *Liberty's Daughters,* 242–50; Kerber, *Women of Republic.*

53. Samuel Miller, "The Appropriate Duty and Ornament of the Female Sex," in *The Columbian Preacher; Or, A Collection of Original Sermons, from Preachers of Eminence in the United States. Embracing the Distinguishing Doctrines of Grace* (Catskill, N.Y., 1808), 253.

54. "An Essay on the Modern Novel," *Port Folio* 2 (10 April 1802): 107.

55. "Novel Reading, a Cause of Female Depravity," *New England Quarterly* 1 (1802): 172–74. A headnote accompanying the article indicates that it was originally published in the *Monthly Mirror* (England) in November 1797.

56. Enos Hitchcock, *Memoirs of the Bloomsgrove Family. In a Series of Letters to a Respectable Citizen of Philadelphia,* 2 vols. (Boston, 1790) 2:29.

57. Dwight, *Travels* 1:518; and Samuel Miller, *A Brief Retrospect of the Eighteenth Century,* 2 vols. (New York, 1803) 2:179.

58. Originally published posthumously and in bowdlerized form, *Mr. Penrose: The Journal of Penrose, Seaman* has been republished with an excellent introduction and notes by David Howard Dickason (Bloomington, Ind., 1969), 358–59.

59. The story of Mrs. Anderson is related in Sukey Vickery's letter of 19 July 1799 to Adeline Hartwell, Sukey Vickery Papers, Manuscript Collection, AAS. See also Cathy N. Davidson, "Female Authorship and Authority: The Case of Sukey Vickery," *Early Amer-*

ican Literature 21 (Spring 1986): 4–28.

60. S. S. B. K. Wood, *Amelia; or, The Influence of Virtue. An Old Man's Story* (Portsmouth, N.H.: William Treadwell, 1802), 103.

61. Norton, *Liberty's Daughters*, 257–94. Compare Cott, *Bonds of Womanhood*, 101–25; Kerber, *Women of Republic*, 185–231; and Wilson, "Illusion of Change," 410–14.

62. Hannah More, *Strictures on the Modern System of Female Education*, 2 vols. (1799; New York, 1813) 2:26.

63. Judith Sargent Murray, *The Gleaner: A Miscellaneous Production. In Three volumes. By Constantia* (Boston, 1798) 3:221.

64. Margaret Smith quoted in Shirley Brice Heath, "Toward an Ethnohistory of Writing in American Education," in *Writing: The Nature, Development, and Teaching of Written Communication*, ed. Marcia Farr Whiteman, 2 vols. (Hillsdale, N.J., 1981) 1:29.

65. AAS copy of Hannah Webster Foster's *The Coquette* (Boston, 1797).

66. AAS copy of *The History of Constantius and Pulchera* (Suffield, Conn., 1801).

67. Diary of Susan Heath, 11 September and 6 October 1812, Massachusetts Historical Society, Boston.

68. Abigail Adams to John Adams, 31 March 1776; and John Adams to Abigail Adams, 14 April 1776, repr. in Alice S. Rossi, ed., *The Feminist Papers: From Adams to de Beauvoir* (New York, 1973), 10–11.

Afterword

How Radical Was the American Revolution?

ALFRED F. YOUNG

CORNWALLIS *turned* NURSE, *and his* MISTRESS *a* SOLDIER.

A political adaption of the popular Anglo-American book of rhymes called *The World Turned Upside Down,* this appeared in an American almanac celebrating Washington's defeat of General Cornwallis in the final battle of the Revolution at Yorktown. The caption is "Cornwallis turned Nurse, and his Mistress a Soldier." The original rhymes, also a song, celebrated a wide range of imaginary reversals. From *The Columbian Almanac for 1782* (Philadelphia, 1782).

These essays, taken with a growing body of recent scholarship, contribute to an understanding of two major unresolved issues in the study of the radicalism of the revolutionary era: the sources of radicalism and the impact of radicalism on the results of the Revolution. I would like to explore both with a view, not to answering, but to establishing a framework within which to address the larger question, How radical was the American Revolution?

This recent scholarship suggests sharply variant alternatives to the long-standing trickle-down or spillover interpretations of radicalism, in which the movements for internal change are viewed as a by-product of the political revolution against Great Britain. In 1926, J. Franklin Jameson spoke of "the stream of revolution once started [which] could not be confined within thin narrow banks but [which] spread abroad upon the land." And in 1967 Bernard Bailyn saw in the Revolution "a movement of thought, rapid, irreversible and irresistible" which "swept past boundaries few had set out to cross, into regions few had wished to enter." In the "contagion of liberty" "a spark" jumped from Whig political ideology to ignite sentiment for antislavery, religious liberty, and the rejection of deference. All historians use metaphors and Jameson and Bailyn provided evocative physical analogies which, as they often do, allowed little room for human agency. If Jameson was vague in identifying the dynamic source of change, Bailyn, as David B. Davis has written, "tend[ed] to exaggerate the autonomous power of ideas" to effect change.[1] Who broke the banks of the river? Which people carried the sparks from one tree of liberty to another?

Recent scholarship suggests a number of propositions that might restore agency to this process and moves us toward a synthesis of the origins of radicalism without, however, suggesting a single paradigm:

First, there were deep roots of radicalism in ideas, values, traditions, and customs held by common people long before the Revolution.

Second, as groups played an active role in the Revolution and became aware of their own interests, they invoked their own traditions in addition to appropriating Whig rhetoric.

Third, experiences over an unusually long revolutionary era contributed to radical impulses, not only in the now well-known decade of resistance before 1775, but during the protracted war from 1775 to 1781 and even more from the mid-1780s on, especially through the 1790s, when the impulses of the French Revolution and the successful black revolution in St. Domingue rekindled American radicalisms.

Fourth, as antagonisms increased, many groups of common people acquired a heightened consciousness of themselves and their distinct interests which enabled them to become a presence in American life.

SOURCES OF RADICALISM
"That each of us may sit down under his own fig-tree and
enjoy the fruits of his own labour"

The first proposition, that there were deep roots of radicalism in
ideas, values, traditions, and customs held by common people which
they brought to the era of the Revolution, has been analyzed by historians within various frameworks: moral econony, *mentalité*, class
ideology, political culture, or "customs in common," in Edward
Thompson's apt phrase for the culture shared by English "plebeians"
in the eighteenth century.[2] Take, for example, the yeoman farmers
who loom large in many of the essays in this volume. A common assumption among early American farmers was that they were entitled to "the fruits of their labor," attained by the "sweat of their brow."
William Manning's aphorism, "labor is the soul [sole] parrant of all
property" was to them a given. Farmers who plowed a furrow, sowed
seeds, and reaped a harvest, or farm women who spun thread from
flax or wool, saw weavers turn it into cloth, which they then made
into clothing, did not need a political economist to instruct them in
the labor theory of value. This is what informed the long-standing
fear, among New England yeomen in particular, of being reduced to
"vassals" under "lordships," a fear that Richard Bushman has established was part of their "vernacular culture." This is what made yeoman farmers so quick to respond to any threat to the security of their
title to land, especially to taxes that threatened to reduce them to
the status of debtors, which could lead to the loss of their land. Political leaders like John and Samuel Adams were successful because
they were attuned to such fears. This was the social nexus of the
agrarian response to Whig political and constitutional rhetoric.[3]

Historians can now pull this red thread through the skein of collective agrarian responses from the late seventeenth century
through the prewar Regulator movements, the political conflicts of
the 1770s with England, and the Shaysism of the 1780s, to the agrarian rebellions and agrarian politics of the 1790s and early 1800s.
This was the radicalism of farmers who were property holders or
would-be property holders and believed they had a right to land,
tools, and other productive property. These were not necessarily
marginal farmers, although many were landowners with uncertain
title to their land, tenants with insecure leases, or backcountry
squatters. Nor did farmers have to be poverty-stricken to become
radical. As often as not, they were landholders with families who
worried about becoming impoverished—a fear of falling—or the sons
of landholders who feared they would be unable to acquire land and

duplicate the success of their fathers. Their goal was personal independence through secure landholding, a goal that merged with the political aspiration for national independence in some regions, making yeoman patriots, and which in other regions decidedly did not, leaving a large number of farmers Tory, neutral, or "disaffected" during the war.

Artisans were imbued with similar values. Also property holders or would-be-property holders, they were men (and sometimes women) who practiced a productive trade as masters ("a man on his own") or as journeymen, working for others who aspired to be masters. They were heirs to the ancient traditions of their trades as well as to a belief in property right tenets long articulated by their forebears among English artisans of the seventeenth and eighteenth centuries.[4] In Philadelphia in 1773 "a Mechanic," writing to his fellow mechanics, argued that the Tea Act was oppressive "whether we have property of our own or not." Here was the "breach" by which the British ministry would "enter the Bulwark of our sacred liberties." At stake was "whether our property, and the dear earned fruits of our own labor are at our own disposal."[5] Artisans believed that their skill was a form of property. "Labour at that time," argued a petition signed by 1,200 Connecticut mechanics in 1792, referring to the years before the Revolution, "was the principal property the citizen possessed."[6] Artisans in the port cities, even more than country folk, lived in fear of becoming dependent, of falling into the poorhouse or becoming recipients of poor relief. Journeymen worried that they might remain wage earners and not rise to the ranks of the independent. Apprentices who ran away had little confidence they could ever climb the ladder into this artisan world.[7]

What values might we expect to find among the free, propertyless wage earners at the bottom? Among merchant seamen, for instance—the largest single group of wage earners in early America? As Admiral Peter Warren testified in 1745 after they fiercely resisted impressment into His Majesty's navy, seamen "have the highest notion of the rights and liberties of Englishmen, and indeed are almost Levellers." Sailors prized their freedom. Jesse Lemisch has established that impressment was a leading cause of their participation in the mob actions of the era of resistance. Marcus Rediker, looking at sailors at sea, concluded that "seamen often brought to the ports a militant attitude towards arbitrary and excessive authority, and a willingness to empathize with the grievances of others, to cooperate for the sake of self defense, and to use direct action, violent if necessary, to accomplish collectively defined goals."[8]

Throughout the colonial era, those in servitude, whether African-

American slaves, immigrant indentured servants from Great Britain, or native-born apprentices, demonstrated what in 1721 the Reverend Cotton Mather of Boston called a "fondness for freedom."[9] Fifty years later a slave in the same city, the African-born Phillis Wheatley, wrote: "In every human Breast, God has implanted a Principle, which we call Love of Freedom. It is impatient of Oppression, and pants for Deliverance; and by the Leave of our modern Egyptians I will assert, that the same Principle lives in us."[10] Slaves, as Peter Wood baldly put it, did not need the example of the Sons of Liberty to inspire them to seek their own freedom.

Slaves of the last half of the eighteenth century warrant being identified as African American. African culture contributed to their consciousness. Most slaves were native-born children, grandchildren, or great-grandchildren of men and women who had been wrenched from Africa; a large number were recent forced migrants from Africa. Tens of thousands of slaves were imported in the decades before the war, and many more from 1783 to 1808. A host of scholars have rediscovered the retentions and survivals from African culture, ranging from marriage and burial customs to folk medicine to house styles and religious systems. Moreover, slaves formed families which served as a channel to pass on their identity to successive generations—the theme of Herbert Gutman's path-breaking research on the history of the black family. When they adopted Anglo-American religions, they blended evangelical Protestantism with African religious practices.[11]

What did slaves aspire to after emancipation? Their lives as workers were a constant reminder that their daily labor was being stolen from them, just as they or their ancestors had been stolen from Africa. The evidence of the revolutionary era, the time of the first emancipation, suggests that no less than white Anglo-American yeomen and artisans they sought the means to secure personal independence. Massachusetts slaves began a 1773 petition with the premise that "they have in common with other men, a natural right to be free, and without molestation, to enjoy such property, as they may accumulate by their industry," moved to a plea that "they may be liberated and made free-men," and ended with the request that they be granted "some part of the unimproved land, belong to this province, for a settlement, that each of us may there quietly sit down under his own-fig-tree, and enjoy the fruits of his own labour." Tens of thousands of slaves fled during the war; many were transported by the British to Nova Scotia in 1783, sought land there, and when they fared poorly made their way back to Africa to the British colony of Sierra Leone in quest of land. In the 1790s, when Robert Carter

began to free the five hundred slaves on his Virginia plantation by
individual acts of manumission, they sought from him land or the
means to pursue a trade they assumed was their right.[12]

  This set of beliefs among both free farmers and artisans and unfree slaves, as their language alone suggests, was often rooted in religion, especially in the evangelical dissenting faiths. Evangelical
religion surfaces in protest throughout these essays. Wood notes that
before the war there were a number of black preachers like Philip
John, who preached "that there should be no more white King's Governor or great men, but the Negroes should live happily and have
laws of their own." Taylor finds that, after the war, "in every agrarian
resistance or rebellion, anti-authoritarian evangelical preachers encouraged, clarified and invested with divine meaning their settlers'
agrarian notions. They were Baptists, New Light Congregational-
ists, ultra-evangelical Antinomians who sought to bypass a learned
clergy in pursuit of direct spiritual encounters." William Manning, although an orthodox Calvinist Congregationalist, envisioned the battle of "the Many" against "the Few" as a war in the imagery of the
Old Testament.

  Religious awakenings reverberated through the revolutionary era.
While historians continue to explore the links between the Great
Awakening (1739–45) and the Revolution, far more attention is being
paid to the waves of enthusiastic religions during and especially after the war.[13] Millennialism, it is now clear, took many forms—
charging, for example, the radical protest of an intercolonial
backcountry rebel like Herman Husband with his vision of a New Jerusalem in the West as a yeoman's utopia.[14] By the early 1800s the
evangelical Baptists and Methodists, on the way to becoming the
most numerous of American denominations, contributed not only to
what Nathan Hatch has called "the democratization of American
Christianity," but to the democratization of American political life.[15]

  Belief systems such as these—a labor theory of value, an evangelical Christian equalitarianism, plebeian notions of the rights and liberties of Englishmen—can be thought of as resources common people
drew upon at times of crisis.

APPROPRIATIONS OF LIBERTY
"Who can have a better right to the land than we
who have fought for it?"

If this commitment to prior source of radical values is valid, it is not
hard to argue the second proposition, namely that in the era of the
Revolution, as groups of ordinary people played an active role in the
Revolution and became aware of their own interests, they invoked

their own traditions as well as the Whig rhetoric of lawyers, ministers, planters, and merchants. There was a synthesis of traditional veins of radical thought with newer currents forged in the experiences of the Revolution that scholars are only now analyzing.

Language reveals the synthesis. The postwar protest by New England farmers who in Taylor's account settled illegally on frontier land in Maine and resisted by force the efforts of the great proprietors to oust them is a rich example of such a synthesis. They held an underlying assumption of a right to land drawn from radical Christian traditions ("God gave the earth to his children") and a sense of a moral economy. ("Wild lands ought to be as free as the common air.") But their military service in the war fortified this claim. ("Who can have a better right to the land then we who have fought for it?") And the fact that the land in dispute was confiscated from England made it all the more common property. ("These lands once belonged to King George. He lost them by the American Revolution & they became the property of the people who defended and won them.")

Other language showed an intricate appropriation of Whig rhetoric. The unfree living in the centers of patriot movements were extraordinarily quick to seize on Whig ideas, especially when patriots shifted the meaning of liberty from traditional English constitutional rights to natural rights, the first transition in the meaning of this keyword that Countryman analyzes. Thus, in Massachusetts, the first petition of slaves for freedom in January 1773 was a plaintive Christian humanitarian plea: "We have no Property! We have no Wives! No Children! We have no City! No Country! But we have a Father in Heaven." The second, in July, spoke of a "natural right to be free" but dwelt on a person's right to his own labor. Even their 1774 petition, in which they spoke of themselves as "a freeborn Pepel [who] have never forfeited this Blessing by aney compact or agreement whatever," continued to blend this Whig theme with Christian values. Not until a 1777 petition, which referred to their patience in presenting "Petition after Petition," did they pick up on their "natural & unalienable right" to freedom. This appropriation was so opportunistic one is tempted to argue that Whig rhetoric was more the occasion than a cause for asserting a claim to liberty.[16]

As individuals picked up ideas that were in the air, they often pushed them far beyond anything intended by patriot leaders. Years later Ebenezer Fox, a Boston-area apprentice cited by Rorabaugh who shipped out on a privateering vessel, wrote in his memoirs: "I thought I was doing myself a great injustice by remaining in bondage when I ought to be free; that the time was come, when I should liberate myself from the thraldom of others and set up a government of my own; or in other words, do what was right in the sight of my own eyes." His words reveal the kind of personal Declaration of Independence from all authority that Henry Thoreau would have appreciated, and that would have made John Adams shudder.

The unequals had to make a leap in their thinking to turn the talk of liberty into a demand for equality for themselves; and the leap is better explained by experience than by any logic inherent in the idea. For George Robert Twelves Hewes, a Boston shoemaker who survives in two as-told-to biographies, the experience of participating in the Boston Massacre, the Boston Tea Party, and countless other events of resistance enabled him to cast off deference. He vividly recalled the deference he earlier felt as an apprentice shoemaker when he called on John Hancock, one of the wealthiest mechants in Boston; and then, a decade later, the sense of equality he felt when (as he remembered it) he worked side by side with Hancock throwing the tea overboard in the Tea Party. It is unlikely that Hancock would have risked arrest at so illegal an event, but Hewes could have mistaken another gentleman for him. For the rest of his life Hewes would remember the Revolution's moments of equality—when he was as good a man as his "betters," whether John Hancock, the customs official Hewes defied, or the ship's officer for whom he refused to take his hat off.[17]

We know enough about Abigail Adams to gain insight into what led one woman to make the leap and therefore to speculate about others. In her "remember the Ladies" letter to John in March 1776, she seemed to be raising the demand to end the tyranny of husbands over their wives for the first time. For more than a decade she had been reading or hearing her husband's rhetoric of "tyranny" and "slavery" and "lords and vassals," but it does not seem that she, John, or anyone else in Massachusetts had publicly applied the principle to the status of women.

What were her experiences? Over the decade she had followed the active participation of the women of Boston and the surrounding countryside in the making of the Revolution and referred to herself as a "politician." She may well have drawn inspiration from the black petitioners and alleged conspirators of 1773–74 who, she felt, "have as good a right to freedom as we have." In 1776, only the month before her letter to John, she had read *Common Sense* with its message to begin the world over again. But perhaps most decisive, for almost two years while her husband was intermittently away in Philadelphia, she had taken on new responsibilities outside the traditional "female sphere": she managed the family farm, boasting she had become "quite a farmeriss," and she had become "school mistress" to her three young children. Thus she had a growing consciousness both of her own capacities and her own inadequacies—how ill-educated she was for the task. It was in the context of such experiences that she lifted her voice to John to "remember the Ladies." Similar wartime experiences would lead other women to make such a leap and verbalize a new consciousness.[18]

SOURCES OF RADICALISM
Promises Unfulfilled

The third proposition, that experiences shaped radical impulses over a very long revolutionary era that extended through the 1780s, the 1790s, and beyond, is becoming more of a commonplace among historians as they think through the life histories of the revolutionary generation. The Revolution did not end in 1776, in 1783, in 1787, or even in 1801. In writing about the great leaders—Washington, Adams, Hamilton, Jefferson, Madison—historians have no problem dealing with their entire political lives, which often stretched over half a century and more. Why not think the same way of the common people who lived out their lives over the same years? For many, their radicalism was the product of their *cumulative* experience over the entire era.

"In Every Revolution," wrote Herman Husband in 1793, "the People at Large are called upon to assist true Liberty," but when "the foreign oppressor is thrown off, learned and designing men" assume power to the detriment of the "laboring people." Husband was a leader of the backcountry rebellion of the Regulators of North Carolina defeated in 1771, the Antifederalists defeated in 1788, and the Pennsylvania Whiskey Rebellion on the defensive when he wrote.[19] If early in the Revolution there was a radicalism of hope expressed by Thomas Paine's plea in *Common Sense* to "begin the world over again," late in the era there was a radicalism of promises not fulfilled or of expectations raised but dashed, often expressed with anger or bitterness.

The experiences of a long war—the longest in American history—generated a variety of radical impulses. If the war is ever "restored to the central position that it had for the Revolutionary generation," as the military historian John Shy urged, some of these experiences may be appreciated.[20] Roughly 200,000 men served in the military, about half in the militia, half in the regular army. The Philadelphia militia, whose artisans, journeymen, and laborers were the base of the movement that pushed Pennsylvania to independence and enacted the most radical constitution of any state "carried their egalitarianism with them into the field" and carried it back to the streets of Philadelphia in the campaign for price controls in 1779–80.[21] The militias elsewhere, even when a cross section of their communities, were too democratic in the eyes of elitist officers. Soldiers of the regular army, who after 1776 were drawn from "the very poorest and most repressed persons in Revolutionary society" scholars now agree were no less patriotic for having their aspirations for a better life tied to the promises of land. Tension between enlisted men and officers was endemic and Baron Von Steuben was astute enough to recognize that he had to teach American officers to adapt to the "genius" of individualistic American enlistees and win their "love and respect." "Continentals," who early in the war often expressed their bitterness at the inequities of army life in drunkenness, desertion, and bounty jumping, as they became more disciplined and cohesive, expressed their protest collectively, climaxing in the mutinies of the New Jersey and Pennsylvania lines in 1781.[22] "After eight years [of war] in which about 200,000 of the masses watched perhaps 20,000 of the so called elite perform more or less incompetently" as officers, John Shy observes wryly "the post war voter had lost much of his habitual deference to men allegedly better than he was."[23]

At sea the rage for privateering gave some 60,000 men (as opposed to a few thousand who served in the Navy) a chance to "make their fortunes and serve their country" as the recruiters beguiled them. It also gave them a taste of legalized piracy, in which captains, like pirate commanders, courted the consent of their crews. And thousands of seamen who were captured, if they survived the horrors of British prisons, had the experience of collective self-government.[24]

In the countryside the Revolution took the character of a civil war for tens of thousands of ordinary Americans—or in Ronald Hoffman's apt phrase, "an uncivil war," especially in parts of the southern backcountry, where it "took on the appearance of a social convulsion." Wherever there was a prior history of intense conflict between colonial elites and common folk—especially in the two Carolinas— patriot elites encountered intense opposition. In Maryland where there was more cohesion, there was still active opposition to large planter leadership by the "disaffected"—poor farmers and tenants. The pattern was similar in New York, where tenants opposed patriot landlords. Even in relatively tranquil Virginia there was opposition, only partially overcome when old elites embraced Patrick Henry. While alignments in the South often produced a patchwork of social classes, the principal experience for many southerners was confronting and thwarting their betters, tidewater or low-country elites.[25]

For slaves the "turbulence of the war" in Sylvia Frey's words, "rocked the slave system to its foundations." The British army was a magnet to slaves, North and South, with General Clinton repeating in 1780 in South Carolina Lord Dunmore's offer of 1775 in Virginia, although the British never risked a generalized appeal that would alarm their slave-owning supporters. In the North the urgencies of recruiting quotas forced patriots to reverse their ban on slaves, but in the end probably more slaves wielded arms for the British than against them, and even more simply took flight. Wherever the fighting was, to use Frey's term, *triagonal*—Whigs-Tories-slaves—and wherever the British army was a presence, slaves seized their chance. And in the southern low country, Philip Morgan points out, "wartime anarchy created a power vacuum in the countryside that allowed slaves to expand their liberty" or autonomy within the system.[26]

In civilian life the war created inequities, as inflation soared and profiteers flourished. Food riots were common in the North, often by crowds composed of women, pitting advocates of a moral economy in support of official governmental efforts at price control against advocates of a political economy of free trade.[27] But if the war was in so many ways a hothouse of antagonisms, it also created new vistas for ordinary people. As David Ramsay, South Carolina's participant historian, wrote in 1789, it set people "to thinking, speaking and acting in a line far beyond that to which they were accustomed. . . . It not only required but created talents."[28] The war circulated soldiers and seamen, bringing them into new worlds. The war thus gave tens of thousands of men and women, slave and free, an enlarged sense of American space and the potential for a new way of life. Radical action requires hope and the knowledge of alternatives, not merely desperation.

For women the war offered experiences out of the "domestic sphere." As many as 20,000 women attached themselves to the army as cooks, laundresses, and nurses, usually following family members. And when men went off to war, women were called upon to clothe them—a traditional role—but they also assumed male roles, managing the farm or trade, repeating Abigail Adams's experience of 1775–76. While the role of "deputy husband" was time-honored, never had so many women assumed it as a patriotic duty.[29]

The experiences of postwar society spawned a radicalism of disappointment. For those who had served in the Army, the inequities of the settlement left a long-simmering resentment. Officers received pensions; and soldiers who were wounded received some recompense. But ordinary soldiers rarely received the bounty lands promised them on enlistment. The government did not enact a pension for enlisted men until 1818, and then only for those "in reduced circumstances," which produced 40,000 claims, a Domesday book of American poverty. And not until 1832 was this means test eliminated and an unrestricted pension law enacted for those who could give "a very full account" of their service. Twenty thousand applied. Historians have only begun to take the measure of the pain, pride and outrage in the pension applications of these survivors of the Revolution.[30]

The hard times of the Confederation era forged a radicalism of desperation: of farmers imprisoned for debt and faced with the loss of their land and property; of mechanics swamped by the flood of British-manufactured imports or ruined in the collapse of American shipbuilding; of migrants into the backcountry frustrated in their quest for land. Petitions rained on the state legislatures demanding "access to land, debtor relief, and remedies to the burden of heavy and regressive taxes." Shaysism was not confined to one state. Among elites, as Gordon Wood has made clear, there was an even greater fear that the radicalism of the "people-out-of-doors" would come "indoors," to dominate state legislatures.[31]

Thus by 1787 there is every reason to believe that the "interests" James Madison analyzed in *The Federalist* no. 10 were also perceived by nonelites. Madison wrote of essentially two different sources of "factions." One source lay in substantial propertied interests: "a landed interest, a manufacturing interest, a mercantile interest, a monied interest." But "the most common and durable source of factions" was "the various and unequal distribution of property. Those who hold and those who are without property have ever formed distinct interests in society. Those who are creditors, and those who are debtors, fall under a like discrimination," thus identifying the key conflicts of the 1780s uppermost in elite minds. The creation of the federal Constitution mobilized the substantial commercial interests as never before. The conflict over ratification mobilized a broader array of interests in opposition, inspiring a populist Antifederalism on a scale that is only now being recognized by scholars.[32]

The Hamiltonian economic program of the 1790s, coming on top of the new Constitution, widened the popular perception of a national ruling class that Kornblith and Murrin posit with rule by the few at the expense of the many. In this context, what David Brion Davis calls "the astonishing American enthusiasm for the French Revolution" is understandable. Once the French Revolution entered domestic politics in the guise of foreign policy issues—the war between revolutionary republican France and monarchist Britain, the Paineite effort to revolutionize Great Britain, the Federalist accommodation with Britain in 1795 and the half-war with France—it inspired new levels of equalitarianism and millennialism. Thomas Paine's *The Rights of Man* seemed to pose the same issues that *Com-*

mon Sense had in 1776. The impulses to radicalism soared. As Davis writes, "sometimes foreign revolutions have reinvigorated Americans' faith in a better world, expanding and redefining the meaning of equality and exposing the hollowness of our own pretensions to social justice."[33]

POPULAR CONSCIOUSNESS
"Class," "Plebeian" or "Democratic"?

The fourth proposition about the sources of radicalism—namely, that as the antagonisms of the revolutionary era increased, many groups of common people acquired a heightened consciousness of themselves which enabled them to establish a presence in American life—is the the most problematic, not to prove, but to formulate. Historians seem to agree that a new kind of popular consciousness—a sense of "we" and "they"—came into being over the revolutionary era. They do not agree how to conceptualize it.

There is a temptation to think of it as a class-consciousness. Edward Thompson's brief formulation of class in the preface to *The Making of the English Working Class* (1963)—very likely the most-quoted passage in modern scholarly discourse about class—has been enormously influential among American scholars. "Class happens," wrote Thompson, "when some men, as a result of common experience (inherited or shared), feel and articulate the identity of their interests as between themselves, and as against other men whose interests are different from (and usually opposed to) theirs." After immersing himself in explorations of popular culture in the British eighteenth century, Thompson drew nuanced distinctions about how classes come into being:

> To put it bluntly, classes do not exist as separate entities, look around, find an enemy class, and then start to struggle. On the contrary, people find themselves in society structured in determined ways (crucially but not exclusively, in productive relations), they experience exploitation (or the need to maintain power over those they exploit), they identify points of antagonistic interest, they commence to struggle around those issues and in the process of struggling they discover themselves as classes, they come to know this discovery as class-consciousness. Class and class-consciousness are always the last, not the first, stage in the real historical process.[34]

Thompson's concept of class continues to provoke controversy which need not be resolved here.[35] The historians writing about class in this volume have differing conceptions of class yet they share

Thompson's emphasis on classes' coming-into-being. They write of the "formation" of the yeomanry as a class or of the yeomanry "reinventing itself as a class" in successive backcountries, of the "making" and "unmaking" of a ruling class or of "bourgeois class formation" affecting changing conceptions of liberty. Scholars from many different vantage points are also identifying "points of antagonistic interest" in the revolutionary era around which Americans "commenced to struggle" and "discovered themselves." The points of struggle, if my analysis of this scholarship is valid, were more extensive and more intense later than earlier in the revolutionary era.

Whether self-discovery led to class-consciousness is open to debate. Thompson, in returning to the study of popular struggles in eighteenth-century England, continues to write of "the patricians and the plebs" and of "a plebeian culture" within a "patrician" society. Others use this vocabulary. Merrill and Wilentz characterize William Manning as a "plebeian democrat" and elsewhere Wilentz has described the artisans of New York as holding to a "plebeian artisan republicanism." Gordon Wood sees a dichotomy between plebeian and patrician in America. While I, too, have fallen back on *plebeian,* on reflection, the term seems anachronistic because the vocabulary of "plebeian" and "patrician" drew on a classical tradition that was fast passing out of fashion by 1800. So much discovery in the United States occurred as groups struggled for a voice in the political process that the terms *republican, democratic,* and *citizen consciousness* have been more compelling to historians than class-consciousness.[36]

American scholars have only begun to explore the language of identities among nonelite groups.[37] My impression is that the older vocabulary that drew distinctions in the society of sorts, ranks, conditions, and estates was fading late in the century; certainly the value-laden "better sort," "middling sort," and "meaner sort" were becoming passé, but that "class" probably did not come into common usage—"working class," "middle class"—until well into the second quarter of the nineteenth century.

In the wake of the Revolution the common language of class among nonelites often expressed a polarity of two major divisions in the society. In the debate over ratifying the Constitution, Amos Singletary, a Massachusetts farmer of little formal education, feared that "lawyers, and men of learning, and moneyed men" will "swallow up us little folks." In New York, Melancton Smith, the chief Antifederalist spokesman, a self-made merchant, thought that the proposed new government would fall into the hands of "the few and the great," while excluding "those of the middling class of life."[38] In the debates of the 1790s the language of radicals suggests they drew the dividing line between the productive and nonproductive classes: "those that labour for a living and those who get one without" or "the Many" and "the Few" (William Manning); "the laboring people" against "learned and designing men" or the "idle rich" (Herman Husband); "the people" versus "the aristocracy" (Thomas Paine in *The Rights of Man*). In newspapers and pamphlets the pseudonyms suggest similar identities: "A Laborer" (William Manning), "A Plebeian" (Melancton Smith), "Rough Hewer" (Abraham Yates, Jr.), "A Ploughjogger" (Jedidiah Peck, indeed a farmer and a sometime Baptist preacher), and "A Farmer," "A Mechanic," ad infinitum.[39]

Clearly, some nonelite groups "discovered themselves" more than others, moving toward a more interest-specific if not class-specific consciousness. The obvious candidate is the most self-conscious urban group of the era. Historians refer to them as *artisans* or *craftsmen*, terms which were little used by anyone. In the colonial era they most often referred to themselves as "tradesmen," while "mechanic" was, more often than not, a term of derision used by those above them. At some point in the 1770s, as conservative elites challenged their right to a voice in public affairs, "mechanics" began to wear that term as a badge of pride. In New York City and Philadelphia there were "mechanic" political tickets and Committees of Mechanics. By the mid-1780s in New York they formed a General Society of Mechanics and Tradesmen (the title bridging old and new usage). In Boston The Association of Tradesmen and Manufacturers, a body with delegates from the various trades, addressed written appeals to "their brethren, the mechanics" in other cities, asking them to join in a campaign for the protection of American manufactures. The emblem of the New Yorkers, adopted by societies in other cities, was an upright brawny arm holding a hammer, with the slogan "By Hammer and Hand All Arts Do Stand," a bold assertion of the primacy of the mechanic arts. Mechanics unquestionably became an influence in political life; they knew it, and political leaders knew it. One hesitates to speak of a mechanic class because mechanics were so heterogeneous. Perhaps historians can agree they had a "mechanic consciousness" and that there was a "mechanic presence," and move on from there.[40]

If such groups "discovered themselves" in conflict, it does not necessarily follow that they remained in constant antagonism with their opponents. On the contrary, because the Revolution was also a war for national liberation, nascent classes formed coalitions with other classes against a common outside enemy. Indeed, the era led to a constant reforming of coalitions, especially in face of a foreign danger that persisted in major crises throughout the era. But entering into coalitions did not necessarily diminish awareness of separate identities. In 1788, for example, the fact that in every major city mechanics as a body joined merchants and professionals to parade in political celebration of the new Constitution was a sign of mechanic consciousness; they marched en masse as mechanics, usually grouped trade by trade with emblems, symbols, or tools of their craft, displaying a consciousness of themselves as craftsmen, mechanics, and citizens.[41]

Furthermore, nascent classes divided internally. In the countryside, with the expansion of a market economy, the distinction Kulikoff draws between market-embedded commercial farmers and non-market-oriented yeomen helps explain political divisions among farmers, for example, over ratifying the commercially oriented Constitution of 1787. In the cities the mechanic trades also divided according to market orientation. By the late eighteenth century free wage labor was becoming the norm in northern cities: imported indentured servitude was drying up, slavery was fading, and apprenticeship was being transformed into a form of cheap labor. As the market system made its inroads on artisan production the conflict between masters and apprentices and masters and journeymen rent the fabric of mechanic cohesion.[42]

While there undoubtedly was a growing sense of commonality among "the laboring classes" embracing town and countryside, urban mechanics usually failed to support agrarians in insurrections, whether it was the tenant uprising in New York in 1766 or Shays's Rebellion in 1786. There was a change in 1794, when the urban Democratic Societies condemned the excise tax more than the whiskey rebels. "The laboring classes" in countryside and city were female as well as male, but radicals who embraced Paine's *Rights of Man* (1791–92) showed no comparable interest in Mary Wollstonecraft's *Vindication of the Rights of Women* (1791). The laboring classes included blacks—in a greater proportion than at any other time in American history—yet neither agrarian nor mechanic radicals welcomed Gabriel's abortive insurrection in 1800, or the efforts of free blacks in northern cities to forge their own community institutions. And the free blacks of Boston volunteered to put down Shays's Rebellion. Thus the multiple radicalisms of the revolutionary era remained separate.

Taken together, the argument advanced in these four propositions suggests new ways of thinking about the sources of radicalism in the revolutionary era. It posits not a single radicalism but multiple radicalisms. It does not see them stemming from one all-pervasive idea or ideology. It assumes a prior array of radical value systems which came into play at that time. The Revolution was itself an incalculable stimulus to radicalism. But if anything, scholars might pursue not a "trickle-down" theory of radicalism but rather one "bubbling up" from below. Radicalism flourished not only in the era of political resistance (1765–1775) but during the war (1775–1783) and especially the postwar era (1783–1801) when a radicalism of frustration replaced a radicalism of hope. The multiple radicalisms of the era were often at odds with each other. These propositions provide a framework for an inquiry into the successes and failures of the radical agendas in the results of the Revolution.

RESULTS OF THE REVOLUTION
A Framework for Analysis

If recent scholarship has, as Linda Kerber writes, increased our "appreciation" of the many radical movements of the Revolution, it leaves open the question of their success. And if the recovery of the groups previously neglected by historians makes the Revolution seem more radical, there is a temptation to say our understanding of the results—especially if we focus on the peoples Kerber called "marginal" and I originally called "outsiders"—makes it seem more conservative. The retention and expansion of slavery, the maintenance of a patriarchal subordination of women, the destructive inroads of a market economy on the laboring classes in the cities, to say nothing of the destructive impact of national expansion on American Indians, were developments central to post-revolutionary society.

Scholars contrasting such results with the democratization of American politics, the opening of economic opportunity, and the surges of equalitarianism—all gains benefiting principally yeomen and mechanics and then women—often end up using words like "contradiction" or "paradox," which still leave us hanging for an explanation. Other historians, by claiming as does Gordon Wood, for example, that however much the Revolution failed "to abolish slavery and change fundamentally the lot of women, [it] made possible the anti-slavery and women's rights movements of the nineteenth century and in fact all our current egalitarian thinking," essentially evade their responsibility for historical analysis.[43]

In the afterword to *The American Revolution* (1976) I suggested that there were several ways to measure the success of popular radical movements, short of their achieving power: by their capacity to articulate a distinct ideology, to endure as movements, and especially to influence those in power and shape events. A compelling case could be made for the impact of radical movements on the elites, creating a sophisticated kind of American conservatism that learned

how to accommodate popular pressures. But the same process of accomodation, I thought, did not work for the "outsiders" to the political system—women, blacks, Indians. The scholarship since then has
convinced me I was not bold enough in asserting the impact of popular movements on the elites and that I was wrong in claiming that
women and blacks had little impact on the Revolution, or the Revolution on them.

As I now see the results of the Revolution, my reflections run
as follows:

First, in response to the upsurges of radicalism, elites attempting to make themselves into a national ruling class, divided as to how
to confront these threats. In the political sphere their responses
ranged on a spectrum from the traditional methods of the English
ruling class—force, deference and influence—to negotiation leading
to accommodation.

Second, the processes of negotiation were most successful with the
middling classes—yeomen and mechanics—who had pushed their
way into the political system, establishing a continuing presence
that elites could not ignore if they wished to govern successfully.

Third, negotiation was pervasive throughout the society, offering
accommodations to groups excluded from the political system—
women and slaves—without destroying the subordination on which
the social and economic system rested. American Indians, the real
outsiders, were powerful enough in certain places and times to force a
kind of accommodation on Anglo-Americans that delayed expansion.

And finally, as a result of the process of accommodation which
made the political system more democratic, radical popular movements divided as to the means to effect change on a spectrum that
ranged from the traditional time-honored, effective, extralegal forms
of opposition to working within the new political system.

Framing the analysis of results in this way—as a process of confrontation, negotiation and accommodation occuring on a range of
separate spheres—offers the possibility of resolving the so-called
contradictions in the outcome of the Revolution. It also leaves room
in the analysis for the integration of the complex ways in which the
transformations leading the United States toward a capitalist society both stimulated and frustrated radical impulses.[44]

ELITES DIVIDE
Accommodation in the Public Sphere

That the would-be ruling classes divided in response to the popular
upheavals in the revolutionary era has been established by scholars,
state by state, for some time; Kornblith and Murrin are the first to

take the risk of generalizing about American ruling classes nationally for this era since William A. Williams. In the colonial era elites varied in their cohesiveness. In many colonies, elite families were ever at each other's throats, often appealing demagogically in elections to artisans or farmers with the vote, uniting only to assert their hegemony over the subordinate classes. The merchant classes were usually fragmented; so were large slaveholders or landlords in the Hudson River Valley. But, in general, elites contained the sporadic threats from below. What was new, from the 1770s on, was a persistent popular democratic presence in politics. How to handle it could divide great aristocratic families within (as with the Carrolls of Maryland) or from their neighbors and kin (as in New York), or divide even the confident ruling gentry (as in Virginia).[45]

The Revolution produced a crisis of confidence among old elites in their capacity to take their chances with democracy (to them, "the rabble" or "the mob") and with the new men responsible to popular constituencies with whom elites now had to compete for power (to them, "upstarts" and "demagogues"). Confidence of this sort was something of a dividing line within elites over the entire revolutionary era: between Whigs and loyalists over separating from Great Britain, among Whigs in state making and constitution making, in the 1790s between Democratic Republicans and Federalists, and after their defeat in 1800, between "old school" and "new school" Federalists.

The metaphors elites used for the threats from below are telling tokens of their different outlooks. Panic-stricken conservatives referred to the people as a beast that had to be driven or as a reptile that would bite, some invoking the classical imagery of "the many headed Hydra."[46] By contrast, Robert R. Livingston, a landlord potentate in New York typical of more risk-taking conservatives, in 1777 used the metaphor of a stream: rulers had to "learn the propriety of Swimming with a Stream which it is impossible to stem"; they should "yield to the torrent if they hoped to direct its course." Thirty years later, Noah Webster scolded his fellow Federalists who had fallen from power because they "attempted to resist the current popular opinion instead of falling into the current with a view to direct it." The since-famous lexicographer was a conciliatory conservative, who in his best-selling speller and dictionary presided over nothing less than the Americanization of the English language.[47]

What was new was that the Revolution nationalized the threat of radicalism which earlier was localized. Neither Shaysism nor the whiskey uproar was confined to one state.[48] The creation of a national government created a national arena for conflicts. And the increase in the number and frequency of newspapers permitted a more rapid dissemination of opinion. Master mechanics communicated from one city to another. Some fifty Democratic Societies came into being in the backcountry as well as eastern cities. One consequence of this minor revolution in communications was that outside events could have a fairly rapid national influence. Successive events in the French Revolution produced common reactions all over theUnited States; the news of successful black revolutionaries in the Caribbean invigorated African-American resistance North and South, alarming slaveholders as well as antislavery advocates.[49]

The torrents of national radicalism required extraordinary skill of the nation's pilots. In the postwar crisis that culminated in the Constitutional Convention of 1787, the elite leaders best able to assume national leadership were men like James Madison, who recognized it as a crisis of "the political system," itself a revealing phrase. Madison was able to negotiate on two fronts: with the conflicting substantial propertied "interests" so well represented in the convention (the haves) and with the radical democratic movements that were a "presence" at the convention, even if they were not present (the have-nots and the have-littles). The framers more or less agreed with Madison that if the Constitution was to last "for the ages," it had to conform to "the genius of the people," a phrase meaning spirit or underlying values. Montesquieu had taught them that. Long-range philosophy aside, there was the short-range political problem of getting the Constitution adopted by ratifying conventions in each state. Nathaniel Gorham of Boston, a merchant sensitive to a mechanic constituency, summed it up: "We must consult the rooted prejudices [of the people] if we expect their concurrence in our propositions."[50]

Bold, sophisticated conservatives had learned a lesson from the Revolution—they had to accommodate democratic-minded constituencies in advance. The Federalists of 1787–88 made two grand accommodations usually missing from civics lessons: the first, in the concessions to democratic rule they built into the Constitution itself; the second, during the process of ratification, when they divided the powerful popular opposition who wanted a less centralized and more democratic structure by promising amendments which they later reduced to the Bill of Rights, which left the essential framework intact. The result was a constitution a nationalist-minded radical like Thomas Paine and a localist plebeian democrat like William Manning could fault but accept. It was "a good one prinsaply, but I have no doubt but that the Convention who made it intended to destroy our free governments by it," Manning wrote. It left the future open; it was, he said, "made like a Fiddle, with but few Strings, but so the ruling Majority could play any tune upon it they please."

The elites who gained power but had the least long-run success were the Hamiltonian Federalists of the 1790s, who adopted England as a model. Hamilton, after getting nowhere in the Constitutional Convention with a proposal for a government of King, Lords, and Commons, and state governors appointed by the national president with a veto power over the states, tried to consolidate a government in the 1790s based on the English system of deference, influence, and force. But deference was on the wane, and any attempt to impose it led to the charge of "aristocracy." Building influence through a funding system and bank produced a backlash against corruption. And force—whether military to put down extralegal opposition like the Whiskey Rebellion or Fries's Rebellion, or political repression like the Sedition Law of 1798 to imprison legal opposition—misjudged the "genius of the people," ushering the Federalists out of power.

The elites with the greatest capacity for survival coalesced as the Democratic Republicans, under the leadership of Madison and Jefferson. The Virginia leaders had mastered the process in their native state by building alliances with the dissenting religions in a ten-year battle to disestablish the Anglican church. They learned how to accommodate nationally: to build a coalition of southern slave-owning planters, yeomen, northern merchants in search of markets to make them independent of Britain, and mechanics and would-be manufacturers. It is not surprising that their principal northern allies were politicians from New York and Pennsylvania like Robert R. Livingston, who once again was ready to swim with the stream. The interests thus brought together could share a common aim of expanding overseas commercial markets for agricultural produce, expanding to the West, and developing American manufactures.[51]

Democratic Republicans shifted to accommodate radical agrarians to their left. In 1786 Madison sought Federal power to contain Shays's Rebellion, while Jefferson was prepared for "a little rebellion now and then," as a warning to rulers. But in 1794 Madison and Jefferson fought the Federalist effort to "censure" the "self created societies" as responsible for the Whiskey Rebellion. Both were more concerned with eliminating grievances than putting down agrarian rebels. And with the vast public domain as a resource they were prepared to accommodate insistent settler demands for land. Both fought the repressive Sedition Law. They also recognized the importance of the mechanics—"the yeomanry of the cities" to Jefferson. However, they could not accommodate African Americans in slavery, or American Indians, and were indifferent to the new voices among American women.

NEGOTIATIONS IN THE PRIVATE SPHERE
African Americans

All this negotiation was in the public sphere. The work of historians in a variety of fields of social history suggests that negotiation also was underway within private spheres (a distinction from the public sphere that was often dissolving). This seems true among many segments of the laboring classes, especially in the 1790s. Masters and apprentices, it is obvious from Rorabaugh's vivid examples, were engaged in unstated negotiations. Masters and apprentices literally signed a contract expressing reciprocal obligations for living and working under the same roof. As apprentice deference eroded, the master had to mend his ways. The stock form of the printed indenture may have read the same, but apprentices forced renegotiation of the unwritten contract. At the same time, journeymen in many trades organized on their own to deal with masters, leading to the first pattern of American strikes by journeymen ("turnouts") and lockouts by masters; in most trades unstated collective bargaining continued to affirm custom.[52] Merchant seamen confronting the masters of their vessels traditionally "used a many-sided process of negotiation and resistance to defend themselves and to protect and expand their privileges and rights," and their hand was very likely strengthened in the revolutionary ferment of the Atlantic world.[53]

In rural areas the armed confrontations between settlers and great proprietors could end in negotiations. In Maine, once the proprietors conceded the right of squatters to acquire land, the conflict could boil down to haggling over the price of land. Leading men in frontier communities often served as middlemen. And on the state level in Massachusetts (which then included Maine) and Pennsylvania, Democratic Republicans proved adept at drafting legislation which accommodated both sides, passing in Pennsylvania literally a "Compromise Act." Here politicians brokered a social conflict, an innovation that in time became a cliché in American politics.[54]

The war enhanced the capacity of slaves to negotiate with their masters. The new scholarship on slavery in the revolutionary era has identified the processes by which slaves won "space" for themselves within an oppressive system. In 1775–76 southern planters clearly were in no position to accommodate the massive upsurge for freedom. Yet during the war they often had no choice; slaves expanded their autonomy within the system, or made good their flight from it. And after the war the low-country blacks, for example, did not readily surrender their wartime gains and "many continued to flaunt their increased autonomy." In the upper South, Maryland and Virginia passed laws that made it easier for individual slaveholders to free their own slaves through manumission, creating the first sizable free black population in the Chesapeake. In subsequent decades, even as slavery grew and expanded over the entire South, "continued renegotiations of the terms under which slaves worked for their masters,"[55] Ira Berlin argues, were central to the system.

In the North, where there were 50,000 slaves on the eve of the Revolution, emancipation on a state-by-state basis was, in Berlin's apt words, "a slow, torturous process" that often dragged out for years. The thrust of recent scholarship is that the insistent black pressures for freedom did as much as white antislavery benevolence to bring about this first emancipation. During and after the war northern slaves seized freedom, by fighting with the British or the patriots or by running away; or they purchased their own freedom and that of their families. In the five northern states with the largest slave populations, the legislatures provided only gradual emancipation for children born of slaves after they reached their twenties, which explains why in 1810 there were still 27,000 slaves in the North compared to 50,000 free blacks. Once free, blacks in the northern states faced a continuing struggle against racism for access to schools, the ballot, and civil rights. It was a grudging emancipation.[56]

By 1820 in the country as a whole the number of freed blacks approached 250,000, while the number of slaves had grown to 1.5 million. Thus, as Berlin sums it up, the Revolution "was not only a stride forward in the expansion of black liberty, [but it] strengthened the plantation regime and slavery grew as never before, spreading across a continent. Thus if the Revolution marked a new birth of freedom, it also launched a great expansion of slavery."[57]

How was this possible? The question is crucial to understanding the Revolution. The argument David Brion Davis first advanced in 1975 remains compelling. "The American colonists were not trapped in an accidental contradiction between slavery and freedom." On the contrary, as they emerged from the Revolution, "slavery was of central importance to both the southern and national economies, and thus to the viability of the 'American system.' " Moreover, "a free society was by no means incompatible with dependent classes of workers. Its central prerequisite was a large class of freeholders, unencumbered by feudal, military or political obligations. Liberty required independence, and independence required freehold property." Chattel slaves provided the property which defined independence, the long-cherished goal of southern farmers.[58] What accounts for the northern acquiescence to southern slavery? Economic interest, the high priority placed on national union, the devotion to private property in Whig ideology, and the growth of racism as the indispensable justification for continuing slavery in a land of liberty—all these contributed to what was perhaps the most fateful accommodation of the revolutionary era.[59]

ACCOMMODATIONS IN THE "DOMESTIC SPHERE"
Women

This pattern of accommodation within a system of subordination assumed a different shape for women. "We are ready to ask," Linda Kerber writes, "whether and how the social relations of the sexes were renegotiated in the crucible of the Revolution." As a result of women's participation in the prewar resistance and in the war, "how much more inclusive American citizenship should be was under negotiation."[60]

Thought about this way, the oft-cited exchange of letters between Abigail and John Adams in 1776 can be viewed as the opening round of a quintessential negotiation. He would hear nothing of equality of rights, but was receptive to her continuing demands for educational opportunities for women. Out of such exchanges—which we can assume were repeated without written record in countless families of the middling sort—came the accommodation Kerber has called "Republican motherhood," in which mothers were endowed with the patriotic responsibility of raising their sons and daughters as virtuous citizens for the new Republic and therefore required a better education. The "role of Republican motherhood," as Kerber recently reflected, "was a conservative stabilizing one, deflecting the radical potential of the revolutionary experience"; at the same time, it contributed to the expansion of education for women, the principal gain of the decades after 1790.[61]

Thus the literate young women able to read novels in Davidson's account were the beneficiaries of the first negotiation. They in turn won another: they defied authority and read the novels. In the long struggle by women for equal rights this may not seem very subversive, but as long as marriage was the chief option open to women, Davidson argues, a woman had "an opportunity to work out in the safe context of her imagination just what she wanted from men and from marriage." This in turn very likely contributed to "matrimonial republicanism," another product of the negotiation between the sexes. How widespread were these changes, how far they extended beyond educated middling women is not clear. Laurel Thatcher Ulrich's skillful recovery of the life of a midwife on the Maine frontier is evidence of a woman who remained "more a colonial goodwife than a Republican Mother"; the recovery of other lives suggests new patterns. Scholars have found it easier to measure the absence of change in laws and institutions; they are only beginning to tap sources that measure changes in women's consciousness.[62]

That some women should articulate independence as a goal is not surprising in an era in which personal independence was the heightened goal of every Tom, Dick, and Harry. Mary Wollstonecraft's *Vindication of the Rights of Women* found a receptive readership among educated American women. "In very many of her sentiments," the Philadelphia Quaker Elizabeth Drinker confided to her diary, "she, as some of our friends say, *speaks my mind.* In some others, I do not always coincide with her. I am not for quite so much independence." John Adams thought Abigail was "a perfect disciple of Wollstonecraft."[63] Through the 1790s Judith Sargent Murray, the most vocal American theorist of women's rights, argued for an independence that pushed at the boundaries of republican motherhood. Her daughters, she wrote, "should be enabled to procure for themselves the necessaries of life; independence should be placed within their grasp." This was partly to protect women from the vicissitudes of widowhood. "The term *helpless widow* might be rendered as unfrequent and inapplicable as that of *helpless widower.*" But Murray was also critical of raising "our girls . . . with one monopolizing consideration . . . an establishment by marriage . . . *An old maid* they are from infancy taught, at least indirectly to consider as a contemptible being." On the contrary, she argued, "marriage should not be presented as the *summum bonum,* or as a certain, or even necessary, event; they should learn to respect a single life, and even regard it as the *most eligible,* except a warm, mutual and judicious attachment has gained the ascendancy in the bosom." But she pushed women no further to break through the barriers of the "domestic sphere."[64]

In an era when most white men had access to the means to achieve independence, most women did not; and most men were not prepared to surrender "our masculine systems," as John Adams put it. Why not? Just as the independence of the slaveholder was defined by the dependence of his slaves, or the independence of the artisan defined by the dependence of his apprentices and journeymen, so the independence of a white male, whatever his occupation, was defined by the dependence of his wife and children. Independence, as Joan Gunderson puts it, "was a condition arrived at by exclusion, by *not* being dependent or enslaved." Personal independence, the life goal of ordinary male Americans, required heading a family, being a property holder, and possessing "a requisite set of mental/moral and/or martial capacities." "All these meanings of independence," Nancy Fraser and Linda Gordon argue, "simultaneously defined contrasting senses of dependence which excluded women, slaves and children."[65]

In "a new narrative" of the Revolution which fully integrates gender, Kerber foresees that the Revolution "will be understood to be more deeply radical than we have heretofore perceived it because its shock reached into the deepest and most private human relations." But it will also be understood to be "more deeply conservative . . . purchasing political stability at the price of backing away from the implications of the sexual politics implied in its own manifestos, just as it backed away from the implications of its principles for changed race relations."[66]

ACCOMMODATIONS
American Indians, Elites, and Frontiersmen

The revolutionary era was a time of unprecedented landed expansion. The new country that emerged from the Revolution expanded with breathtaking speed over a vast geographic area. This expansion produced a triangular confrontation of American Indians, eastern national elites, and western settlers that led to alternating national policies of accommodation and warfare and to deep divisions within native American societies.

The range of accommodation with native Americans was limited by an ethnocentrism that made the most well-meaning Anglo-Americans incapable of coexisting with Indians as they were. During and after the war, in which most Indians fought on the side of the British, their traditional protectors, the dominant attitude among whites James Merrell finds encapsulated in such toasts and slogans as "Civilization or death to all American Savages" or "Civilization or extinction." But Anglo-American leaders had not calculated on the Indians' will for independence or their capacity to defend it.[67]

In the decades before and after the war, native American societies had experienced movements of spiritual revitalization—in David Dowd's words, "Great Awakenings"—that reinforced political and military resistance. For example, behind Pontiac, the secular leader of the Indian confederacy of the 1760s, lay Neolin, the Delaware prophet. The Revolutionary War which produced "a near unanimity of the trans-Appalachian struggle against the United States" enhanced pan-Indianism. The tactics of Revolutionary War leaders such as the scorched-earth decimation of Iroquois villages (which earned George Washington the reputation among the Iroquois as "town destroyer") put native Americans in no mood to accommodate the victorious United States.[68]

In the peace treaty, the British, as Francis Jennings puts it, "passed the card called sovereignty" over Indian land, "a legal fiction," to the new nation. But spokesmen for the Iroquois Confederacy in the north said they were "a free People subject to no Power upon earth," while the southern tribes insisted they had done nothing "to forfeit our Independence and natural Rights." Confronted with Indian power, national political leaders rapidly shifted, recognizing Indian claims to sovereignty, literally negotiating treaties, and promising, in the Northwest Ordinance of 1787, that "the utmost good faith shall always be observed towards the Indians; their land and property shall never be taken from them without their consent."[69]

The corollary of this accommodation was to bring the "blessings of civilization" to American Indians. This meant, as Merrell writes, that "Indian men would adopt plow agriculture, women would abandon the field for the home, and all would give up their heathen ways for Christ." The symbol was engraved on the silver peace medal U.S. presidents bestowed on cooperating chieftains: a native American male throwing a broken arrow to the ground before President Washington, who is in his general's uniform, sword at his side; and in the background, a man, perhaps the same Indian, guiding a plough pulled by two oxen, tilling a field.[70]

The pressures of western agrarians forced a change on national policy-makers. An aggressive policy toward Indians had been a persistent demand of the most radical backcountry movements from Bacon's Rebellion in Virginia in 1676, to the Paxton Boys of Pennsylvania in 1764, to the Whiskey Rebels of 1794. In fact the radical philosophy by which settlers justified their claim to vacant land against absentee proprietors with legal title was applied to Indians. The tillers of the soil, whose labor gave it value, were alone entitled to the land. Indians, in the eyes of farmers, did nothing to improve the "howling wilderness." The same class antagonism informed the backcountryman's attitude toward absentee land proprietors and eastern opponents of an aggressive policy toward the Indians. The Tennessee territorial legislature in 1794 reminded Congress that "citizens who live in poverty on the extreme frontiers were as entitled to be protected in their lives, their families and little property, as those who were in luxury, ease and affluence in the great and opulent eastern cities." In the 1790s eastern elites with their own agendas for expansion, bent to these pressures, sanctioning war on a massive scale.[71]

Among radical agrarians there were some muted voices of protest. William Manning was not the only agrarian who objected to the cost of the wars against the Indians: from 1791 to 1796 the five million dollars spent on the western wars were five-sixths of the total American budget. Herman Husband, a radical Bible-reading millennialist, wanted peaceful negotiations with Indians, who in his eyes were among the lost tribes of Israel. The settlers on the Maine frontier in their guerrilla war against the proprietors sometimes assumed Indian disguises, identifying themselves with the liberty-loving (sometimes terrifying) first inhabitants of the soil. Euro-Americans who practised accommodation with Indians, living in what Richard White has called a "middle ground"—fur traders, captives who became converts, and other migrants in multi-ethnic villages—were few in number. Thus there were no effective voices challenging the alternatives of "civilization or extinction" that in reality were "alternative routes to obliteration."[72]

Anglo-American pressures forced people into their own internal processes of accommodation. The names historians have attached to the divisions—accommodationists versus nativists, progressives versus conservatives—varied but the patterns were similiar. Tribal societies were divided among those who would accommodate by negotiating away land rights and moving on, those who were willing to adopt the white man's ways, including Christianity and plow agriculture, and those who rejected them or sought selective adaptation of Anglo-American ways. New waves of spiritual revival led by prophets and visionaries fed the movements for militant resistance and the revitalization of Indian societies. In the early 1800s, the Shawnee prophet Tenskwatawa made it possible for his brother, Tecumseh, to renew a confederacy and mount a powerful but unsuccessful military offensive against the United States. Where military resistance was no longer feasible, as among the Senecas, the prophet Handsome Lake laid the basis for collective action that led to moral and social reform. In this context the divisions within Indian societies confronting imperial expansion bear some resemblance to the divisions within the Anglo-American society of the same era.[73]

The Democratic Republicans, once in national power, offered their own mixture of benevolence and belligerence, paving the way for the next step, physical removal from the eastern United States. In 1783, 150,000 Indians lived east of the Mississippi; by 1844, less than one-fourth remained. That the Mashpees, faced with removal from Cape Cod, Massachusetts, appealed to the Constitution—"We as a tribe will rule ourselves, and have a right to do so; for all men are born free and equal, says the Constitution of the country"—was a token of the continuing appropriation of revolutionary ideals but not of their vitality.[74]

RADICAL DIVISIONS

The processes of accommodation in the political system contributed to a division within radical popular movements as to the best means

for effecting change. The norm inherited from colonial times was extralegal action: mob actions in the cities and Regulator movements
in the countryside. The period of political resistance (1765–75) expanded the frequency, size, leadership of crowds, and the repetoire of
popular rituals. There were more self-led crowds, more spontaneous
actions, and more class-specific crowds. Colonial crowds did not fit a
single model of the consensual expression of the will of the community. The crowds of the revolutionary era were even more diverse.[75]

In the eyes of the common people the success of the Revolution le-
gitimized extralegal action, and the war sanctioned violence, endow-
ing both with the aura of patriotism. After the war popular rituals
were transmitted to new protesters by oral tradition: symbolic actions such as effigy burnings and the erection of liberty poles, acts of
physical intimidation such as tar and feathering and warnings by
apocryphal avenging figures, and "rough music" to punish offenders
of community norms. If any single act became symbolic of the Revolution as a whole, it may have been the Boston Tea Party.[76]

The democratization of the political culture, the accommodations
by elites, combined with a quasi-revolution in communications, undoubtedly had an effect in channeling protest into a now more open
political system. Petitioning to state legislatures, which very likely
was on a greater scale than in the colonial era, lost the tone of
supplication.[77] Yet extralegal action was hardly abandoned; it
seemed to run parallel to the legal. In the 1790s in western Pennsylvania, farmers formed Democratic societies, passed resolutions,
and sent petitions to the federal government. Simultaneously, they
resorted to tar-and-feathering tax collectors, erecting liberty poles,
and parading thousands-strong through Pittsburgh to intimidate local elites. They were prepared for military resistance, but confronted
by a massive federal mobilization of force, the rebels debated strategy and withdrew.[78]

Resorting to force produced a crisis in confidence within popular
movements over achieving their ends within the system, the mirror
image of the crisis in confidence among elites over taking their
chances with democracy. Clearly, a kind of constitutional democratic
radicalism came into being. William Manning, the plebeian democrat
who had opposed Shays's Rebellion, would have members of his proposed national laboring society take an oath to support the government against insurrections. The aim of the society was to educate
"the Many" to make use of their electoral power to oust "the Few."
Other yeomen, who had no reason for confidence in legislative or judicial systems, continued to resort to force.

Among the mechanic classes in the cities there was more of a

break with traditional modes of mob action. It was said of John Jay
in 1795, after the news of his treaty arrived in the United States,
that he could have traveled from Maine to Georgia by the light of his
burning effigies. And in Baltimore in 1807 journeymen shoemakers
debated whether tarring and feathering their anglophile Federalist
foreman was not a legitimate extension of republican principles.[79]
But respectable mechanics and tradesmen fashioned new, affirmative, nonviolent rituals: they paraded in civic festivals, attended
Fourth of July ceremonies, and celebrated the victories of the French
Revolution at dinners. They also took part in politics, and those qualified to vote—a large proportion of the total—cast ballots in increasing numbers. The ballot box was not the coffin of a plebeian citizen
consciousness. The assembly election of 1796 in New York City,
Hamilton reported with anguish, "in the eyes of the common people
was a question between the rich and the poor."[80]

This division as to means was a persisting issue in the subsequent
history of American radicalism: whether to use physical force of nonviolent persuasion, whether to take part in politics, and if so,
whether to work within existing parties, or to form new ones. Merely
to list the alternatives is to summon up images of the splits within
abolitionism, the leading radical movement of the pre–Civil War era,
and later within socialism, one of the leading radical movements of
the industrial era.

If by the end of the eighteenth century, African-American slaves in
the South had fewer legal paths to freedom, it might be argued they
had enlarged their range of illegal options. The war and the rise of
free black communities made flight more possible and more successful than ever before. But collective insurrection was now a possibility,
inspired variously by the example of successful rebellion in St.
Domingue, a new wave of evangelical religion, the emergence of an
artisan class among slaves, and the example of the first viable free
black communities. There is a temptation to speak of a new cycle of
insurrection after the turn of the century.

Gabriel Prosser's failed conspiracy in Richmond, Virginia, in the
summer of 1800, which to Gov. James Monroe was "unquestionably
the most serious and formidable conspiracy we have ever known of
that kind," was led by urban artisans. St. George Tucker, an antislavery Virginian, measured how far black people had come in the quarter of a century since 1775. In response to Lord Dunmore's plea,
slaves had acted individually by running away; in 1800 they showed
they were capable of "acting in concert"—to a degree Tucker found
"astonishing." In 1775 they "fought for freedom merely as a good; now
they also claim it as a right." At his trial one rebel said, "I have noth-

ing more to offer than what George Washington would have had to
offer, had he been taken by the British and put on trial by them. I
have ventured my life in endeavoring to obtain the liberty of my
countryman, and am a willing sacrifice in their cause."[81] On the Virginia–North Carolina border a threat of insurrection followed in
1801–02. While conspiracies would dot the subsequent landscape of
southern slavery, for most slaves opposition meant everyday resistance in the work process—the quintessential negotiation to force
accommodation—running away, or the cultural resistance implicit in
sustaining the family and the invisible church.[82]

Among advocates of women's rights, by contrast, it is difficult to
detect a split as to means. There clearly were differences among articulate women. Women who read Mary Wollstonecraft or Judith
Sargent Murray divided as to how much "independence" they should
claim. Women disagreed over how much and what kind of education
they should have. Some women actively supported Federalists; others, the Democratic Republicans. The novels written by women
ranged widely in their "feminism." However, that women aired their
differences in newspapers, magazines, and novels or privately in correspondence, diaries, and conversations suggests the boundaries of
women's activities. Compared to women in the French Revolution,
women in America had only begun to act collectively in public. In the
1790s women became active in church societies and benevolent organizations. Yet by 1800 it is not quite possible to speak of a women's
movement much less a women's rights movement.[83]

Women who expressed their opinions may have divided between
optimists and pessimists. In his 1798 feminist novel *Alcuin* Charles
Brockden Brown captured a mood of disillusionment in the words he
put in the mouth of Mrs. Carter, an educated Philadelphia widow, in
response to the question "Are you a Federalist?" "What have I as a
woman to do with politics?" she answers brusquely. The law which
"annihilates the political existence of at least half of the community
[treats women] as if we were pigs or sheep." On the other hand, Murray, writing in the same year, saw "young women . . . at the dawn of
a new era in female history," and many of the first female graduates
of the schools and academies echoed her. It would be several decades
before hope would combine with bitterness to inspire the radicalism
of collective action.[84]

1776
Twenty-five Years Later

How successful were the multiple radicalisms that emerged in 1775–
76 and flourished in the 1780s and 1790s? I have argued that over

the long revolutionary era one of the best tests of the success of radical movements is their impact on the elites. In 1801 the Democratic Republicans, led by the more accommodating of the two national elites, won power. How far did they then carry the processes of accommodation in the different spheres of American life?

Some of the players are the same. Thomas Jefferson characterized his election over John Adams as "the revolution of 1800," and "as real a revolution in the principles of our government as that of 1776 was in its form." The country had rejected Federalist rule by coercion; the "reign of terror" was over. Adams had been less able in 1800 than in 1776 to navigate the democratic torrent. He confronted far less "veneration for persons in authority" in 1800 than in 1776. The "people-out-of-doors" had come indoors to vote, to elect new men of their own kind to Congress as well as the state legislatures. Adams had to confront the likes of Irish-born Matthew Lyon in the House of Representatives. Lyon had come to the colonies an indentured servant, made his way to wealth as a manufacturer in frontier Vermont, was elected to Congress on the fourth try as a Democratic Republican, was sentenced to jail under the Sedition Act for criticizing President Adams, and was returned to Congress by his constituents with an even greater majority.[85]

All of the demons Adams feared in 1776 were more of a menace at the turn of the century. Yeoman farmers who in 1775 had closed the courts in western Massachusetts were likely in 1800 to be waging guerrilla war against their great proprietors in Maine. As one of them said, "We once defended this land at the point of a bayonet & if drove to the necessity are now equally united, ready & zealous to defend it again the same way." Apprentices were "disobedient" enough to threaten the system of apprenticeship. The "insolence" of individual slaves had escalated to collective conspiracy for rebellion. And while in 1776 Abigail Adams had raised the issue of women's rights privately in a letter to her husband, Murray publicly urged women to cultivate "a noble ardour of independence" in her newspaper essays, subsequently published in three volumes (to which the Adamses subscribed).

In power the Jeffersonian elite would accommodate only some of these popular movements. Would-be yeoman farmers hungry for land could anticipate revisions in federal land laws making the public domain available in smaller parcels at lower prices. And when an expansionist president acquired the Louisiana Territory, he could claim to have fulfilled the expectation of his inaugural address of land "for the thousandth generation to come." Mechanics could be optimistic when they submitted to Congress in 1801 a petition for protection for

American manufactures with the same wording they had submitted in 1789.

Others had less reason for optimism. The journeymen shoemakers of Philadelphia, a hundred of whom began a long strike in 1799, the first of a half a dozen such strikes that would take place in as many cities in the next decade or so, would be tried and convicted for conspiracy. They drew more opposition than support from local Democratic Republicans. William Manning still tried after 1801 to get his proposal for a national society of laboring men published. Vigilance of the Many against the Few apparently was necessary, no matter who was in power. Reformers with a host of causes were in motion in the states and cities, hoping to expand the suffrage and the number of elective offices, to curb the common law or restrict lawyers, and to expand public schools. Some were native-born, inspired by the new evangelical religions; others were "Jacobin" émigrés from Great Britain anxious to fulfill the promise of Thomas Paine's *Rights of Man* or *Age of Reason*. All these reformers composed, in effect, a left wing among local Democratic Republicans, although they were not necessarily Jeffersonians.[86]

Nationally Jeffersonians wanted to contain, not accommodate, the radical thrusts for freedom from southern slaves. Jefferson had not published a word of public criticism of slavery since *Notes on Virginia* in the 1780s. His antislavery sentiment, already withering on the vine of his racism, froze with the news of rebellions in St. Dominque, even before Gabriel's conspiracy at home. Jefferson differed with Gov. James Monroe only in how far Virginia had to go to deter future rebellions; in 1800 after twenty-six conspirators had been executed, he told Monroe "there had been hanging enough." Confronted as president with the Napoleonic effort to overthrow the successful slave revolutionaries in their West Indies colony, Jefferson consistently "pressed for the devastation and destruction of the black Jacobins."[87]

Women could expect less support from Jefferson than Adams. "Our good ladies," Jefferson rejoiced to Anne Willing Bingham of Philadelphia, after reporting the activities of women in France, "have been too wise to wrinkle their foreheads with politics. They are contented to soothe and calm the minds of their husbands returning ruffled from political debate." Bingham disagreed, but only here and there a few maverick Republicans—Benjamin Rush, James Sullivan, Charles Brockden Brown—took a public stand on women's issues.[88]

The limits of Jeffersonian accommodation were soon made clear to the American Indians. To a visiting delegation, the philosopher-scientist expressed the hope that "we shall see your people become disposed to cultivate the earth, to raise herds of the useful animals,

and to spin and weave for their food and clothing." To the territorial
governor of Ohio, Jefferson revealed his underlying rationale: "Our
settlements will gradually circumscribe and approach the Indians &
they will in time either incorporate with us as citizens of the U.S or
remove beyond the Mississippi." Inside a velvet glove he kept a
mailed fist. "We presume our strength and their weakness is now so
visible," he remarked in 1803, "that they must see we have only to
shut our hand to crush them." The "empire for liberty" Jefferson envisioned was for white male yeoman farmers and their families.[89]

*H*ow radical was the American Revolution? Or, if you prefer, how
much transformation was there as a result of the Revolution? The
central concept I have advanced of a negotiation among contending
groups, "classes," and individuals offers a number of advantages as
an analytical tool or as a heuristic principle of investigation. It differs from the old progressive and conflict interpretations, which focused primarily on the political and saw outright victory for one side
and defeat for the other (The Constitution as Thermidor). It differs
from the old consensus interpretation in analyzing results as the
product of conflict. It avoids the weakness of intellectual or ideological interpretations that posit a single cluster of ideas from which all
change emanates. It acknowledges the systems or structures that
framed what people did, but assigns priority to the agency of people
in effecting change and renewing their struggles even in the face
of defeat.

It enables us to encompass more of the multiple dimensions of
the Revolution: as a colonial struggle for liberation from imperial
rule, in which there were coalitions of nascent "classes" in both co-
operative and antagonistic relationships, and as a series of internal
struggles in separate but often overlapping spheres. It allows us to
measure the results of these struggles, not at one stopping point,
but as an ongoing process, in which negotiations were often renewed
and sometimes faded. It further permits us to measure results in
many different spheres of life, private as well as public. And it enables us to recognize that while the Revolution was indeed radical,
there is no single answer to the question, How radical was the American Revolution?

NOTES

ACKNOWLEDGMENTS: I am very much indebted to the scholars who
read drafts of this essay and the introduction for challenging my in-

terpretations, correcting my errors, pushing me to clarify my thoughts, and giving me the benefit of their expertise in their fields. Ira Berlin, Linda Kerber, and Gary Nash patiently went through several drafts of both the introduction and afterword. Scholars who read earlier versions of this essay are Edward Countryman, Emory Evans, Ronald Hoffman, Frederick Hoxie, Allan Kulikoff, Jesse Lemisch, Michael Merrill, Philip Morgan, Marcus Rediker, and Sean Wilentz. None of them bears responsibility for the errors of my ways. Members of the seminars in early American history at the University of Maryland and the Philadelphia Center for Early American Studies also provided valuable criticism.

1. J. Franklin Jameson, *The American Revolution Considered as A Social Movement* (Princeton, 1926), 9; Bernard Bailyn, *The Ideological Origins of the American Revolution* (Cambridge, Mass., 1967), chap. 6; David Brion Davis, *The Problem of Slavery in the Age of Revolution, 1770–1823* (Ithaca, N.Y., 1975), 274n.

2. E. P. Thompson, "The Moral Economy of the English Crowd in the Eighteenth Century," *Past and Present* 50 (1971): 76–136, reprinted in Thompson, *Customs in Common: Studies in Traditional Popular Culture* (New York, 1992), chap. 4, with a reply to his critics, "The Moral Economy Reviewed," chap. 5; James Henretta, "Families and Farms: *Mentalité* in Pre-Industrial America," *William and Mary Quarterly*, 3d series (hereafter cited as *WMQ*), 35 (1978): 3–22.

3. Richard L. Bushman, "Massachusetts Farmers and the Revolution," in Richard M. Jellison, ed., *Society, Freedom and Conscience* (New York, 1976), 77–124; Bushman, *King and People in Provincial Massachusetts* (Chapel Hill, N.C., 1985), chap. 5.

4. See John Rule, "The Property of Skill in the Period of Manufacture," in Patrick Joyce, ed., *The Historical Meaning of Work* (New York, 1987), 99–118; Ronald Schultz, "The Small-Producer Tradition and the Moral Origins of Artisan Radicalism in Philadelphia, 1720–1810," *Past and Present* 127 (1990): 84–116; and Peter Linebaugh, *The London Hanged: Crime and Civil Society in the Eighteenth Century* (New York, 1992), for artisan customs.

5. "To the Tradesmen, Mechanics & c. of Pennsylvania," (Philadelphia, 4 Dec. 1773), broadside.

6. James P. Walsh, " 'Mechanics and Citizens' : The Connecticut Artisan Protest of 1792," *WMQ* 42 (1985): 66–89.

7. Gary B. Nash, "Artisans and Politics in Eighteenth Century Philadelphia," in Margaret C. Jacob and James R. Jacob, eds., *The Origins of Anglo-American Radicalism* (London, 1984, Atlantic Highlands, N.J., 1991), 258–78; Nash, *The Urban Crucible: Social*

Change, Political Consciousness, and the Origins of the American Revolution (Cambridge, Mass., 1979); Alfred F. Young, " 'Sul Martello e Sulla Mano so Fondano tutte le Arti' : Gli Artigiani e la Rivoluzione" [" 'By Hammer and Hand All Arts do Stand': Artisans and the Revolution"], *Rivista di Storia Contemporanea* 1 (1982): 1–32; Young, "The Emergence of American Artisan Consciousness: The Revolutionary Era" (Paper presented at The Second Labor History Symposium of the George Meany Memorial Archives, 1990).

8. Jesse Lemisch, "Jack Tar in the Streets: Merchant Seamen in the Politics of Revolutionary America," *WMQ* 25 (1968): 371–407; Lemisch, *Jack Tar vs. John Bull: The Role of New York's Seamen in Precipitating the Revolution* (New Brunswick, N.J., forthcoming); Admiral Warren to the Duke of Newcastle, 18 June 1745, cited in Marcus Rediker, "A Motley Crew of Rebels: Sailors, Slaves, and the Coming of the American Revolution," in Ronald Hoffman and Peter J. Albert, eds., *"The Transforming Hand of Revolution": Reconsidering the American Revolution as a Social Movement* (Charlottesville, Va., forthcoming); Rediker, *Between the Devil and the Deep Blue Sea: Merchant Seamen, Pirates, and the Anglo-American Maritime World, 1700–1750* (Cambridge, 1987); Rediker, " 'Good Hands, Stout Heart and Fast Feet': The History and Culture of Working People in Early America," in Geoff Ely and William Hunt, eds., *Reviving the English Revolution: Reflection and Elaborations on the Work of Christopher Hill* (London, 1988), 221–49.

9. Lawrence W. Towner, " 'A Fondness for Freedom': Servant Protest in Puritan Society," *WMQ* 19 (1962), 201–19; Bernard Bailyn, "Voyagers in Flight: A Sketchbook of Runaway Servants, 1774–1775," in Bailyn, *Voyagers to the West: A Passage in the Peopling of America on the Eve of the Revolution* (New York, 1986), 352ff; Jonathan Prude, "To Look upon the 'Lower Sort': Runaway Ads and the Appearance of Unfree Laborers in America, 1750–1800," *Journal of American History* 78 (1991): 124–59.

10. Phillis Wheatley to Samson Occom, 11 Feb. 1774, in *Massachusetts Gazette*, 21 March 1774, reprinted in Julian D. Mason, Jr., ed., *The Poems of Phillis Wheatley* revised and enlarged ed. (Chapel Hill, N.C., 1989), 203–4.

11. Ira Berlin, "Time, Space, and the Evolution of Afro-American Society on British Mainland North America," *American Historical Review*, 85 (1980): 47–78; Melville Herskovits, *The Myth of the Negro Past* (New York, 1941); Gerald W. Mullin, *Flight and Rebellion: Slave Resistance in Eighteenth-Century Virginia* (New York, 1972); Peter H. Wood, *Black Majority: Negroes in Colonial South Carolina from 1670 through the Stono Rebellion* (New York, 1974);

Herbert G. Gutman, *The Black Family in Slavery and Freedom, 1750–1825* (New York, 1976); John Michael Vlach, *The Afro-American Tradition in Decorative Arts* (Cleveland, 1978); Mechal Sobel, *Trabelin' On: The Slave Journey to an Afro-Baptist Faith* (Westport, Conn., 1979); Allan Kulikoff, *Tobacco and Slaves: The Development of Southern Cultures in the Chesapeake, 1660–1800* (Chapel Hill, N.C., 1986); Sobel, *The World They Made Together: Black and White Values in Eighteenth Century Virginia* (Princeton, 1987); William D. Piersen, *Black Yankees: The Development of an Afro-American Subculture in Eighteenth-Century New England* (Amherst, Mass., 1988); Jon Butler, *Awash in a Sea of Faith: Christianizing the American People* (Cambridge, Mass., 1990), chap. 5.

12. A Petition To His Excellency Thomas Hutchinson, Esq., *Massachusetts Spy*, 29 July 1773; Gary Nash, "Thomas Peters: Millwright and Deliverer," in Nash and David Sweet, eds., *Struggle and Survival in Colonial America* (Berkeley, 1981), 69–85; James St. G. Walker, *The Black Loyalists: The Search for a Promised Land in Nova Scotia and Sierra Leone* (New York, 1976); Hannah [Harris, a weaver] to Robert Carter, 5 April 1792, in Alfred F. Young and Terry Fife with Mary Janzen, *We the People: Voices and Images of the New Nation* (Philadelphia, 1993), chap. 6.

13. David Lovejoy, " 'Desperate Enthusiasm': Early Signs of American Radicalism"; Patrica Bonomi, " 'A Just Opposition': The Great Awakening as a Radical Model"; Rhys Isaac, "Radicalised Religion and Changing Life Styles: Virginia in the Period of the American Revolution," in Jacob and Jacob, eds., *Origins of Radicalism*, 214–55; Gregory H. Nobles, *Divisions Throughout the Whole: Politics and Society in Hampshire County, Massachusetts, 1740–1775* (New York, 1983); Richard Beeman, *The Evolution of the Southern Backcountry: A Case Study of Lunenberg County, Virginia, 1746–1832* (Philadelphia, 1984); Lovejoy, *Religious Enthusiasm in the New World: Heresy to Revolution* (Cambridge, Mass., 1985); Bonomi, *Under the Cope of Heaven: Religion, Society, and Politics in Colonial America* (New York, 1986); Harry S. Stout, *The New England Soul: Preaching and Religious Culture in Colonial New England* (New York, 1986); Butler, *Awash in a Sea of Faith;* John Brooke, *The Heart of the Commonwealth: Society and Political Culture in Worcester County, Massachusetts, 1713–1861* (Cambridge, Eng., 1989); Ronald Hoffman and Peter Albert, eds., *Religion in a Revolutionary Age* (Charlottesville, Va., forthcoming).

14. Ruth H. Bloch, *Visionary Republic: Millennial Themes in American Thought, 1765–1800* (Cambridge, Eng., 1985); Mark H. Jones, "Herman Husband: Millenarian, Carolina Regulator, and

Whiskey Rebel" (Ph.D. diss., Northern Illinois University, 1982).

15. Stephen A. Marini, *Radical Sects of Revolutionary New England* (Cambridge, Mass., 1982); Nathan O. Hatch, *The Democratization of American Christianity* (New Haven, 1989).

16. Various petitions are reprinted in Herbert Aptheker, ed., *Documentary History of the Negro People In the United States*, 2 vols. (New York, 1951) 1: 5–9; and Robert Twombley, "Black Resistance to Slavery in Massachusetts," in William L. O'Neill, ed., *Insights and Parallels* (Minneapolis, 1973), 41–52; Thomas J. Davis, "Emancipation Rhetoric, Natural Rights and Revolutionary New England: A Note on Four Black Petitions in Massachusetts, 1773–1777," *New England Quarterly* 62 (1989): 248–63.

17. Alfred F. Young, "George Robert Twelves Hewes (1742–1840): A Boston Shoemaker and the Memory of the American Revolution," *WMQ* 38 (1981): 561–623.

18. Alfred F. Young, "The Women of Boston: 'Persons of Consequence' in the Making of the American Revolution, 1765–76," in Harriet Applewhite and Darlene G. Levy, eds., *Women and Politics in the Age of the Democratic Revolution* (Ann Arbor, Mich., 1990), 213–18; for variant interpretations, Edith B. Gelles, "The Abigail Industry," *WMQ* 45 (1988), 656–83.

19. Herman Husband, "Manuscript Sermons," 48–49, cited in Mark H. Jones, "The Western 'New Jerusalem': Herman Husband's Utopian Vision" (unpub. MS.).

20. John Shy, "The American Revolution: The Military Conflict Considered as a Revolutionary War," in Stephen G. Kurtz and James H. Hutson, eds., *Essays on the American Revolution* (Chapel Hill, N.C., and New York, 1973), 124.

21. Stephen Rosswurm, *Arms, Country, and Class: The Philadelphia Militia and the "Lower Sort" during the American Revolution* (New Brunswick, N.J., 1987), 111; Rosswurm, "The Philadelphia Militia, 1775–1783: Active Duty and Active Radicalism," in Ronald Hoffman and Peter J. Albert, eds., *Arms and Independence: The Military Character of the American Revolution* (Charlottesville, Va., 1984), 75–118.

22. Don C. Higginbotham, "The Early American Way of War: Reconaissance and Appraisal," *WMQ* 44 (1987), 230–73; James Kirby Martin, "A 'Most Undisciplined, Profligate Crew': Protest and Defiance in the Continental Ranks," in Hoffman and Albert, eds., *Arms and Independence*, 119–40; Martin and Mark E. Lender, *A Respectable Army: The Military Origins of the Republic, 1763–1789* (Arlington Heights, Ill., 1982); Charles Royster, *A Revolutionary People at War: The Continental Army and American Character, 1775–1783*

(Chapel Hill, N.C., 1979).

23. John Shy "The Legacy of the American Revolutionary War," in Larry Gerlach, comp., *Legacies of the American Revolution* (Logan, Utah, 1978), 43–60.

24. Jesse Lemisch, "Listening to the 'Inarticulate': William Widger's Dream and the Loyalties of American Revolutionary Seamen in British Prisons," *Journal of Social History* 3 (1969): 1–29.

25. Rachel N. Klein, "Frontier Planters and the American Revolution: The South Carolina Backcountry, 1775–1782"; Jeffrey J. Crow, "Liberty Men and Loyalists: Disorder and Disaffection in the North Carolina Backcountry"; Emory G. Evans, "Trouble in the Backcountry: Disaffection in Southwest Virginia during the American Revolution"; and Richard R. Beeman "The Political Response to Social Conflict in the Southern Backcountry: A Comparative View of Virginia and the Carolinas during the Revolution," in Ronald Hoffman, Thad Tate, and Peter J. Albert, eds., *An Uncivil War: The Southern Backcountry during the American Revolution* (Charlottesville, Va., 1985), 37–69, 125–78, 179–212, 213–39; Jeffrey J. Crow and Larry E. Tise, eds., *The Southern Experience in the American Revolution* (Chapel Hill, N.C., 1978); Ronald Hoffman, *A Spirit of Dissension: Economics, Politics and the Revolution in Maryland* (Baltimore, 1973); Richard R. Beeman, *Patrick Henry: A Biography* (New York, 1974).

26. Frey, *Water from the Rock,* chaps. 3–5, quotation 326; Benjamin Quarles, *The Negro in the American Revolution* (Chapel Hill, N.C., 1961), chaps. 7–9; Philip D. Morgan, "Black Society in the Lowcountry, 1760–1810," in Ira Berlin and Ronald Hoffman, eds., *Slavery and Freedom in the Age of the American Revolution* (Charlottesville, Va., 1983), 49–82; Graham Hodges, "Black Revolt in New York City and the Neutral Zone: 1775–1783," in Paul Gilje and William Pencak, eds., *New York City in the Age of the Constitution* (New York, 1992), 20–48.

27. Barbara Clark Smith, "Food Rioters and the American Revolution," *WMQ* (forthcoming); Smith, *After the Revolution: The Smithsonian History of Everyday Life in the Eighteenth Century* (New York, 1985), chap. 1; Smith, *The Politics of Spectatorship in Revolutionary America* (forthcoming); Rosswurm, *Arms, Country, Class,* chap. 7.

28. David Ramsay, *The History of the American Revolution,* 2 vols. (Philadelphia, 1789), 2:315.

29. Mary Beth Norton, *Liberty's Daughters: The Revolutionary Experiences of American Women, 1750–1800* (Boston, 1980); Linda K. Kerber, " 'I Have Don . . . much to Carrey on the War': Women and

the Shaping of Republican Ideology after the American Revolution," in Applewhite and Levy, eds., *Women and Politics,* 227–57; compare Laurel Thatcher Ulrich, *Good Wives: Image and Reality in the Lives of Women in Northern New England, 1650–1750* (New York, 1980).

30. John Resch, *Suffering Soldiers: Revolutionary War Veterans and Political Culture in the Early Republic* (forthcoming); John C. Dann, ed., *The Revolution Remembered: Eyewitness Accounts of the War for Independence* (Chicago, 1990), introduction; Jesse Lemisch, "The American Revolution and the American Dream: A Life of Andrew Sherburne, A Pensioner of the Navy of the Revolution," in Lemisch, *The American Revolution Seen from the Bottom Up* (New York, forthcoming).

31. Ruth Bogin, "Petitioning and the New Moral Economy of Post-Revolutionary America," *WMQ* 45 (1988): 391–425; Gregory H. Nobles, "Breaking into the Backcountry: New Approaches to the Early American Frontier, 1750–1800," *WMQ* 46 (1989): 641–70; Gordon Wood, *The Creation of the American Republic, 1776–1787* (Chapel Hill, N.C., 1969), chaps. 7–11; Robert A. Gross, ed., *In Debt to Daniel Shays: The Bicentennial of an Agrarian Rebellion* (Charlottesville, Va., 1993).

32. James Madison, *The Federalist,* 2 vols. (New York, 1788, available in many editions), no. 10; compare to an earlier memorandum, Madison "Vices of the Political System," April 1987, in William T. Hutchinson, et al., eds., *The Papers of James Madison,* 16 vols. (Chicago, 1962), 9:345–58; Merrill Jensen, John Kaminski, Gaspare J. Saladino, and Richard Lefler, eds., *The Documentary History of the Ratification of the Constitution,* 9 vols. of 20 planned (Madison, Wis., 1976–); Herbert J. Storing, ed., *The Complete Anti-Federalist,* 7 vols. (Chicago, 1981); Saul Cornell, "Aristocracy Assailed: The Ideology of Backcountry Anti-Federalism," *Journal of American History* 76 (1990): 1148–72.

33. David Brion Davis, "American Equality and Foreign Revolutions," *Journal of American History* 76 (1989): 729–52; Davis, *Revolutions: Reflections on American Equality and Foreign Liberations* (Cambridge, Mass., 1990).

34. E. P. Thompson, *The Making of the English Working Class* (London, 1963); Thompson, "Eighteenth Century English Society: Class Struggle without Class," *Social History* 3 (1978): 133–65, quotation, 149.

35. For discussion of class in Thompson see William H. Sewell, Jr., "How Classes Are Made: Critical Reflections on E. P. Thompson's Theory of Working Class Formation," in Harvey J. Kaye and Keith McClelland, eds., *E. P. Thompson: Critical Perspectives* (Philadel-

phia, 1990), 50–77; Kaye, *The British Marxist Historians: An Intro-*
ductory Analysis (Cambridge, Eng., 1984); Bryan D. Palmer, *Descent*
into Discourse: The Reification of Language and the Writing of Social
History (Philadelphia, 1990), chap. 4; for related discussion of class
consciousness in American history: Alan Dawley, "E. P. Thompson
and the Peculiarities of the Americans," *Radical History Review* 10
(1978–79): 33–59; "Interview with Herbert Gutman" in Gutman,
Power and Culture: Essays on the American Working Class, Ira Berlin,
ed. (New York, 1987), 329–56; Sean Wilentz, "Against Exceptionalism:
Class Consciousness and the American Labor Movement, 1790–1920,"
International Labor and Working Class History 26 (1984): 1–24.

36. E. P. Thompson, "Patrician Society, Plebeian Culture," *Jour-*
nal of Social History 7 (1974): 382–405; Thompson, *Customs in Com-*
mon, 87–96; Alfred F. Young, "English Plebeian Culture and
Eighteenth-Century American Radicalism," in Jacob and Jacob, eds.,
Origins of Radicalism, 185–212; Sean Wilentz, *Chants Democratic:*
New York City and the Rise of the American Working Class, 1788–
1850, (New York, 1984); Gordon Wood, *The Radicalism of the Amer-*
ican Revolution (New York, 1992), chap. 2.

37. For recent analysis: Stuart M. Blumin, *The Emergence of the*
Middle Class: Social Experience in the American City, 1760–1900
(Cambridge, Eng., 1989); Allan Kulikoff, "The Languages of Class in
Rural America," in Kulikoff, *The Agrarian Origins of American Cap-*
italism (Charlottesville, Va., 1992), chap. 4; Gregory Kaster, " 'Not
for a Class?' The 19th-Century American Labor Jeremiad," *Mid*
America: An Historical Review 70 (1988): 125–39; for the pathbreak-
ing English scholarship, Asa Briggs, "The Language of 'Class' in
Early Nineteenth Century England," in Briggs and John Saville,
eds., *Essays in Labor History* (London, 1967), 43–73; and Gareth
Stedman Jones, *Languages of Class: Studies in English Working*
Class History, 1832–1982 (Cambridge, Eng., 1983).

38. Jonathan Elliot, ed. *The Debates in the Several State Con-*
ventions, on the Adoption of the Constitution, 5 vols. (Philadelphia,
1836), vol. 1, 100–102; (Amos Singletary); vol. 2, 245–48 (Melancton Smith).

39. I have drawn my impressions from reading the newspapers.
For two works that lean heavily on newspapers see Donald H. Stewart, *The Opposition Press of the Federalist Period* (Albany, N.Y.,
1969); and Alfred F. Young, *The Democratic Republicans of New York:*
The Origins, 1763–1797 (Chapel Hill, N.C., 1967).

40. In addition to the works cited in note 7, for bibliography
on recent artisan studies, see Sean Wilentz, "The Rise of the American Working Class, 1776–1877," in J. Carroll Moody and Alice

Kessler-Harris, eds., *Perspectives on American Labor History: The Problem of Synthesis* (DeKalb, Ill., 1989), 83–90; Gary J. Kornblith, "The Artisanal Response to Capitalist Transformation," *Journal of the Early Republic* 10 (1990): 315–21.

41. Young, "English Plebeian Culture," 200–206; Sean Wilentz, "Artisan Republican Festivals and the Rise of Class Conflict in New York City, 1788–1837," in Michael H. Frisch and Daniel J. Walkowitz, eds., *Working Class America* (Urbana, Ill., 1983), 37–77.

42. Sharon V. Salinger, *'To Serve Well and Faithfully': Labor and Indentured Servants in Pennsylvania, 1682–1800* (Cambridge, Eng., 1987); Billy G. Smith, *The "Lower Sort": Philadelphia's Laboring People, 1750–1800* (Ithaca, N.Y., 1990).

43. G. Wood, *Radicalism of Revolution*, 7; Bernard Bailyn, "The Central Themes of the American Revolution," in Kurtz and Hutson, eds., *Essays on Revolution*, 30–31.

44. For recent work on this theme: Joyce Appleby, *Liberalism and Republicanism in the Historical Imagination* (Cambridge, Mass., 1992); James Henretta, *The Origins of American Capitalism: Collected Essays* (Boston, 1992); Kulikoff, *Agrarian Origins of American Capitalism;* Michael Merrill, *The Anti-Capitalist Origins of the United States: Essays in the Political Economy of Early America* (Ithaca, N.Y., forthcoming).

45. William A. Williams, *The Contours of American History* (Cleveland and New York, 1961, 1988); Hoffman, *Spirit of Dissension;* Edward Countryman, *A People in Revolution: The American Revolution and Political Society in New York, 1760–1790* (Baltimore, 1981); Staughton Lynd, "A Ruling Class on the Defensive," in *Class Conflict, Slavery, and the United States Constitution: Ten Essays* (Indianapolis, 1968); Rhys Isaac, *The Transformation of Virginia, 1740–1790* (Chapel Hill, N.C., 1982).

46. Peter Linebaugh and Marcus Rediker, "The Many Headed Hydra: Sailors, Slaves and the Atlantic Working Class in the Eighteenth Century," in Colin Howell and Richard J. Twomey, eds., *Jack Tar in History: Essays in the History of Maritime Life and Labour* (Fredericton, New Brunswick, 1991), 11–36.

47. Livingston cited in Young, *Democratic Republicans*, 15; Webster cited in Joseph J. Ellis, *After the Revolution: Profiles of Early American Culture* (New York, 1979), chap. 6, 203.

48. Barbara Karsky, "Agrarian Radicalism in the Late Revolutionary Period (1780–1795)" in Erich Angermann et al., eds., *New Wine in Old Skins: A Comparative View of Socio-Political Structures and Values Affecting the American Revolution* (Stuttgart, 1976), 87–114; David P. Szatmary, *Shays' Rebellion: The Making of an Agrarian*

Insurrection (Amherst, Mass., 1980); Thomas P. Slaughter, *The Whiskey Rebellion: Frontier Epilogue to the American Revolution* (New York, 1986); Stephen R. Boyd, ed., *The Whiskey Rebellion: Past and Present Perspectives* (Westport, Conn., 1985); Jeffrey J. Crow, "The Whiskey Rebellion in North Carolina," *North Carolina Historical Review* 66 (1989): 1–28.

49. Richard D. Brown, *Knowledge Is Power: The Diffusion of Information in Early America, 1770–1865* (New York, 1989); Philip S. Foner, ed., *The Democratic-Republican Societies, 1790–1800: A Documentary Sourcebook of Constitutions, Declarations, Addresses, Resolutions, and Toasts* (Westport, Conn., 1976); Winthrop D. Jordan, *White over Black: American Attitudes toward the Negro, 1550–1812* (Chapel Hill, N.C., 1968), chap. 10.

50. The argument in this and the succeeding paragraph is developed in Alfred F. Young, "Conservatives, the Constitution, and the 'Spirit of Accomodation,' " in Robert A. Goldwin and William A. Schambra, eds., *How Democratic is the Constitution?* (Washington, D.C., 1980), 117–47, and in revised form in "The Framers of the Constitution and the 'Genius of the People' " in *Radical History Review* 42 (1988) with commentary by Barbara Clark Smith, Linda K. Kerber, Michael Merrill, Peter Dimock, William Forbath, and James Henretta, 7–47.

51. Williams, *Contours of American History*, 149–223; John R. Nelson, Jr., *Liberty and Property: Political Economy and Policymaking in the New Nation, 1789–1812* (Baltimore, 1987); Joyce Appleby, *Capitalism and a New Social Order: The Republican Vision of the 1790s* (New York, 1984); Steven Watts, *The Republic Reborn: War and the Making of Liberal America, 1790–1820* (Baltimore, 1987).

52. Howard B. Rock, *Artisans of the New Republic: The Tradesmen of New York City in the Age of Jefferson* (New York, 1979); Rock, ed., *The New York City Artisan, 1789–1825: A Documentary History* (Albany, N.Y., 1989); Wilentz, *Chants Democratic*, chaps. 1, 2.

53. Rediker, *Devil and the Deep*, 291.

54. Alan Taylor, *Liberty Men and Great Proprietors: The Revolutionary Settlement in the Maine Frontier, 1760–1820* (Chapel Hill, N.C., 1990), chaps. 8, 9.

55. Frey, *Water from the Rock*, chaps. 7–9; Phillip D. Morgan, "Black Society in the Low Country, 1760–1810," in Berlin and Hoffman, eds., *Slavery and Freedom*, 83–142; Richard Dunn, "Black Society in the Chesapeake 1776–1810," in ibid., 49–82; Ira Berlin, "Rethinking Afro-American Slavery in Mainland North America" (Paper presented to the Southern Historical Association 1991).

56. Ira Berlin, "A History of Slavery," MS in progress, chap. 6;

Gary B. Nash, *Race and Revolution* (Madison, Wis., 1990); Nash, *Forging Freedom: The Formation of Philadelphia's Black Community, 1720–1840* (Cambridge, Mass., 1988); Nash and Jean R. Soderland, *Freedom by Degrees: Emancipation and its Aftermath in Pennsylvania* (New York, 1990); Shane White, *Somewhat More Independent: The End of Slavery in New York City, 1770–1810* (Athens, Ga., 1991).

57. Berlin and Hoffman, eds., *Slavery and Freedom,* xv.

58. Davis, *Problem of Slavery,* chap. 6, quotations at 256, 259, 262.; Edmund S. Morgan, *American Slavery, American Freedom: The Ordeal of Colonial Virginia* (New York, 1975).

59. Nash, *Race and Revolution,* chap. 2; Jordan, *White Over Black,* pts. 4, 5; Paul Finkelman, "Slavery and the Constitutional Convention: Making a Covenant with Death," in Richard Beeman, Stephen Botein, and Edward C. Carter II, eds., *Beyond Confederation: Origins of the Constitution and American National Identity* (Chapel Hill, N.C., 1987), 188–225; Staughton Lynd, "The Compromise of 1787," *Political Science Quarterly* 81 (1966): 225–50.

60. Linda K. Kerber, " 'History Can Do It No Justice': Women and the Reinterpretation of the American Revolution," in Ronald Hoffman and Peter J. Albert, eds., *Women in the Age of the American Revolution* (Charlottesville, Va., 1989), 3–42, quotation at 10.

61. Linda K. Kerber, "The Republican Mother: Women and the Enlightenment—An American Perspective," *American Quarterly* 28 (1976): 187–205; Kerber, " 'I have Don . . . much,' " 227–57; Jan Lewis, "The Republican Wife: Virtue and Seduction in the Early Republic," *WMQ* 44 (1987): 689–721.

62. Laurel Thatcher Ulrich, *A Midwife's Tale: The Life of Martha Ballard, Based on Her Diary, 1785–1812* (New York, 1990); for scholarship emphasizing the limitations of reform: Joan Hoff Wilson, "The Illusion of Change: Women and the American Revolution," in Alfred F. Young, ed., *The American Revolution: Explorations in the History of American Radicalism* (DeKalb, 1976), 383–445; Christine Stansell, *City of Women: Sex and Class in New York, 1789–1860* (New York, 1986); Elaine F. Crane, "Dependence in the Era of Independence: The Role of Women in a Republican Society," in Jack P. Greene, ed., *The American Revolution: Its Character and Limits* (New York, 1987), 253–75; Marylynn Salmon, *Women and the Law of Property in Early America* (Chapel Hill, N.C., 1986); for scholarship registering changes in consciousness, Mary Beth Norton, "The Evolution of White Women's Experience in Early America," *American Historical Review* 89 (1984): 593–619; Joan Jensen, *Loosening the Bonds: Mid-Atlantic Farm Women, 1750–1850* (New Haven, 1986); Lee Chambers-

Schiller, *Liberty a Better Husband: Single Women in America, The Generations of 1740–1820* (New Haven, 1989); William J. Gilmore, *Reading Becomes a Necessity of Life: Material and Cultural Life in Rural New England, 1780–1835* (Knoxville, Tenn., 1989).

63. Elaine F. Crane, ed., *The Diary of Elizabeth Drinker,* 3 vols. (Boston, 1991), 22 April 1796.; Charles W. Akers, *Abigail Adams: An American Woman* (Boston, 1980), 116.

64. Judith Sargent Murray, *The Gleaner,* 3 vols. (Boston, 1798), 1:167, 168, 193; 3:219; for the fullest analysis of Murray see Kerber, " 'I have Don . . . much,' " 238–44.

65. Joan R. Gunderson, "Independence, Citizenship, and the American Revolution," *Signs* 13 (1987): 59–77; Ruth H. Bloch, "The Gendered Meanings of Virtue in Revolutionary America," ibid., 37–58; Nancy Fraser and Linda Gordon, "Contract vs. Charity: Participation and Provision: A Reconsideration of 'Social Citizenship' " (Paper presented at Newberry Library Family and Community History Center Seminar, 1992).

66. Kerber, " 'Do It No Justice,' " 41.

67. James H. Merrell, "Declarations of Independence: Indian-White Relations in the New Nation," in Greene, ed., *American Revolution,* 197–223.

68. Gregory Evans Dowd, *A Spirited Resistance: The North American Indian Struggle for Unity, 1745–1815* (Baltimore, 1992).

69. Merrell, "Declarations of Independence," 197; Francis Jennings, "The Indians' Revolution," in Young, ed., *The American Revolution,* 341.

70. Merrell, "Declarations of Independence," 204; for the peace medal, Young and Fife, *We the People,* chap. 7.

71. Cited in Reginald Horsman, "The Image of the Indian in the Age of the American Revolution," *Newberry Library Center for the History of the American Indian Occasional Papers Series,* No. 6 (1983), 5; Alan Taylor, "Land and Liberty on the Post-Revolutionary Frontier," in David T. Konig, ed., *The Possession of Liberty in the Early American Republic* (Stanford, Calif., forthcoming).

72. James P. Whittenberg, "Herman Husband's Plan for Peace between the United States and the Indians, 1792," *WMQ,* 34 (1977): 647–50; Taylor, *Liberty Men and Great Proprietors,* chap. 7, "White Indians"; Richard White, *The Middle Ground: Indians, Empires, and Republicans in the Great Lakes Region, 1650–1815* (Cambridge, Eng., 1991).

73. Dowd, *A Spirited Resistance;* R. David Edmunds, ed., *American Indian Leaders: Studies in Diversity* (Lincoln, Neb., 1980); Edmunds, *The Shawnee Prophet* (Lincoln, Neb. 1983); Edmunds,

Tecumseh and the Quest for Indian Leadership (Boston, 1984); Anthony F. C. Wallace, *The Death and Rebirth of the Seneca* (New York, 1969); Joel W. Martin, *Sacred Revolt: The Muskogees' Struggle for a New World* (Boston, 1991); James H. Merrell, *The Indians' New World: Catawbas and Their Neighbors from European Contact through the Era of Removal* (Chapel Hill, N.C., 1989); for the continuing failure of scholars to integrate Indian history, Merrell, "Some Thoughts on Colonial Historians and American Indians," *WMQ* 41 (1989): 94–119. The pathbreaking synthesis for the colonial era is Gary B. Nash, *Red, White, and Black: The Peoples of Early America* (Englewood Cliffs, N.J., 1974, 3d. ed, 1991); the most recent synthesis is Francis Jennings, *The Founders of America* (New York, 1992); the new history is collected in Ronald Hoffman and Frederick Hoxie, eds., *Native Americans and the Early Republic* (Charlottesville, Va., forthcoming).

74. Bernard W. Sheehan, *Seeds of Extinction: Jeffersonian Philanthropy and the American Indian* (Chapel Hill, N.C., 1973); the Mashpees cited in Merrell, "Declarations of Independence," 217; Richard Drinnon, *Facing West: The Metaphysics of Indian-Hating and Empire-Building* (New York, 1980), Part 2.

75. Thomas P. Slaughter, "Crowds in Eighteenth Century America: Reflections and New Directions," *Pennsylvania Magazine of History and Biography,* 115 (1991): 3–34; Paul A. Gilje, *The Road to Mobocracy: Popular Disorder in New York City, 1763–1834* (Chapel Hill, N.C., 1987).

76. Bryan D. Palmer, "Discordant Music: Charivari and White-capping in North America," *Labour/Le Travailleur,* 1 (1978): 5–62; Susan G. Davis, *Parades and Power: Street Theater in Nineteenth Century Philadelphia* (Berkeley, Calif., 1986); Samuel Kinser, *Carnival, American Style: Mardi Gras at New Orleans and Mobile* (Chicago, 1990).

77. Bogin, "Petitioning," *WMQ* 45 (1988): 391–425; Edmund S. Morgan, *Inventing the People: The Rise of Popular Sovereignty in England and America* (New York, 1988), chap. 9.

78. Dorothy Fennell, "From Rebelliousness to Insurrection: A Social History of the Whiskey Rebellion, 1765–1802" (Ph.D. diss., University of Pittsburgh, 1981).

79. Charles G. Steffen, *The Mechanics of Baltimore: Workers and Politics in the Age of Revolution, 1763–1812* (Urbana, Ill., 1984), 217–21.

80. Simon P. Newman, "American Popular Political Culture in the Age of the French Revolution," (Ph.D. diss., Princeton, 1991); Newman, " 'A Truly American Festival': The Politics of July Fourth

Celebrations in Philadelphia, 1777–1801," *WMQ* (forthcoming); Young, *Democratic Republicans,* chap. 22.

81. Frey, *Water from the Rock,* 257, 320; Douglas R. Egerton, "Gabriel's Conspiracy and the Election of 1800," *Journal of Southern History* 56 (1990): 191–214; Mullin, *Slave Resistance,* chap. 5, Tucker cited at 157; Eugene Genovese, *From Rebellion to Revolution: Afro-American Slaves Revolts in the Making of the Modern World* (Baton Rouge, La., 1979); Jeffrey J. Crow, "Slave Rebelliousness and Social Conflict in North Carolina, 1775–1802," *WMQ* 37 (1980): 79–102.

82. Frey, *Water from the Rock,* chaps. 7–9; Mary Beth Norton, Herbert G. Gutman, and Ira Berlin, "The Afro-American Family in the Age of Revolution" and Albert J. Roboteau, "The Slave Church in the Era of the American Revolution," in Berlin and Hoffman, eds., *Slavery and Freedom,* 175–213; Jacqueline Jones, "Race, Sex, and Self-Evident Truths: The Status of Slave Women during the Era of the American Revolution," in Hoffman and Albert, eds., *Women in Revolution,* 293–337.

83. Paula Baker, "The Domestication of Politics: Women and American Political Society, 1780–1920," *American Historical Review* 89 (1984): 620–47; Anne M. Boylan, "Women and Politics in the Era Before Seneca Falls," *Journal of the Early Republic* 10 (1990): 363–82; Susan Branson, "Politics and Gender: The Political Consciousness of Philadelphia Women in the 1790s," (Ph.D. diss., Northern Illinois University, 1992).

84. Charles Brockden Brown, *Alcuin: A Dialogue* (New York, 1798), cited in Branson, "Politics and Gender," 70–74; Murray, *The Gleaner,* 3:188–89.

85. Thomas Jefferson to Spencer Roane, 6 Sept. 1819, cited in Dumas Malone, *Jefferson the President: First Term, 1801–1805* (Boston, 1970), 26; Aleine Austin, *Matthew Lyon: "New Man" of the Democratic Revolution, 1749–1822* (University Park, Pa., 1981).

86. Richard J. Twomey, *Jacobins and Jeffersonians: Anglo-American Radicalism in the United States 1790–1820* (New York, 1989); Hatch, *Democratization of Christianity,* chap. 2; Richard E. Ellis, *The Jeffersonian Crisis: Courts and Politics in the Young Republic* (New York, 1971); Michael Durey, "Thomas Paine's Apostles: Radical Emigrés and the Triumph of Jeffersonian Republicanism," *WMQ* 44 (1987): 661–88.

87. Thomas Jefferson to James Monroe, 20 Sept. 1800, cited in Egerton, "Gabriel's Conspiracy," 214; Michael Zuckerman, "The Color of Counter-Revolution: Thomas Jefferson and the Rebellion in San Domingo," in Loretta Valtz Mannucci, ed., *The Languages of Revolution,* (Milan Group in Early American History *Quaderno*

2, University of Milan, 1989), 83–107; Jordan, *White Over Black,* chap. 12.

88. Thomas Jefferson cited in Norton, *Liberty's Daughters,* 190–91. Compare to the equalitarianism of the Massachusetts Republican James Sullivan, in Linda K. Kerber, "The Paradox of Women's Citizenship in the Early Republic: The Case of *Martin vs. Massachusetts,* 1805," *American Historical Review* 97 (1992): 349–78.

89. Thomas Jefferson, "Address," 7 Jan. 1802; Jefferson to Gov. William Henry Harrison, 27 Feb. 1803, cited in Malone, *Jefferson the President,* 273–75; Sheehan, *Seeds of Extinction,* chaps. 5–9. For Jefferson's radicalism compare Richard Matthews, *The Radical Politics of Thomas Jefferson: A Revisionist View* (Lawrence, Kan., 1984) to Leonard Levy, *Jefferson and Civil Liberties: The Darker Side* (Cambridge, Mass., 1963); Levy, *Emergence of a Free Press* (New York, 1985) and the works cited above by David Brion Davis, Winthrop Jordan, and Bernard Sheehan.

Contributors

EDWARD COUNTRYMAN (Ph.D., Cornell University, 1971) teaches at Southern Methodist University. He is the author of *A People in Revolution: The American Revolution and Political Society in New York, 1760–1790* (Baltimore: Johns Hopkins University Press, 1981; New York: W. W. Norton, 1989), winner of the Bancroft Prize, and *The American Revolution* (New York: Hill & Wang, 1985). He is coauthor of *Who Built America?* (New York: Pantheon Books, 1992), vol. 1, and contributing editor of *The British Film Institute Companion to the Western* (London: Andre Deutcsh, 1988).

CATHY N. DAVIDSON (Ph.D., State University of New York at Binghamton, 1974) teaches in the English Department at Duke University and is editor of the journal *American Literature.* She is the author of *Revolution and the Word: The Rise of the Novel in America* (New York: Oxford University Press, 1986), and *Reading in America: Literature and Social History.* (Baltimore: Johns Hopkins University Press, 1988). She is 1993 President of the American Studies Association.

GARY J. KORNBLITH (Ph.D., Princeton University, 1983) teaches at Oberlin College. His articles have appeared in *Journal of the Early Republic, Business History Review, Massachusetts Review, Essex Institute Historical Collections,* and *Henry Ford Museum & Greenfield Village Herald.* He is presently working on a book, *Joseph T. Buckingham and the Making of the Boston Middle Class.*

ALLAN KULIKOFF (Ph.D., Brandeis University, 1976) teaches at Northern Illinois University. He is the author of *Tobacco and Slaves: The Development of Southern Cultures in the Chesapeake, 1680–1800.* (Chapel Hill: University of North Carolina Press, 1986), winner of the Francis Simkins Award and the John Dunning Prize. His essays are collected in *The Agrarian Origins of American Capitalism* (Charlottesville: University Press of Virginia, 1992).

MICHAEL MERRILL (Ph.D., Columbia University, 1985) teaches in the Labor Education Department at Rutgers University. He is the author of *Revolutionary America: Agrarianism and Equal Rights in the Early Republic* (Ithaca: Cornell University Press, forthcoming). He collaborated with Sean Wilentz on *The Key of Liberty: The Life and Democratic Writings of William Manning, "A Laborer," 1747–1814* (Cambridge: Harvard University Press, 1993).

JOHN M. MURRIN (Ph.D., Yale University, 1966) teaches at Princeton University. He is coauthor and coeditor of *Saints and Revolutionaries: Essays in Early American History* (New York: W. W. Norton, 1984). His essays have appeared in *History and Theory, William and Mary Quarterly, Reviews in American History* and other journals. His collected essays will be published by Oxford University Press.

W. J. RORABAUGH (Ph.D., University of California at Berkeley, 1976) teaches at the University of Washington. He is the author of *The Alcoholic Republic: An American Tradition* (New York: Oxford University Press, 1979), *The Craft Apprentice: From Franklin to the Machine Age in America* (New York: Oxford University Press, 1986), and *Berkeley at War: The 1960s* (New York: Oxford University Press, 1989).

ALAN TAYLOR (Ph.D., Brandeis, 1986) teaches at Boston University. He is the author of *Liberty Men and Great Proprietors: The Revolutionary Settlement on the Maine Frontier, 1760–1820* (Chapel Hill: University of North Carolina Press, 1990) and of *William Cooper's Town: Power and Persuasion on the Early American Frontier* (New York: Alfred A. Knopf, forthcoming).

SEAN WILENTZ (Ph.D., Yale University, 1980) teaches at Princeton University. He is the author of *Chants Democratic: New York City and the Rise of the American Working Class, 1788–1850* (New York: Oxford University Press, 1984), winner of the Albert J. Beveridge and Frederick Jackson Turner awards. He is coauthor with Paul Johnson of *The Kingdom of Matthias* (New York: Oxford University Press, forthcoming) and with Michael Merrill of *The Key of Liberty: The Life and Democratic Writings of William Manning, "A Laborer," 1747–1814* (Cambridge: Harvard University Press, 1993).

PETER H. WOOD (Ph.D., Harvard University, 1972) teaches at Duke University. He is the author of *Black Majority: Negroes in Colonial South Carolina from 1670 through the Stono Rebellion* (New York: Alfred A. Knopf, 1974). He is coauthor with Karen Dalton of

Winslow Homer's Images of Blacks: The Civil War and Reconstruction Years (Austin: University of Texas Press, 1988) and with Gregory Waselkov and Thomas Hatley of *Powhatan's Mantle: Indians in the Colonial Southeast* (Lincoln: University of Nebraska Press, 1989).

ALFRED F. YOUNG is editor of the series *Explorations in the History of American Radicalism,* 3 vols. (Dekalb: Northern Illinois University Press, 1968–93) and co-general editor with Leonard Levy of *The American Heritage Series,* 45 vols., (Indianapolis: Bobbs Merrill, 1965–77). He is the coauthor with Terry Fife and Mary Janzen of *We the People: Voices and Images of the New Nation* (Philadelphia: Temple University Press, 1993) and coeditor with Robert Karrow of *Past Imperfect: The Essays of Lawrence W. Towner on History, Libraries, and the Humanities* (Chicago: University of Chicago Press, 1993). His book *The Democratic Republicans of New York: The Origins, 1765–1797* (Chapel Hill: University of North Carolina Press, 1968), received the Jamestown Award from the Institute of Early American History and Culture.

Index